…ITION

THE COMPLETE HANDBOOK OF
NOVEL WRITING

EVERYTHING YOU NEED TO KNOW TO CREATE & SELL YOUR WORK

THE EDITORS OF WRITER'S DIGEST

INCLUDES INTERVIEWS WITH AND ARTICLES BY:

JOE HILL

ALICE HOFFMAN

JANE FRIEDMAN

HUGH HOWEY

JODI PICOULT

PATRICIA CORNWELL

ROBERT CRAIS

GARTH STEIN

ANNE RICE

DAVID BALDACCI

DENNIS LEHANE

GEORGE R.R. MARTIN

STEPHEN KING

JOJO MOYES

LEIGH MICHAELS

STEVE ALMOND

LEE CHILD

JERRY B. JENKINS

HALLIE EPHRON

EMMA DONOGHUE

KHALED HOSSEINI

JANE SMILEY

3RD EDITION

THE COMPLETE HANDBOOK OF
NOVEL WRITING

EVERYTHING YOU NEED TO KNOW TO CREATE & SELL YOUR WORK

THE EDITORS OF WRITER'S DIGEST

WRITER'S DIGEST
BOOKS

WritersDigest.*com*
Cincinnati, Ohio

For more resources for writers, visit www.writersdigest.com.

20 19 18 17 16   5 4 3 2 1

Distributed in Canada by Fraser Direct
100 Armstrong Avenue
Georgetown, Ontario, Canada L7G 5S4
Tel: (905) 877-4411

Distributed in the U.K. and Europe by F+W Media International
Brunel House, Newton Abbot, Devon, TQ12 4PU, England
Tel: (+44) 1626-323200, Fax: (+44) 1626-323319
E-mail: postmaster@davidandcharles.co.uk
Library of Congress Cataloging-in-Publication Data

ISBN-13: 978-1-4403-4839-6

Edited by Rachel Randall
Designed by Alexis Estoye
Production coordinated by Debbie Thomas

Table of Contents

Part One
THE ART AND CRAFT OF A STRONG NARRATIVE

Part Two

THE WRITING PROCESS

Part Three

EXPLORING NOVEL GENRES

Part Four

FINDING AND CULTIVATING A MARKET FOR YOUR WORK

Part Five

INTERVIEWS WITH NOVELISTS

THE ART AND CRAFT OF A STRONG NARRATIVE

BEST-SELLING ADVICE
Inspiration and Ideas

"Don't try to figure out what other people want to hear from you; figure out what you have to say. It's the one and only thing you have to offer."

—Barbara Kingsolver

"Everybody walks past a thousand story ideas every day. The good writers are the ones who see five or six of them. Most people don't see any."

—Orson Scott Card

"Write while the heat is in you. … The writer who postpones the recording of his thoughts uses an iron which has cooled to burn a hole with."

—Henry David Thoreau

"But the truth is, it's not the idea, it's never the idea, it's always what you do with it."

—Neil Gaiman

"If you stuff yourself full of poems, essays, plays, stories, novels, films, comic strips, magazines, music, you automatically explode every morning like Old Faithful. I have never had a dry spell in my life, mainly because I feed myself well, to the point of bursting. I wake early and hear my morning voices leaping around in my head like jumping beans. I get out of bed quickly, to trap them before they escape.

—Ray Bradbury

"Every idea is my last. I feel sure of it. So, I try to do the best with each as it comes and that's where my responsibility ends. But I just don't wait for ideas. I look for them. Constantly. And if I don't use the ideas that I find, they're going to quit showing up."

—Peg Bracken

"Good writing is remembering detail. Most people want to forget. Don't forget things that were painful or embarrassing or silly. Turn them into a story that tells the truth."

—Paula Danziger

"Don't put down too many roots in terms of a domicile. I have lived in four countries and I think my life as a writer and our family's life have been enriched by this. I think a writer has to experience new environments. There is that adage: No man can really succeed if he doesn't move away from where he was born. I believe it is particularly true for the writer."

—Arthur Hailey

"A writer need not devour a whole sheep in order to know what mutton tastes like, but he must at least eat a chop. Unless he gets his facts right, his imagination will lead him into all kinds of nonsense, and the facts he is most likely to get right are the facts of his own experience."

—W. Somerset Maugham

"Sit and quiet yourself. Luxuriate in a certain memory and the details will come. Let the images flow. You'll be amazed at what will come out on paper. I'm still learning what it is about the past that I want to write. I don't worry about it. It will emerge. It will insist on being told.

—Frank McCourt

66 My advice is not to wait to be struck by an idea. If you're a writer, you sit down and damn well decide to have an idea. That's the way to get an idea."

—Andy Rooney

"I have never felt like I was creating anything. For me, writing is like walking through a desert and all at once, poking up through the hardpan, I see the top of a chimney. I know there's a house under there, and I'm pretty sure that I can dig it up if I want. That's how I feel. It's like the stories are already there. What they pay me for is the leap of faith that says: 'If I sit down and do this, everything will come out okay.'"

—Stephen King

"As writers we live life twice, like a cow that eats its food once and then regurgitates it to chew and digest it again. We have a second chance at biting into our experience and examining it. … This is our life and it's not going to last forever. There isn't time to talk about someday writing that short story or poem or novel. Slow down now, touch what is around you, and out of care and compassion for each moment and detail, put pen to paper and begin to write. 99

—Natalie Goldberg

1

TRAINING YOUR IDEAS

···

How to Keep Your Inspiration from Running Wild

────────

N.M. Kelby

After Truman Capote nearly destroyed himself writing his groundbreaking best-seller *In Cold Blood* in 1965, he was quoted as saying that his next book, a novel tentatively titled *Answered Prayers*, would be easy by comparison. "It's all in my head!"

And that was the problem. Capote was a perfectionist, and the novel in his head was an untamed beast. His standards were so impossibly high that when he died in 1984, he'd spent the better part of nineteen years writing, rewriting, missing deadlines, publishing excerpts, drinking himself into a frenzy—and never finishing the work.

What writer hasn't had a difficult time putting an idea into words—especially an idea for something as complex as a novel? I often have a million ideas bouncing around in my head like puppies at the pound. I want to write about themes of love, usually reckless love, and mystery. I want to be profound and funny, too. I want to take readers to places they've never imagined and make them feel things they haven't felt before. And, to top it all off, I want to make the words themselves do extraordinary things—to, for instance, evoke the precise sound of an ancient jazz quartet playing a Sunday brunch in the wrong end of the French Quarter.

Of course, I also want the resulting work to be a bestseller.

Sound familiar?

The desire to write The Great American Novel is like an overactive beast that needs obedience school. If you've ever had a dog, you know what I mean. Dogs are pack animals. You're supposed to be the leader. You're supposed to be in charge. If you're not, you're in trouble. Dogs will run wild unless you focus them with a calm, centered mind, an assertive hand, and a strong sense of purpose.

The same is true with your novel. Ideas often start with boundless energy, vying for your attention. But when you get them on the page, they don't always match your original vision. A plotline feels contrived. An emotion falls flat. When this happens, you can easily feel defeated. You work and rework a paragraph or chapter, but it just isn't doing all the things you need it to do. When your ideas run wild, it's too easy for them to frustrate and eventually overwhelm you.

This is where many writers give up. But you shouldn't.

Instead, learn how to tame your beast.

ESTABLISH A CALM, CENTERED MIND

The television is blaring. Your loved one has no idea where the car keys are. Your neighbor is giving salsa lessons in his backyard. You live in a swirl of noise and confusion, so how can you possibly cultivate a quiet place within you to write? Easy. Take out a rolled-up newspaper and whack your world on its hindquarters— not hard, but just enough to get everyone's attention, including your own. Nonexistent boundaries, unfocused expectations, and lack of routine are the writer's downfall. You need to be your own pack leader.

Make your work space your sanctuary. Keep office hours. Close the door if you can. If you can't, put on earphones and listen to music. Writing is a meditation on life. You need to feel alone in the world so that you can be objective about it.

Don't ever panic. Keep in mind that even great writers like F. Scott Fitzgerald and Ernest Hemingway needed editing. You can always go back and fix what doesn't work. Nothing is perfect the first time.

Don't despair. Some writing days are better than others. If you feel stuck, move on or just take a break and come back to it tomorrow. A night's sleep often makes a world of difference.

Don't place yourself in competitive situations while you're working on a book. Losing a "first-chapter" contest or workshopping a book-in-progress can lead to second-guessing. It's best to finish your draft before you ask for any critical evaluation. Sometimes when you're progressing through the early stages of a novel, writing groups can do more harm than good.

While working on your draft, don't compare it to the latest bestseller in your genre. The best way to write a best-selling book is to write a book that you could give to anyone, including your mother-in-law and that salsa-dancing neighbor. Novels that truly work are books in which people can see their own hearts.

They're books that make people feel that you're writing about them. The best way to write such a genuine work is to write from an authentic part of yourself rather than be distracted by what's selling and why.

Think of yourself as an athlete. Exercise. Eat right. If you're driving yourself crazy with work, stop and invite a friend to meet for coffee. Balance is key.

Don't be afraid to set your own pace and create your own work in a way that makes the most sense for you. Yes, your favorite author puts out a book a year, but you don't need to. Create a process that works for you, and write in your own time frame.

STUDY YOUR BREED

Just as you can't easily train a Chihuahua to retrieve ducks—it's just not in its nature—you can't write a book without thinking about what the reader demands from the genre. Every book, just like every breed, brings with it a certain set of natural expectations. Historical romance must address history. Mysteries must have some level of, well, mystery. Literary books are usually not plot focused.

Understanding the "breed" of your book is the first step in bringing your novel to the page. Once you create a clearly defined set of expectations, you can train yourself to stay within them—and soon you'll be able to sit, roll over, and fetch with the best of them.

When Nancy Horan wrote the bestseller *Loving Frank*, a historically imagined novel about the tragic love affair of Frank Lloyd Wright and Mamah Borthwick Cheney, she chose a task with a rather large laundry list of expectations. She had to, first and foremost, create characters based on real people. In the case of Mamah, not much had been written about her, and only a few documents had been left behind. What was widely known was that Mamah was a great beauty who had left her young children and perfectly respectable husband for Frank—and who had done so in an era when those choices were especially taboo. Horan's challenge, then, was to make the woman sympathetic while imagining the great pain and suffering Mamah's decision must have caused both herself and those around her. Horan's Mamah also had to have intellect and spirit so that she didn't seem like a mindless follower of the architect.

In effect, Horan had to crawl into Mamah's psyche and make it her own.

Of course, Frank's character also had to be handled with care. History has not always been kind to him. Biographers have depicted him as arrogant, vain, unreliable, and largely unschooled (because of his lack of structural training, many of his buildings are beautiful but flawed); he was not an easy subject to endear to modern readers. But Horan's instinct as a writer told her that the reader needed to see Wright as a man Mamah could fall in love with and needed to understand why she would leave her seemingly perfect life for a troubled (and married) man.

Then Horan had to take historical considerations into account. She had to stay true to the era in every possible detail. In the early twentieth century, not only were affairs conducted via telegram rather than text message, but adultery was seen as a crime. What's more, Horan had to explain Wright's architecture and his aesthetic viewpoint in a way that was intelligent, fresh, simple, and yet not so simple as to bore those already knowledgeable about Wright's work.

All of these expectations for Horan's historical novel could have been outlined even before she wrote a word, showing her a clear path from idea to page.

So, you see, readers' expectations for your genre are a good place to start and a general guideline that will help you throw out ideas that won't fit.

Once you've established your readers' expectations as a framework, you need to decide *how* to tell your story.

Consider *The Wonderful Wizard of Oz* and *Wicked: The Life and Times of the Wicked Witch of the West*. Both books are set in the same world. L. Frank Baum's hero in *The Wonderful Wizard of Oz* is Dorothy. Gregory Maguire's *Wicked* includes Dorothy's falling house as an unfortunate incident, but his hero is the Wicked Witch. The book is sympathetic to her plight—and that changes everything.

While Baum's message is simple—"There's no place like home"—Maguire creates a tale with a complex message about the nature of good and evil. The two books couldn't be more different. And both have been wildly successful.

There's a myriad of ways to tell each and every story; don't be afraid to make yours unique.

TRAIN YOUR FOCUS

Once you've built your framework, you need to be ruthless. Everything in a novel must work to tell the tale. Think of your book like a television news segment. If the story is about a murder, you'll usually see a shot of where the murder took place or where the body was found, a photo of the victim, an interview with a witness who heard something or knew the victim, and a sound bite from the police officers investigating the story. The fact that the victim liked dogs wouldn't usually be included unless the barking of his dog alerted the neighbors, who then found the body. Every element in a news story works to tell the tale, and that should also be true for your novel.

You'll probably start by pursuing more ideas than you have room for in your story, but when it comes time to write, remember that you can't stuff things into the narrative just because you like them. For example, let's say you originally wanted to write about a chef. You've spent three months researching culinary school, but after completing the first draft you realize that this character no longer fits within the framework of your science fiction thriller and you're going to have to cut him. It's painful, but it must be done.

Of course, if you did spend three months researching something, it's very difficult to toss that work away—so don't. Maybe you'll write half of your book and discover that it really does fit, but you just couldn't see it at first. Or maybe you'll discover that you'd rather write about a chef, and so you create a new framework. Never throw anything away. I like to keep all my research in Moleskine notebooks. I also glue postcards and business cards onto the pages. If I see a name that strikes my fancy, I'll jot it down. Sometimes photographs go in, too. When I'm finished, the notebook is crammed full of ideas—just like my head used to be. Some I can use now; some I save for later.

WALK YOUR INNER DOG

A calm, centered mind; "breed" wisdom; and the discipline to shape your focus— let's look at how this model works in the real world.

Say you've just read an article about a sixteen-year-old boy who lived in a lifeboat in shark-infested waters for 227 days before he was rescued. As soon as you read the story, you can imagine yourself living it. You can feel this boy's fear and begin to understand what it would take to survive all those days in open water. Perhaps you decide the idea has a *Robinson Crusoe* feeling to it. Like Daniel Defoe's book, it's an adventure—and so this becomes your model. You now know what "breed" of story you're working with.

Next you have to consider what the reader expects from an adventure story and what the facts of the situation are. Given the reality of a boy living at sea in a lifeboat, the novel, like *Crusoe*, must deal with overcoming great obstacles through hard work and patience. You might also imagine that a boy adrift on a raft would begin to wonder about the nature of God, as he is certainly at odds with the whims of nature.

So when you sit down to write this story you could think of it as a reinvented version of *Crusoe*—unless you throw a 450-pound Bengal tiger in the mix. With a dangerous and hungry cat on board, you now have *Life of Pi*, Yann Martel's rumination on the nature of adventure, survival, faith, and truth. Martel added his unique take to this simple story, based on subjects he's interested in, such as faith and zoology. By being true to himself and his vision of the world, he boldly created a fable that became an international bestseller.

While you write a book, it's art. When you're finished, it's business. Never confuse the two. Art encourages you to take risks, re-create reality, embrace adventure, and break all the rules—it makes you want to soar. Business is about sales, sales, and sales—and it makes you jumpy. You'll never tame your beast if you write while wondering how many books you can sell.

Don't worry about failing. Be fearless about taming your best ideas and tossing out those that don't fit your model. Choose paths that illuminate your unique take on the world. Once you're in the habit of walking your inner dog, you never know where it might lead you.

FROM IDEA TO PAGE IN FOUR SIMPLE STEPS

Nothing is more exciting than the promise of a story in your head, but to get it on the page you need to figure out exactly what you need to do to make it work. You need to realistically outline. You need to set up a game plan to hook your audience and keep their attention. And you need to throw out those scenes and details that bog down readers. Here are some simple steps to help you build the frame on which you hang your story.

1. **ALWAYS BEGIN WITH YOUR PROTAGONIST.** Readers need to discover who the hero is and why they should root for him. Introduce your protagonist, either directly or indirectly, within the first 300 words.
2. **ESTABLISH TIME AND PLACE.** Your readers should know exactly where they are. If they don't, they will lose focus and may stop reading. They have to trust that you are in control of the story. Nobody likes to be left alone in the dark.
3. **ANNOUNCE THE STAKES.** Great prose will go a long way—about 2,500 words, more or less. After that, even the most literary readers want to know why they're reading. A simple sentence can do the trick. At the end of the first section of *The Things They Carried*, Tim O'Brien writes of the letters that Jimmy Cross received from a girl back home named Martha. He mentions that they're signed "Love, Martha," but acknowledges that using the word *love* is a custom and nothing more. At the end of this sec-

tion, O'Brien writes, "Slowly, a bit distracted, he would get up and move among his men, checking the perimeter, then at full dark he would return to his hole and watch the night and wonder if Martha was a virgin." Right there, the author lets us know what's really on this young man's mind—and at the heart of the story.

4. **ORGANIZE.** Once you have structured your story around the beginning you've set in place, look at all the bits of writing you've done and all the notes you've taken and ask, "Where the heck was I going with this?" If you don't know, or if the direction you're headed now doesn't match where you were going when you set out, focus on better defining those areas before you continue.

N.M. Kelby (www.nmkelby.com) is the critically acclaimed author of several novels, including *The Pink Suit*, *White Truffles in Winter*, and *In the Company of Angels*. She is the recipient of numerous prestigious grants and awards, including a Bush Artist Fellowship in Literature, a Florida Book Award, and both a Florida and Minnesota State Arts Board Fellowship.

2

BEND IT, AMP IT, DRIVE IT, STRIP IT

How to Develop Any Idea into a Great Story

Elizabeth Sims

A while ago I attended an inventors' club meeting. Some of the members had already launched successful products and were working on more, while others were merely beginners with great ideas. The beginners were commiserating about how hard it is to deal with financing, raw materials, manufacturing, promotion, and all the rest, when one of the experienced inventors suddenly stood up. "Look," he said impatiently, "ideas are a dime a dozen. It's the *development* that puts you over the top. Do what you have to do to make it real and get it to market."

I was surprised, because I'd always thought that a brilliant idea could make you a fortune. But I quickly realized my new friend was right: Idea is just the beginning.

Fiction writers have a lot in common with those inventors. It's not hard to get inspired by a great concept, to take it to your table or toolshed or cellar and do some brainstorming, and even to start putting the story on paper—but eventually, many of us lose traction. Why? Because development doesn't happen on its own. In fact, I've come to think that idea development is the number one skill an author should have.

How do great authors develop stunning narratives, break from tradition, and advance the form of their fiction? They take whatever basic ideas they've got, then move them away from the typical. No matter your starting point—a love story, buddy tale, mystery, quest—you can do like the great innovators do: Bend it. Amp it. Drive it. Strip it.

Bend. Amp. Drive. Strip.

It's BADS, baby, it's BADS.

BEND IT

Chuck Palahniuk is on record as saying he drew heavily from *The Great Gatsby* to create his novel *Fight Club*. I've read both books (multiple times) but would not have perceived that parallel. He said, "Really, what I was writing was just *The Great Gatsby* updated a little. It was "apostolic" fiction—where a surviving apostle tells the story of his hero. There are two men and a woman. And one man, the hero, is shot to death." Palahniuk transformed a traditional love story set in the high society of America's Roaring Twenties into a violent and bloody tale of sexual obsession, cultism, and social disruption set in a rotten world.

He bent the ideas behind *Gatsby* into something all his own.

The next time you get a great idea for a story, don't stop there. Bend your initial concept, making it more unique—and more powerful—with every turn:

- **GET OUT OF YOUR HEAD AND INTO YOUR PELVIS.** Give your characters inner yearnings (sexual or otherwise) they don't understand and can't deal with cognitively. Palahniuk gave his apostolic main character an unnamable urge, a gland-level longing that drives him to pretend to be a cancer patient and participate in support groups where hugging and crying are not only okay but expected. Breaking the taboo against exploiting nonexistent pain does more than give the character relief: It moves the story forward in huge leaps.
- **BRAINSTORM WHO YOUR CHARACTERS MIGHT BE BY REIMAGINING THEIR MOTIVATIONS.** Let's say you've come up with the idea that your main character is an insomniac who needs chocolate to fall asleep. Bend that urge into something that is totally disquieting to anybody *but* your protagonist. Wouldn't it be more compelling if she has to, say, shoplift an expensive item precisely one hour before bedtime?
- **BREAK AWAY FROM FAMILIAR PARAMETERS.** Most authors write characters with backgrounds similar to their own, at least with respect to class, education, and money. Throw that out. Write billionaires, bums, addicts, the hopeless, the heroic. Give them crappy, selfish habits, resentments, grudges. Mix traits. Make feral creatures out of urban sophisticates and urban sophisticates out of feral creatures.

- **ADD INSANITY.** The key to making a character believably and compellingly crazy is to give him a way to rationalize his behavior, from the slightly weird to the outrageous. Is your character actually nuts, or is there something else going on? How can anybody tell? Crazy characters need a lot of resources to keep them out of trouble—and can have a major impact on everybody else. Have fun with that.
- **QUESTION CONVENTION.** Use existential questions to bend the life lessons your readers think they've already learned: What is suffering? What is pleasure? What is a waste? What is worthwhile? Can something be both, or neither? Invite your characters to reject common wisdom and look for answers themselves.

AMP IT

Brief Encounter is a British film adapted from Nöel Coward's play *Still Life*. It's the story of two quiet people who meet and fall in love in spite of being married to others, but then, conscience stricken, break off the relationship before it really gets going. The small, exquisite tragedy resonated with the genteel, romantic codes of conduct valued in prewar England.

But then along comes Tennessee Williams with his play *Cat on a Hot Tin Roof*, a love story that has similar themes at its core but rips us away from any semblance of civilization. Could Williams ever amp drama! For one thing, he knew that a story about noble ideals wouldn't cut it anymore. Setting his play in the emotionally brutal mélange of the postwar American South, he slashed into the secret marrow of his protagonists and antagonists alike, exposing the weaknesses and delusions that bind people together on the surface while tearing them apart below decks.

Take the essence of your story, and amp it:

- **ADD CHARACTERS AND PILE ON THE EMOTION.** Playwrights used to limit the number of characters in their stories, not wanting to overcrowd the stage. But when Williams crams six or eight people onto the scene at once and sets them all at one another's throats, we get a chance to *feel* their emotional claustrophobia and unwanted interdependence. Amp up your action by adding cunning, vindictiveness, jealousy, fear of exposure, stupidity, even death.
- **MAKE EVEN MINOR CHARACTERS FIERCE AND ELEMENTAL.** Consider Mae and Gooper's five children in *Cat on a Hot Tin Roof*, whom lesser

authors would describe (boringly) as "brats" and leave offstage. Before you even see them, you witness their havoc (ruining Maggie's dress) and listen to Maggie call them "no-neck monsters." You don't even have to meet them to fear them. Then Williams gives them stage time, every second of which makes you squirm with discomfort.

- **EXPOSE INTERNAL BLEEDING.** The deepest, most painful wounds are the invisible ones humans inflict on one another and themselves in a hundred ways: betrayal, selfishness, abandonment. Strive to write characters who feel vulnerable to pain, whose secrets are so close to the surface that they can't afford to be polite. Put in a truth teller and watch the inner flesh rip and sizzle.
- **CREATE BLOOD TIES.** Kinship is story gold. Take your pick of, and take your time with, its darker aspects: scapegoating, favoritism, jealousy. A blood link can instantly heighten *any* conflict, because kinship is the one thing in life you can't change or walk away from. Make your characters learn this the hard way.

DRIVE IT

Many great modern stories spring from the same seeds as old folk tales. The subjugation of young women, for instance, is not only one of the oldest oppressions, it's one of the most pernicious—hence, it still resonates with audiences of all sorts. We first meet Cinderella in the scullery, a slave to the rough demands of her stepmother and older stepsisters. When Cinderella tries to take some initiative to improve her situation, she's squelched and punished. (I might add that the step-relationship is especially lush ground for storytellers, given the schizophrenic strength of the half-kin, half-stranger link.)

Margaret Atwood, in her landmark dystopian novel *The Handmaid's Tale*, steers the Cinderella archetype away from any home whatsoever and from any relationships, besides. She multiplies Cinderella a thousand times, and all the Cinderellas are kept alive for the sole asset they possess that can't be synthesized (at least, not yet!): their fertile wombs. Their purpose is to procreate a society that would be better off dead. And there are no handsome princes to come along and change anything.

Atwood drove Cinderella to a point almost—but not quite—beyond recognition. And that's the power.

You, too, can make gut-wrenching magic out of your fiction by driving your tale to a conclusion further than you ever thought it could go:

- **START AT THE CRUX OF YOUR PREMISE AND HIT THE GAS.** Agents and editors often tell new writers, "Don't start at the beginning, start in the middle," which usually means, "Don't waste pages setting up the core of your story." Wise advice. Try *starting* at your knottiest point, and then drive it forward using the same techniques that got your concept there. Everybody's bloody and panting, everybody's heart is broken, everybody's hanging on by their fingernails. Now what? Let the story begin!
- **MAKE IT BIGGER THAN THE INDIVIDUAL.** How would an organization intimidate and subjugate? Make it legal; go step by small step. Lawlessness isn't as frightening as a breakdown of the social order with the wrong people in charge. An organization can be as small as a truck stop, a fraternity house, or a bridal party. Let everything seem normal at first, and then gradually let things devolve, deteriorate, go wrong. Make your characters passengers trapped on a train that's barreling toward disaster.
- **ADD THE COMPLICITY OF A VICTIM.** Polite, politically correct society isn't at all comfortable with a victim being complicit in his own oppression. Good! The discomfort comes from the fact that everybody knows but doesn't *want* to know that such perversion of the human spirit exists; it's real because self-deceit is real. Break the taboo and use it to *make* your tale breathtaking, like a ship breaking apart on a reef.
- **PUT IN AN IMPOSSIBLE CHOICE.** The women in Atwood's novel live an impossible choice every day: Do they go along, or rebel? To go along is to destroy yourself from within; to rebel is to invite certain destruction from without. An impossible choice can confront someone who's being black-mailed, or someone who absolutely must have two conflicting things, or any number of other possibilities. And it can steer your story in new directions like nothing else.

STRIP IT

War has been the seed of innumerable creative works. In developing *War and Peace*, Leo Tolstoy put in everything he could think of because war is so big. To represent the French invasion of Russia and the accompanying Napoleonic era, he wrote an epic that followed dozens of characters. The sheer, pounding weight of detail in *War and Peace* helps us understand the impact of war on individuals and the institutions they thought to be unshakable.

But Ernest Hemingway, a young man reeling from his own experiences in World War I, stripped away everything he could think of because war is as small as one man. Confronted with the realities of war, he wrote what came to him, then stripped it and sanded it until nothing but hard, bright pieces were left. The result, *In Our Time*, is a collection of vignettes and short stories that evokes the immediate horror and lingering pain of that most awful of human activities.

When it starts to seem as if no number of words can truly represent the reality of anything, explore what might happen if you strip down your idea to allow the miniature to suggest the infinite:

- **ADOPT A MINIMALIST ATTITUDE.** If you've so far taken to heart my BAD advice (!), you might have a notebook or file with ideas, hunks of story, character notes, lists of heart-clutching moments you want to put in. Great material! Now, instead of trying to develop all that further by squeezing out more, look closely at what you have. Sort through it for gems, or what could become gems with some tough love. Seek quality over quantity. Continue to apply this mentality throughout your writing and revision.
- **CONVEY EMOTION THROUGH ACTION, NOT DESCRIPTION.** Inexperienced storytellers often try—alas, unsuccessfully—to do what Tolstoy did well: to not only show what happens but to tell in deep, ruminative detail how everybody feels about it. To Siberia with that! Do like Papa Hemingway: When Joe's dad in "My Old Man" gets crushed to death on the horse track, Hemingway simply lets Joe tell us that the cops held him back, and what his father's dead face looked like, and that it was pretty hard to stop crying right then. You, too, can present life-and-death emotion without saying a word about it. Adopting this approach from the outset of your idea development can save you a lot of writing and rewriting later.
- **USE SMALL PARTICULARS TO BRING BIG THINGS TO LIFE.** A mushroom cloud, or a burned, crying baby? A wedding with a cast of thousands, or the intimate taste of a lover? A travelogue, or the feel of acceleration down a mountain road? It's not too early to start thinking about your details. Be choosy. What makes *your* heart quicken? Those glancing moments may offer up all the description you need.

When you implement these techniques, don't bear down hard on any one; take a light, relaxed approach and allow idea to build on idea. If you do that, your innate creativity will take over. It knows what it's doing! At times when you're really rolling, your ideas will seem to develop themselves; they'll pop brighter and bite deeper.

And like the best inventors, who combine brilliant ideas with the guts and drive to make them reality, you won't be stuck drumming your fingers on the drafting table. You'll be producing well-developed stories with the optimum chance of success.

Elizabeth Sims is the author of the Rita Farmer Mysteries and the Lambda Award–winning Lillian Byrd Crime Series, and she has written short stories, poems, and essays for numerous publications. She writes frequently for *Writer's Digest* magazine, where she is a contributing editor. Her book on writing craft, *You've Got a Book in You: A Stress-Free Guide to Writing the Book of Your Dreams*, was published by Writer's Digest Books in 2013.

The Complete Handbook of Novel Writing

3

THE TAMING OF THE MUSE

Encouraging Inspiration Through Craft and Play

Paula Munier

When it comes to courting the muse, writers are as superstitious as baseball players. Rituals, icons, and talismans abound, all designed to stay on the good side of the muse, who when pleased will let you go with the flow, fire up your imagination, and ward off potential evils, like flat prose and plot holes and writer's block.

Leo Tolstoy and Friedrich Nietzsche both insisted that the best way to summon the muse is to take a walk. William Burroughs wrote down all his dreams because he believed that his muse visited him while he was asleep. Ken Kesey's muse was William Faulkner, whom he read to "get going" when he sat down to write.

Some writers beckon the muse with beauty: Amy Tan places historical artifacts related to her work-in-progress on her desk; Alice Hoffman paints her writing room the color that resonates with her current project. Others rely on particular tools: John Steinbeck used only round pencils—not hexagonal ones— and Elmore Leonard wrote all his novels on legal pads. And, perhaps most famously, many writers lured the muse with liquor: Tennessee Williams said he couldn't write without wine, and Norman Mailer needed a can of beer to "prime" himself. In fact, so many writers have relied on plying the muse with booze that alcoholism has often been called "the writer's disease."

While you may view all these muse-related rites and remedies as so much nonsense, you can't deny that inspired work is work that stirs the hearts of editors, agents, and readers. In short, inspired work sells. So let's take a look at how you can draw on inspiration as you master your craft.

FEEDING THE BEAST

Woodcrafters know that it's not enough to build something well—the most successful pieces are beautiful *and* well built. Form is as important as function.

The Shakers, whose furniture represents perhaps the ultimate expression of form meeting function, considered the construction of each piece an act of prayer inspired by the grace of God. You may not consider your writing an act of prayer or call upon the grace of God or the blessing of the muse to inspire you, but if you do, you are honoring the very meaning of the word *inspiration*, which comes from the Latin *inspiratio*, meaning "breath of God (or god)" or "divine guidance."

For best results, however, you need to define your god or muse. An angry, vengeful, Old Testament God or a scolding-harpie muse will not serve your work well—and may shut down your creativity completely. What you need is a little fun.

You read that right. *Fun*. If you find writing torturous and soul killing, then you should do something else. The same is true if you are writing to become rich and famous. There are far less stressful and taxing paths to fame and fortune. If you're in the writing game to make money, quit now—and take up investment banking. If you're in the writing game to become a household name, quit now—and pull a Kim Kardashian.

The only reason to be a writer is because (1) you love writing and/or (2) you couldn't stop writing even if you tried—and you've already tried. If the latter applies to you, then you need to learn to enjoy the process. You need to make it fun. It *needs* to be fun—or, at the very least, engrossing. That's what inspiration is all about.

If you're not engaging yourself, how can you possibly expect to engage the reader? If you're not amusing yourself, how can you possibly expect to amuse the reader? If you're not entertaining yourself, how can you possibly expect to entertain the reader?

STORMING YOUR BRAIN

Whether you believe that God (or some universal force) took six days or millions of years to create the Earth, you have to admit that, from a storyteller's point of view, it looks like the guy had a good time doing it. What an imagination: He created an amazing setting with deserts and mountains and swamps and seas and storms and earthquakes and germs and bugs and mammals and Cro-Magnon man, and then he threw in some plot elements like evolution and ice ages. Finally he gave our Homo sapiens hero—or is he the villain?—free will, curiosity, and seemingly equal, if conflicting, propensities for generosity and violence. Then he sat back and let the fur fly. Look at the world we live in—this is a world created by a playful God, worthy of the act of creation.

Playing God is the writer's job. We all think we'd like to be God—and daydream about what life would be like were we really in charge of the universe. If I were the boss of you and everything else, there'd be no fast food and no parking meters, and there'd be more librarians than lawyers, more poets than politicians, and free Wi-Fi and college and yoga for everyone and . . . . See? That sounds great, until the responsibility of it hits us. What's to be done about war and world hunger and that wastrel down the street who refuses to clean up his yard?

Deciding who lives and who dies in our stories is just part of that responsibility—a duty that can stop us in our tracks, leading to sleepless nights, unfinished manuscripts, and very expensive therapy sessions. But playing God can also be fun—provided your imagination is fully on board.

The playful god is the one who happily creates entire worlds from scratch, selecting the setting, populating it with characters and creatures, good and bad, and subjecting them all to feast and famine, love and war, death and dinosaurs, and disasters both natural and unnatural. He's the philologist who designs Middleearth down to the smallest detail—from the exquisitely intricate cartography, to the extravagant cast of dragons, dwarves, hobbits, elves, men, orcs, wizards, and wargs, to the numerous complex languages spoken by the aforementioned denizens of his fictive dream (J.R.R. Tolkien). She's the American scientist from Arizona who imagines a smart and sexy genre-bending historical science-fiction adventure-romance epic about an English ex-combat nurse in postwar northern Britain who is propelled back to eighteenth-century Scotland, where she finds herself caught in the middle of the ongoing skirmishes between the ruling English and the rebellious Highland Scots (Diana Gabaldon).

SEDUCING YOUR SUBCONSCIOUS

As we've seen, writers will resort to interesting and sometimes intense means of inviting the muse to bless their work. Thanks to ongoing developments and discoveries in brain science, we can avail ourselves of certain techniques that can put us in touch with our subconscious mind, the veritable playground of the storytelling gods, home to our intuition, emotions, dreams, memories, the collective unconscious, and more.

I've always envied visual artists because they seem to have a direct line to their subconscious. From where I sit as a writer, it looks like they just show up at the studio and plug right into their unconscious minds—and out it pours onto the canvas. Think of Jackson Pollock dribbling and drabbling paint at will, subconsciously re-creating the fractal patterns of nature years before fractals were discovered. I once spent an entire afternoon in front of Pollock's *One: Number 31, 1950* at the Museum of Modern Art, gazing at the work in silent reverence and watching people from all over the world seek it out and gaze along with me.

They say that writing is the most difficult of the arts because it does not appeal directly to a sense. Music appeals directly to our sense of hearing, painting to our sense of sight, the culinary arts to our senses of smell and taste, the textile arts to our sense of touch. When practitioners of these sense-related arts play—Miles Davis jamming on the trumpet, Martha Graham choreographing a dance, Chef Emeril Lagasse "takin' it up a notch" in the kitchen, Christo and Jeanne-Claude stringing saffron flags from 7,503 gates in New York City's Central Park—they can count on directly appealing to the senses of their audience in a way writers cannot.

Writing must undergo a translation in the reader's brain before it can be processed and understood. Typically the writer produces a series of black symbols on a white surface—letters on a page or screen—which must be interpreted by the reader. With any luck, that interpretation corresponds closely to the meaning the writer intended. This extra step puts us writers at a distance from our audience—a distance that other artists do not have to take into account.

All the more reason we should capitalize on our subconscious minds when we write. Here are some techniques that may help you:

- **TAKE A WALK.** The writers who begin their day's work with a long walk are too numerous to list here, but you can count Julia Cameron, Henry David Thoreau, and Jean-Jacques Rousseau among them. What's more, three forty-minute walks a week can actually grow your hippocampus, the part of your brain that forms, stores, and organizes your memories, according to a recent study by the University of Pittsburgh.
- **WARM UP.** You can warm up your writing muscles by entertaining your muse, just as the warm-up band entertains the audience before the concert headliner takes the stage. Try doing a crossword puzzle, writing a letter, or penning a haiku. For me, writing light verse works every time.
- **MEDITATE.** Meditation enhances creativity—and creativity is your muse at work. Meditate for thirty-five minutes before you sit down to write, and

you'll experience a boost in both divergent thinking (generating new ideas) and convergent thinking (focusing on solving one problem at a time), according to a recent study by Leiden University. Both divergent and convergent thinking are critical to good storytelling. Storytellers who have benefited from meditation include Kurt Vonnegut and Alice Walker.

- **SOUND IT OUT.** Music benefits the brain as well; studies show that listening to music can make you happier, relieve anxiety and depression, and activate the parts of the brain involved in movement, memory, planning, and attention, according to recent studies cited in *Trends in Cognitive Science*. Charles Bukowski listened to classical music on the radio as he wrote; Hunter Thompson preferred The Rolling Stones. Whatever floats your muse.

- **PLAY IT OUT.** If you play an instrument, all the better. According to researchers at Boston Children's Hospital, playing an instrument regularly boosts what is called the brain's executive functioning, which includes problem-solving skills and the ability to focus. The most famous writer band—or perhaps the only writer band—is probably the Rock Bottom Remainders, whose members include Stephen King, Amy Tan, Dave Barry, and Mitch Albom.

- **USE YOUR HANDS.** Writing by hand boasts cognitive benefits that typing does not, according to a growing number of studies from such venerable institutions as the University of Washington, Indiana University, and Duke University. The finger movements involved in handwriting switch on the parts of the brain related to language, memory, thinking, and idea generation. Many writers always keep legal pads or index cards close at hand, on which they scribble notes for their works-in-progress. I have a big sketch notebook for each project, in which I jot down notes, draw maps, create family trees, plot out storylines, and paste pictures of characters and houses and whatever else my stories need. I use pens and pencils, colored pencils and magic markers, sticky notes and paper clips. The more toys, the better, as far as your subconscious is concerned.

- **SLEEP ON IT.** Anticipation can be half the fun. When you're sleeping, your conscious mind goes dormant, too—but your subconscious mind remains awake. Before you go to sleep, ruminate about your characters, the storyline, those big scenes you've yet to write. Get your subconscious excited about your story—and then let it do the work while you get a good night's rest, just like John Steinbeck liked to do.

THREE NO-BRAINER RULES FOR YOUR BRAIN

1. **KEEP IT REAL.** The subconscious mind cannot distinguish between reality and visualization. So when you visualize yourself sitting down to write every afternoon at 3 p.m. or pounding out ten pages every night or plotting a thriller with more twists and turns than Hitchcock, your subconscious believes you—so make your visualizations as true to life as possible.
2. **KEEP IT SIMPLE.** Your brain can focus best on only one habit at a time. So if you are focused on summoning the muse—that is, acquiring the creativity habit—don't try to lose weight or quit smoking or take up running at the same time. Give yourself two weeks to six months to establish your connection with the muse before devoting attention to other habits.
3. **KEEP IT POSITIVE.** The subconscious mind cannot process negation, so be sure that when you sweet-talk your muse, you use positive statements: "I am an imaginative writer" (rather than "I am not a boring writer").

INSPIRATION ON DEMAND

When I think of a writer at play, I think of Ray Bradbury. I met him once, early in my career, at the Santa Barbara Writers Conference. Bradbury was the Dalai Lama of writers, an enlightened storyteller almost childlike in his enthusiasm for his craft. His joy was contagious; he made you feel good about being a writer and challenged you to enjoy the actual process of writing as much as he did. As he told us—and I took it to heart—"the first thing a writer should be is *excited.*"

If you need reminding what excitement looks like, spend some time with children. Any child at play will do, but small children are best—they have not yet had excitement shamed out of them. Think of toddlers digging for wiggling worms in the backyard, kindergartners set loose with finger paints and rolls of blank paper, school-age kids in the sun on the beach building castles and forts out of sand and sea. Even teenagers—out of the grown-ups' earshot—will drop the adolescent masks of apathy when texting or rapping or hanging out playing video games.

As a writer, it is your mission to recapture that childlike enthusiasm for play. This capacity for play is also a capacity for joy. I'm not saying that every word you write has to be a fun and happy experience—just a playful experience, the mere prospect of which excites you.

Excitement is often made up of equal parts anxiety, anticipation, and, ultimately, exhilaration. Watch a toddler learn to walk: the fearful first steps into the void, the frustration of the inevitable fall, the overwhelming determination to succeed, and, at long last, the unparalleled delight in the final wobbling that marks victory.

The toddler's path is the path of every creative person. The trick is to rekindle the excitement that fuels the toddler in your writer's soul. For toddlers, learning to walk is a game they must win. Sure, they could continue to crawl—the safer and more reliable form of travel—but one by one, they pull themselves up and master the art of walking. And then, much to their parents' trepidation, they win the ultimate boon: They run!

Life for a toddler is one exciting moment after another—serious play that reaps serious rewards. When I was a child, I spent a lot of time with the neighborhood kids playing war. (Before you judge us too harshly, note that my neighborhood was an armed camp, as I spent most of my childhood on Army bases, where war was the dominant metaphor of our young lives. We played war the way other kids played hide-and-seek and kick the can.)

I was a good soldier. But, cursed with a short attention span, I would often grow tired of war games and try to convince my pals to play school instead. Of course, I always insisted on being the teacher, which may have explained their reluctance to play along. I liked being the boss, running playtime for me and my playmates— and my commanding play proved good preparation for the writing life.

For when you're writing, you're playing, but you're in *command* of that play. If you're writing a thriller, the game could be a suspenseful, terrifying game of cat and mouse. If you're writing a romance, the game of love could be a dark, tragic tale of unrequited passion—or a boy-meets-girl fable with a meet-cute moment and a happy ending worthy of Nora Ephron. If you're writing a family drama, the game could be a domestic war that makes *Who's Afraid of Virginia Woolf?* look like child's play.

Speaking of play, there's a reason that even dramas as serious as the aforementioned Edward Albee masterpiece *Who's Afraid of Virginia Woolf?* are called plays. Think about it: In the theater, plays are comprised of words and actions written by one person and performed on a stage by actors portraying imaginary men and women doing imaginary things in imaginary places in order to entertain the audience. As a storyteller, you do the same thing—only you do it without the benefit of the stage or the actors or the audience. You sit alone in a room making up imaginary people doing imaginary things in imaginary places. That's playing—whether you enjoy the process or not. So you may as well take a cue from our friend Ray Bradbury and enjoy the hell out of it.

"INSPIRATION MEETS CRAFT" EQUALS "PRACTICE MEETS PLAY"

Having fun when you write means rediscovering your sense of play. Look to the games you loved as a child—especially the ones you played when left on your own—for clues on how to develop a playful attitude toward your work.

As an only child, I spent a lot of time alone. Especially in the summer, when we typically moved to a new place—with no school in session and many kids on vacation, I was forced to amuse myself. So I went on a lot of long walks in the woods with my little poodle Rogue, climbed a lot of apple trees, ate a lot of sour apples, and read a lot of books high in the branches, my faithful dog in wait below. I've replicated this playtime in my adult writing life. As long as I have apples, books, and a dog by my side, I can usually settle down to write quite happily. When the muse eludes me, I take a long walk in the woods.

Your sense of play is critical to establishing and maintaining a regular writing practice. In order to master your craft, you have to work at it day after day, week after week, month after month, year after year. The paradox here is simply this: To do something well, you have to like doing it enough to devote enough time to do it well—and yet to like doing something, you have to do it well enough to like doing it. Most of us like doing things we're good at—and eventually we stop doing things we feel we're not very good at.

Play and practice go hand in hand, just like inspiration and craft. Or at least they should. Dorothy Parker famously said that she hated writing but loved having written—and many writers have joined that chorus since. But let's remember that she drank to excess.

Better to be one of those writers who loves the writing process—and can't get enough of it. When it comes to role models, you're better off choosing Ray Bradbury over Dorothy Parker any day.

After all, it was Bradbury who said, "You must stay drunk on writing so reality cannot destroy you."

Paula Munier is the senior literary agent and content strategist at Talcott Notch Literary Services. A well-published journalist, author, copywriter, and ghostwriter, Paula has penned countless new stories, articles, essays, collateral, and blogs, and has authored or co-authored more than a dozen books, including *Plot Perfect*, *Writing with Quiet Hands*, and *The Writer's Guide to Beginnings*.

4

TESTING THE STRENGTH OF YOUR STORY IDEAS

....

How to Ensure Your Idea Can
Carry the Weight of a Novel

————————

Fred White

"I have a great idea for a story," you exclaim to a friend or spouse or just to yourself, only to have that idea lose steam after jotting down the opening paragraph. It's not uncommon for a writer to spend months or even years on a novel, drafting dozens, maybe even hundreds, of pages before realizing that the story isn't holding together or lacks distinction, or that the conflict is not strong enough or does not hinge upon a worthwhile goal, or that the characters lack flesh and blood.

You can decrease the likelihood of writing yourself into a corner by testing your story idea with key questions before you start drafting or even outlining. Questioning is an effective way of generating content; think of the journalists' famous "5Ws + H" (Who, What, When, Where, Why, and How). I propose that fiction writers employ their own set of content-generating questions, trading in the 5Ws + H for CCSP: Conflict, Characters, Setting, and Purpose.

1. Does your idea involve strong **CONFLICT**?
2. Are your **CHARACTERS** true to life?
3. Is the **SETTING** distinctive?
4. Is there a recognizable **PURPOSE**?

Before I explain how to use these questions to test the efficacy of your story idea, let's back up a bit by posing two preliminary questions: First, *Do you have a promising story idea to begin with?* Find out now by stating your idea in a single sentence. If you can't come up with anything that sounds like a story worth reading, then keep trying until you do.

> My story is about a psychiatrist who falls in love with one of his married patients.

Do we have a possible story premise here? Perhaps. Let's flesh it out a little more to get a clearer picture.

> My story is about a psychiatrist who succumbs to the amorous advances of one of his married patients, violating his code of ethics and that of his profession. (It is not uncommon for patients to become infatuated with their psychiatrists, and he realizes this.) But he also begins to suspect that her affections may be faked, that she wants to seduce him as revenge on his wife for having once slept with her husband—a secret the psychiatrist uncovers when he stumbles upon his wife's phone records.

The elaborated idea now shows a more developed conflict situation, one that sets itself apart, by virtue of the unexpected revelation, from the many other doctor-falls-in-love-with-patient stories out there.

The second preliminary question is this: *Have you researched your subject thoroughly?* If you're writing a novel about a psychiatrist, then you need to know a fair amount about psychiatry, psychoanalysis, and how psychiatrists typically interact with their patients. Your research should include not just background reading but interviews with practicing psychiatrists and people who have undergone psychoanalysis. Never give short shrift to research; a good novel or short story, whether a police procedural or an espionage thriller or a visionary tale of Martian exploration, rests on a solid foundation of factuality.

The basic story elements are now ready to be tested using the four CCSP questions. As you will see, each of these basic questions will serve as a springboard for more specific questions.

1. DOES YOUR IDEA INVOLVE STRONG CONFLICT?

"Story" implies conflict: clashing goals, values, and desires; uncertainties; and the consequences of one's decisions. Life is filled with conflict, but for conflict to work in a novel it must be in *urgent* need of being resolved, and it must be *difficult* to resolve. Urgency and difficulty are the elements that give strength to the conflict. Your protagonist will likely face several daunting obstacles that she must resolve. Think of Dan Brown's protagonist Robert Langdon, who, in *Inferno*, follows clue after clue (some of them false) that he hopes will lead him to the terrible thing the (presumed) antagonist has set up that may or may not destroy humankind. Of course, if your story focuses more on human relationships, the obstacles will probably be less explicit but equally daunting. For instance, in Ken Kesey's *One Flew over the Cuckoo's Nest*, Randle McMurphy tries to convince Nurse Ratched that her (and by extension the hospital's) treatment of mentally ill people makes the patients worse, not better.

To return to the psychiatrist who is attracted to his married patient, the conflict involves not only his professional ethics but the woman's marital situation. When probing the strength of this conflict situation, dig deeper. The following more specific, probing questions would likely arise as you explore possible consequences, goals, and plot twists.

- What would be the *consequences* of developing a romantic relationship with his married patient? (Possibilities: The woman sees an opportunity for blackmail, the patient's husband finds out and seeks revenge, the psychiatrist's ability to treat the woman becomes compromised just when he is gaining insight into her illness, the woman has an irrational hatred of men—which is why she sought a psychiatrist in the first place, and so on.)
- What *goal* does the psychiatrist hope to attain? (Possibilities: preserve his integrity and hers; honor his obligation as a healer; refuse to treat the woman because he has gained insight into her motives; etc.) And because unexpected outcomes in fiction often make the reading experience doubly rewarding, don't feel obligated to follow through with only the ideas you've generated here. If you happen upon a surprising idea in the midst of drafting and it works, run with it.
- What ironic *twists and turns* can you give to the conflict to make the story more distinctive? (Possibility: The woman's mental problem is that she feels compelled to ensnare professional men into compromising their standards— the very problem for which she is seeking psychiatric help.)

For a novel, you might also adapt the above questions to the characters in a subplot, one involving, say, the psychiatrist's childhood or the patient's history of mental illness, her relationships with men, and so on.

To examine the dynamics of conflict further, let's consider a different story idea, one dealing with a timely social problem: A high school teacher tries to stop a student from bullying a gay student. The main conflict is between the teacher, who worries that the bullying may lead to criminal violence, and the bully, who regards the gay student as a threat to his religious convictions—or perhaps to homoerotic impulses he denies. Is the conflict strong enough? Again, keeping both difficulty and urgency in mind, the following four secondary questions will help you decide.

1. What happens if the bullying student's parents interfere with the teacher's goal? (Difficulty factor)
2. What actions should the teacher take, before it's too late, that would make the bullying student (and/or his parents) realize the harm his bullying can cause? (Urgency factor)
3. How will the teacher get the other students to take a vocal stance against bullying, even though she knows many of them are against homosexuality? (Difficulty factor)
4. What must the teacher, the bullied student's parents, and/or fellow students do to keep the bullied student from harming himself or others? (Urgency + Difficulty factors)

By posing these probing questions and responding to them, you generate sufficient content for a novel.

2. ARE YOUR CHARACTERS TRUE TO LIFE?

Good fiction shows human nature for what it is: flawed, heroic, struggling, joyous, hateful, corrupt, self-serving, self-sacrificing, rebellious, and dozens of other attributes that make up the human condition. Good fiction also enables us to vicariously experience life through the psyches of people who are different from ourselves and yet possess enough shared qualities for us to identify with them. This is why reading fiction can foster compassion and tolerance. True, fiction—especially genre fiction—sometimes draws sharp distinctions between heroes and villains, good and evil, but character complexity should still emerge even in the most formulaic thriller or murder mystery. Characters become memorable when their actions and decisions, noble or ignoble, ring true, enabling us to put ourselves in their shoes. By asking whether your characters are true to life, you also raise this secondary question: What does it take for readers to identify with the people in your story, especially your main character?

In the story about the psychiatrist's struggle between his romantic feelings toward his patient and his professional ethics, you want your readers to empathize with, to vicariously experience, his emotional turmoil (and the patient's as well). It is by skillfully combining dialogue, internal monologue, and narration that your characters will become evocative. If you want to dramatize the psychiatrist's conflicting impulses, you might describe his powerful longing to make love to his patient; yet when he speaks to her, his words utterly belie those feelings. He might stonily tell her, "Please do not come here again."

In the story about the teacher and the gay-bashing bully, you may want to indicate that the bully secretly resents his strict religious upbringing. Maybe his aggressive behavior is compensation for his own so-called "effeminate" tendencies. A scene in which his father ridicules him for enjoying, say, ballet dancing, can add psychological complexity to the character.

Other questions that should arise from your efforts to make your characters true to life include the following:

1. How do I describe their physical and behavioral characteristics in a way that will make them more prominent? (Possibilities: conspicuous aspects of their appearance such as scars, tattoos, or hairstyle; quirky behavior traits such as hand-wringing, walking with a limp, or a peculiar manner of speech)
2. How can I describe my characters in a way that suggests a particular personality or psychological disorder? (Possibilities: nail-biting, which might suggest a neurotic personality; inability or unwillingness to make eye contact, which might suggest a lack of confidence or a guilty conscience)

3. IS THE SETTING DISTINCTIVE?

The setting (physical as well as circumstantial) contributes much to the reader's holistic experience of the story. In *Nineteen Eighty-Four*, George Orwell quickly establishes a dystopian setting with just a few masterful brushstrokes in the opening paragraphs. The clock striking thirteen (implying a militaristic government), the oversized posters of Big Brother throughout Winston Smith's apartment building, the unreliable elevator ("… the electric current was cut off during daylight hours. It was part of the economy drive in preparation for Hate Week.")—these background details pull the reader into the world of the story. Similarly, F. Scott Fitzgerald's description of the opulence of Jay Gatsby's mansion sheds light on Gatsby's obsessive desire to win back the heart of Daisy Buchanan (whose heart can be stirred only by opulence). Or consider how Edgar Allan Poe's description of the decrepit house in "The Fall of the House of Usher" serves as a projection of Roderick Usher's inner decrepit state. A fully delineated setting is a powerful tool for adding depth and intrigue to a story.

Test the efficacy of the setting in your story idea with these questions.

1. How can I make my story's setting a reflection of the conflict situation?
2. How does the setting serve as a projection of the protagonist's personality?
3. How does the setting contribute to the mood or atmosphere of the story?

The office of the love-smitten psychiatrist, for example, might contain a photograph of Sigmund Freud or a reproduction of the Hippocratic oath to indicate his commitment to upholding the highest standards of his medical profession. At the same time, the oath would come to represent the conflict between professional obligation and the irrational impulses of the heart.

As for the teacher who is determined to stop a student from bullying someone whose sexual orientation differs from the norm (or whose very presence is an affront to the student's religious upbringing), you might choose to set a chapter or scene in the school gym or classroom, or in the bully's home, where an important facet of the teenager's conflicted personality can be played out to maximum effect.

4. DOES THE IDEA FULFILL A CLEAR PURPOSE?

When readers wonder about the point of a story (or more bluntly ask, "So what?") they are wondering about its purpose or theme. Why does it matter whether the psychiatrist cuts off his romance with his patient or insists that upholding one's integrity is more important than giving in to the demands of the heart? Why does it matter whether the teacher decides to carry out her plan to stop the student from bullying a gay student, despite warnings from his parents not to interfere?

Sometimes writers get carried away with making the purpose too explicit, in which case the story becomes preachy or pedantic. Testing to determine if your story idea fulfills a clear purpose will quite likely trigger these questions.

1. How should the principal characters—the protagonist and antagonist—convey their respective convictions or values?
2. How will the reader come to realize that the protagonist's convictions are the most honorable or sensible under the circumstances?

The psychiatrist in the first scenario and the teacher in the second are both committed to the ethics of their respective professions (as well as to their own personal code of ethics), but the situation each one faces—the female patient who tries to seduce him; the bully whose actions demand action outside the protocols of teacher-student interaction—put these ethical commitments to a severe test, which makes for gripping storytelling.

By way of conclusion, I offer a cautionary note: As with all art, the art of fiction defies formulation. Stories can unfold in unpredictable ways, and that's a good thing; unpredictability often leads to flashes of original insight that make stories distinctive and memorable. The idea-testing guidelines I've presented are designed to get you to think deeply about conflict, character, setting, and theme. Human beings are subtle, complex, and unpredictable, and one of the challenges of art is to capture that subtlety, complexity, and unpredictability while still adhering to story design. To be a good writer of fiction, one should be a student of human behavior, to be ever curious about what makes people do what they do—or fail to do what they long to do.

Fred White is a professor of English emeritus at Santa Clara University, where he taught courses in composition and literature for more than thirty years. He is the author of *The Daily Writer*, *Where Do You Get Your Ideas?*, and *The Writer's Idea Thesaurus*, among others. He also has written scores of critical articles, essays, and fiction pieces over his distinguished career.

5

FIRE UP YOUR FICTION

Igniting Your Novel with Passion and Purpose

Donald Maass

Many fiction manuscripts submitted to my literary agency feel lackluster. Much genre fiction feels tired. Many mainstream and literary novels also strike me as stale. Even when well written, too often manuscripts fail to engage and excite me.

What is missing when a manuscript hugs the wall and refuses to dance? Originality is not the key. It can't be, otherwise no wounded detective would ever have a chance and every new vampire series would be dead on arrival. Even overpublished clichés can sometimes break out and sell big. The same is true of look-alike mainstream and literary fiction.

The issue, then, is not whether a story has a cool new premise. Whether hiking a well-worn trail or blazing uncharted wilderness, when a manuscript succeeds it is invariably fired by inspiration. Passion comes through on the page.

How does that passion get there? Here are some exercises to apply to your novel-in-progress. They are designed to dig up what matters in your story and infuse it in your manuscript in effective—but not obvious—ways.

FIND THE UNCOMMON IN COMMON EXPERIENCE

To get passion into your story, do it through your characters. What angers you can anger them. What lifts them up will inspire us in turn. Even ordinary people can be poets, prophets, and saints. That's true in life, so why not in your fiction?

Here is an exercise designed to discover and utilize what is universal in the experience of your characters, especially when they are regular folk like you and me.

Write down what comes to mind when you read the prompts below.

1. Is your story realistic? Are your characters ordinary people?
2. What in the world of your story makes you angry? What are we not seeing? What is the most important question? What puzzle has no answer? What is dangerous in this world? What causes pain?
3. Where in the world of your story is there unexpected grace? What is beautiful? Who is an unrecognized hero? What needs to be saved?
4. Give your feelings to a character. Who can stand for something? Who can turn the plot's main problem into a cause?
5. Create a situation in which this character must defend, explain, or justify his actions. How is the plot's main problem larger than it looks? Why does it matter to us all?

Find places in your manuscript to incorporate the emotions, opinions, and ideas generated in the prompts above.

FIND THE COMMON IN UNCOMMON EXPERIENCE

What if your protagonist is already a genuine hero? If your hero or heroine is an above-average, courageous, principled, and unstoppable doer of good, then you may believe that you don't have a problem. Cheering will begin automatically, right?

Wrong. Perfect heroes and heroines are unrealistic. Readers know that. They can't strongly bond with such characters. To connect, they need to feel that such paragons are real.

That is also true for the world of your story. The rarefied stratosphere of national politics, international intrigue, or any other out-of-the-ordinary milieu will not draw readers in unless they find some way to relate to it.

The following are steps you can take to humanize your hero and make the exotic world of your story real for us ordinary mortals.

1. Is your story about uncommon events? Are your characters out of the ordinary?
2. Find for your hero a failing that is human, a universal frustration, a humbling setback, or any experience that everyone has had. Add this early in the manuscript.
3. What in the world of the story is timelessly true? What cannot be changed? How is basic human nature exhibited? What is the same today as it was one hundred years ago and will be the same one hundred years ahead?

4. What does your protagonist do the same way everyone else does it? What is his lucky charm? Give this character a motto. What did she learn from her mom or dad?

5. Create a situation in which your exceptional protagonist is in over his head, feels unprepared, is simply lost, or in any other way must admit to himself that he's not perfect.

Find places in your manuscript to incorporate the results of the steps above.

DEVELOP THE MORAL OF THE STORY

What if your novel already has a driving message? Suppose its purpose is in some way to wake us up. That's great, but your message will harden your readers' hearts if you lecture or preach. To avoid that, let the *story* be your lesson. The teacher is your central plot problem. The students should be your characters.

Here are ways to use those elements to make your point.

1. Is there a moral or lesson in your story?
2. When does your protagonist realize she got something wrong?
3. Who in the story can, at the end, see things in a completely different way?
4. At the end, how is your hero better off?
5. At the end, what does your hero regret?
6. Who, in the midst of the story, is certain there is no solution or any way to fully comprehend the problem?
7. Why is the problem good, timely, universal, or fated?

Find places in your manuscript to incorporate the results of the questions above.

BUILD THE FIRE IN FICTION

Did you ever get lost in the middle of writing a manuscript? Have you ever wondered, deep in revisions, if your story holds together or still makes sense? Have you ever lost steam?

Steal from life. That's what it's for, isn't it? How often, when something bad happened to you, did you think to yourself, *At least this will be good material for a story some day*?

Well, now's your chance. The details and specifics of what has happened to you are tools with which you can make every scene personal and powerful. Use the following prompts whenever you are stuck or running low on inspiration.

1. Choose any scene that seems weak or wandering. Who is the point-of-view character?
2. Identify whatever this character feels most strongly in this scene. Fury? Futility? Betrayal? Hope? Joy? Arousal? Shame? Grief? Pride? Self-loathing? Security?
3. Recall a time when you most strongly felt the emotion you identified in the last step. When precisely did this happen? Who was there? What was around you? What do you remember best about the moment? What would you most like to forget? What was the quality of the light? What exactly was said? What were the smallest and largest things that were done?
4. In this experience from your life, what twisted the knife or put the icing on the cake? The situation would have stirred this feeling anyway, but what *really* provoked it?
5. What were you thinking when the importance of this experience struck you?

Give the details of your experience to your character, right now, in this very scene.

Donald Maass founded the Donald Maass Literary Agency in New York in 1980. His agency sells more than 150 novels every year to major publishers in the U.S. and overseas. He is the author of *The Career Novelist, Writing the Breakout Novel, Writing the Breakout Novel Workbook, The Fire in Fiction, The Breakout Novelist, Writing 21st Century Fiction,* and *The Emotional Craft of Fiction.* He is a past president of the Association of Authors' Representatives, Inc.

BEST-SELLING ADVICE
Plot and Structure

"Plot is people. Human emotions and desires founded on the realities of life, working at cross purposes, getting hotter and fiercer as they strike against each other until finally there's an explosion—that's plot."

—Leigh Brackett

"Remember: Plot is no more than footprints left in the snow after your characters have run by on their way to incredible destinations."

—Ray Bradbury

"Plot, or evolution, is life responding to environment; and not only is this response always in terms of conflict, but the really great struggle, the epic struggle of creation, is the inner fight of the individual whereby the soul builds up character."

—William Wallace Cook

"To me, everything in a novel comes down to people making choices. You must figure out in advance what those choices are going to be."

—Marion Zimmer Bradley

"The problem for me is finding my own plots. They take a long time. ... I like to have it happen, just like in our own lives. We don't always know where they're going, and if we make formal decisions on a given night, if we sit down and put a list of things we're going to do on a piece of paper, they almost never work out right.

—Norman Mailer

"I make a very tight outline of everything I write before I write it. … By writing an outline you really are writing in a way, because you're creating the structure of what you're going to do. Once I really know what I'm going to write, I don't find the actual writing takes all that long."

—Tom Wolfe

"For a book to really work, form and function must go hand in hand, just like with buildings, as any decent architect will tell you."

—Tracy Chevalier

"Transitions are critically important. I want the reader to turn the page without thinking she's turning the page. It must flow seamlessly."

—Janet Evanovich

"Sometimes one can overanalyze, and I try not to do that. To a great degree, much of the structure has got to come naturally out of the writing. I think if you try to preordain, you're going to stifle yourself. You've got a general idea, but the rest has to come naturally out of the writing, the narrative, the character, and the situation."

—Robert Ludlum

"There is no finer form of fiction than the mystery. It has structure, a storyline, and a sense of place and pace. It is the one genre where the reader and the writer are pitted against each other. Readers don't want to guess the ending, but they don't want to be so baffled that it annoys them. … The research you do is crucial. In mystery fiction, you have to tell the truth. You can't fool the reader and expect to get away with it.

—Sue Grafton

" Too many writers think that all you need to do is write well—but that's only part of what a good book is. Above all, a good book tells a good story. Focus on the story first. Ask yourself, 'Will other people find this story so interesting that they will tell others about it?' Remember: A best-selling book usually follows a simple rule, 'It's a wonderful story, wonderfully told'; not, 'It's a wonderfully told story.'"

—Nicholas Sparks

"We're past the age of heroes and hero kings. If we can't make up stories about ordinary people, who can we make them up about? ... Most of our lives are basically mundane and dull, and it's up to the writer to find ways to make them interesting. "

—John Updike

6

THE HERO'S JOURNEY

Implementing the Classic Storytelling Model

Paula Munier

All stories—whether you're entertaining your friends at the watercooler with a story about the bachelorette party you attended in Las Vegas or amusing your child with a bedtime fairy tale—are made up of three parts: beginning, middle and end. The three-act structure is the classic storytelling model: from "Once upon a time" to "happily ever after," and all the good stuff in between.

Once you understand and begin implementing the basic three acts, you can then refine the structure further. One way to do this is by following the hero's journey, in which the main character undergoes a meaningful transformation over the course of the narrative. But before we dive into this approach, let's explore the three-act structure at its most basic level.

EXPLORING THE THREE-ACT STRUCTURE

Breaking down a story into three acts is the first step in plotting. *Beginning, middle, end*: These are terms we've heard and used all our lives, but defining them in regard to storytelling is not as simple as you might think.

- **THE BEGINNING:** The beginning of your story is the point at which everything is about to change. It's the first step of the journey, the first fork in the road, the first turn in the right (or wrong) direction. The beginning is "Once upon a time, there was protagonist X—and then Y happened, changing everything for X."
- **THE MIDDLE:** In the middle, X must overcome the obstacles, master the skills, and learn the lessons needed to brave the ultimate test: Y Squared, the climax of the story (which will come at the end). The middle is the meat of

the story, in which all the twists and turns and detours on the journey home to the end challenge X to be his best—or worst—self.

- **THE END:** If X survives the middle, he's ready for the end. It's as if your protagonist has trained for the Olympics, and now all the obstacles he has overcome and skills he has mastered and lessons he has learned have armed him for the final contest, which is the mother of all trials and tribulations: Y *Squared*. *Y Squared* is X's worst nightmare—and to survive, X needs to become his best self, once and for all.

Let's take a look at how that breakdown works in two archetypal stories that are very different from one another—in length, genre, origin, audience, and so on—and yet structurally have much in common.

Cinderella

This classic fairy tale remains one of the most popular stories of all time. It gives us a likable heroine in Cinderella, a determined and cruel villain in the wicked stepmother, and perfectly mirrored secondary characters in the two ugly stepsisters.

> **ACT ONE (BEGINNING):** Cinderella's wicked stepmother won't let her go to the ball.
>
> **ACT TWO (MIDDLE):** The Fairy Godmother helps Cinderella get to the ball in style, where she meets Prince Charming, falls in love, and loses the glass slipper.
>
> **ACT THREE (END):** Cinderella is forced back into a life of servitude. Prince Charming shows up with the glass slipper and slips it on Cinderella's foot for a perfect fit. They get married and live happily ever after.

Star Wars

Star Wars is an epic tale of grand scope, but at its heart it's a coming-of-age story about a young man looking for adventure—and finding himself.

> **ACT ONE (BEGINNING):** When Princess Leia is captured, she sends out a plea for help. After his aunt and uncle are murdered, Luke Skywalker answers Leia's call—and joins Obi-Wan to rescue the princess and destroy the Death Star.
>
> **ACT TWO (MIDDLE):** Luke becomes a Jedi knight under Obi-Wan's tutelage. Together they enlist the help of Han Solo and Chewbacca to rescue Princess Leia.

ACT THREE (END): The rebel forces plan their attack on the Death Star. During the conflict, Luke must trust the Force in order to destroy the Death Star.

REFINING THE THREE-ACT STRUCTURE

Once you've determined the basic beginning, middle, and end of your story, you can build your plot by breaking each of those three acts into smaller units. One way to refine the three-act structure is by incorporating the hero's journey. This is a character-driven approach that describes the transformation the protagonist must experience over the course of the story. If you prefer reading and writing character-driven stories, the hero's journey approach may resonate with you. Or, if your story is plot driven and you know your characters could use some development, looking at your story as a hero's journey may help you create more well-rounded characters.

Famed mythologist Joseph Campbell introduced the journey of the archetypal hero in his seminal work, *The Hero with a Thousand Faces.* Campbell defines the hero's journey as a story in which the protagonist embarks on an adventure and faces trials and revelations that demand everything of him. He rises to the challenge and is transformed in the process.

THE HERO'S JOURNEY, STEP BY STEP

The hero's journey comprises three acts, and each act is made up of the steps the hero must undertake on a journey that will change him irrevocably and make him whole.

The steps of the hero's journey represent the stages of the hero's transformation. Let's examine this transformation step by step. (Note: There are various terminologies for the steps of the hero's journey. Here, I use a simple, updated transformational terminology for modern stories.)

ACT ONE (BEGINNING)

THE STATUS QUO: When we meet our hero, we see him in his everyday world, before he undertakes the journey that will change his life.

THE CATALYST: This is the event that calls for our hero to act, leave his everyday world behind, and embark upon a journey into the unknown.

DENIAL: Typically our hero balks at this call to adventure and rejects the opportunity outright—often out of fear or hesitation or pride.

ENCOUNTER WITH THE GURU: Every hero needs a mentor, someone whose knowledge and wisdom are vital to the hero's transformation. This sage adviser can help him navigate the twists and turns of life and, most important, the hazardous journey ahead.

ACCEPTANCE AND ACTION: This is the event that prompts the hero to change his mind and accept the new reality of his life. He decides to act, which means leaving his everyday world behind and crossing the physical and psychological threshold into a new world.

ACT TWO (MIDDLE)

TRIALS AND TRIBULATIONS, FRIENDS AND FOES: In this new world, our hero encounters the people who will aid him along his journey—and those who will thwart him. The tests that challenge him will help him determine friend from foe.

THE EDGE OF THE ABYSS: Now our hero is poised at the edge of the second threshold, but before he crosses it, he must regroup, rest, and plan his next course of action.

THE PLUNGE: The hero takes the plunge into the abyss, facing his greatest fear in a confrontation with death—literal or metaphorical.

THE PAYOFF: Having survived the abyss, the hero earns his prize.

ACT THREE (END)

THE WAY THROUGH: At this point in the story, the hero is on the road back to prepare for the biggest test of all. He may be running from the forces unleashed in Act Two—which is why the way through is often a chase scene.

THE TRUE TEST: This is the final test, the one in which the hero must prove that he has truly learned his lesson.

RETURN TO THE NEW NORMAL: Our hero comes home, transformed by his journey, with his reward—physical and metaphorical—in hand.

Let's refine the three acts of *Star Wars* using this approach. Notice how the stages of the hero's journey are slightly out of order in *Star Wars*. This demonstrates that the steps of the journey do not necessarily have to appear in the exact order outlined above, nor do they all have to appear in your story. The hero's journey is meant to be used as a guide, not a straightjacket.

ACT ONE (BEGINNING)

THE STATUS QUO: Luke Skywalker is bored at home on the farm with his aunt and uncle.

THE CATALYST: Luke finds a message from the kidnapped Princess Leia.

ENCOUNTER WITH THE GURU: Luke meets Ben, a.k.a. Obi-Wan Kenobi.

DENIAL: Obi-Wan offers to train Luke as a Jedi knight, but Luke refuses.

ACCEPTANCE AND ACTION: Stormtroopers kill Luke's family, and he begins his training as a Jedi knight.

ACT TWO (MIDDLE)

TRIALS AND TRIBULATIONS, FRIENDS AND FOES: Luke travels with Obi-Wan, C-3PO, and R2-D2 to the cantina and meets Han Solo and Chewbacca.

THE EDGE OF THE ABYSS: Luke and the team board the Death Star to save the princess.

THE PLUNGE: Luke encounters a series of ordeals, including the monster in the sewage, the collapsing trash room, attacking stormtroopers, and so on.

THE PAYOFF: Luke saves the princess.

ACT THREE (END)

THE WAY THROUGH: Luke and company evade Darth Vader and go home to prepare for the attack on the Death Star.

THE TRUE TEST: Luke uses the Force to destroy the Death Star.

RETURN TO THE NEW NORMAL: Luke comes home to a hero's welcome.

The hero's journey approach to the three-act structure is a classic storytelling model that outlines the hero's transformation (or dramatic arc) in the same way that humans have been telling these stories for millennia. Outline your hero's transformation according to the hero's journey and your story will resonate with readers, just like the myths of old.

USING THE HERO'S JOURNEY IN YOUR OWN WORK

To identify the steps of the hero's journey in your story, ask the following questions, stage by stage.

ACT ONE (BEGINNING)

- **THE STATUS QUO:** What constitutes your hero's ordinary world? All work and no play? Single and looking for love in all the wrong places? Stuck in the suburbs dreaming of Paris?
- **THE CATALYST:** What happens to wake up your character? Does he get fired? Flunk an exam? Find out his wife is having an affair? Get kidnapped? Get dumped? Murder his boss? Meet a cute girl? Get a new job offer out of town?
- **DENIAL:** Does your heroine act on this catalyst right away? Or balk? What excuses does she come up with to ignore what's happening? Why does she fail to act?

- **ENCOUNTER WITH THE GURU:** Who's your hero's mentor, adviser, or confidante? His mother? His boss? Sibling? Best friend? Pastor? Neighbor? Co-worker? How does this person guide your hero?
- **ACCEPTANCE AND ACTION:** What happens to change your heroine's mind? Why does she accept what's happening and decide to act now? What does she do? Where does she go? What new world must she enter?

ACT TWO (MIDDLE)

- **TRIALS AND TRIBULATIONS, FRIENDS AND FOES:** Who does your hero meet on his journey, in this new world? Who are his friends? His foes? How do they help—or hinder—him? What new skills must he master? What lessons must he learn? What obstacles must he overcome?
- **THE EDGE OF THE ABYSS:** What's the big challenge that faces your heroine now? How will she prepare for it—mentally, physically, and spiritually? What are her plans?
- **THE PLUNGE:** What plunge does your hero take? Does he risk declaring his love? Storming the castle? Righting a wrong? What fears must he overcome? How does he confront death—literally or metaphorically?
- **THE PAYOFF:** How is your heroine's brave plunge rewarded? Fame? Fortune? Sex? Love? Commitment? What's her Holy Grail?

ACT THREE (END)

- **THE WAY THROUGH:** Who's chasing your hero now? Are your hero's enemies or demons hot on his heels? How will your hero prepare for the next test, the biggest one of all?
- **THE TRUE TEST:** What is the test that will prove once and for all that your heroine has truly learned her lesson? How will she pass this test? *Why* will she pass?
- **RETURN TO THE NEW NORMAL:** What is the symbol of your hero's victory? A diamond ring? A crown? A Swiss bank account? Now that your hero is home safe and sound, his transformation complete, how will he celebrate that transformation? A wedding? A reunion? A graduation? Keys to the city? An island getaway in the Caribbean?

The Complete Handbook of Novel Writing

7

THE TWO PILLARS OF NOVEL STRUCTURE

How to Build a Sturdy Platform for Your Story

James Scott Bell

Structure is translation software for your imagination.

You, the writer, have a story you want to tell. You feel it, see it, populate it with characters. But turning all that raw material into a novel isn't simply a matter of putting it into words on a page or screen. You have to "translate" it into a form that readers can relate to.

That's what structure does. And if you ignore it or mess with it, you risk frustrating—or worse, losing—readers.

I was amused many years ago when a writing teacher of some repute shouted in front of an auditorium that there was no such thing as structure. He went on and on about this. Later, when I looked at his materials and the terms he had used to designate various story beats, guess how they unfolded? Yep, in a perfect, traditional three-act structure.

When it comes to the writing process, fiction writers tend to fall into two camps: those who prefer to outline before they write, and those who find outlines too constricting. The pillars of structure are equally useful tools for both types of writers. If you're a writer who likes to outline, you can learn to set up a strong story by mapping out a few key structural scenes from the start. And if you like flying by the seat of your pants, you can continue to be as free as you like with your first draft. Write hot. Just understand that later, you *will* have to think about structuring what you've written—because manuscripts that ignore structure are almost always filed under *unsold*.

But what, you may ask, *about authors who purposely play with structure—some to the point their books are called "experimental"?* Suffice to say that these authors usually know exactly why they are doing so—and they accept as a consequence that their books might not be as popular with the reading public as novels that have structure working in their favor. At the very least, every author should understand structure fully before playing around with it. (This advice also applies to hand grenades.)

A BRIDGE TO SOMEWHERE

My favorite visual representation of story structure is the suspension bridge:

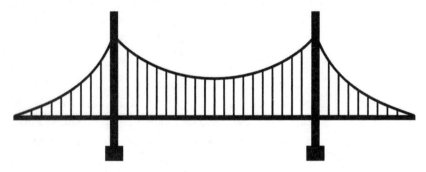

The key foundational elements here are the two pillars, or pylons. These pillars are set down in bedrock, allowing the suspension cables to support a solid and secure platform—the bridge itself.

Think about it: Every story has to begin, and every story has to end. And the middle has to hold the reader's interest. The craft of structure tells you how to begin with a bang, knock readers out at the end, and keep them turning pages all the way through. When you ignore structure, your novel can feel like one of those rope bridges swinging wildly in the wind over a 1,000-foot gorge. Not many readers will want to go across.

THE FIRST PILLAR

The beginning of a novel tells us who the main characters are and introduces the situation at hand (the story world). It sets the tone and the stakes. But the novel does not take off or become "the story" until it passes that first pillar. Think of it as a Doorway of No Return. The feeling must be that your lead character, once she passes through, cannot go home again until the major problem of the plot is solved.

Let's use *Gone with the Wind* as an example. In the first act, Scarlett O'Hara is sitting on her porch, flirting with Brent and Stuart Tarleton. We get to know her as a selfish, scheming, privileged antebellum coquette. She uses her charms to enrapture the men around her and play them like carp on a hook. A sister of the Tarleton twins says Scarlett is "a fast piece if ever I saw one."

If this novel were a thousand pages of Scarlett's flirtatious ways, we'd never make it past page 10. A successful novel is about *high-stakes trouble.* True character is revealed only in crisis, so Margaret Mitchell gives us some opening trouble (what I call the Opening Disturbance): Scarlett learns that Ashley is going to marry Melanie.

That trouble alone might be enough for a category romance, but not for a sprawling epic of the Old South. Something must force Scarlett into a fight for her very way of life, and that's what the first pillar is about: It thrusts Scarlett into Act Two. That event is, of course, the outbreak of the Civil War.

We first catch sight of this pillar in *Gone with the Wind* when Charles Hamilton hastens to Scarlett at the big barbecue at Twelve Oaks:

> "Have you heard? Paul Wilson just rode over from Jonesboro with the news!"
>
> He paused, breathless, as he came up to her. She said nothing and only stared at him.
>
> "Mr. Lincoln has called for men, soldiers––I mean volunteers––seventy-five thousand of them!"

The South, of course, sees this as provocation. Charles tells Scarlett it will mean fighting: "But don't you fret, Miss Scarlett, it'll be over in a month and we'll have them howling."

The Civil War is a shattering occurrence that Scarlett cannot ignore or wish away. She would rather stay in the Old South and preserve Tara, her family home, and her familiar way of life. In mythic terms, Scarlett would like to remain in the "ordinary world." But the outbreak of war *forces* Scarlett into the "dark world" of Act Two.

That's why it's useful to think of this as a Doorway of *No Return.* There is no way back to the old, comfortable world. Scarlett has to face major troubles now—and not just about matters of the heart. She will need to save her family and her land. She will need money and cleverness. She must overcome or be overcome.

In the classic three-act story structure, Act Two is all about "death stakes." That is, one of three aspects of death must be on the line: physical, professional, or psychological.

For Scarlett, it's psychological death (though her life *is* in danger at various points). If she doesn't preserve Tara and her vision of the Old South, she will "die inside," so to speak. *Gone with the Wind*'s story question is, *Will Scarlett grow from her old self into the self she needs to be?* She doesn't want this fight. But she is pushed into the death stakes because of the war.

The timing of the first pillar should be before the 1/5 mark of your book. In movies, it's common to divide the acts into a 1/4-1/2-1/4 structure. But in novels it's best to have that first doorway appear earlier. In a fast-moving novel like *The Hunger Games*, it can happen quickly. It's in chapter one that Katniss hears her sister's name chosen for the games, and in the beginning of chapter two, she volunteers to take her place.

Gone with the Wind is more than one thousand pages long. The Civil War breaks out at about the 1/10 mark.

Here are some other examples of the first pillar in popular novels:

- In Thomas Harris's *The Silence of the Lambs*, Clarice Starling is thrust into a cat-and-mouse game with Hannibal Lecter because it might be the only way to solve a serial killer case.
- Detective Sam Spade takes on Brigid O'Shaughnessy as a client in Dashiell Hammett's *The Maltese Falcon*.
- In Harper Lee's *To Kill a Mockingbird*, Atticus Finch accepts the job of defending a black man accused of raping a white girl. For his daughter, Scout Finch (the story's narrator), this means events thrust her into a dark world of prejudice and injustice. She can't remain an innocent.

Look at your own novel-in-progress and ask the following questions:

- Have you given readers a character worth following?
- Have you created a disturbance for that character in the opening pages?
- Have you established the death stakes of the story?
- Have you created a scene that will force the character into the confrontation of Act Two?
- Is that scene strong enough—to the point that the lead character cannot resist going into the battle?
- Does the first Doorway of No Return occur before the 1/5 mark of your story?

THE SECOND PILLAR

The second pillar is another kind of Doorway of No Return: *It makes possible or inevitable* the final battle and resolution.

Act Two, between the two pillars, is where the major action of the story takes place. The stakes are death (physical, professional, or psychological), and the lead has to fight (literally or figuratively). Remember: The first door has been slammed shut. The second act is a series of actions where the character confronts and resists death, and is opposed by counterforces.

Then the second pillar, or doorway, happens. This is often an event that feels like a major crisis or setback. Or it can be a clue or discovery. Regardless, it pushes the lead character into Act Three. It forces the final battle, the resolution. Indeed, it makes it possible.

Returning to the example of *Gone with the Wind*, Scarlett has many battles in Act Two. She needs to get out of Atlanta with Melanie before the Yankees take over. She needs to get money to save Tara from onerous taxes. She needs to figure out how to handle that charmer Rhett Butler, who keeps showing up in her life. These matters relate to the overall story question, the test (and growth) of Scarlett O'Hara's character.

All of this leads to the second pillar: the crisis that occurs when Scarlett marries Rhett. Scarlett still believes "*she belonged to Ashley, forever and ever,*" and yet she says yes to Rhett's proposal. Why? Because it "was almost as if he had willed the word and she had spoken it without her own volition."

This marriage makes inevitable the final battle in Scarlett's heart, and the crisis intensifies. Rhett finally realizes Scarlett will never give up on Ashley and decides to leave the marriage. Scarlett, however, has a realization of her own: that she has been living for a false dream, and that home and Rhett are what she truly needs. But it will, of course, be too late. Rhett doesn't give a damn, and Scarlett will have to go back to Tara to think about getting him back. Tomorrow.

Here are some other examples of the second pillar:

- Lecter tells Clarice that Buffalo Bill covets what he sees every day (clue). This information leads her to the killer.
- The bullet-ridden body of a ship's captain collapses in Sam Spade's office. Inside the bundle he was carrying is the black bird (major discovery).
- Tom Robinson, an innocent black man, is found guilty of rape by an all-white jury, despite the evidence to the contrary (setback).

Look at your own novel-in-progress and ask the following questions:

- Have you created a major final crisis or setback the lead must overcome?
- Alternatively (or additionally), have you presented a clue or discovery that is key to the story's resolution?
- Does this final Doorway of No Return make the resolution possible or inevitable (or both)?

THE OTHER SIDE

The two pillars of structure will never let you down. In defining the three acts of your story and creating points of no return for your characters (and your readers), they will guarantee that the platform of your story is strong. And they will free you to be as creative as you like with the elements of your story—characters, voice, scenes—without fear of falling off a rope bridge into the Valley of Unread Novels.

Let the construction begin.

James Scott Bell is the author of the number one bestseller for writers, *Plot and Structure*, and numerous thrillers, including *Romeo's Rules*, *Try Dying*, and *Don't Leave Me*. In addition to his traditional novels, Jim has self-published in a variety of forms. His novella *One More Lie* was the first self-published work to be nominated for an International Thriller Writers Award. He served as the fiction columnist for *Writer's Digest* magazine and has written highly popular craft books, including *Write Your Novel from the Middle*, *Super Structure*, *The Art of War for Writers*, and *Conflict and Suspense*.

8

WEAVING IN A SEAMLESS BACKSTORY

Creating the Tapestry of Your Character's Past

Karen Dionne

My first science thriller, *Freezing Point*, opens with the crew of a fishing trawler braving rough seas off the coast of St. John's, Newfoundland:

> The wind howled around the solitary trawler like an angry god. Inside the wheelhouse, Ben Maki braced himself as an errant wave hit broadside and the trawler listed heavily to starboard. Sleet spattered the windows on the port side. White patches of sea ice told him they were close. The captain grinned—at least, Ben hoped it was a smile; the expression could have been a grimace as it wrapped around an unlit cigar.

Who is Ben Maki? Why is he on this ship? What does he hope to accomplish? Readers won't find the answers to those questions in my opening pages. Why not? Because the answers are part of the novel's backstory.

Backstory refers to the characters' history and other story elements that underlie the situation at the start of the book. Backstory helps to establish the setting and makes the reader care about what happens to the characters.

But as authors, we need to be careful: Backstory by definition takes the story backward. Whether we employ flashbacks, character musings and recollections, or passages of exposition to reveal what came before, every instance of backstory stops our novel's forward momentum and risks leaving our stories, well, dead in the water.

TOO MUCH, TOO SOON

One of the most common mistakes I note when I'm called upon to offer comments on aspiring authors' manuscripts is that the author has included too much backstory in the opening pages. Sometimes the novel plods along page after page as the author diligently works to set up the story, and I have to force myself to keep reading. Other times, the novel gets off to a terrific start, but just as the author has carried me breathlessly through that first tension-filled chapter and I start thinking, *This author can really write*, the second chapter falls into storytelling mode—and I don't mean storytelling in a good way!

Including backstory in the opening pages is the same as saying to the reader, "Wait a minute—hold on. Before I tell you the story, first there's something about these characters and this situation that you need to know."

In actuality, there's very little readers need to know about our characters' history and motivations that they won't learn over the course of the book. Interrupting our story to tell the reader about something that happened *before* it began works against the very thing we're trying so hard to accomplish: engaging readers and sweeping them up into the world of our novel.

I love showing authors how they're unwittingly sabotaging their stories up front and then watching their lightbulbs go off, because the problem has such an easy fix: *All they have to do is isolate the instances of unnecessary backstory and take them out.*

If you don't have an experienced reader to look to for help, this solution might sound easier said than done. It helps to remember that strong novel openings are cinematic. Moviegoers don't question what they're shown on the screen as the film begins, because they're literally watching the story play out in front of them.

Likewise, throwing our readers into our narratives without explaining how the characters got to that point is enough to establish the story's reality. Putting my characters on that ship and showing what happens to them when the iceberg they lasso rolls unexpectedly and their ship turns upside down is sufficient. I have the whole rest of the book to show why they were there in the first place.

TIMING IS EVERYTHING

Managing backstory in a novel is a matter of control. A good storyteller has no trouble thinking up rich histories for his characters. But a good novelist holds these details back, revealing them only at the time that best serves the story.

"Rushing the backstory is a terrible waste," says Garth Stein, *New York Times* best-selling author of *The Art of Racing in the Rain*. "Many writers try to get too much out too soon. If the earthquake is going to happen today, don't start your story two days ago, even though something important happened to your protagonist two days ago. Start it with the earthquake. Then, the previous two days become the backstory that will inform our hero's actions in the 'now'—the fight he had with his wife, the fact that he has no gas in his car (or cash), or that his kids are stuck at summer camp and he has to get to them. Tension between what the reader knows and what the reader doesn't know will then serve to propel your reader through your story."

In addition to gumming up the trajectory of the narrative with unnecessary details, writers who reveal too much too soon interfere with what Stein calls "the reader's game of anticipation and prediction." He explains: "Part of the reading experience is the predictive game readers play. As readers, we are always trying to glean the reason for an action, and we put together our own backstory based on the clues a writer gives us. Sometimes those things turn out to be true, sometimes they don't. That's the fun part. When we discover the author's truth, we can compare it with what we predicted and see how it measures up."

If backstory in a novel's opening pages is a problem, why do so many newer writers include it? Most often it's because they don't realize that as they sit down to begin their novel, they're not actually writing the story—not yet. Those early pages might *look* like a novel, but they're really prep work.

"Writing backstory *feels* like storytelling," says *New York Times* best-selling novelist Jamie Ford (*Hotel on the Corner of Bitter and Sweet*), "but it isn't. It's regurgitating facts or dolling up aspects of worldbuilding—basically plugging in what that author already knows, hoping it will entertain and enlighten the reader. Instead it has the opposite effect. Less is more. Backstory is like creating a connect-the-dots picture—you just need the dots. The reader will draw the lines."

As we begin writing, we're grounding ourselves in the story, exploring our characters, creating their histories as we discover who they are and what they want. These early writings are a crucial part of the process. As authors, we need to know everything that came before and why our characters act as they do.

Our readers, however, do not. Answering their questions too early and too easily takes away a large part of the incentive for them to keep reading.

Examine your opening pages with a critical eye and ask: Does the reader really need to know this fact about the character? Or is this detail something that

I find interesting but isn't crucial to the story? Will the story fall apart if I withhold this information?

If your conclusion is that the reader absolutely needs to know a particular detail about the situation or the character, then ask yourself: Does the reader need to know this *now*, in the opening pages? Or can I reveal it later, after the reader is more engaged with the characters and has fully invested in the story? Is there a better way to introduce this crucial bit of backstory, aside from simply relating it? Can I accomplish the same thing more subtly by using hints and innuendos, thus allowing the reader to use her imagination to fill in the gaps and participate more fully in the story?

A good opening sets the scene, introduces the characters, and sets the story in motion. What it never does is answer the question, "Why?" *Why* the characters behave and think as they do, and how they came to this point in the opening, are questions that will be answered throughout the book.

THE RIGHT BALANCE

How can you discern which instances of backstory are crucial to the story and which are not? Folio Literary Management's Jeff Kleinman offers a simple answer: "Backstory is the stuff the author figures the reader should know—*not stuff the character desperately wants to tell the reader.* If it's critical to the character, it's critical to the reader, and then it's not backstory."

Read Kleinman's comment again. Good storytelling has nothing to do with what the author wants to say, and everything to do with what the characters need to say. As authors, we don't speak in our own voices; rather, we're speaking for our characters. Thus, it's perfectly all right to have a character say, "I grew up in a small town in New Jersey," or "I was the middle child in a religiously conservative family"—as long as this detail is something the character desperately wants to tell the reader.

Consider Stein's *The Art of Racing in the Rain*, which is narrated by a dog. In the opening paragraph, clearly, there's something the narrator urgently wants readers to know:

> Gestures are all that I have; sometimes they must be grand in nature. And while I occasionally step over the line and into the world of the melodramatic, it is what I must do in order to communicate clearly and effectively. In order to make my point understood without question. I have no words I can rely on because, much to my dismay, my tongue was designed long and flat and loose,

and therefore, is a horribly ineffective tool for pushing food around my mouth while chewing, and an even less effective tool for making clever and complicated polysyllabic sounds that can be linked together to form sentences. And that's why I'm here now waiting for Denny to come home—he should be here soon—lying on the cool tiles of the kitchen floor in a puddle of my own urine.

Aside from showing us that Stein's canine narrator is wonderfully self-aware, this opening raises more questions than it answers. All we know is that the dog is planning something—a "grand gesture"—and that it somehow involves lying in a puddle of urine while waiting for his master to come home.

This is the "now" of the story, as Stein puts it. "Think of your story as having two elements," he says. "There's the 'now,' which is the immediacy of the drama that's being played out before us, and there's the 'then,' which is the 'how we got here' of the story—or the backstory, if you prefer."

If you're realizing that you've inadvertently loaded the beginning of your novel with backstory, don't despair. "My editor always says, 'Cut this from the beginning and weave it into the narrative,'" Ford admits, "so I fight those same backstory battles."

WHEN IN DOUBT

For authors struggling with backstory, Kleinman has this advice: "In almost all cases, if it's backstory, it needs to be cut."

This might seem drastic. If you're not yet convinced, I offer this challenge: Comb through your opening chapters looking for backstory. Remove every instance, and see if your story doesn't read better.

I speak from experience. In addition to representing Stein and other successful authors, Kleinman is my agent. When I sent him the final draft of my first novel, the opening chapter included several paragraphs of backstory that I believed the reader needed to know in order to understand what was happening. More specifically: who Ben Maki was, why he was on that ship, and what he hoped to accomplish.

But Kleinman flagged all of these instances as unnecessary. He is a talented editor as well as a wonderful literary agent, and I trust his judgment. So I took his advice and removed every shred of backstory from the opening pages.

Later, after my novel sold and my Berkley editor sent *Freezing Point* out to select readers in hopes of garnering endorsement blurbs, *New York Times* best-selling thriller author Douglas Preston wrote, "The opening chapter is superb, a truly beautiful piece of work, one of the best I've read in a long time."

No matter where we begin our stories, there's always something that came before. Listen to your characters. Figure out what they desperately want to tell readers. Then hold these details back as long as you can. Reveal them gradually throughout your novel in clever, imaginative ways, and your story will remain firmly and engagingly in the "now."

Karen Dionne is the author of *The Marsh King's Daughter*, (G.P. Putnam's Sons, 2017), a dark psychological suspense novel set in Michigan's Upper Peninsula wilderness. She is the co-founder of the online writers community Backspace, and organizes the Salt Cay Writers Retreat held every other year on a private island in the Bahamas. She is a member of the International Thriller Writers, where she served on the board of directors as Vice President, Technology.

The Complete Handbook of Novel Writing

9

THE ESSENTIAL ENDGAME STRUCTURE

Techniques for Ending Your Novel Effectively

Larry Brooks

There are more than a few writers and teachers out there, many of them orders of magnitude more famous than I am (not hard to do), who don't like to compartmentalize or even attempt to define the sequential parts and essential milestones of a story's structure. Too formulaic, they say. Takes the fun and creativity out of it, they claim. A write-by-the-numbers strategy for hacks, a vocal few plead.

When they do talk about story structure, they tend to dress it up with descriptions that are less engineering-speak in nature—"the hero's journey" … "the inciting incident" … "the turn"—and are more appropriate to a lit class at Oxford. Makes them sound—or more accurately, *feel*—more writerly. Or perhaps they just aren't used to accessing their left brain for this very right-brained thing we call storytelling.

What's interesting is that the stories these writers create or use as examples in their teaching follow pretty much the same structural paradigm. And given that this isn't an exact science, that puts them in this left-brained ballgame whether they want to wear the uniform or not.

None of how story structure is labeled out there in Workshop Land is inherently wrong, nor does it really matter. What you call it is far less important than how you implement it—and the extent to which you understand it.

Thank God for screenwriters. Because they call it like it is. In fact, most of them think Oxford is a loafer.

THE FOUR PARTS OF EFFECTIVE STORYTELLING

I prefer to call story structure what it is: four parts, four unique contexts and discrete missions for the scenes in them, divided by two major plot points and a midpoint. Call them plot twists if you want to; the folks at Oxford won't know. Throw in a compelling hero's need and quest. Then formidable obstacles that block the hero's path. A couple of pinch points. A hero who learns and grows, someone we can empathize with and root for. Scenes that comprise the connective tissue among them all.

Then execute all of it in context to a fresh and compelling conceptual idea, a clear thematic intention, an interesting worldview, and a clever take on the plot.

I dunno, it all sounds pretty creative to me.

In other words, a blueprint for storytelling. One that, when understood and marinated in artful nuance and dished with clean writing, becomes nothing less than the Holy Grail, the magic pill of writing a novel.

Not remotely easy. But, perhaps for the first time, eminently clear. Then we come to Part Four: the finale of your story. And guess what? There is no blueprint for it. And no rules, either. Well, okay, there's one.

GUIDELINES FOR A COMPELLING ENDING

The one rule of Part Four—the resolution of your story—is that no new expositional information may enter the story once it has been triggered. If something appears in the final act, it must have been foreshadowed, referenced, or already in play. This includes characters.

Aside from that one tenet, punishable by rejection slip if you dismiss it, you're on your own to craft the ending of your story. And in so doing, the enlightened writer observes the following guidelines and professional preferences.

Guideline 1: The Hero Is a Catalyst

The hero of the story should emerge and engage as the primary catalyst in Part Four. He needs to step up and take the lead. He can't merely sit around and observe or just narrate, he can't settle for a supporting role, and, most of all, he can't be rescued.

I've seen all these things, many times, in unpublished manuscripts. I've rarely seen one in a published book. It happens, but never in a title anybody remembers.

Guideline 2: The Hero Grows Internally

The hero should demonstrate that he has conquered the inner demons that have stood in his way in the past. The emerging victory may have begun in Part Three, but it's put into use by the hero in Part Four. Usually Part Three shows the inner demon trying for one last moment of supremacy over the psyche of the hero, but this becomes the point at which the hero understands what must be done differently moving forward, and then demonstrates that this has been learned during the Part Four dénouement.

The hero applies that inner learning curve, which the reader has witnessed over the course of the story, toward an attack on the exterior conflict that has heretofore blocked the path.

Guideline 3: A New and Better Hero Emerges

The hero should demonstrate courage, creativity, out-of-the-box thinking, even brilliance in setting the cogs in motion that will resolve the story. This is where the protagonist earns the right to be called a hero.

The more the reader *feels* the ending through that heroism—which depends on the degree to which you've emotionally vested the reader prior to Part Four—the more effective the ending will be. This is the key to a successful story, the pot of gold at the end of your narrative rainbow. If you can make the reader cry, make her cheer and applaud, make her remember, make her *feel*, you've done your job as a storyteller.

If you can cause all of those emotions to surface, you just might have a book contract on your hands.

A PLAN FOR PART FOUR'S EXECUTION

Here's the real magic of Part Four: If you've done your job well in the first three quarters of your story, if you've plotted with powerful milestones that are in context to a compelling and empathetic hero's quest and evolving arc, chances are you'll intuitively know how your story needs to end when you get there. Or, if not intuitively, then after some serious introspection and long walks in the woods with a digital recorder.

And by "get there," I'm not suggesting you write the first three parts and then see where you are.

Fact is—and this is for anyone who thinks what is recommended above sounds like organic storytelling development—unless you develop your story over the first three quartiles using your story's key principles, parts, and milestones as benchmarks, you'll be more lost in Part Four than you may even have realized. Only by having an executed story plan as a baseline for the perhaps somewhat slightly more organic unfolding of Part Four does this process stand a chance.

That said, it's better to plan Part Four ahead of time, too. Even if you get a better idea for how to end your story along the way, this provides the richest landscape for that to happen.

What I'm saying is that you should strategize and plot all your main story points beforehand—even if you aren't yet sure of your ending—and in the process of developing the first three parts you'll find that the final act begins to crystallize as part of the process.

If you engage in story planning through a series of drafts rather than an outline, you'll need to write enough drafts to finally understand what Part Four should be. Same process, different tolerances for pain.

But there's risk in that. If you are a drafter, the likelihood of you settling for mediocrity is orders of magnitude greater. The prospect of rewriting the first three hundred pages does that to a writer.

SAVE YOUR STORY FROM COMING TO A BAD END

Too many stories end badly. And yet they somehow get published and even succeed to some degree. That's because the rest of the story—the structure of it and the compelling essence of the character—triumphs to an extent that the ending doesn't make or break the story at all. It just is.

Bad endings are far more common with established authors than they are for new ones because new authors rarely publish a book in which the ending isn't one of the best things about the reading experience. A bad ending—unsatisfying, flat, illogical, or just plain wrong—will get you rejected faster than misspelling the editor's name.

Your goal should be to make your ending a home run, especially if this is your first novel. Because the reverse is true, as well—a killer ending might soften the editorial reader to things that only a proven pro would get away with.

Story structure empowers an effective ending. If you can't craft one after a requisite deep immersion into the infrastructure of the first three parts, you haven't yet gone deep enough.

WHY STRUCTURE MATTERS

Every once in a while you'll read about a neophyte swimmer getting into trouble in deep water, and then, when a more experienced swimmer paddles out to help, he fights off the rescue with all his waning strength.

The thing about panic and resistance is that it can get you killed. What can kill you even quicker is not even knowing that you need rescuing.

The analogy hits home because every now and then, more often than you'd think, I encounter writers who just won't accept the unimpeachable truth and validity of story structure. They fight it off as if their writing dream is being mugged. They reject it as formulaic and therefore unworthy. Maybe they once heard a famous author—one who doesn't even realize the extent to which he is applying these principles in his work—talk about the spiritual, magical way he writes stories, sometimes actually bragging about all the rewriting he does to make it right.

Make no mistake, a rewrite is always a corrective measure. Nothing to brag about.

Virtually every published novel is, in fact, a natural product of solid story architecture, regardless of how it got there. To believe otherwise is like saying the aesthetic beauty of the halls of Versailles has nothing to do with poured concrete foundations and seamless masonry. With architecture. Or that, back in the day, there wasn't an actual blueprint for it all. Or that the pouring of those foundations was a no-brainer to the extent it didn't warrant intellectual energy of any kind.

These architectural atheists swear that writing a novel is, or should be, a process of random exploration, that their bliss resides in following characters down blind alleys and allowing them to set their own pace, with no real knowledge of where they're going.

This is like saying the joy of playing golf is wandering around the course, crisscrossing fairways, club in hand, hitting balls at assorted greens as you please. I don't dispute the inherent kick in such an approach. There's an innate kick in a lot of things: drugs, alcohol, sex with ex-spouses, Russian roulette … but that doesn't make them smart or productive.

Chances are, these folks are confusing process with product. If you're only in it for the process, that's one thing. Just don't expect to get published within this century.

Writing without bringing a solid grasp of story structure to the keyboard is like performing surgery without having gone to medical school. You can write like Shakespeare in love and have the imagination of Tim Burton on crack, but if your stories aren't built on solid and accepted structure—which means you don't get to *invent your own* structural paradigm—you'll be wallpapering your padded cell with rejection slips.

I'm not saying you *must* outline your stories. That's not what story structure means. What I am saying is that you do have to apply the *principles* of story structure to the narrative development process, outline or no outline. Organic or totally left-brained. At least, if you want to publish. That's just a fact.

Larry Brooks is the author of three number one niche bestsellers on amazon.com and other venues and lists: *Story Engineering, Story Physics,* and *Story Fix,* all from Writer's Digest Books. He is also the creator of the fiction-writing craft site storyfix.com, and speaks frequently at conferences and workshops internationally. He has published six critically acclaimed novels, all psychological thrillers (Turner Publishing), including a *USA Today* bestseller.

The Complete Handbook of Novel Writing

10

SUPPORTING STORIES

Adding Depth to Your Novel Through Subplots

Jessica Page Morrell

Subplots are miniature stories woven into the main story, complete and intriguing in their own right, serving to contrast, reinforce, or divert attention from the main plot. These mini plots contain beginnings, middles, and ends, and support the protagonist's emotional growth, further the dramatic action, and reflect or echo the significance of theme and premise.

Subplots can be centered on main characters in actions that fall outside of the main storyline, or they can be centered on secondary characters. Sometimes a combination of both is used. These stories-within-stories can run the entire length of the plot and be resolved near or in the climax, or they can have a short run and end long before the climax. They can also serve as magnifying glasses, underlining the actions of the main plot or providing relief from it when, for example, a story has violence, tragedy, or other elements that can seem relentless.

REASONS FOR USING SUBPLOTS

Subplots are often so intricately embedded into the main events that you don't even notice they're there. But if you dissect some of your favorite novels, you'll likely discover how the subplots expand the scope, provide extra highs and lows, and create verisimilitude. In the best stories, the characters appear rich, the action is weighted with thematic significance, and the whole is sprinkled with magic. Subplots, which are typically based on issues, concerns, or characters' agendas, can add to all these elements by:

- proving that your protagonist's life and the story world are complicated and teeming

- weaving the stories of two or three secondary characters into the protagonist's situation, thus revealing sides of the protagonist that cannot always be shown in the main action
- taking the pressure off the main storyline so that it does not become overly gloomy or exhausting
- introducing comic relief and hilarity (when appropriate)
- adding complexity to the story by introducing complications, problems, and more decisions and choices to be made
- revealing the growth and change in the protagonist
- fleshing out the story by building the fictional world between plot points
- providing social and political context
- enhancing theme and proving the premise
- adding to tension or suspense
- keeping the main plot from being resolved too soon, by sidetracking the protagonist or events from time to time
- deepening characters by revealing their opinions on things happening in the world—values and philosophies not connected to the main plot
- driving the story forward with more questions that need answering and more events and consequences that need resolution

Because readers want to believe in your fictional world and the situations that exist there, subplots serve a vital role. The events, diversions, and brief interludes found in subplots make fiction feel true to life and keep a plot from being too predictable.

Here is a litmus test of sorts to help you decide if a given subplot is necessary to your story: If a subplot can be removed without creating a hole in the story, it is not needed.

Writers often discover that subplots evolve as they develop the story, as if the characters are whispering suggestions. If your subplot evolves naturally from the main story and is not gratuitous or an afterthought, it will be more believable.

Subplots can revolve around everyday actions like shopping trips, phone calls, intimate moments, and displays of friendship. For example, Robert B. Parker's Spenser series features a large, gruff, and macho detective with an equally masculine sidekick, Hawk. The men work out together and go to elegant bars and restaurants, where they drink top-shelf Champagne or imported beers. Spenser is a gourmet cook and has a lover, Susan, who is a psychologist, while Hawk dates equally educated and fabulous women. These activities and relationships prevent the characters from becoming detective stereotypes and provide respite, moments to discuss the case, and opportunities to interject humor.

CREATING COMPLICATIONS

As conflict drives fiction, complications are necessary to entangle the character in ever-more-vexing dilemmas, difficulties, and situations. Complications are actions that enter the story world and change the course of the story. The most notable complication is the one associated with the inciting incident, the first change that opens the story, sets it into motion, and causes imbalance. As your story moves along, things keep getting worse for your protagonist, and often these worsening situations are created by complication-based subplots.

The best complications are unexpected but realistic, and somehow expand the story. They can be positive or negative; can thwart either the protagonist or antagonist; can stem from other characters, events, or discoveries; and can be based on anything from mistakes and misunderstandings to bad weather and physical threats.

Negative complications create problems for the protagonist and supporting characters, and make solving the main conflict more difficult by providing new obstacles that must be overcome along the way. Complications create a dizzying effect and add nail-biting moments to fiction.

If you've ever watched a daytime soap opera, you've noticed that there is no single plotline. Instead, there are many interconnections, complications, and linking storylines. In television dramas that feature an ensemble cast, such as *Downton Abbey*, *Grey's Anatomy*, or *Homeland*, the storylines are so interwoven with subplots that it is sometimes difficult to separate out the main story. In these dramas, the characters also deal with issues with family members, personal health problems, romances that bloom and die, troubled children, competition, or strife among co-workers. That list is only a beginning—the subplot possibilities for a large cast are endless.

If you watch television dramas, you might want to spend a week or so keeping track of subplots in your favorite shows. Number and name the subplots, and notice which ones last for an entire season or throughout the series. This small exercise proves the importance of secondary actions in making the whole complicated and captivating.

ENLARGING THE STORY WORLD

Authors most often use subplots to broaden the world of the story. Without sub-plots, a novel can become like the South Pole, where only penguins are able to survive—a vast, white, harsh environment with a single species to focus on. You need other creatures—especially predators—for conflict, interest, and variety.

Elinor Lipman's *Isabel's Bed* includes a number of subplots that enhance the scope of the story world. The main story centers on Harriet, who moves to Cape Cod to ghostwrite Isabel's scandalous life story. One of the subplots traces Harriet and Isabel's attempts to find and understand true love. Another subplot is about women's friendships and how beautiful women relate to other women. Yet another (hilarious) subplot focuses on writing groups, casting a satiric eye on these sometimes dysfunctional gatherings of scribes.

Jane Smiley's *Good Faith* is about the real estate industry during the Reagan administration. The main storyline follows the rise and fall of the fortunes of forty-year-old Joe Stratford, who's divorced and lives alone. The main plot fol-lows the classic "stranger comes to town" scenario. The stranger is Marcus Burns, a former IRS agent who now works as an investment counselor and who pulls Joe into a business deal. A number of subplots reflect the era and paint a picture of the real estate industry and other interests that intersect with it. One subplot reflects the implosion of the unregulated savings and loan industry, while an-other looks at the dangers of day trading and gold speculating. Smiley's forte is transforming her research into readable drama; her subplots, even if they teach how golf courses are built and land development works, never feel like instruc-tion but like part of a large, entertaining world.

CONNECTING CHARACTERS

In novels written with an ensemble cast, there is usually a single connecting thread—a family, a place, an event, a company, a war—that holds together a com-plicated series of ongoing subplots running alongside the main storyline. The late best-selling Irish author Maeve Binchy made this sort of novel her staple. Her novels are especially noted for well-rounded secondary characters, complexity, cleverly entwined subplots, and characters that combine to create a fully real-ized world. One such novel is *Scarlet Feather*, which follows one year in a start-up catering business in Dublin.

The main story centers on the business, beginning on New Year's Eve, when partners Tom Feather and Cathy Scarlet discover a location for their operation and buy the building. The business gets off to a roaring start, but that doesn't last, and their personal lives also begin to fall apart. Written in an omniscient viewpoint, with each chapter devoted to a single month, events in the catering business serve as the main thread and include a fairy-tale wedding, party disasters, a robbery, slow-paying customers, and cooking on a live television show. These events move forward, intricately woven among the following subplots that simmer along with the gourmet meals:

- Cathy's husband, Neil, is a workaholic lawyer who doesn't really support her.
- Neil's interfering mother doesn't think Cathy is good enough for him.
- Cathy's mother was once Neil's mother's maid.
- Tom's relationship with the beautiful Marcella is floundering.
- Muttie Scarlet, Cathy's father, has good and bad luck betting on the horses.
- Marcella longs to be a model, but she's too old for high fashion.
- Tom's father ends up in the hospital with a heart attack.
- Cathy becomes pregnant and then suffers a miscarriage.
- Neil's niece and nephew, nine-year-old twins who continually wreak havoc, disappear.

Binchy pulled off the complicated story structure by using many half-scenes, flipping from place to place and character to character with few explanations and transitions, relying heavily on dialogue, using minimal setting details, and keeping most fully realized scenes short. Because the viewpoint is omniscient, she was able to slip into many of the characters' thoughts while zigzagging among dozens of lives.

This sort of novel would be difficult for most beginning writers to attempt, but it still can be instructive to examine, especially if you yearn to write in depth about a huge cast of characters. Notice how quickly Binchy's narrative moves in and out of scenes. Also note that her dialogue contains a liberal dose of subtext, every character has an agenda, her protagonists are sympathetically drawn, and the main storyline reflects enough knowledge of the food business to be convincing.

SUBPLOT MISSTEPS TO AVOID

Finding a balance between your main storyline and your subplots requires skilled craftsmanship. You might face tough decisions about what to include and what to leave out. Here are a few cautionary guidelines to help you on your way.

- **DON'T DANGLE SUBPLOTS LIKE LOOSE THREADS.** If your story has more than one subplot, it typically works best not to resolve them all at the same time. Tying up too many loose ends in the climax tends to be messy and steals the focus from the main ending.
- **DON'T FOLLOW A SUBPLOT WITH THE SAME FOCUS AND WORD COUNT THAT YOU DEVOTE TO THE MAIN STORY.** Pay attention to proportion when devising subplots. Generally, they should never take up more scenes than main plots.
- **NEVER TOSS A SUBPLOT INTO A STORY TO TAKE UP SPACE OR ADD TO THE WORD COUNT.** They should always be specific to the story and highlight some aspect of character, storyline, theme, or premise.
- **DON'T FORGET TO PROVIDE YOUR SUBPLOTS WITH RISING AND FALLING ACTION.** Subplots are based on actions and events that cause your characters to shape new behaviors, emotions, or thoughts. As in the main storyline, the most significant events are those that result in a character's emotional change.
- **DON'T LET YOUR SUBPLOTS WEAKEN THE MAIN STORYLINE.** In novels, when you use multiple viewpoints or alternating time frames, the story will split off and widen into separate segments. The same can happen with subplots—but they can send the story skittering off on a tangent, and that tangent, unless well crafted, can be distracting or seem extraneous.

CREATING SUBPLOTS THAT MATTER

Subplots are not tossed into a story willy-nilly as if you're sowing grass seed. Some might appear in your imagination along with the main storyline, while others will develop as you get to know your characters.

To help yourself imagine the intertwining events, people, and relationships, draw a diagram of your storyline and the related subplots. While there are many options for creating this diagram, and you might want to create more than one, here's a fairly simple way to begin: Write your protagonist's name in bold letters in the center of a piece of paper. From this name, create a web or wheel with spokes, connecting your protagonist to everyone else in the story. Place your antagonist on the page, add secondary characters, and sketch a line to connect them to the protagonist. Be sure to connect each relationship in the story by calling out significant subplots and conflicts.

In addition to (or instead of) creating a web, you can write a brief outline that summarizes a subplot. For example, suppose your main storyline surrounds Jennifer's search for her sister, Brenda, who disappeared from her college dorm.

Meanwhile, a romance subplot is woven in to complicate matters. Your subplot outline can be fairly simple, such as:

> A few weeks after Brenda disappears, Sam and Jennifer meet at a party and discover they both have a passion for microbrews and mah-jongg. The two start spending time together, but then Sam has a family emergency and travels to Pennsylvania without contacting Jennifer before he leaves. While he's away, Jennifer, feeling rejected, confused, and angry, starts dating her old boyfriend, Justin, who promises to help her with her search. Justin begins pressing her to marry him. As strange clues about Jennifer's sister's whereabouts pile up, Sam returns; he and Jennifer argue about the state of their relationship and decide to call it quits.
>
> Sam and Jennifer meet three months later at a mah-jongg tournament, where they are teamed together and beat all their rivals. Jennifer is wearing an engagement ring, so their banter is forced. Later, during a celebration, Sam observes Jennifer with Justin and can tell that he's not right for her. In a bold move, Sam tells her this.
>
> In the main storyline, Jennifer discovers that her sister was murdered and, realizing that life is fragile and remembering how her sister always took risks, she breaks off her engagement and resumes a relationship with Sam.

If your subplots are based on your protagonist, begin the most important one in the early chapters after you launch the main storyline. If you have a subplot that involves a secondary character, it's often best to delay starting it until the reader is familiar with the main characters and the milieu of the story and understands the story question. The main storyline must be established with a firm foundation before these subplots take off so that the reader isn't confused.

When constructing your story, envision the plot and subplot more as a web or maze than as parallel lines like a railroad track. The best plots zigzag back and forth between main story and subplot. You don't write the main plot, then stop it to write the subplot, then drop out of that sequence to return to the main plot. Instead, the subplots *intersect* with the main storyline, and vice versa.

Subplots are most easily devised from the characters nearest the protagonist. Thus, when you look for subplots, you needn't look far. In Janet Evanovich's Stephanie Plum series, Stephanie's on-again, off-again romance with Joe Morelli and her dangerous attraction to Ranger provide the main subplot. But the protagonist's wacky family also provides subplots and comic relief.

Here's a tip: Use the characters closest to your protagonist; the closer the emotional ties between the subplot character and your protagonist, the greater depth your story will have.

Subplots are a powerful tool for plotting, but they require forethought and planning. Since a single plotline often cannot carry enough interest in a novel, you have exciting choices to make when you devise your crowded, fascinating world. Choose wisely with your theme and premise in mind, and, when possible, merge your subplots with your protagonist's main actions.

Jessica Page Morrell understands both sides of the editorial desk as a developmental editor and author and has a deeply practical approach to writing and teaching. She writes with depth, wit, and clarity on topics related to writing and creativity, along with other topics, and is the author of *Thanks, But This Isn't For Us: A (Sort of) Compassionate Guide to Why Your Writing is Being Rejected*; *Bullies, Bastards & Bitches: How to Write the Bad Guys in Fiction*; *The Writer's I Ching: Wisdom for the Creative Life*; *Voices from the Street*; *Between the Lines: Master The Subtle Elements Of Fiction Writing*; and *Writing Out the Storm*. Her work also appears in eight anthologies and *The Writer* and *Writer's Digest* magazines. Morrell founded and coordinates writing conferences, has been creating columns about the writing life since 1998, and is a popular speaker at writers' conferences in North America and Ireland. Morrell lives in Portland, Oregon, where she is surrounded by writers and gardens and watches the sky in all its moods.

11

BEHIND THE SCENE

....

Five Techniques for Crafting Stronger Scenes

James Scott Bell

A great story premise will not stand without solid scenes to prop it up. Colorful characters can flit across the page, but unless they are engaged in pitched battle, the reader simply won't care.

Don't let your scenes fall into cliché or monotony. Always look for ways to freshen them up. Here are five techniques to help you do that.

1. MAKE YOUR DIALOGUE FLOW

Try writing a scene in only dialogue. Let it flow. Don't think much about it. When you're finished, you can look back and figure out what the scene is really about.

I once wrote a scene between competing lawyers. Part of it went like this:

> "You think you can get away with that?"
> "Whatever works."
> "Disbarment works, too."
> "You want to try to prove that? Know what that'll make you look like?"
> "Don't presume to know what I will or will not do."
> "I know you better than your wife, Phil."

That last line of dialogue came out of nowhere. Why did the character say that? I could have just edited it out, of course, but it seemed far better to explore the implications. They led to a plot point in which the one lawyer revealed he'd had an investigator tailing Phil for six months—and had pictures, places, and dates Phil would not want revealed to his wife.

All that just from playing with dialogue. Try it, and you'll discover undercurrents for your scene you didn't know existed.

2. CUT OR HIDE EXPOSITION

Any time the author gives information in narrative form, the immediate story is put on hold. This exposition, if you don't watch it, can bloat and choke off a good scene.

Look for exposition you don't need. If it's not crucial for the moment, delay it. If it's not crucial for the overall story, cut it. The more important information can often be "hidden" by putting it into either dialogue or a character's thoughts.

3. FLIP THE OBVIOUS

Our minds work by reaching for the most familiar choices available. For writers, that usually means a cliché. So learn to flip things.

If your characters are mere archetypes, your scenes won't engage the readers. Imagine a truck driver rumbling down the highway at midnight, holding the steering wheel in one hand and a cup of hot coffee in the other.

Got that?

I'll bet the first image that came to mind was of a burly male, probably wearing a baseball cap or cowboy hat. That's a familiar image of a trucker. It's a cliché, and therefore not very interesting. But what if you flipped it around? What if the trucker was a woman?

Try it.

Now you have an image to play with. But I'll wager you still pictured a rather "tough" woman, because all truckers are tough, right?

Flip that around. Put this woman in a nice evening dress. What does that do for your image? Why is she dressed that way? Where is she going? Who is after her?

You can also play this game with descriptions and dialogue:

> "It's about time we started the meeting," Johnson said. "Let's do an agenda check."
>
> "Right," Smith said. "First up is the Norwood project. Second, the P&L statement. Third, staffing."

Stop a moment and flip the obvious response:

> "It's about time we started the meeting," Johnson said. "Let's do an agenda check."
>
> "Do it yourself," Smith said.

The nice part about this exercise is that even if you decide to stick with your original dialogue, the list you come up with provides you with possible subtext or insights about your character.

Play this game and you're guaranteed to yield fresh material for your characters, dialogue, and, of course, scenes.

4. APPLY THE CLOSED-EYES TECHNIQUE

Describing a physical setting in rich detail is crucial to a vivid scene. Where do such details come from? Say your hero has just entered a house where a friend lives. Close your eyes and "see" this house. Then record what you see as if you were a reporter on the scene. Describe all of the details as they are revealed to you. Then edit out what you don't need. By doing it this way, you'll give yourself plenty of good raw material to work with.

5. KNOW WHAT YOU'RE AIMING FOR

Every scene in your novel should have a bull's-eye moment or exchange to aim toward. A bull's-eye can be a few lines of dialogue that turn the action around or reveal something striking. It can be as subtle as a moment of realization or as explicit as a gunshot to the heart. Many times it is found in the last paragraph or two.

Identify that bull's-eye moment so you know what you're writing toward. Then hit the target. You may be a little off center in the first draft, but that's what rewriting is for. You'll hit it the second or third time.

START YOUR NOVEL RIGHT NOW

As soon as an idea jells in my head, I want to start writing. I've got a lot of ideas at various stages, and sometimes I just want to venture, Kerouac-style, into the land of be-bop-prose rhapsody.

So I've developed a mini-plan of action that lets me write a little while also pushing me to the next stage of my preplanning.

If you're one of the impatient ones, maybe these steps will work for you, too.

WRITE A LOGLINE
Don't settle for plain vanilla. Work a one-line concept summary of your idea until it juices you.

An insurance salesman and a hot, upper-crust woman plot to murder her husband for double the insurance payout.

EXPAND THE LOGLINE INTO BACK-COVER COPY

Your cover copy doesn't have to be perfect, but it does have to excite you enough to keep going.

> Slick insurance man Walter Neff thinks he's got the world on a string. And then he meets Phyllis Dietrichson, the hot young wife of one of his clients. Maybe it's that anklet she wears. Or maybe it's the smell of honeysuckle in the air.
> Whatever it is, it's murder.
> Driven by lust and greed, Walter helps Phyllis plan her husband's murder. Walter knows how to make it look like an accident so Phyllis can collect under the double indemnity clause.
> But there's one problem, and his name is Barton Keyes. A legendary insurance investigator, he can sniff out a fraud from miles away. Walter knows everything has to be perfect. And so it seems.
> Until that night on the train …

WRITE THE OPENING DISTURBANCE

You know enough about your characters to do this. Get a visual in your mind. Cast the characters. You can use any actor, living or dead.

For Walter, you might imagine, say, Fred MacMurray. Or Mickey Rooney. For Phyllis, maybe you'll think of Barbara Stanwyck or Kate Winslet.

Now write an opening chapter.

WRITE THE NEXT SCENE

Make more trouble, or write the characters' reaction to what just happened.

BRAINSTORM

Quick—make a list of twenty things that could happen next. Don't think too much. Then brainstorm about your lead character. Deepen her. Give her inner struggles and conflicts.

Now plan three more scenes.

WRITE THOSE SCENES

Now you will be in a great position to judge your story. Take a week just to experiment, rewrite things, try a different point of view, outline. Play.

Your novel will grow naturally. And you've hardly broken a sweat.

BEST-SELLING ADVICE
Characters

" Begin with an individual, and before you know it you have created a type; begin with a type, and you find you have created—nothing."

—F. Scott Fitzgerald

"Don't expect the puppets of your mind to become the people of your story. If they are not realities in your own mind, there is no mysterious alchemy in ink and paper that will turn wooden figures into flesh and blood."

—Leslie Gordon Barnard

"When writing a novel a writer should create living people; people, not characters. A character is a caricature."

—Ernest Hemingway

"People do not spring forth out of the blue, fully formed—they become themselves slowly, day by day, starting from babyhood. They are the result of both environment and heredity, and your fictional characters, in order to be believable, must be also."

—Lois Duncan

"A genuine creation should have character as well as be one; should have central heating, so to say, as well as exterior lighting. "

—James Hilton

" The character on the page determines the prose—its music, its rhythms, the range and limit of its vocabulary—yet, at the outset at least, I determine the character. It usually happens that the fictitious character, once released, acquires a life and will of his or her own, so the prose, too, acquires its own inexplicable fluidity. This is one of the reasons I write: to 'hear' a voice not quite my own, yet summoned forth by way of my own."

—Joyce Carol Oates

"I said the hell with Plot. I'm going to write stories about people that interest me, the way I see them. I'm sick of formula. I'm sick of Hero, Heroine, Heavy. I'm sick of neat, tidy, emasculated emotions, with every little puppet jerking through the paces of what ought to be and not what is. I'm sick of Characters. I'm going to write about men and women, all classes, types and conditions, within the limits of my own capabilities. People with faults, with nasty tempers, with weaknesses and loves and hates and fears and gripes against each other. People I can believe in because I know and understand them. People who aren't like anybody else's characters because they are themselves, like 'em or don't. … And all of a sudden I began to sell."

—Leigh Brackett

"When I was a Hollywood press agent, I learned how the Hollywood casting system worked. There was a roster of actors who were always perfect as doctors or lawyers or laborers, and the directors just picked the types they needed and stuffed them into film after film. I do the same [with my characters], book after book."

—Richard Condon

"When you are dealing with the blackest side of the human soul, you have to have someone who has performed heroically to balance that out. You have to have a hero.

—Ann Rule

"The writer must always leave room for the characters to grow and change. If you move your characters from plot point to plot point, like painting by the numbers, they often remain stick figures. They will never take on a life of their own. The most exciting thing is when you find a character doing something surprising or unplanned. Like a character saying to me: 'Hey, Richard, you may think I work for you, but I don't. I'm my own person.'"

—Richard North Patterson

"Writers shouldn't fall in love with characters so much that they lose sight of what they're trying to accomplish. The idea is to write a whole story, a whole book. A writer has to be able to look at that story and see whether or not a character works, whether or not a character needs further definition.

—Stephen Coonts

12

CHARACTER STUDY

Populating Your Fiction with an Authentic Cast

Alice Hoffman

It's often said that all characters in a dream are pieces of the dreamer's consciousness; the dreamer is every character in her own dreams, including the cat and the dog. It's also true that every character in a writer's fiction is a piece of that writer's consciousness. Fully imagined characters—that is to say, characters who aren't based on real people—are drawn from our own subconscious. We should know these people deeply because in some way, whether a character is a mass murderer or a nun, we are them.

In concentrating on what's inside a character at the deepest level, there's often a story within the story about the character—one the reader may never know, but one that the writer must always know. A character's interior trauma or past experience is the core around which everything else is built. By writing so closely to a character's spirit, the drafting process needs to be free enough to allow the writer to enter into another person's consciousness. In a way, this is the greatest accomplishment for a writer in building character: When it's possible to "think inside someone else's head," we know we've succeeded in breathing life into a fictional person. Once this happens, we can stand back. The character can control his fate.

There are teachers who may tell you to write about what you know and to write about people you've seen, met, eavesdropped on, or sat down at a table with for a family dinner. But if a writer knows the inner truth of an emotional experience, he can write about it in every setting. As fiction writers, we can be inside the experience of every situation and every character. A woman doesn't have to be a man to write about one, even in the first person, and vice versa. The art of being a writer of fiction, as opposed to nonfiction or memoir, is to be yourself and yet have the ability to imagine yourself in another's circumstances. My mentor, Albert Guerard, always told his students that a writer didn't have to experience something to write about it; he only had to be able to imagine it. And I'd add that we also have to be able to feel it.

My method of character building is from the inside out—not necessarily the color of eyes and hair, the height and weight, but rather questions like these: How does a person sleep at night? What does he fear? Does he run from lightning or rush toward it?

One of the best devices in terms of imagining characters in an ongoing project such as a novel, which can take months or years to write, is to live inside the characters—to take them with you into the outside world, to experience real life in, say, a Starbucks or an airport, both as yourself and as your character. This means thinking about your character's reactions while you react as yourself. As fiction writers we split ourselves into parts: The self and the characters we write about all abide within us. At times, during the process of writing, it's possible to experience the disintegration of the self. This is the ecstasy of writing and of art, of losing oneself in the process of creating.

The moment when you know that your characters are fully alive is when they begin to make their own choices; this happened to me with my novel *Seventh Heaven*. In outline after outline, list after list, my character Nora Silk was planning to get involved with a police officer. But one day she did the oddest thing—she fell in love with someone completely unexpected. I tried to rewrite her into doing what I willed, what I wanted, but Nora Silk now had a mind of her own. I should have known she'd do as she pleased from the moment she entered my novel, driving fast and taking directions from no one.

> Nora Silk was trying to keep up with the moving van, but every time she stepped down hard on the gas and hit sixty-five miles an hour the Volkswagen shimmied for no reason at all. Nora had to hold tight to the steering wheel whenever the tires edged into the fast lane. She looked past the heat waves and concentrated on driving until she heard the pop of the cigarette lighter.

My first experience with the intensity of writing characters that seemed real was when I finished my first novel, *Property Of.* Fittingly, I dreamed about a ceremony in which my characters were leaving me, and I awoke in tears. It's a loss to finish with a character you've put so much time and energy into, and, of course, so much of yourself. But, like dreams, there's an endless supply of characters waiting to be created and named.

Alice Hoffman has published twenty-three novels, three books of short fiction, and eight books for children and young adults. Her novel *Here on Earth* was an Oprah Book Club pick in 1998. Her novels have received mention as notable books of the year by *The New York Times, Entertainment Weekly, The Los Angeles Times, Library Journal,* and *People.* Her most recent novel, *The Marriage of Opposites,* was an immediate *New York Times* bestseller.

13

UNEARTHING YOUR CHARACTER

Drilling Down to the Core Personality

Jeff Gerke

Are you just like anyone else? I mean *just* like, as in no one, including your mother, could tell you apart from the other person?

I'm guessing not. Even identical twins are different from one another—though on the genetic level they are technically clones. The closer you look the more differences emerge. No two people are identical.

So why do we see novels peopled with identical characters? Why is there so little variation or even creativity among characters in so many novels?

Oh, sure, the characters in these novels might be different on the surface. One is male, and the other is female. One is old, and the other is young. One is Asian, and the other is Caucasian. One has long hair, tats, and sundry piercings, while the other is a choir boy with a crew cut. But these are just costuming details. They hardly distinguish personality. Ideally, they are an *expression* of personality, but that's not the same.

Then you get differences in attitude. One is mean, and the other is nice. One is anxious, and the other is relaxed. One is bitter, and the other is forgiving.

Or differences in agenda. One is after someone's job, and the other is content where he is. One wants to have a baby, and the other wishes she could get rid of her nine kids.

Sometimes you see differences in speech that the author hopes will constitute the person's entire character: the surfer dude and the low rider and the butch and the New Ager and the hillbilly.

Blech. Even taken together, these things do not add up to a *personality*—neither in fiction nor in life.

Worse, we often see outright stereotypes in fiction. The kindly old man, the rebellious teenager, the floozy, the greasy politician, the authoritarian military man.

But even if you had an angry floozy with red hair, an Australian accent, and the goal to sleep her way up the corporate ladder, you still don't necessarily have a real character.

Without selecting a core personality for your characters, most likely all the people in your book *will feel the same.* The peaceful ex-Marine with a lisp and the desire to just get by on the minimum may, to the author, seem different from the floozy, but at his core, at the spot where his actual personality should shine through, he will feel just like the floozy to the reader. As will the crook, the pedophile, the mailman, and the FedEx clerk.

Because without an authentic character personality, no amount of external decoration can conceal the fact that the mannequin under it all is the same mannequin under all the others.

The difference these characters are lacking, the difference your characters must have from one another, is core personality.

GETTING TO THE HEART OF THE MATTER

When I had set myself the challenge to create an ensemble cast of characters for my Operation: Firebrand novels—and succeeded in landing a three-book publishing contract to bring these people to life—I pretty much panicked.

What have I gotten myself into? I don't know how to make differentiated characters! Think, Jeff, think. How do you make characters seem different? Well, who studies differences in character? Psychologists. Yeah, yeah! I'll run to the bookstore and look up personality types in the psychology section. Psychologists are supposed to know what makes people tick—and what makes them different. And wait, I've done those personality self-tests before. I'll look into those, too.

I walked out of the store with a book worth its weight in gold, if you'll excuse the cliché. I found it in the psychology section. It's a temperament studies book called *Please Understand Me II* by David Keirsey. Though it is not a book designed for novelists, fiction writers can gain a great deal from it. In it, Keirsey works with the Myers-Briggs temperament classifications.

The thing that separates *Please Understand Me II* from other books based on the Myers-Briggs framework is that Keirsey describes how these temperaments

The Complete Handbook of Novel Writing

will behave in so many arenas: career, marriage, hobbies, parenting, conversation, and more. Keirsey describes in marvelous detail what each type aspires to, what kind of language each type uses, what type of work each type gravitates toward, and which type-to-type pairings work best (and worst) in relationships. Lots of grist for the novelist's mill.

The Myers-Briggs model divides all personalities into four broad categories, and further divides each category into four subcategories, resulting in sixteen possible character types.

You don't need to use *Please Understand Me II*—or even the Myers-Briggs temperaments—to create your characters. But you need to find some model to serve as the basis for your characters' core personalities.

A couple of other great resources that cover personality types—and are more geared to novelists—are *45 Master Characters* by Victoria Schmidt and *The Writer's Guide to Character Traits* by Linda Edelstein, Ph.D.

Now, using a personality type for the basis of your character may not sound very impressive. You may find yourself saying, *If we're using stock characters, how can we create original characters for our fiction?* But there's a bit more to it than that. A character type represents a core temperament, but then you add layer upon layer to round out your character and bring your fictional person to life. By building characters in this way, no two characters you create will ever be the same, even if they're based on the same temperament type.

CORE PERSONALITY TEMPERAMENTS

Your first step in creating a character is to choose a core personality temperament. I'm going to assume here that you're building your protagonist, but the principles apply to all your major characters. You don't have to go through the entire process for every character in your novel, by the way, just the top three to six.

Let's look at a brief explanation of the Myers-Briggs model to get an idea of how to form a core personality type for your character. As you read through these descriptions, keep in mind the character you're creating. Which of these types seems closest to what you want to do with this character? Remember: You're not trying to find yourself in these descriptions (although it might be good for you to do that once, just to get it out of your system), but to find your *character*.

The Myers-Briggs Type Indicator (MBTI) categorizes all personality types in terms of four dichotomies, or either-or choices. Everyone, for example, is either an extrovert or an introvert. That's one of the four dichotomies. The other three either-or dichotomies are sensing versus intuition, thinking versus feeling, and judgment versus perception.

From these, the Myers-Briggs system assigns letters:

- Extrovert (E) or Introvert (I)
- Sensing (S) or Intuition (N)
- Thinking (T) or Feeling (F)
- Judgment (J) or Perception (P)

According to the system, everyone is on one side or the other of each of these little seesaws. Someone might be an extroverted, sensing, thinking judger (ESTJ); an introverted, intuiting, feeling perceiver (INFP); and so forth. There are sixteen possible combinations of the letters and traits.

That means there are sixteen core personality types. As we've seen already, that doesn't mean there are only sixteen possible characters to use in fiction. Though, speaking of my own particular weaknesses, having sixteen differentiated characters in my beginning fiction would've been a sixteen-fold improvement!

The Sixteen Types

Here are brief summaries of the sixteen Myers-Briggs personality types. These only scratch the surface. I recommend you use one of the books mentioned in this chapter or find another source to help you select your main characters' core personality types. You will get a much fuller description of personality than space allows me to provide here.

- **INFP:** sees the world as full of wonder, as through rose-colored glasses; must have work that has a meaningful purpose; idealistic
- **ENFJ:** organized and decisive; works to build harmony in personal relationships; empathetic; sees potential in everyone
- **ISFJ:** a serious observer of other people; has an overwhelming desire to serve others; often taken advantage of; responsible
- **ESTP:** tolerant and flexible; prefers actions over words; the doer, not the thinker; spontaneous; impulsive; competitive
- **INFJ:** true activist for a worthy cause; good insights into other people; remembers specifics about people who are important to him
- **ESTJ:** the person self-appointed to keep everyone in line; prefers facts to opinions; stays with the tried and true; practical
- **ENFP:** idea person; warm and enthusiastic; enjoys work that involves variety and experimentation.

- **ISTJ:** quietly thorough and dependable; always seeking to clearly understand things; punctual to a fault; can seem cold
- **ESFJ:** generous entertainer; lover of holidays and special occasions; natural leader; good delegator; encourager; cooperative
- **ENTP:** ingenious; outspoken; easily bored by routine; challenges status quo; institutes change; clever; incisive
- **INTP:** obsessed with achieving logical consistency of thought; natural and creative scientist; looks for the logical explanation
- **ENTJ:** organizes groups to meet task-oriented goals; vision caster; always seems to find herself leading; spots inefficiencies and fixes them
- **INTJ:** system builder; both imaginative and reliable; natural strategist; long-range planner; independent and original
- **ISTP:** doesn't do something unless it's a big project into which he can throw himself utterly; great "big problem" solver
- **ESFP:** exuberant; outgoing; lover of life; hedonistic; partier; scattered; into the "new"; Johnny on the spot; chatty
- **ISFP:** sensitive; caring; all about feelings (hers and other people's); moody; quiet; kind; doesn't like conflict; needs her own space

SELECTING YOUR CHARACTER'S TEMPERAMENT

When I'm creating a new character, I turn to *Please Understand Me II*. The author has grouped the sixteen types into four main temperament groups. I read those general group descriptions first. Usually doing that will get me into the neighborhood of what I'm sensing this character should be.

Then I'll dig deeper by reading the four types within the main category I've selected. Again, I'll keep reading until I get an internal check that says, "Nah, that's not her." If I get all the way through the description without finding anything that triggers that internal check, I know I'm on to something. Indeed, most times I'll encounter one or more items that ring true about this character. I'll go, "Yes! That's totally her!"

Whether you use the Myers-Briggs model or some other study of character type, reading the general descriptions will help narrow your search. You can then dig deeper to find more traits that fit your character until you have a match.

Once I have a match, I begin writing notes. You might not do it this way, but I like to write down the parts of that personality description that resonate with me when I consider the character. I may not know how I'll use the idea in the story—I might not even know what my story is yet!—but I know I'll want to work it in somehow because I've found something that is intrinsically, almost poetically, *right* about her.

If you prefer plotting to characterization and you experience one of these Zen-like moments of rightness, you will find yourself oddly geeked over something you'd never given a great deal of thought to: characters. And then you're hooked.

I said before that if you follow this process thoroughly, your characters won't all be the same, even if they're based on the same temperament. That's because you'll be reading through the type descriptions with a different person in mind each time. For instance, as you're trying to find the core personality of your mother character, you'll notice different elements than when you read through the descriptions for, say, your second lieutenant character in Vietnam. It will never seem like you're reading the same description twice.

USING YOUR OWN TEMPERAMENT

If you're like most novelists, you'll automatically base your protagonist on *yourself*. It's certainly an understandable temptation.

But I would advise you not to choose your own temperament for your main character—at least for the first few times through this process.

The problem with basing your protagonist on your own personality type is that you can't really see yourself. You are the least objective person on the planet when it comes to the subject of you. You may perceive yourself as outgoing and fun, while the rest of the world sees you as the antisocial toadstool you really are. (I'm joking, but you get the point.)

And if you don't have a clear sense of who you are—and, let's face it, most people do not—how can you write a consistent fictional character if that character is based on you? When it comes to writing characters for your novel, one of your largest blind spots is most likely your own personality.

If you simply must model the main character after your core personality, then study the description of that type carefully. Be sure you're adhering to how your personality type normally behaves, even if *you* wouldn't do it that way. If you veer off the path, internal consistency of character will forever elude you in your novel, and you won't even know where you lost it, much less how to get it back.

Also, if you decide to use your own temperament for the hero, don't let any other character in the book have the same temperament. You'll need to raise a barrier around your protagonist, metaphorically speaking, to make sure your personality doesn't seep into the personalities of one or more (or all) of the other characters in your book.

COMMENCE LAYERING

If you haven't already chosen a base personality type for the character you're building, do so now. If you're having trouble choosing between two or three, just pick one of the candidates and run with it. If you find yourself scrunching your face and thinking, *That really doesn't seem like her,* then go back and try one of the other candidates.

In a pinch, you can always take a bit of one of the types to add to another type that the character seems most like, because real people sometimes score highly on two or more types. But it will make it harder to keep track of who this person really is and how she would really behave.

When you settle on your character's type, review the description thoroughly, writing down ideas that occur to you based on those details. Note how this person behaves in public, what she aspires to, what she'd like to be seen as, what she values, what types she best gets along with, what types rub her the wrong way, what careers she would gravitate to, what kind of spouse and parent she will be.

Take extensive notes for how these things could come into play in your story. You may not use them all in the book, but they'll get you in the right frame of mind for who this person is.

Then, equipped with this ocean of thought about this character, you can soak in it as you're writing. If you lose touch with who this person is, return to these notes and bask awhile. Wade around in the ideas you first had that gave you those *a-ha*! moments as you dreamed her up.

Jeff Gerke loves to empower novelists to tell the stories burning holes in their hearts. He does so through his how-to books for Writer's Digest, through the many writers conferences he teaches at every year, and through his own freelance mentoring and editing services at jeffgerke.com. He is the founder and former owner of Marcher Lord Press, a small science fiction and fantasy publishing company, and he is the author of multiple novels, including the Operation: Firebrand trilogy of military thrillers.

14

THE OUTER LIMITS

How to Stretch Your Character

David Corbett

Most of us at some point in our reading lives have come upon a scene where one of the characters does something so odd it doesn't just defy expectation, it stops us cold.

We're not pleasantly intrigued, we're baffled—or annoyed. The dreamlike illusion we've enjoyed up to that point has been ruptured not in some Brechtian breach of the fourth wall but through plain bad writing. We scratch our heads, thinking, *The character just wouldn't do that.*

As writers, we don't ever want our readers to feel that kind of disconnect—but that doesn't mean our characters should be neatly and easily defined, either. Pushing our characters to their limits, in fact, is what makes for compelling fiction.

So how, then, can we determine the limits of what's believable in how a character behaves?

CHARACTER IN CONTEXT

In life, when someone we know acts "out of character," the subtext is almost always *Something must be wrong.* The strange behavior, we assume, must be the result of some strain of which we're unaware.

Sometimes we learn the person has a health problem. Sometimes we learn he was under the influence. The intoxicant may be drink or drugs, the pressure of fear, or the rush of love (or some other kind of rapture), but the result is the compromise of the person's inhibitions.

In the most unsettling cases, we come to realize we don't know the person as well as we thought. The behavior we found puzzling resulted from an aspect of personality we simply didn't know, recognize, or understand. (This kind of revelation isn't limited to others. You may even have shocked yourself on occasion, behaving in a way that made you think, *Where the heck did that come from?*) One great advantage reality has over fiction is that it doesn't have to make sense. It just happens. In the case of real people, there's no stopping the movement of time to say, "*I don't buy that.*"

The great challenge of fiction is creating characters who feel logically, emotionally, and psychologically consistent—who make sense—but retain the enigmatic power to surprise.

It should come as no shock that the trick is to learn from real life.

Just like their real-world avatars, characters who defy our expectations are almost always either:

- under a strain
- feeling free of some customary inhibition
- revealing something about themselves they've previously concealed

Put otherwise, the key factor in the seemingly strange behavior is normally one of the following:

- conflict
- permission
- deceit or disclosure

CONFLICT: I WOULDN'T DO THIS IF I DIDN'T HAVE TO

When the principal motivator for the unexpected act is conflict, the character enters the scene with a strong desire and a plan for achieving it, only to run smack into an equal—or overpowering—counterforce. As the character learns his plan is insufficient, ill conceived, even ridiculous, he tosses aside this element or that—or pitches the whole thing overboard—and is forced to adapt and improvise.

The limits of what the character can do in the service of improvisation are defined first by the parameters of her mental and emotional makeup. But those parameters acquire elasticity depending on the depth of the character's desire, the ferocity of the opposition, and the stakes.

For example, in the film *Three Days of the Condor*, Joseph Turner (played by Robert Redford) is a mild-mannered analyst. But when he returns from lunch one day to discover his co-workers murdered, he kidnaps Kathy Hale (played by Faye Dunaway) as he tries to find a safe place to regroup. Turner's not "the kind of guy" who under any other circumstances would abduct a woman. But his behavior is believable because his adversaries are ruthless. He's not acting as he *might*; he's acting as he *must*. And the real key to the credibility of his otherwise out-of-character behavior is that he himself acknowledges the abnormality of what he's doing.

Likewise, in Tennessee Williams's *A Streetcar Named Desire*, Blanche DuBois is desperate to find not just a resting place but a home with her sister, Stella. It becomes obvious, however, that Stella's heart and home now belong to her husband. Blanche struggles harder and harder to get Stella to come out and say it—"my home is your home"—using flattery, nostalgia, guilt, sisterly simpatico, humor, but her efforts continue to fail. Finally, there's nothing to do but something wildly out of character; Blanche tells her sister the unvarnished truth: "You're all I've got in the world." But, being Blanche, she can't help but add a little manipulative dig: "And you're not glad to see me."

These scenes work because the characters don't improvise wildly; they start with the familiar, using tactics they know well. The level of strangeness rises in sync with their desperation as the conflicts build and those tried-and-true methods fail.

The scenes also succeed because on some level the characters express or recognize the unusualness of what they're doing. Turner apologizes. Blanche quickly reverts to form.

PERMISSION: AS LONG AS YOU SAY IT'S OKAY

Drink doesn't just steady the nerves. It grants the drinker tacit permission to let her inhibitions down, act as she pleases, and say what she feels. And the "uncharacteristic" behavior is usually something that, when the person is sober, is kept under wraps.

In *Streetcar*, drink isn't just an intoxicant for Blanche, it's an indulgent friend who assures her it's all right: She can return to her fantasy world of romance and mystery and forget the scandalous realties that have rendered her homeless, penniless, and the subject of scorn.

Looked at more broadly, the role of permission reveals how much we frame our conduct around our circumstances. Propriety, duty, conformity, habit—they

The Complete Handbook of Novel Writing

limit what we believe we're allowed to do or say. But then we go on holiday—wherever, however—and the rules of gravity no longer apply.

In the film *Rachel, Rachel*, Rachel Cameron (played by Joanne Woodward) is a middle-aged spinster in a small Connecticut town. She lives wrapped in a straightjacket of righteous conformity—until a man shows up and she falls in love. She takes her holiday right there at home, finally letting herself feel the pleasure she's been denying herself for decades.

Here the issue isn't adaptation in the face of *present* conflict. It's exploration or discovery of a suppressed, unsettling, or even dangerous side of the personality that's been there all along, though it's been unexpressed. But that raises the question of *why* it's been unexpressed, which often leads to *past* conflict.

You won't know how far you can push a character's liberated feelings without exploring her backstory: Why has this side of her personality been denied? When was the last time she demonstrated it? What happened? Who in the character's past enforced that prohibition? In answering such questions, envision a crucial scene: a self-absorbed parent ignoring a long-anticipated performance; a judgmental teacher launching into a tirade over an innocent mistake; a so-called friend mocking the latest love interest. Let that one vivid scene stand for a history of abuse, neglect, or being shut down.

And when the suppressed behavior at last finds expression, keep that internal naysayer in mind. As when faced with present conflict, the character might not suddenly leap from the familiar to the unrecognizable in one reckless bound but instead experiment, her boldness growing with her confidence. Then again, the behavior she's kept under wraps may escape with explosive force, as though to destroy the image of that person who, for years, has been saying, over and over with insidious force, *no.*

DECEIT OR DISCLOSURE: THAT WASN'T REALLY ME

Here the inexplicable conduct hasn't been repressed—it's been deliberately hidden. Of the three types of surprise behavior we've covered, this one lends itself best to a sudden, big reveal. It's also the easiest and most straightforward to portray.

In *The Scarlet Pimpernel*, Marguerite St. Just is baffled by what's become of the brave, charming man she married. Sir Percy Blakeney has become a parody of himself, playing the part of the slow-witted dandy. Ultimately Marguerite discovers the foppery is a disguise, intended to conceal Sir Percy's role as the leader of a band of noblemen dedicated to saving the lives of aristocrats facing death under the Reign of Terror.

In Daphne du Maurier's *Rebecca*, the gentile Maxim de Winter erupts in inexplicable bursts of caustic temper that take on such a menacing aspect that he seems increasingly likely to crack apart. In the story's crucial revelation, he at last confesses why this is—his wife Rebecca's death wasn't an accident after all.

Once we know the puzzling behavior results from something that has been concealed, we accept it readily, unless for some other reason it feels unbelievable. The paraplegic may very well get up and dance, but if he does, it better be magic or deception at play. Anything else is just bad writing.

IF I DID THIS MORE OFTEN I'D BE BETTER AT IT

Regardless of what's prompting your character to reach her limits, strange behavior shouldn't come easily. Characters who demonstrate instant skill or comfort with something they've never tried before reside largely in the realm of schlock. The less familiar the behavior, the clumsier and more uncomfortable it should be. Trying anything out of the ordinary means complication, difficulty, intensified focus. Portray that in your scenes, and you'll increase tension, enhance suspense, and intensify reader empathy.

THE ROLE OF CONTRADICTIONS

What much of the behavior we're discussing exemplifies is the capacity of human beings to be contradictory.

Simply stated, a contradiction is something about a person that piques our interest because it betrays what we expect, given what else we know or observe about him.

Once you train your eye to look for contradictions, they crop up virtually everywhere, expressing a paradox of human nature: that people do one thing *and* exactly the opposite; they're this, but they're also that.

In Jungian psychology, this largely unexplored, contradictory aspect of the personality is referred to as the Shadow. Psychic wholeness requires integrating into the conscious personality the nebulous traits embodied in the Shadow, and a great many stories are premised on exactly that kind of self-realization.

That said, some of the contradictions that prove useful in characterization are not psychological but physical: a bully's squeaky voice, the ballerina's chubby knees. But the most interesting contradictions always reflect something internal, even dispositional: A man is both garrulous and shy, outgoing but suspicious, brutal but childlike. Omar Little from the television show *The Wire* isn't just a shotgun-toting vigilante; he's also an openly gay man who treats his lovers with startling affection and tenderness. The effect: We never know which half of the personality will assert itself in any given situation. That's suspense—the best kind.

Some contradictions are behavioral: We feel divided—optimistic and yet wary, accepting and yet guarded. Other contradictions reflect the need to act properly in a variety of contrasting social situations: the dinner table, the office, the stadium, the chapel, the bedroom. We feel differing degrees of freedom to "be ourselves" in each of these environments, depending on who else is present.

Beyond purposes of verisimilitude, contradictions serve two key dramatic purposes:

1. They defy expectation and thus pique our interest.
2. They provide a straightforward method for depicting complexity and depth. Specifically, they provide a means to portray:

   - subtext (the tension between the expressed and the unexpressed, the visible and the concealed)
   - the situational subtleties of social life ("I must be many things to many people")
   - the conflict between both conscious and unconscious behavior
   - suspense (we want to know what the contradiction means and why it's there)

But again, there are limits to what is credible. Contradictions that seem implausible may enhance a comedic portrayal—the mob boss with the Yorkie, the cop who's terrified of cats, the chain-smoking nun—but they can undermine a dramatic one if handled carelessly. Ask whether the contradiction draws you, the writer, toward the character or permits you an emotional distance. If the latter, you're "looking at" the character rather than emotionally engaging with her, and the characteristic you're considering is likely not working. If you can justify the contradiction, root it in backstory and unearth scenes from your imagination that reveal how this character developed these seemingly irreconcilable inclinations. That way, it will become less conceptual and more intuitive and organic.

EMOTION, INTUITION, AND TRUST

The temptation when writing scenes in which characters do the unexpected is to stop and explain what just happened. Many writers think, not without some merit, that to leave things incomplete, ambiguous, or untidy is sloppiness. Though there's much to admire in this sort of rigor, in the realm of characterization it's sadly misplaced.

Where rigor is necessary is in how vividly, creatively, and comprehensively we conceive our characters. We don't get to know someone new through a recitation of biological data; we get to know him by interacting with him, especially during emotional or demanding times. So, too, we get to know a character by engaging with him in meaningful scenes that reveal the most significant aspects of his life: his wants and contradictions and secrets and wounds, his attachment to friends and family and his fear of his enemies, his schooling and sense of home, his loves and hatreds, his shame and pride and guilt and sense of joy. As important as a character's choices and motivations are in any scene—what he does and why—they don't exist in a vacuum.

This way of understanding the character—through emotionally significant scenes, and not information—allows us to engage with the character on the level of intuition, not intellect. This permits us to envision our characters clearly and feel as though we're in dialogue with them, observing them as we observe a dream—*not* controlling them like marionettes. And it's precisely "plot puppets" that most routinely exhibit traits that feel "out of character."

Readers shouldn't be vexed by a character's behavior, but they should never feel entirely comfortable, either, or they'll be several steps ahead of the story at every turn.

Explaining your character kills her. Whatever she does, readers need to feel her actions arise not from some single, explainable source but from the whole of her personality. And the deeper you understand that whole, the more likely you'll be able to portray convincingly the unexpected in her behavior.

So where is that fine line between being puzzled by behavior and finding it contrived? The answer lies in letting the behavior emerge *from the character*, not the writer. We need to create enough of a vivid intuition of a character that the possibility for real, unpredictable, unpremeditated action *on the character's part* seems credible. And this requires envisioning the character in emotionally demanding scenes, filled with conflict, pathos, and risk. In the end, it's not so much a question of how far the character will go but how thoroughly you're willing to connect with her.

David Corbett is the award-winning author of five novels, a novella, and the story collection *Thirteen Confessions*. His most recent novel is *The Mercy of the Night*. His instruction guide book, *The Art of Character*, has been called "a writer's bible."

15

COMPLICATING YOUR CHARACTERS

Creating Complex Motivations and Backstories

Joseph Bates

You might be afraid that simple motivations lead to simplistic characters—that once you've discovered what your character really wants is, say, a big piece of cheesecake, all he has to do is run through your novel screaming, "I want cheesecake!" (Detective One: "This is a grisly crime scene, Fred. One of the worst. I'm afraid we've got a serial killer on our hands here." Detective Two: "But what about *cheesecake*?!")

That's not the case, of course. Complex characters can, do, and should emerge from the simplest motivations, for two main reasons:

1. Guided by simple motivations, our actions in pursuit of those motivations are complex and occasionally contradictory or self-defeating.
2. Simple motivations don't necessarily mean *pure or noble*.

The prime example of both of these is Melville's Captain Ahab, who has one, and only one, single-minded motivation: to kill the white whale that stole his leg. But his actions in trying to achieve this goal are terrifying and risk not just his own life and his ship, but the lives of his entire crew as well. And while his motivation is clear, his need for vengeance is anything but noble, fueled by some of the worst—and most prevalent—instincts in man. His straightforward motivation leads to actions that reveal the complexity and the darker side of human nature.

But even with a character like Frodo in *The Lord of the Rings*, who has a rather pure motivation, the conflicts he faces and the actions he takes reveal his complexity. Frodo is not an epic hero, greater than us. He is fragile and vulnerable, and occasionally makes the wrong move in spite of the fact that he's doing his best and doing it for the right reason; he's even occasionally tempted to keep the One Ring for himself and use its power. To put it another way, he's like us. And this is why Tolkien gives Frodo the Ring rather than, say, the warrior-king Aragorn. Aragorn comes very close to being larger than life in the trilogy, and in his strong hands we might feel that taking the One Ring to Mordor is a done deal. Instead, Tolkien hands the One Ring to a hobbit—small in size, big in heart, no expert in combat, seemingly the character in the novel *least* likely to accomplish what needs to be done. This is the reason we connect with the story. There is something at risk in handing the Ring to Frodo, and because there's real risk, there's also real reason to *hope* for a good outcome.

Let's consider how to complicate your own characters in a similar way, by imbuing them with desire and then putting obstacles in their way (including, of course, *themselves*).

DEEPENING THE PROTAGONIST'S CHARACTER

At the beginning of the book, your main character is defined by his internal motivation: what he values and wants. But as you begin moving him through the events in the novel— as he faces conflicts and other characters—you'll start to see him as a human being, someone who wants something but does not always act in ways that will achieve the goal or that are in his best interests.

Let's consider a hypothetical example of a man who tries to woo the love of his life away from another. This is a pretty clear and straightforward motivation. But our hypothetical character messes up in almost every way: He shows up to his would-be lover's work to serenade her and interrupts an important meeting; maybe he hires a skywriter to announce his love from on high, via smoke message, but the pilot is drunk and misspells her name or writes something obscene; finally we put him in a bar where he is wooed by another girl, takes her back home, and then is caught with his pants down by his true love. Though the same simple motivation is present throughout, our poor character—like all our poor characters—is only human, meaning that he makes mistakes, underreacts or overreacts, and misjudges in epic fashion. He tries his best, fails, tries again, and in the process he becomes real.

When building your protagonist, start from the baseline and then test her, seeing how she acts and reacts. Establish her character clearly at the start of the novel. When she says or does things that surprise you midway through the book, don't fret but rejoice. She has begun to reveal herself to you as a full person, catching you off guard in terms of who she is and what she's capable of. This is perfectly acceptable and, in fact, cause for celebration, as long as her ultimate goal or motivation continues to drive her actions.

DEEPENING THE ANTAGONIST'S CHARACTER

In certain situations and genres, the conflict your protagonist faces might take the form of a person—an antagonist—standing in the main character's way. Antagonists walk a peculiar line: In one sense, they clearly fall into the category of supporting character, as their existence helps define the protagonist and his quest more clearly; yet antagonists also feel like major characters and sometimes even threaten to steal the show. This is especially the case with books in a series, where the hero stays the same and the villain changes with each new installment; the tendency can be to do something dynamic with each new antagonist to add variety, and as a result the villains become increasingly more outrageous and scene-stealing even as the protagonist holds steady and perhaps begins to look a little washed-out by comparison.

There are two things to remember—and keep in stride—when crafting an antagonist. The first is that the antagonist is, like every other major and minor character in your book, a full person with his own motivations, wants, and goals. Your antagonist can't be one-dimensional. Even if his goal is straightforward and simple, it just so happens that his earnest want or goal is in direct conflict with what your protagonist wants (and thus what *we* want to happen in the story). The villain, as you'll sometimes hear said, is the hero of his own story. He's going after a goal just as your hero is, no matter how misguided his motivation.

Now for the second thing to remember: The villain may be the hero of his own story, but this story ain't it. Because we see everything in your fictional world through the lens and perspective of your protagonist, the antagonist is clearly in opposition, clearly a hurdle. If we wanted to—and now we're playing the role of critic, or maybe therapist, for just a minute—we could see the antagonist's side of things. But for the most part, we're *not* inclined, because we want the protagonist, the hero, to succeed.

Those of you working in genres may be hesitant to think of your antagonist as a person—if you're writing a mystery where there's a sadistic killer on the loose, for example, you don't want to condone sadism by making your killer an otherwise okay guy. Or if you're working in epic fantasy or science fiction or horror, you want your bad guys to be bad guys, darn it, as close to pure evil as you can manage. To this point I'll say that the needs of your story and genre certainly *will* affect the way you craft an antagonist, but I'd beware of making your villain the embodiment of pure evil for the same reason you should avoid making your protagonist an exemplar of pure virtue: Readers can't identify with such extremes, because no one in real life is purely evil or purely good. Thus, at a baseline, your antagonist must be in some way *attractive* to readers, in some subversive way seductive, so that rather than being repelled by him we're intrigued enough to move closer, even if we're thankful we can shut the book if we ever get *too* close. Besides, unchecked evil isn't very frightening; readers can simply say, *Well, I'm never going to encounter that.* But evil that shows up with a smile and then knocks you over the head is terrifying. That's the kind of evil we *might* encounter, and that's a thought that could keep us up at night.

The most important thing to keep in mind is that this is the protagonist's story. And even if your antagonist is a fuller character than the *other* secondary characters in the book and gets more page time, he's still there to help us see, understand, and ultimately sympathize with the hero.

DEEPENING CHARACTER THROUGH BACKSTORY

Backstory is an important part of developing complex characters and offers a sense of depth, the feeling that our characters are real people with lives and histories that often have a bearing on the present problems faced in the novel. But backstory can also be tricky for a writer: It's far too easy to flash back to the past and get stuck there, wondering how in the world you're going to return to the present action of the story. Or you might feel the need to identify and explain *every* past action that bears on the current situation. Part of this comes from our psychology-influenced culture, which tends to see our actions and personalities as the result of past events and traumas. The contemporary fiction writer has probably been trained to find the difficult childhood experience, for example, that now explains why your character is a philanderer, addict, martyr, murderer, or saint. This inclination is a statement of our times.

But even more than a reflection of the contemporary mind-set, effective backstory is valuable in that it furthers our story's sense of verisimilitude—that our characters, and even our larger fictional world, really exist. A person without a past is perhaps common to slasher films and spaghetti westerns, but in the real world the places we go and people we meet all have a discernable (or at least assumed) history, depth, and perspective. Adding these dimensions to our characters and fictional world makes both seem more real to readers. However, when our narrative seems to be *stuck* in the past or obsessed with it, the sense of verisimilitude is destroyed, and readers are left wondering which "story" is the important one: the one in the past or the one in the present.

The first step in balancing backstory is recognizing that it falls into two distinct categories: incidental and direct.

Incidental Backstory

Incidental backstory is used primarily for purposes of description, to deepen our immediate understanding of a person, place, or thing. I call this backstory "incidental" to make the point that, while it is often quite useful in establishing verisimilitude in your fiction, you've *chosen* to give backstory as a way of making the person, place, or thing relatable, even though you might have done the same work by using a different tack.

A good example of incidental backstory comes early in Jeffrey Eugenides's *The Virgin Suicides*, in which the first-person plural narrators—a group of neighborhood boys who are now men in their thirties—recall the fateful summer from their youths when the Lisbon girls, five beautiful sisters from their community, took their own lives. Because the boys were outside the Lisbon home and thus never had the intimate access to know what, exactly, was going on behind closed doors, the narrators have had to piece the account together from secondhand sources like their friend Paul Baldino, the son of a reputed mobster, who claimed to have been inside the Lisbon home the night of the first Lisbon girl's suicide attempt. To explain *how* Baldino was inside the home, Eugenides gives this brief bit of incidental backstory:

> A few years earlier, behind the spiked Baldino fence patrolled by two identical white German shepherds, a group of workmen had appeared one morning. They hung tarpaulins over ladders to obscure what they did, and after three days, when they whisked the tarps away, there, in the middle of the lawn, stood an artificial tree trunk. It was made of cement, painted to look like bark, complete with fake knothole and two lopped limbs pointing at the sky with the fervor of amputee stubs. In the middle of the tree, a chainsawed wedge contained a metal grill.
>
> Paul Baldino said it was a barbecue, and we believed him. But, as time passed, we noticed that no one ever used it. ... Soon the rumor began to circulate that the tree trunk was an escape tunnel, that it led to a hideaway along the river where Sammy the Shark kept a speedboat ... . Then, a few months

after the rumors began, Paul Baldino began emerging in people's basements, through the storm sewers.

The backstory here, as you can see, serves a specific descriptive, atmospheric, and logistical purpose, and it does the trick wonderfully. But is it strictly *necessary* to give this bit of history? No. All Eugenides needs to do is find some way to put Paul Baldino inside the Lisbon home so he can report on finding Cecelia, the oldest Lisbon girl, in the bathtub with her wrists cut. Eugenides could have set this up without giving the story of the mobsters and secret passageways; he could just as easily have Baldino be a Peeping Tom or a cat burglar. The incidental backstory is a choice—an artful one that provides readers with another glimpse of the town and its inhabitants, another piece of local folklore to add depth to the collective voice. The reason we, as authors, *choose* to go with incidental backstory is because we think it does the trick *best*, though we recognize we might accomplish the same thing without involving history at all.

Direct Backstory

Direct backstory, on the other hand, has a crucial bearing on, and relevance to, the present action in the story—information that's substantive rather than descriptive or atmospheric. The burden of this kind of backstory, since it's needed for the reader's full understanding of the character, is to find interesting ways of delivering it so that it doesn't feel like an information dump or summary. In fact, all past action that you bring into your story has to be delivered with as much focus and momentum as the present action; even when the story dives into the past, readers have to be invested in the present narrative moment.

Of course, there are many ways of delivering direct backstory. Sometimes you'll want to flash back and give us the past event in scene. Other times, direct backstory might be revealed through quick asides in the narration, in dialogue between characters, or in a character's subtle actions or reactions to certain situations that suggest the deeper meaning beneath. It's up to you to choose how you give the past what it requires, but make sure that whenever you go backward, you move your story *forward*.

The biggest challenge most writers have in balancing backstory is confusing incidental backstory and direct backstory, spending pages in the past building up some moment they *believe* to be important but that's actually descriptive or atmospheric. My favorite example of what seems to be direct backstory, but is revealed to be incidental, comes from Vladimir Nabokov's *Lolita*, wherein the predatory Humbert Humbert wants to dissuade readers from psychoanalyzing the untimely death of his young mother.

> My very photogenic mother died in a freak accident (picnic, lightning) when I was three. ...

No need to whip the wind around, blow the checkered tablecloth into the air, or cull dark clouds into thunderheads when "(picnic, lightning)" does the trick. Sometimes, of course, your backstory will be more substantive and require pages, precision, and patience. But sometimes it will be incidental, requiring only a short aside. As you think about your ideas regarding backstory, make sure you can differentiate between incidental and direct, and know when each is called for.

UPPING THE READER'S EMOTIONAL INVESTMENT

The reason we begin our novel in the internal motivation of the protagonist—and the reason we're continually reminded of that motivation as we move through the external conflicts faced by the protagonist—is because this is how readers directly and emotionally relate to the quest. Few, if any, readers will have faced the specific external conflicts we make our character face in the novel, but all of them will have faced the *internal* motivation and conflicts associated with the character's external quest: for instance, wanting to protect someone we love, and not knowing if we can; wanting to win someone's heart, and not knowing if we will; wanting to be happy, safe, accepted, appreciated, loved, etc. These are things *all* of us want at our core, and when these are put in jeopardy by the conflicts your character faces, readers feel the anxiety, too.

Taken to their conclusion at the end of the novel, these familiar wants and needs begin to form the bigger organizing principle of theme when put at risk through conflict and confrontation. But as you navigate the long second act of your book, trying to amp up forward momentum and raise the stakes, it's important that you continue to make the connection back to the character as a person, back to what he wants and what's really at risk. Think about those books that most affected *you* as a reader: What was it about the character's struggle that you felt *personally* connected to, that moved you to either anger or tears? What were the specific moments in those books where you felt most exhilarated and full of hope, or where you feared that all was lost? Do you still think about those moments? Can you still conjure the emotion you felt as you read?

When the events in your book matter in some meaningful way to your protagonist, they become meaningful to readers. In turn, readers will bring their personal experiences, hopes, and fears to bear on the text. Furthermore, they *want* to do so—the intimate, personal relationship engendered by narrative is unlike an audience's relationship to any other art form. It feels intimate and real. Let it.

Joseph Bates is the author of *Tomorrowland: Stories* (Curbside Splendor, 2013) and *Writing Your Novel from Start to Finish* (Writer's Digest Books, 2015). His short fiction has appeared in such journals as *The Rumpus, New Ohio Review, Identity Theory, South Carolina Review, Fresh Boiled Peanuts,* and *InDigest Magazine.* He is a consulting fiction editor with Miami University Press and teaches in the creative writing program at Miami University in Oxford, Ohio. Visit him online at www.josephbates.net.

16

STATUS

What No One Is Teaching You
About Characterization

Steven James

One of the most effective ways of creating unforgettable characters is something most writers have never even heard of.

Managing status.

I first learned about status years ago while studying physical comedy, mime, and improvisation. I remember listening to acting instructor Keith Johnstone (author of *Impro* and *Impro for Storytellers*) explain how dominance and submission affect actors on stage and how stillness raises status. As he spoke, I kept thinking of how essential it is for writers to capture the same characterizations on the page.

Since then, I've been on the lookout for ways to fine-tune the status of my characters. Here are four essential principles I've discovered.

1. VARIABLE STATUS IS THE KEY TO DIMENSIONALITY

So what exactly is status?

Simply put, in every social interaction, one person has (or attempts to have) a more dominant role. Those in authority or those who want to exert authority use a collection of verbal and nonverbal cues to gain and maintain higher status. But it's not just authority figures who do this. In daily life all of us are constantly adjusting and negotiating the amount of status we portray as we face different situations and interact with different people.

Novelists have the daunting task of showing this dynamic of shifting submission and dominance through dialogue, posture, pauses, communication patterns, body language, action, and, when applicable, the character's thoughts.

- Dominant individuals have confidence, a relaxed demeanor, loose and easy gestures and gait. Submissive people constrict themselves—their stride, voice, posture, gestures.
- Typically, the closer a person's hand is to his mouth during a conversation, the less status he has. Looking down, crossing your legs, biting your lip, and holding your hands in front of your face are all ways of hiding. Concealment lowers status.
- Eye contact is a powerful way of maintaining dominance. Although cultures differ, in North America we make prolonged eye contact when we wish to intimidate, control, threaten, or seduce.
- Stillness is power. Dominant people delay before replying to questions, not because they can't think of anything to say but to control the conversation. They blink less frequently than submissive people and keep their heads still as they speak. The more fidgety, bedraggled, or frazzled a person is, the less status he has. In movies the protagonist will often smoke so he has an excuse to be slow in answering questions as he pauses to take a drag from his cigarette—a high-status play.
- Submissive people apologize more and agree more than dominant people. They try to please and placate and are easily intimidated. To act as if I need something from you lowers my status. To let you know that you can be helpful to me raises my status.
- The most effective negotiators tend to mirror the status of the people with whom they're doing business. This way they neither appear too aggressive (intimidatingly high status) or too willing to give in and compromise (unimpressively low status).

Think about the roles you play in relating to your boss, your lover, your children, the bellhop you meet at the hotel. You step onto the court of your son's basketball game to be a referee and enter one role; you go on a date with your spouse and enter another. Golfing with your buddies, visiting your mother at the nursing home, giving that big presentation at work—all of these situations require a certain set of behaviors and call forth differing degrees of confidence and status.

As an interesting exercise in evaluating status, watch a presidential debate with the sound turned off. If you're like most people, you'll be able to read signs of status quite easily when you look for them in other people.

Status varies with respect to three things: relationship (a father has higher relational status than his ten-year-old daughter), position (a boss has higher positional status than her employees), and situation (if you're attacked by a team of highly trained ninjas and you've never studied martial arts, you'd have quite a bit lower situational status than your nunchucks-wielding assailants). Banter between friends and mutual sarcasm are signs of equal status. Vying for power in the relationship is not.

Although the level of relational, positional, and situational status might be out of our hands, our response to it is not. Status can be shown through tension, how characters handle setbacks, or just in how they deal with everyday encounters with other people. The daughter might manipulate her father, the employee might quit, and you might summon up enough moxie to frighten off those ninjas. So in determining status, choices matter more than circumstances.

When readers complain that a character is one-dimensional, flat, or "cardboard," they may not realize that they're actually noting the character's unchanging status, regardless of the social context in which she appears. She might always be angry or ruthless or heroic or any number of things, but the more uniformly she responds to everyone and everything, the less interesting she'll be to readers.

People in real life are complex.

Fictional characters need to be as well.

We understand a person's characterization, whether in real life or in fiction, by seeing how that person responds in different situations to different people.

So what's the key to a well-rounded character?

Simple: She doesn't have the same status in every situation.

To create a fascinating and memorable protagonist, readers must see her status vary as she interacts with the other characters in the story.

Dimensionality is brought out by showing the subtle shifts in status as the character relates to others within different contexts. To show complexity of characterization, we need to see the character in a variety of relationships or conversations.

In my novels featuring FBI Special Agent Patrick Bowers, whenever he's at a crime scene or standing up to a bad guy, he always has the highest status. He will never back down, he will never give in, he will never give up.

However, to have dimensionality he also needs relationships in which he has *low* status. As a single dad, he struggles with knowing how to handle his sharp-witted and surly teenage daughter, and, lacking some social graces, he fumbles for the right things to say to the women he's attracted to. Without his daughter or a love interest to reveal those *low-status* aspects of his characterization, he would be one-dimensional and certainly not engaging enough to build a series around.

If you want readers to emotionally invest in your protagonist, you'll need to find some areas of his life where he has a weakness, low status, or something to overcome. Remember: Even Indiana Jones was afraid of snakes, and Superman—the highest-status superhero ever created—is defenseless against Kryptonite.

2. WORD CHOICE DETERMINES CHARACTERIZATION

In theater the phrase "stealing the scene" refers to instances in which another person upstages the star. Actually, it's just another way of saying that the star (or protagonist) no longer has the highest status.

When this happens onstage, it'll annoy the star.

When it happens in your novel, it'll turn off your readers.

You can shatter hundreds of pages of careful characterization with one poorly chosen word. A person with high status might shout, holler, call, or yell, but if he screams, screeches, bawls, or squeals, his status is lowered. Similarly, a character who quivers, trembles, whines, or pleads has lower status than one who tries to control the pain. For example:

> Parker drew the blade across Sylvia's arm. She shrieked and begged him to stop.

> Parker drew the blade across Sylvia's arm. She clenched her teeth, refusing to give him the satisfaction of seeing her cry.

In the first example, Sylvia's uncontrolled reaction lowers her status beneath that of her assailant. In the second, however, her resolve raises her status above that of Parker, who has evidently failed to intimidate her. Rather than appearing victimized, she has become heroic: Yes, he could make her bleed, but he could not make her cry. That's a woman with high status.

While an antagonist might have higher situational, relational, or positional status, your protagonist must never *act* in a way (that is, make choices) that lowers his status below that of the antagonist.

Take a moment to let that sink in.

You might find it helpful to imagine high-status movie stars playing the part of your protagonist. I'm not sure about you, but I have a hard time imagining Liam Neeson, Jason Statham, or Bruce Willis pleading for mercy or screaming for help.

Choices, more than anything else, will determine status.

So while editing your story, continually ask yourself what you want readers to feel about each character. Do you want them to be on this character's side? To cheer for him? Fear him? Despise him? Discount him? Every action, every word of dialogue, every gesture—even every speaker attribution—communicates a certain level of status.

Make sure the words you choose support the impression you're trying to make. Don't undermine all of your efforts to create a strong protagonist by using the wrong verb. If Betty *stomps* across the floor (showing lack of self-control) or *struts* across it (implying the need for attention), she'll have lower status than someone who *strides* across it (showing composure and confidence).

Even punctuation affects status.

> "I know you heard me! Move away from Anna! If you lay a hand on her, I guarantee you will regret it!"

> "I know you heard me. Move away from Anna. If you lay a hand on her, I guarantee you will regret it."

In the first example, the exclamation points make the speaker seem frantic or desperate. In the second, the periods show that he is controlled, measured, authoritative. That's how a hero responds.

A wimpy protagonist isn't interesting.

A wimpy antagonist isn't frightening.

In marketable fiction, both heroes and villains need high status. When villains aren't frightening or heroes aren't inspiring, it's almost always because the author has let them act in a way that undermines their status.

3. PROTAGONISTS NEED OPPORTUNITIES TO BE HEROIC

When I was writing my second novel, one section gave me a particularly difficult time. Agent Bowers is at the scene of a suicide when Detective Dunn, a street-smart local homicide cop, shows up. Dunn is tough. He's used to calling the shots, to having the highest status.

In this scene, he makes an aggressive high-status move by getting in Bowers's face and then taunting him. I struggled with showing that, as bold and brash as Dunn is, my hero still has higher status. After thrashing through numerous drafts, here's how the encounter finally played out (from Bowers's point of view).

> Dunn stepped close enough for me to smell his garlicky breath.

The Complete Handbook of Novel Writing

"This is my city. The next time you and your pencil-pushing lawyer buddies from Quantico decide to stick your nose into an ongoing investigation, at least have the courtesy to go through the proper channels."

"I'd suggest you back away," I said. "Now."

He backed up slowly.

Agent Bowers refuses to be baited and isn't intimidated by Dunn's aggressive posturing. If he were, readers would lose faith in him and side with Dunn. Instead, Bowers remains calm and, by exhibiting poise and self-control, induces Dunn's submission. (Incidentally, by adding the speaker attribution "I said," I inserted a slight pause in Bowers's response, subtly adding to his status even more. To see the difference, read the sentence aloud with and without the pause.)

At the end of the scene, when Dunn steps back, there's no doubt in the mind of the readers who is in charge.

Readers won't empathize with a weak protagonist. They expect protagonists who have strength of conviction, moral courage, and noble aspirations. It's true, of course, that during the story the protagonist might be struggling to grow in these areas, but readers need to see her as someone worth cheering for along the way. If you're grappling with how to do that, try one of these methods.

- **HAVE YOUR PROTAGONIST SACRIFICE FOR THE GOOD OF OTHERS.** This might come in the form of a physical sacrifice (stepping in front of a bullet), a financial sacrifice (anonymously paying another's debt), a material sacrifice (volunteering for the Peace Corps), or an emotional sacrifice (forgiving someone for a deep offense).
- **HAVE HER STAND UP FOR THE OPPRESSED.** I've noticed that some authors try to show how "tough" their protagonist is by portraying her as cold or unfeeling—especially at a crime scene. Bad idea. Most of the time, readers want the hero (or heroine) to be compassionate and life affirming.

  Let's say your medical examiner is at that crime scene and one of the other cops gestures toward the corpse and quips, "They stab 'em, you slab 'em." Your protagonist needs to uphold the value of human life. She might reproach the cop or remind him of the victim's grieving family. Conversely, if you had her say those words and make light of something as precious as life itself and she gets rebuked by someone else, you'll end up devastating her status.
- **HAVE HER TURN THE OTHER CHEEK.** If someone slaps your protagonist and she refuses to fight back, her self-control raises her status above that of the attacker. Strength isn't shown only by what a person can do but by what she *could do* but *refrains from doing*. Self-restraint always raises status.

4. STATUS CRYSTALLIZES AS THE STORY ESCALATES

As your story builds toward its climax, the status of both your hero and your villain will also rise. The bad guy will become increasingly coldhearted or unstoppable, and the good guy will need to summon unprecedented strength or courage to save the day.

Status has more to do with actions than motives, so even though the hero and villain have completely different agendas, you can raise the status of either of them by giving him more self-control, courage, and resolve.

Remember: Stillness is power, so to make a villain more imposing, let him slow down. Show readers that he's in no hurry to commit his evil deed—he has such high status that he can walk slowly and still catch the person fleeing frantically through the woods.

Those with high status accomplish the most with the least amount of effort.

A terrifying villain doesn't violently yank someone's hair back and twist her head around to make her look him in the eye. Instead, he might entwine his hand in her hair and slowly force her to look at him, even as she struggles to get free. But for him it is no effort. Yes, he could jerk her head back, but he chooses not to. Instead, slowly and methodically he forces her to submit.

Villains are less frightening when they're self-congratulatory, impressed with their own plans, swaggering, or showing off, because all of these actions lower their status.

You actually *lower* a villain's status by giving him the need to prove himself. Sadistic, chortling, hand-wringing villains aren't nearly as unnerving as calm, relentless ones who are indifferent to the suffering of others. The more they admire themselves, the lower their status becomes.

Villains are made more believable and more frightening when, instead of taking pleasure in other people's pain, they treat the suffering of others with indifference.

If your story calls for multiple villains, stagger their status so the top-tier bad guy has the highest status and is therefore the most threatening and dangerous person for your protagonist to encounter at the story's climax.

To summarize: Think of every relationship and social encounter as a transaction of status. Give your protagonist a variety of relationships that reveal different status dynamics and bring out deeper dimensionality. Be sure to sharpen status differentiations as your story progresses and build toward that satisfying and surprising climax.

LOW STATUS	HIGH STATUS
- Arrogance	+ Confidence
- Loss of control	+ Self-control
- Crying or weeping often	+ Reserved, might cry over the death of a loved one
- Screaming	+ Shouting, calling, speaking calmly
- Quivering, trembling, begging	+ Resisting giving in to the pain, never begs
- Slouching	+ Good posture
- Tense	+ At ease, relaxed
- Averts eye contact	+ Steady gaze
- Postures, shows off	+ Exhibits poise, feels no need to impress others
- Brags, narcissistic	+ Doesn't draw attention to self, humble
- Shrinks from danger	+ Rises to the occasion
- Cowardly	+ Courageous
- Shy	+ Outgoing
- Self-congratulatory	+ Self-effacing
- Needy	+ Self-reliant
- Argumentative, interrupts others	+ Listens attentively
- Tries to be cool	+ Can't help but be cool
- Worries about reputation	+ Cares more about ideals
- Dependent	+ Independent but also relational
- Vies for control	+ Naturally has control
- Gives in to pressure, conforms	+ Sets trends
- Makes threats	+ Takes action
- Impressed with himself, self-congratulatory	+ Lifts up and encourages others
- Worried about what others think	+ Doesn't care what others think
- Sadistic	+ Compassionate

Steven James is the best-selling, critically acclaimed author of thirteen novels. He has a master's degree in storytelling and is a contributing editor to *Writer's Digest*. Best known for his psychological thrillers, he has received more than a dozen honors and awards for his novels, including three Christy Awards for best suspense. His book *The Queen* was a finalist for an International Thriller Award. His groundbreaking book on the craft of fiction, *Story Trumps Structure: How to Write Unforgettable Fiction by Breaking the Rules*, won a 2015 Storytelling World Award, recognizing it as one of the year's best resources for storytellers. His second book on fiction craft, *Troubleshooting Your Novel: Essential Techniques for Identifying and Solving Manuscript Problems*, was released in September 2016.

17

THE MAIN INTRODUCTION

Revealing Your Character's
Key Elements from the Start

Jordan Rosenfeld

The first third of your narrative is all about establishing the nuts and bolts of characters and their basic conflicts and plot problems, and setting into motion all the seeds for conflict and challenges to come. In these opening scenes, readers are meeting your characters—and, most important of all, your protagonist(s)— just as if they were new guests over for dinner. Their words, actions, and reactions to one another all serve as primary introductions, and these first impressions set the stage for their behavior deeper into the book.

While you probably know that you need to craft opening scenes that reveal who your character is (a smack-talking hooligan with seductive eyes and a mop of brown curls, or a lonely librarian who reads mystery novels and winds up investigating an actual crime), it's important to recognize that in this first section of your narrative, you also need to establish the following:

- **INVOLVEMENT:** What is your protagonist's relationship to the events of the significant opening scene or situation that will launch your plot? Is the event his fault? Is it centered on her in some way? Did he accidentally stumble into it? Is she integral to it?
- **THE STAKES:** What your protagonist stands to lose or gain as a result of these events needs to create the tension and drama that will propel your story forward.
- **DESIRES:** What your protagonist desires, from material goods to deep and abiding love, will inform the stakes and his intentions.

- **FEARS:** What your protagonist most fears, from bodily harm to not obtaining those desires, will also inform the stakes, which you must continue to raise.
- **MOTIVATION:** What reasons does he have to act upon the inciting events? What is he driven by?
- **CHALLENGES:** How does the significant situation challenge her life, views, status, relationships, needs, and so on?

Let's look at each of these key points, illustrating them with examples from the early scenes in Andre Dubus III's acclaimed novel *House of Sand and Fog*.

INVOLVEMENT

Co-protagonist Kathy Nicolo (married name Lazaro) is a cleaning woman whose self-absorbed husband divorced her eight months ago. Since then, her life has been a wreck: She barely scrapes by financially, and her stability as a recovered alcoholic and addict is severely tested. The only material thing of significance to her is the house she inherited from her father, where she lives.

How is she involved in the significant situation? In the first scene she wakes up to find a locksmith and a cop at her door with a notice of eviction for back taxes. She protests that the notice is an error, but it's futile; until she can prove in court that she has done nothing wrong, they have the right to evict her, and they do. Kathy must move into a motel while she sorts things out. In the time it takes her to get a lawyer, her house goes up for auction and is purchased by co-protagonist Colonel Behrani, a once-wealthy man from Iran who is now a struggling immigrant with iron pride.

Though Dubus does a thorough job of developing both characters fully and weaving their stories together seamlessly, for simplicity's sake let's focus on Kathy's storyline. It's pretty clear what Kathy's relationship to the significant situation is: She's been evicted from her house. Although Kathy claims it's a mistake, readers don't have enough evidence yet to know if this is true. She seems volatile, and readers aren't sure if she's trustworthy; she *could* be the kind of woman who fails to pay taxes:

> "That's all right 'cause I'm not leaving." My throat felt dry and stiff.
>
> The locksmith looked up from his work on my back door.
>
> Deputy Burdon rested one hand on the countertop, and he had an understanding expression on his face, but I hated him anyway. "I'm afraid you have

no choice, Mrs. Lazaro. All your things will be auctioned off with the property. Do you want that?"

"*Look*, I *inherited* this house from my father, it's paid for. You can't evict me!" My eyes filled up and the men began to blur. "I never *owed* a … tax. You have no right to do this."

THE STAKES

The stakes are pretty clear: Without her house, she has nowhere to go but to a motel, and on her small income, that expense is a big one—Kathy could quickly wind up in dire straits. This evokes some sympathy for the woman, even though readers don't really know her yet.

Your stakes must be equally clear; don't make readers guess. Let them see from the start exactly what is at stake for your protagonist. Does he stand to be kicked out of his tribe if he speaks his mind, lose his worldly possessions if he loses his job, or lose his child visitation rights if he can't pay child support? These questions and their answers must be enacted in scenes in the first part of your narrative.

Set your stakes using this simple two-prong approach:

- Show what the protagonist has to gain.
- Show what the protagonist stands to lose.

DESIRES

Next, through passages of interior monologue, readers get a peek into Kathy's desires, which center mostly on her relationships. She remembers the few rare good times before her husband Nick left her; she reflects on the days with her first husband, Donnie, when she was barely an adult and became addicted to cocaine. The readers feel her palpable loneliness—she's so lonely that even the bad memories are a comfort to her. Her desire for love makes plausible her yearning to connect with Lester Burdon, the deputy who first came to evict her:

"I thought I'd check in on you, see how you're holding up."

He sounded like he meant it, and he seemed even softer than the day before when he'd led those men in kicking me out of my house. When we got to his car, a Toyota station wagon parked at the edge of the lot near the chain-link fence, I kind of hoped he'd keep talking; Connie Walsh was the first person

I'd had a real conversation with in over eight months, and that was more of an interrogation than a talk. I wanted one, even with a sheriff's deputy in the fog.

Kathy's pressing desire to be loved will get her into a lot of trouble later in the narrative. Her other, more immediate desire—to get her house back—is much more straightforward and will drive her actions in much of the rest of the narrative.

Desires will come in many shapes in your narrative and can be expressed or shown:

- in dialogue between characters
- in the form of thoughts (interior monologue), as in the example above
- in subtle actions—your protagonists may simply take what they desire, or try to

What matters is that readers have a feeling for what these desires are, straight away. Desires and motivations must fuel a character's intentions in every scene; they help give purpose to the characters' actions, so you'll want to make them as clear as possible.

ASSESSING YOUR CHARACTER AT THE END OF YOUR OPENING SCENES

The scenes at the start of your story are all about potential conflict. Reread them and ask yourself: Have I destabilized my protagonist, given him problems and conflicts that begin to worry both him and my readers? Has my protagonist been directly involved in a significant situation that has brought initial conflict and challenges? Make sure your protagonist is showing signs that he feels tested, forced into action, and driven toward change. Nothing should yet be too conclusive, too fixed in stone. If it is, readers will have little motivation to keep reading.

FEARS

Kathy's fears are a bit less direct, but they simmer in the subtext of the scenes. Readers know that she is a recovering addict with a penchant for men who like to control her. This tells readers that Kathy is not a person with high self-esteem or someone who feels particularly in control of her own life. Readers see that she is someone who prefers dependence on others over independence, and that the act of being out of her house throws her whole life into chaos. Kathy is afraid to be alone and afraid to be an adult in the world, to take responsibility for herself. These fears will get her into trouble in the middle of the novel.

Your protagonist should have some kind of fear, whether it's a rational one, such as fear of fire, or an irrational one, like a fear of butterflies or the color yellow, because those innocuous things can trigger memories of terrible experiences. No character should be too brave—even heroes have weaknesses. Establish what your character is afraid of early on, because in the middle of the narrative, you're going to exploit those fears. You can establish fear:

- through speech (for instance, he can admit to a friend that he is terrified of spiders)
- through behavior (your protagonist sees a passenger jet overhead and hits the dirt like she is about to be bombed)
- through a flashback scene in which readers see that the protagonist was traumatized by a specific event

Fear is as much a part of your protagonist's motivations as desire, and it is through both fear and desire that you exert change on your characters.

MOTIVATION

Kathy's surface motivation is pretty clear: She's motivated to get her house back because it's all she has, and she sees it as the cornerstone of her ability to live a stable life. This motivation leads her to get legal aid and fight for what is hers. But Kathy is also motivated by older, deeper issues regarding her family and her relationship to her parents. These motivations are the ones that cause her to get involved with Lester Burdon, a married man and a cop; they also cause her to become volatile and enraged at Colonel Behrani, who has her house; and they begin to set the stage for the drama that unfolds in the second part of the narrative. Your protagonist's motivations will be clear to the reader so long as you do the following:

- make clear your the protagonist's desires
- make clear the protagonist's fears
- offer opportunities to thwart the desires and trigger the fears

Motivations—which stem directly from your protagonist's fears and desires— are the foundation of scene intentions. Once you know how your protagonist is

The Complete Handbook of Novel Writing

motivated, and by what forces, you can direct him to act in every scene in a way appropriate to the circumstances of your plot.

CHALLENGES

Kathy's challenges are myriad. She lacks money and resources, she has a weakness for using alcohol to drown her feelings, she is attracted to men who are bad for her, and she is literally challenged by Colonel Behrani's takeover of her home.

Challenges are the situations in which you thwart your protagonist's desires and trigger his fears, and they are good and necessary. The more of them you can comfortably create—that is, the more you can conjure that pertain to your plot and make sense to your character—the better, because they evoke a sense of urgency and concern in your reader. In the first part of your narrative, your job is to set up which intentions are going to be opposed, leading the way to the middle of your story, where these intentions will meet with greater opposition and create more conflict. Do your job well, and you'll have crafted a protagonist readers want to read more about.

Jordan Rosenfeld is the author of the writing guides *Writing the Intimate Character: Create Unique, Compelling Characters Through Mastery of Point of View*; *Writing Deep Scenes: Plotting Your Story Through Action, Emotion, and Theme*, with Martha Alderson; *A Writer's Guide to Persistence: How to Create a Lasting and Productive Writing Practice*; *Make a Scene: Crafting a Powerful Story One Scene at a Time*; and *Write Free: Attracting the Creative Life*, with Rebecca Lawton. She is also the author of the suspense novels *Women in Red*, *Forged in Grace*, and *Night Oracle*.

BEST-SELLING ADVICE
Craft and Style

" Make your novel readable. Make it easy to read, pleasant to read. This doesn't mean flowery passages, ambitious flights of pyrotechnic verbiage; it means strong, simple, natural sentences."

—Laurence D'Orsay

"The difference between the almost right word and the right word is really a large matter—'tis the difference between the lightning-bug and the lightning."

—Mark Twain

"You have to follow your own voice. You have to be yourself when you write. In effect, you have to announce, 'This is me, this is what I stand for, this is what you get when you read me. I'm doing the best I can—buy me or not—but this is who I am as a writer.'"

—David Morrell

"I think I succeeded as a writer because I did not come out of an English department. I used to write in the chemistry department. And I wrote some good stuff. If I had been in the English department, the prof would have looked at my short stories, congratulated me on my talent, and then showed me how Joyce or Hemingway handled the same elements of the short story. The prof would have placed me in competition with the greatest writers of all time, and that would have ended my writing career.

—Kurt Vonnegut

" What a writer has to do is write what hasn't been written before or beat dead men at what they have done."

—Ernest Hemingway

"Oftentimes an originator of new language forms is called 'pretentious' by jealous talents. But it ain't watcha write, it's the way atcha write it."

—Jack Kerouac

"You should really stay true to your own style. When I first started writing, everybody said to me, 'Your style just isn't right because you don't use the really flowery language that romances have.' My romances—compared to what's out there—are very strange, very odd, very different. And I think that's one of the reasons they're selling."

—Jude Deveraux

"Writing is like being in love. You never get better at it or learn more about it. The day you think you do is the day you lose it. Robert Frost called his work a lover's quarrel with the world. It's ongoing. It has neither a beginning nor an end. You don't have to worry about learning things. The fire of one's art burns all the impurities from the vessel that contains it."

—James Lee Burke

"We, and I think I'm speaking for many writers, don't know what it is that sometimes comes to make our books alive. All we can do is to write dutifully and day after day, every day, giving our work the very best of what we are capable. I don't think that we can consciously put the magic in; it doesn't work that way. When the magic comes, it's a gift. **"**

—Madeleine L'Engle

18

TRANSFORM YOUR NOVEL INTO A SYMPHONY

How to Orchestrate Theme, Emotion, Character, and More

Elizabeth Sims

As an author and writing coach, I'm always searching for new ways to understand the novel form. Recently, while standing with my drums, cymbals, and bells in the back row of the orchestra I play in, it struck me that music, specifically the symphony form, is an apt analogy for the interplay of harmonizing elements that must come together in the crafting of a novel.

Some symphonies are crowd-pleasers: Beethoven's Fifth, Dvorak's *The New World*, Berlioz's *Symphonie Fantastique*. And some require a bit more effort to get in touch with: Ives's Fourth and Mahler's Seventh, perhaps.

It's the same way with novels, which is why my local library buys twelve copies each of the latest bodice rippers but carries next to nothing by the German existentialists.

The vast instrumental sweep of a symphony exists purely to engage the listener's emotions, to give pleasure, to entertain, to provoke, to challenge, perhaps to tell a story in the most abstract of terms. To achieve this, every composer writes as dramatic a score as possible, full of conflict, interplay, development, and transformation. The process is as important as the tools.

Given that we, as novelists, must also engage our readers' emotions first and foremost, we can learn much from the symphonic form. And we can learn even more from the deep, rich process of composing. Because I think, too often, writers get fragmented by considering the elements of fiction individually: theme, setting, character, dialogue, and so forth. We can get so enamored by a slick premise or an exotic setting that we forget that a successful novel, like a great symphony, is vastly more than the sum of its parts; it's how they come together in harmony.

Here's how to orchestrate all the instruments, melodies, and dynamics at work in your novel like a master composer.

THEME: YOUR NOVEL'S MELODY

Theme is the seed from which a symphony grows. The most compelling symphonies begin with a basic, uncluttered melody, which is then developed, repeated, explicated, obscured, revealed, torn to bits, resurrected. A major symphony can feature several themes, which play together and transform one another before resolving. The best composers can make incredible music out of small, humble melodies, and they do it by bringing theme to bear on all the other elements of the symphony. This is a terrific lesson for authors, because theme is also the defining element of the novel.

For instance, two themes Harper Lee worked into *To Kill a Mockingbird* are *good versus evil* and *one brave individual can make a difference*. Lee developed these themes individually and together: We see that the good intentions of the townspeople can't overcome the evil of a few determined individuals, and that someone who is brave enough to act is needed. Enter Atticus Finch; enter Boo Radley, the mockingbird. Furthermore, Lee developed her themes in conjunction with her characters and setting: an impoverished white family, an honorable black man caught in the wrong place at the wrong time, the Jim Crow South.

How can you take your theme to symphonic levels?

PUT SERIOUS THOUGHT INTO THEMES FROM THE START. Only when you have a firm grasp on what your themes are can you powerfully compose the harmonies around them.

Simple is best when it comes to theme. Why? Because a simple theme can be expanded and ornamented, but a complex theme is difficult to simplify without destroying it. *The power of love* is a terrific simple theme that can take you from zero to Alpha Centauri, while *a person who has been abused will never truly love unless she gets lots of counseling* isn't likely to be much of a springboard beyond itself.

LET THEME GROW AND DEVELOP WITH YOUR CHARACTERS. *The power of love*, being pure and easy to understand, can work in tandem with many other themes. For an example, let's choose *life is random and unfair*.

Now, if you want to start with a bang, you could put a couple of honeymooners on a plane and make it crash. However, if you start with an attractive businessman who exchanges exasperated glances with a beautiful actress in the security line at the airport, then put both of them in the coffee line together, where they find they have instant chemistry (the power of love emerges, a small but thrilling melody), and suddenly he proposes on the spot, and on impulse she accepts because she's on the rebound (complexity builds), and they board the plane and plan their life together, lost in each other's eyes—and *then* the plane falls out of the sky ... now you've got something. You've established *and* intensified your *power of love* theme before adding the second theme, *life is random and unfair*. From there you can get into obstacles overcome, lessons learned, beauty discovered.

Let's say the couple is found alive in the fiery wreckage, but they are permanently disfigured—her face is gravely damaged and he's lost his hands. What variations you can play! Readers with romantic streaks will want the couple's love to grow after this catastrophe, to be proven real, forged on the anvil of adversity. You could do this, and you could further test their love by inflicting yet more misfortune on them: a reconstructive surgery gone wrong, a stillborn child. In consciously making theme work on character, when your characters then respond to those situations, you can make character work on theme. (Love is rejected, only to be found again; love is shown to be less powerful than fear; one character's idea of love differs from another's; etc.)

LET THEME DRIVE PLOT. In my novel *The Extra*, I wanted dogs to be symbolically tied to my themes, and I wanted to have fun doing it. I constructed a subplot where a prizewinning beagle stud goes missing and a detective reluctantly agrees to find it. Beyond that, I put in references to dogs throughout the novel: It's sweltering hot ("the dog days"); in the night skies, Sirius, the dog star, is rising; the protagonist's child wants a dog and goes to some lengths to get one; a feral pack of canines roams the city; and so on. These dogs come together sooner or later (for instance, the missing stud is found to have joined the feral pack) so that the big themes harmonize with the small, symbolic ones: Tenacity and fatal secrecy are both further illustrated by the dog elements.

ELEVATE YOUR STORY BY ADDING THEMATIC DETAILS TO YOUR SETTINGS. Let's say one of your themes is *abandonment*, and one of your settings is a pool hall. You could describe the pool hall as shunned by polite society; it could be populated by derelicts; it could be in a part of town forgotten by the urban redevelopment projects. Themes can also interact ironically with your settings; for example, the theme of abandonment can be brought to a luxury condo in Honolulu—far from being warm, this dwelling might be cold and sterile, abandoned by human feeling.

YOUR ENSEMBLE: A STAGE FULL OF VOICES

A great composer, in writing a symphony, will be sure to differentiate between the voices of the ensemble. Think of the whole orchestra playing the exact same scale, all together, slowly—it might sound pleasant enough, but it will also sound bland.

The act of highlighting different instruments lets the composer create the ultimate in musical riches: conflict. A composer will write solos for individual voices, bringing them to bear on the themes and variations of the sonic material: the plangent cello, the vainglorious trumpet, the clashing cymbals, the luminous French horn, the piercing piccolo. The instruments play duets, trios; they chase one another in scherzos; they mock one another in rondos; they fight one another in fugues.

Particularly noteworthy ensemble-cast novels are Ernest Hemingway's *The Sun Also Rises*, Muriel Spark's *The Girls of Slender Means*, Katherine Anne Porter's *Ship of Fools*, and James Ellroy's *L.A. Confidential*. In these books the authors establish their characters rapidly and distinctly, give them star turns, and let group dynamics form alliances, then shift, destroy, and re-create them.

LISTEN TO YOUR CHARACTERS. Treat your ensemble of characters as if it has the massive range of an orchestra. Listen to their voices with your deepest self as you write; open your core to them. Go on and get a little metaphysical! Just as composers can be inspired by the instruments at their disposal, so it can be with your characters and you.

GIVE THEM SOLOS. An easy way to highlight and develop a character—and leave him open for conflict with others—is to give him periodic solo passages. Letting him go off on his own could be as simple as a short passage of inner monologue or as complex as a subplot.

Let's say we want to explore how gutsy our maimed businessman is. He could decide to pursue competitive sports or to go on a spiritual quest into the wilderness. Perhaps he takes along a hired nursing aide, and what began as a solo turns into a duet. Perhaps the aide turns out to be a con artist or a maniac or an inventor who, gazing at a thunderstorm one afternoon during his own solo turn, makes a mental breakthrough that results in a partnership in which he and the businessman develop prosthetic hands the likes of which the world has never seen.

PASS THE SPOTLIGHT. A literal, and perfectly effective, way to switch solos from one character to the next is to shift the point of view. You can do this either by writing separate sections from different characters' POVs, as Kathryn Stockett did in *The Help*, or by using an omniscient POV and concentrating on individual characters from time to time (action scenes are great for passing the spotlight). Either way, this technique can generate wonderful tension.

If you're employing the protagonist's first-person POV exclusively, try bringing other characters in and out of your hero's life in high relief. For instance, to give a murder suspect a solo, you can have your detective protagonist interview her, drawing out information. While doing so he observes her intensely, from personal presentation to vocabulary to body language. He raises questions, draws conclusions, and prepares a plan of action.

Do this, and you will immediately see new ways your characters can harmonize, clash, and crescendo.

TEMPO, DYNAMICS, AND MOOD: POWERFUL TOOLS

Good symphonic composers will use the full dynamic range of the ensemble, from one lone small voice—say, an oboe introducing a mournful melody from the obscure center of the orchestra—to the full ensemble in maximum *fortissimo*, detonating chords in a rapid finale.

When an entire orchestra plays a passage very softly, suspense builds. We know the musicians have the power to blast us out of our seats, yet there they are, whispering to us, beckoning slowly. They know what's coming, but we don't, and we sit spellbound with the tense joy of anticipation.

Some thriller authors are masters at varying their dynamics and tempo to heart-clutching effect. John D. MacDonald's *Cape Fear* (formerly titled *The Executioners*), for instance, cranks the volume up and down, alternating between scary and reassuring, between fast and slow action, while swinging the variances wider and wider, as we helplessly, masochistically, wait for the final payoff.

BE OVERT. Write a storm scene followed by a quiet love scene, followed by a messenger with devastating news, followed by a winning lottery ticket. An action sequence like a car chase can certainly represent a dynamic shift, but so can a silent multimillion-dollar museum heist.

CHANGE KEYS. Generally speaking, major keys furnish harmony, a mood of communion or playfulness, and minor keys challenge harmony with a darker atmosphere. Consider the first sentence of Anita Brookner's quiet, Man Booker Prize–winning novel, *Hotel du Lac*: "From the window all that could be seen was a receding area of grey." I'd certainly call that an opening in a minor key. Brookner exploits and expands that atmosphere in electron-microscope detail, so that we get thirsty for some major-key relief, which comes soon enough in the form of the subtle yet needle-sharp wit the author is loved for.

A good simple way to shift atmosphere is to use description to foretell what is to come. Something like this:

> We laughed and hugged, relief flooding us like cool water. A minute later, however, a large, fast-moving shadow passed overhead. "What the hell was that?" Philip said. "All the birds are supposed to be dead."

USE THE SMALL STUFF. A small but effective atmosphere-changing tool is sentence structure: Short, blunt sentences on the heels of a long, flowing passage change the rhythm, the feel. Another is dialogue: Imagine a conversation between a person who is angry and a person who is not. Right away you can see how their vocabulary and diction can establish suspense, develop a scene, and lead to action.

YOUR FINALE: EMOTION AMPLIFIED

Over and over, I counsel aspiring novelists to take their time writing their climax and wrap-up. I'm reminded here of a quotation from Emerson: "Adopt the pace of nature: Her secret is patience." Be like top composers and authors, and don't rush your payoffs. That doesn't mean to make your climactic scenes slow; it means to give them your full attention. Don't hurry the reader through them.

An audience will instinctively appreciate any sort of resolution. But they will feel it deeply and emotionally only if they are given disharmony and discordance first. The contrast provides context, and this makes a huge difference.

So, as you build to the end, take away your readers' soft bed and let them sleep on rocks for a night or two. They will positively kiss their pillows once you take them home again.

The world offers us countless ways to stimulate our creativity as novelists. I believe that the metaphor of music is largely untapped by fiction writers, and I think we've just scratched the surface of a lode of riches here. Try some of these ideas, and then dig into them in your own way.

Do a good job, and you'll get a standing ovation—and play to a packed house next time.

19

SOMETHING TO SAY

Weaving Theme into Your Novel

Donald Maass

Have you ever been trapped at a party talking with someone who has nothing to say? You look for excuses to slip away. So do readers. When they run across a novel that has nothing to say, they snap it closed—or perhaps hurl it across the room. Fiction readers expect to be engaged on deeper levels.

Fact one: All stories are moral. All stories have underlying values. If they didn't, we wouldn't bother listening. Whether they are danced around a campfire or packaged in sleek trade paperbacks, they are the glue that holds together our fragile human enterprise.

Fact two: Readers tend to seek out the novels that are in accord with their beliefs. Techno-thriller readers are largely military personnel; science fiction readership is heavy with scientists; romance readers are largely women; mystery and thriller readers skew somewhat conservative. The number of fiction readers who deliberately seek to have their morals tested and minds changed are few.

Yet the picture is not that simple. Most readers may not want to be converted, but they do want to be stretched. They want to see the world through different eyes. They crave insight. Thus, it's not true to say that fiction readers are looking only for what is comfortable, familiar, and politically pleasing.

Hence, fact three: Fiction is the most engrossing when it pulls readers into points of view that are compelling, detailed, and different. Characters' beliefs are what engage readers on those deeper levels. For the characters to have those beliefs, the author must be able and willing to share them, too, at least for a time.

If a powerful problem is a novel's spine, then a powerful theme is its animating spirit. How can you infuse your novel with such a theme? It starts with *you* having something to say.

HAVING SOMETHING TO SAY

I do not believe that you have no opinions. It is simply not possible that you have never observed a fact of human nature or uncovered a social irony. You no doubt also have some thoughts on the meaning of the universe itself. You are an aware, observant, and discerning person. You are a novelist.

What you may not have done is allow yourself to become deeply passionate about something you believe to be true. That is natural. It is not easy to vigorously express your views, especially in our postmodern, politically correct era. We fear offending others. We respect other people's views. We listen and defer. We weigh pros and cons, and sit cooperatively through countless meetings.

We admire those who respect others, but we admire even more people who take a stand. Do you remember Tiananmen Square? Chinese students rallied for democratic reform, and the world was moved. What stirred us most deeply, though, was the image of the nameless man who lay down in the path of a rolling tank. A similar uncompromising idealism has made Howard Roark in Ayn Rand's *The Fountainhead* (1943) one of the great characters in modern fiction. In every new generation, he inspires devotion.

A novelist needs courage, too: the courage to say something passionately. A *breakout* novelist believes that what she has to say is not just *worth* saying but is something that *must* be said. It is a truth that the world needs to hear, an insight without which we would find ourselves diminished.

What do you care about? What gets your blood boiling? What makes you roar with laughter? What human suffering have you seen that makes you wince in sympathetic pain? That is the stuff of exceptional novels. Stories lacking fire cannot fire readers.

BUILDING A THEME STEP-BY-STEP

One problem with talking about theme is that any discussion necessarily makes "theme" sound like something extra added to a story at the end, like cheese baked on top of a casserole. But I feel it's beneficial to work in advance on the moral forces moving underneath your story.

To avoid a preachy tone, it may be helpful not to grapple with theme on a global scale but rather first to examine individual scenes. Pick at random a scene from your current novel. Any scene. What is happening? A point-of-view character, in all likelihood your protagonist, is experiencing something: a problem or some complication of the central conflict. Good. Now ask yourself this question: *Why is this character here?* I do not mean the plot reasons. I mean the inner reasons, her motivations.

List them. You will probably find that at the top of your list are the character's immediate needs: her physical and emotional requirements. Further down the list probably are the character's secondary needs: information, support, avoidance, comfort, curiosity, and so on. Finally, down at the bottom of the list are the higher motivations, the ones that are not immediately relevant and that would sound a bit silly to include in your scene: the search for truth, a thirst for justice, a need to hope, a longing for love.

Next, reverse the list. That's right: Write it out again, starting with the reasons at the bottom of your original list. Now rewrite your scene so that your character is motivated first by the reasons at the top of your new list, and last by your original reasons. The scene feels a little different, doesn't it? Motivating your characters according to higher values will do that. It adds passion to action.

You need to enhance motivation if you want to give your protagonist the inner fire that, developed step-by-step through your manuscript, results in a powerful theme. Understatement and restraint are good. However, when high motives are made believable and integral, it's like sending a ten-thousand-volt electric current through your novel. It will light it up like a beacon in the dark.

PRESENTING INESCAPABLE MORAL DILEMMAS

One problem that can sink a novel is a failure to draw a clear line between good and bad. Most readers are moral people. They turn to fiction—really, to any form of storytelling—for affirmation of the values we hold in common. They long to know that what they believe is right. Contemporary life offers few opportunities to take a strong moral stand, but fiction deals heavily with such moments.

Now, I am not arguing for a revival of the moral fable or the novel of social conscience so popular in the nineteenth century. Certainly, contemporary novels can have a sharp moral tone—especially social satires like Joseph Heller's *Catch-22* or Tom Wolfe's *The Bonfire of the Vanities*—but, in general, as readers we prefer that our fiction make its point in a restrained rather than an overt fashion. That means keeping the message out of the mouth of the author and instead conveying it through the actions of the novel's characters.

If you think about it, many successful stories box their characters into a situation with inescapable moral choices and dilemmas. Facing a moral choice—that is, a choice between two rights or two wrongs—is one of the most powerful conflicts any novel can present. Does the protagonist of your current novel face such a choice? What would make that decision more difficult? As a mental exercise, pile on those difficulties. Are there ways to build on them earlier in the novel? The more fundamental and inescapable you can make a moral choice, the more impact it will have.

What does your protagonist believe? What truths are his rocks and foundations? Are there ways to undermine those beliefs, maybe even to subvert them altogether? Can you make it so that your protagonist comes to believe the opposite? Many plot-driven novels do a good job with outward problems but stint on their protagonists' inner journeys. Many character-driven novels do a good job detailing their characters' inner lives but don't twist, torment, and challenge them to extremes. Protagonists without flaws or blind spots feel bland. The same is true of characters' moral lives. What has your protagonist gotten wrong? What deeper truth has she not yet seen?

Many novelists are rightly wary of moral content. It is too easy to turn preachy. It is essential, then, that the moral outlook of your protagonist is embedded in her actions. One of the most highly moral science fiction writers of our time is Orson Scott Card. While his convictions are clear, in his best work they emerge from the action of the story rather than from his characters' mouths. In his Nebula and Hugo Award–winning novel *Ender's Game*, young Andrew "Ender" Wiggin is taken from his family and put into a military training school, where he is conditioned with highly stressful virtual warfare simulations. At the climax of the novel, following a thousand-to-one-odds battle in which the enemy's home planet is destroyed, Ender learns that what had seemed to be a computer game is not a simulation at all. Ender, a child genius, has been fighting an actual alien invasion. The fighter pilots he wasted in order to win really died.

Card's novel has volumes to say about children, computer games, and the human culture of violence, but nowhere in the novel are these themes stated overtly. Instead, Card allows the story itself to send the message.

What about your protagonist? What's his worst mistake? What injustice reduces her to helpless rage? What's the one thing he refuses to do? What action defines all for which she stands? Test your protagonist to the utmost. If you do, your story will soar.

DEVELOPING A UNIVERSAL THEME

If an author has effectively constructed a moral conflict, first planting its seeds and then bringing it to a simultaneous climax with the outer events of the plot, the overall effect will probably be a well- and long-remembered message. Notice the word *probably* in that last sentence. Some messages are memorable; others are not. Why? The answer is linked to what makes a theme universal.

A widely believed message, moral, or point is in one sense universal, but that does not guarantee it will have impact. Half-hour family sitcoms usually present a familiar moral, but usually it is forgotten by the time the final credits roll, because the sitcom message is often simplistic and weakly dramatized. What matters more than whether a point is widely accepted is whether it is developed in depth.

"Love conquers all" is pretty much the theme of all romance fiction. Much of the time, it doesn't have a high impact. A great romance novel makes love matter more than anything else in the world. Specifically, one love—*this* love. Every hero and heroine on the romance shelves belong together, but not all have us hoping, cheering, and biting our nails to know whether they'll unite. For that to matter to readers, it's got to matter to those characters in ways particular and profound.

The same is true in mystery novels. The typical theme in this genre is "justice must be done." Sure. And in all mystery novels, it is. But how often do we quake with rage and fear that evil will win? Not often. For that to happen, the protagonist's own rage and fear must grip our hearts and rattle our nerves. Conversely, the antagonist's point of view must be as compelling. What makes your antagonist right? That question can be as important as discovering the worst thing that your protagonist can do wrong.

What about the truly original theme, though? Is it possible for readers to accept a point that is unfamiliar, perhaps even unpopular? Certainly. Few novelists want to say exactly what has been said before. Most would like to be visionary. That is fine, and indeed it is one of the purposes of literary fiction, as opposed to genre fiction, the thematic purpose of which is to validate familiar beliefs. But there are ways to make an unpopular point compelling, and there are ways to make it repellant.

The key, again, is your protagonist. If we believe in him, we will believe what he believes. Consider the antihero. Mystery novelist Donald E. Westlake scored a major critical and sales success with his novel *The Ax*. In it, paper company executive Burke Devore, out of work for two years and desperate, decides to raise his chances for a new job by murdering his competition one by one. Late in the novel, Devore justifies his actions in a ringing, if ironic, endorsement of current American values:

> Every era, and every nation, has its own characteristic morality, its own code of ethics, depending on what the people think is important. There have been

times and places when honor was considered the most sacred of qualities, and times and places that gave every concern to grace. The Age of Reason promoted reason to be the highest of values, and some peoples—the Italians, the Irish— have always felt that feeling, emotion, sentiment was the most important. In the early days of America, the work ethic was our greatest expression of morality, and then for a while property values were valued above everything else, but there's been another more recent change. Today, our moral code is based on the idea that the end justifies the means.

There was a time when that was considered improper, the end justifying the means, but that time is over. We not only believe it, we say it. Our government leaders always defend their actions on the basis of their goals. And every single CEO who has commented in public on the blizzard of downsizings sweeping America has explained himself with some variant on the same idea: The end justifies the means.

The end of what I'm doing, the purpose, the goal, is good, clearly good. I want to take care of my family; I want to be a productive part of society; I want to put my skills to use; I want to work and pay my own way and not be a burden to the taxpayers. The means to that end has been difficult, but I've kept my eye on the goal, the purpose. The end justifies the means. Like the CEOs, I have nothing to feel sorry for.

You know, I almost agree with him! Westlake makes a fresh comment upon our values by having Devore say what we expect him to say, but calmly and rationally do the opposite of what we want. Devore is wrong—but Westlake is original.

So, do you now have a better idea of what your current novel is about? Do you have a plan for revising it to make its themes stronger? If not, don't worry. Writing is, if nothing else, an act of discovery. The important thing is to ensure, somewhere along the way, that you are angry, weeping, or determined to show your readers something that is imperative for them to experience.

An indifferent author cannot excite me. An author who is fired up, however— or, rather, who fires up his characters as his proxies—stands a much better chance of crafting a story that will hold me spellbound. Think of the main characters of some of the last century's best-selling novels and series: Travis McGee, Howard Roark, Scarlett O'Hara, George Smiley, and so on. They are not diffident, deferential people. They are principled, opinionated, and passionate. They do not sit on the sidelines. They act. Their inner fire fires us—as well as the sales of their authors' books. Their viewpoints inspire us, their opinions linger in our minds, and their beliefs mingle with our own.

20

SIX POWERFUL WAYS TO MAINTAIN SUSPENSE

....
Keep Your Readers Captivated

Steven James

Thriller? Mystery? Literary fiction? It's all the same: Building apprehension in the minds of your readers is one of the most effective keys to engaging them early in your novel and keeping them flipping pages late into the night.

Simply put, if you don't hook your readers, they won't get into the story. So if you don't drive the story forward by making readers worry about your main character, they won't have a reason to keep reading.

Think: Worry equals suspense.

The best part is, the secrets for ratcheting up the suspense are easy to implement. Here are six of the most effective.

1. PUT CHARACTERS THAT READERS CARE ABOUT IN JEOPARDY

Four factors are necessary for suspense: reader empathy, reader concern, impending danger, and escalating tension.

We create reader empathy by giving the character a desire, a wound, or an internal struggle that readers can identify with. The more they empathize, the closer their connection with the story will be. Once they care about and identify with a character, readers will be invested when they see the character struggling to get what he most desires.

We want readers to worry about whether the character will get what he wants. Only when readers know what the character wants will they know what's at stake.

And only when they know what's at stake will they be engaged in the story. To get readers more invested in your novel, make clear: (1) What your character desires (love, freedom, adventure, forgiveness, etc.); (2) what is keeping him from getting it; and (3) what terrible consequences will result if he *doesn't* get it.

Suspense builds as danger approaches. Readers experience apprehension when a character they care about is in peril. This doesn't have to be a life-and-death situation. Depending on your genre, the threat may involve the character's physical, psychological, emotional, spiritual, or relational well-being. Whatever your genre, show that something terrible is about to happen—then postpone the resolution to sustain the suspense.

We need to escalate the tension in our stories until it reaches a satisfying climax. Raise the stakes by making the danger more imminent, intimate, personal, and devastating. So if the moon explodes in Act One, the entire galaxy better be at risk by Act Three. If tension doesn't escalate, the suspense you've been developing will evaporate.

It's like inflating a balloon. You can't let the air out of your story; instead, you keep blowing more in, tightening the tension until it looks like the balloon is going to pop at any second.

Then blow in more.

And more.

Until the reader can hardly stand it.

Incidentally, this is one reason why adding sex scenes to your story is actually counterintuitive to building suspense. By releasing all the romantic or sexual tension you've been building, you let air out of the balloon. If you want to titillate, add sex; if you want to build suspense, postpone it.

2. INCLUDE MORE PROMISES AND LESS ACTION

Suspense happens in the stillness of your story, in the gaps between the action sequences, in the moments between the *promise* of something dreadful and its arrival.

When I was writing my novel *The Bishop*, I began with the goal of letting the entire story span only fifty-two hours. I thought that by packing everything into a tight time frame I would really make the story suspenseful.

As I worked on the book, however, I realized that there was so much that needed to happen to build to the climax that if I kept to my fifty-two-hour time frame, events would need to occur one after another so quickly that there

The Complete Handbook of Novel Writing

wouldn't be space for suspense to happen among them. Finally, I added another twenty-four hours to the story to create the opportunity for the promises and payoffs that would make the story suspenseful.

If readers complain that "nothing is happening" in a story, they don't typically mean that *no action is occurring*, but rather that *no promises are being made*.

Contrary to what you may have heard, the problem of reader boredom isn't solved by adding action, but by building on apprehension. Suspense is anticipation; action is payoff. You don't increase suspense by "making things happen," but by promising that they will. Instead of asking, "What needs to happen?" ask, "What can I promise will go wrong?"

Stories are much more than reports of events. Stories are about transformations. We have to show readers where things are going—what situation, character, or relationship is going to be transformed.

Of course, depending on your genre, promises can be comedic, romantic, horrific, or dramatic. For example, two lovers plan to meet in a meadow to elope. That's a promise.

But the young man's rival finds out and says to himself, "If I can't have her, no one can." Then he heads to the field and hides, waiting for them, dagger in hand.

The lovers arrive, clueless about the danger ...

Milk that moment; make the most of the suspense it offers.

And then show us what happens in that meadow. In other words ...

3. KEEP EVERY PROMISE YOU MAKE

In tandem with making promises is the obligation of keeping them. The bigger the promise, the bigger the payoff. For example, in my first novel I had the killer tell a woman whom he'd abducted, "Your death will be remembered for decades." That's a huge promise to readers. I'd better fulfill it by making her death memorable or terrifying. In another book I had a character tell the hero that the villain had "a twist waiting for you at the end that you would never expect."

Another huge promise. Readers think, *Okay, buddy. Let's see if you deliver.*

That's what you want.

So you'd better deliver.

Remember: A huge promise without the fulfillment isn't suspense—it's disappointment.

Every word in your story is a promise to the reader about the significance of that word to the story as a whole. This is where so many authors—both of suspense novels and of fiction in other genres—fumble the ball. If you spend three paragraphs describing a woman's crimson-colored sweater, that sweater better be vital to the story. If not, you're telling readers, "Oh, by the way, I wasted your time. Yeah, that part really wasn't important to the story."

Never disrespect your readers like that.

When stories falter it's often because the writers didn't make big enough promises, didn't fulfill them when readers wanted them to be fulfilled, or broke promises by never fulfilling them at all.

Here's a great way to break your promise to the reader: Start your story with a prologue, say, in which a woman is running on a beach by herself, and there are werewolves on the loose. Let's see if you can guess what's going to happen. Hmm … what a twist this is going to be—she gets attacked by the werewolves! Wow. What a fresh, original idea that was.

How is that a broken promise? Because it was predictable. Readers want to predict what will happen, *but they want to be wrong.* They're only satisfied when the writer gives them more than they anticipate, not less.

I'm always annoyed when an author introduces a character, gives me background information on where she went to college, what she studied, her love interests, her favorite snack food and so on, and then kills her off right away or fails to give her any significant role in the story.

When readers invest their time, they want that investment to pay off.

Make big promises.

Then keep them.

4. LET THE CHARACTERS TELL READERS THEIR PLANS

I know, this seems counterintuitive. Why would we want readers to know what's going to happen? Doesn't that give the ending away?

I'm not talking about revealing your secrets or letting readers know the twists that your story has in store. Instead, just show readers the agenda, and you'll be making a promise that something will either go wrong to screw up the schedule or that plans will fall into place in a way that propels the story (and the tension) forward.

Simply by having your characters tell readers their schedules, you create a promise that can create anticipation and build suspense:

"I'll see you later at the 4 o'clock briefing."

"Let's meet at Rialto's for supper at eight."

> "All right, here's what I have lined up for the rest of the morning: Follow up on the fingerprints, track down Adrian, and then stop by the prison and have a little chat with Donnie 'The Midnight Slayer' Jackson."

A story moves through action sequences to moments of reorientation when the characters process what just happened and make a decision that leads to the next scene. We do this in real life as well—we experience something moving or profound, we process it, and then we decide how to respond. Problem is, in those moments of reflection, a story can drag and the suspense can be lost. During every interlude between scenes a promise must be either made or kept.

And, if you resolve one question or plot thread (that is, you keep a promise you made earlier), you must introduce another twist or moral dilemma (in other words, make another promise).

When a story lags it's almost always because of missing tension (there's no unmet desire on the part of the characters) or not enough escalation (there's too much repetition). To fix this, show us how deeply the character wants something but cannot get it, and escalate the story by making the desire even more difficult to get.

5. CUT DOWN ON THE VIOLENCE

The more violence there is, the less it will mean.

This was a problem I faced with my thriller *The Knight*. In the story, a killer is reenacting ten crimes from a thirteenth-century manuscript that was condemned by the church. If I showed all ten crimes, the story would have certainly included lots of gruesome violence, but the murders would have gotten boring after a while. Instead, my investigator finds out about the killings partway through the crime spree, and he has to try and stop the killer before the final grisly crime.

A murder is not suspense. An abduction with the threat of a murder is.

If you want readers to emotionally distance themselves from the story, show one murder after another, after another, after another; but if you want to build tension, cut down on the violence and increase the readers' apprehension about a future violent act.

The scariest stories often contain very little violence.

And, of course, different genre elements dictate different means of suspense. In a mystery you might find out that a person was beheaded. This occurs before the narrative begins, so the focus of the story is on solving the crime. If you're writing a horror story, you'll show the beheading itself—in all of its gory detail.

If you're writing suspense, the characters in the story will find out that someone is going to be beheaded, and they must find a way to stop it.

Reader expectations, and the depth and breadth of what is at stake in the story, will determine the amount of mystery, horror, or suspense you'll want to include. Nearly all genres include some scenes with them. As a writer, it's vital that you become aware of how you shape those sequences to create the desired effect on your reader—curiosity, dread, or apprehension.

CREATING SUSPENSE USING GENRE ELEMENTS

	MYSTERY	HORROR	SUSPENSE
TIMING OF CRIME OR CRISIS EVENT	The violence occurs before the story starts.	Readers can see it happening.	Readers anticipate that it will happen.
NARRATIVE QUESTION	Who was responsible for the crime?	How will the character die?	How can the crisis or impending crime be averted?
READER ORIENTATION	Readers may lag behind the detective in understanding the clues.	Readers view the action; they're in on the secret.	Readers know about danger that the characters do not.
READER APPEAL	Head (intellectual curiosity)	Gut (visceral reaction)	Heart (worry or concern)

Also, remember that valuing human life increases suspense. Because readers only feel suspense when they care about what happens to a character, we want to heighten their concern by heightening the impact of the tragedy. Show how valuable life is. The more murders your story contains, the more life will seem cheap, and if it's cheap, readers won't be concerned if it's lost.

6. BE ONE STEP AHEAD OF YOUR READERS

When I write my novels I'm constantly asking myself what readers are hoping for, wondering about, or questioning at each point in the story. Our job as writers is to give them what they want, when they want it—or to add a twist so that we give them more than they ever bargained for.

Here are some ways to do that by amping up the suspense:

- **AS YOU DEVELOP YOUR STORY, APPEAL TO READERS' FEARS AND PHOBIAS.** (Phobias are irrational fears, so to be afraid of a cobra is not a phobia, but to be afraid of all snakes is.) Most people are afraid of helplessness in the face of danger. Many are afraid of needles, the dark, drowning, heights, and so on. Think of the things that frighten you most, and you can be sure many of your readers will fear them as well.

- **MAKE SURE YOU DESCRIBE THE SETTING OF YOUR STORY'S CLIMAX BEFORE YOU REACH THAT PART OF THE STORY.** In other words, let someone visit it earlier and foreshadow everything you'll need for readers to picture the scene when the climax arrives. Otherwise, you'll end up stalling out the story to describe the setting, when you should be pushing through to the climax.
- **COUNTDOWNS AND DEADLINES CAN BE HELPFUL BUT CAN WORK AGAINST YOU IF THEY DON'T FEED THE STORY'S ESCALATION.** For example, having every chapter of your book start one hour closer to the climax is a gimmick that gets old after a while because it's repetitious and predictable—two things that kill escalation. Instead, start your countdown in the middle of the book. To escalate a countdown, shorten the time available to solve the problem.
- **AS YOU BUILD TOWARD THE CLIMAX, ISOLATE YOUR MAIN CHARACTER.** Remove his tools, escape routes, and support system (buddies, mentors, helpers, or defenders). This forces him to become self-reliant and makes it easier for you to put him at a disadvantage in his final confrontation with evil.
- **MAKE IT PERSONAL.** Don't just have a person get abducted—let it be the main character's son. Don't just let New York City be in danger—let Gramma live there.

No matter what you write, good prose really is all about sharpening the suspense. Follow these six secrets, and you'll keep your readers up way past their bedtime.

21

MAKE YOUR SETTING
A CHARACTER

How to Create a Rich, Immersive Story World

Donald Maass

In great fiction, the setting lives from the very first pages. Such places not only *feel* extremely real, they are dynamic. They change. They affect the characters in the story. They become metaphors, possibly even actors in the drama.

Powerfully portrayed settings seem to have a life of their own, but how is that effect achieved? *Make your setting a character* is a common piece of advice given to fiction writers, yet beyond invoking all five senses when describing the scenery, there's not a lot of info out there about exactly how to do it.

The trick is not to find a fresh setting or a unique way to portray a familiar place; rather, it is to discover in your setting *what is unique for your characters, if not for you.*

You must go beyond description, beyond dialect, beyond local foods to bring setting into the story in a way that integrates it into the very fabric of your characters' experience.

LINK DETAILS AND EMOTIONS

As a child, did you have a special summer place? A beach house or a lake cabin? One that's been in the family for years, rich in history, stocked with croquet mallets, special iced tea glasses, and a rusty rotary lawn mower?

For me the special summer place was my great uncle Robert's farm on a hillside near Reading, Pennsylvania. "Uncle Locker," as we called him, was, as far as I knew, born old. He loved his John Deere tractor but didn't particularly like children, especially not after my younger brother dropped the tin dipping cup down the front yard well.

Uncle Locker raised sheep. He stocked the lower pond with trout. He had connected a Revolutionary War–era log cabin with a Victorian–era farmhouse, erecting a soaring brick-floored, high-windowed living room between them. In that living room was a candy dish that each day magically refilled itself with M&M's. (I suspect now that it was my great aunt Margaret who was the magician.)

In the evenings Uncle Locker would read the newspaper on the glassed-in porch, classical symphonies crackling on his portable transistor radio as summer lightning flashed across the valley. That, today, is my mental image of perfect contentment. When I hear a radio crackle in a storm, I relax. I miss my Uncle Locker with a sharp pang.

Now, let me ask you this: Without looking back over what you just read, what do you remember best about what I wrote? Was it a detail, like the dipping cup, the M&M's, or the lightning? Or was it the feeling of contentment that, for me, accompanies an approaching storm? Whatever your answer, I would argue that you remember what you remember not because of the details themselves or the emotions they invoke in me, but because *both* those details and personal feelings are present.

In other words, it is the combination of setting details and the emotions attached to them that, together, make a place a living thing. Setting comes alive partly in its details and partly in the way that the story's characters experience it. Either element alone is fine, but both working together deliver a sense of place without parallel.

MEASURE CHANGE OVER TIME

There are other ways to bring setting alive. One of them is to measure the change in a place over time. Of course, most places don't change much—only the people observing them do.

Kristin Hannah's *On Mystic Lake* is a heading-home-to-heal novel. The lake in question is on Washington State's Olympic Peninsula. However, the wounded heroine of the story, Annie Colwater, is a native of the suburbs of Los Angeles.

In the first part of the novel, Annie, immediately after her seventeen-year-old daughter's departure for a semester in Europe, is devastated to learn that her husband wants a divorce. Don't be shocked, but he has taken up with a younger woman at the office. It's a humdrum setup, yet Hannah deftly uses the very ordinariness of Annie's world as a starting point for building tension. In this passage near the novel's beginning, she details springtime in L.A.:

> It was March, the doldrums of the year, still and quiet and gray, but the wind had already begun to warm, bringing with it the promise of spring. Trees that only last week had been naked and brittle seemed to have grown six inches over the span of a single moonless night, and sometimes, if the sunlight hit a limb just so, you could see the red bud of new life stirring at the tips of the crackly brown bark. Any day, the hills behind Malibu would blossom, and for a few short weeks this would be the prettiest place on Earth.
>
> Like the plants and animals, the children of Southern California sensed the coming of the sun. They had begun to dream of ice cream and Popsicles and last year's cutoffs. Even determined city dwellers, who lived in glass and concrete high-rises in places with pretentious names like Century City, found themselves veering into the nursery aisles of their local supermarkets. Small, potted geraniums began appearing in the metal shopping carts, alongside the sundried tomatoes and the bottles of Evian water.
>
> For nineteen years, Annie Colwater had awaited spring with the breathless anticipation of a young girl at her first dance. She ordered bulbs from distant lands and shopped for hand-painted ceramic pots to hold her favorite annuals.
>
> But now, all she felt was dread, and a vague, formless panic. ... What did a mother do when her only child left home?

L.A. always feels pretty much the same to me—but then again, I grew up in New England. Shows you how much I know. Who knew that the change of seasons could be measured by visions of Popsicles and cutoffs? By showing me the minute seasonal changes that a SoCal native would notice, Hannah nails spring as seen by Annie Colwater. But that's not all. This spring, Annie's usual "breathless anticipation" is replaced by dread. The contrast is jarring—in a good way.

REALIZE THAT HISTORY IS PERSONAL

Historical novelists think a lot about what makes the period of their novels different from present day. They research it endlessly. Indeed, many historical novelists say that is their favorite part of the process. When the research is done and writing begins, though, how do they create a sense of the times on the page? "*With details*" is the common answer, but which details, exactly, and how many of them?

And what if the period of your novel is not terribly far back in history? If your story is set in the 1970s, is it enough to mention Watergate, or do you need to be even more specific about disco, VWs, horizontally striped polo shirts, and oil shocks? How about contemporary stories? Does one need to convey a sense of the times when the times are our own?

To start to answer those questions, read the op-ed pages in the newspaper. Does everyone see our times in the same way? No. Outlooks vary. That should also be true for your fictional characters. What is your hero's take on our times? As in so many aspects of novel construction, creating a sense of the times first requires filtering the world through your characters.

Joseph Kanon's richly layered debut mystery novel, *Los Alamos*, won the 1998 Mystery Writers of America Edgar Award for Best First Novel. He followed with *The Prodigal Spy*, *The Good German*, and the tragic and complicated *Alibi*.

Alibi is set in Venice in 1946, immediately after the close of World War II. Rich Americans are returning to Europe, among them widow Grace Miller, who migrates south to Venice, having found Paris too depressing. Grace invites her son Adam, the novel's hero and narrator, who has been newly released from his post-war service as a Nazi hunter in Germany. As the novel opens, Adam tells of his mother's return to the expatriate life:

> After the war, my mother took a house in Venice. She'd gone first to Paris, hoping to pick up the threads of her old life, but Paris had become grim, grumbling about shortages, even her friends worn and evasive. The city was still at war, this time with itself, and everything she'd come back for—the big flat on the Rue du Bac, the cafés, the market on the Raspail, memories all burnished after five years to a rich glow—now seemed pinched and sour, dingy under a permanent cover of gray cloud.
>
> After two weeks she fled south. Venice at least would look the same, and it reminded her of my father, the early years when they idled away afternoons on the Lido and danced at night. In the photographs they were always tanned, sitting on beach chairs in front of striped changing huts, clowning with friends, everyone in caftans or bulky one-piece woolen bathing suits. Cole Porter had been there, writing patter songs, and since my mother knew Linda, there were a lot of evenings drinking around the piano, that summer when they'd just married. When her train from Paris finally crossed over the lagoon, the sun was so bright on the water that for a few dazzling minutes it actually seemed to be that first summer. Bertie, another figure in the Lido pictures, met her at the station in a motorboat, and as they swung down the Grand Canal, the sun so bright, the palazzos as glorious as ever, the whole improbable city just the same after all these years, she thought she might be happy again.

There are several things to note in this highly atmospheric opening. First, Kanon weaves an undercurrent of tension through these two paragraphs, a tension that derives from his mother's longing for ... well, what? Paris is dissatisfying. Venice, seemingly untouched by the war, is full of sunlight and memories. A mood of nostalgia would be enough here, but Kanon himself is not satisfied with a mere rosy glow. Venice is "improbable," and Grace's lift of spirit is tinged with doubt: "She thought she might be happy again."

That word *might* is a calculated choice. Do you get the feeling that Adam's mother will not re-create in Venice the happiness of the prewar party of the 1920s and 1930s? You are correct. Grace is courted by a distinguished Italian doctor, Gianni Maglione, whom Adam immediately dislikes—with good reason, as it turns out. When Adam begins a love affair with Claudia Grassini, a Jewish woman who survived the camps by becoming a fascist's mistress, he is drawn into a tragic conflict. Claudia accuses Dr. Maglione of wartime collaboration and, worse, condemning her own father to death at Auschwitz. Adam's mother wishes to leave the past buried, but Adam, given his background and love for Claudia, cannot leave it alone.

Kanon's opening also effectively evokes Europe in the immediate aftermath of the war. Paris is "grim" and "grumbling." Grace's Paris is specific, too: Kanon mentions not just the city's streets, cafés, and markets but Grace's flat on the "Rue du Bac" and the market on the "Raspail." For all I know, Kanon could be completely making up those places. It doesn't matter. It is their specificity that brings this Paris of food shortages and long memories alive.

Venice, by contrast, is full of false sunlight and sweet memories. These memories are highly specific: afternoons on the Lido, striped changing huts, Cole Porter. Kanon plucks from his research a few choice tidbits that hint at a life of gay carelessness and privilege. His narrator's casual familiarity with them contributes to the passage's reality. But it's not only that. The details and the mood, Grace's naive longing, and Adam's cynical foreknowledge all roll together into a couple of paragraphs that create a unique moment in time.

SEE THROUGH CHARACTERS' EYES

Let's dig deeper into the relationship between character and setting. Is there a technique more powerful than infusing a character with a strong opinion about his place or time? Yes. Infusing *two* characters with that.

Novelist Thomas Kelly focuses on working-class heroes and gritty New York settings. In *Empire Rising*, Kelly builds his panoramic, multiple-point-of-view novel around the construction of the Empire State Building in the 1930s. One principle point of view is that of Irish-American steelworker Michael Briody. In the novel's opening scene, Briody is chosen to pound in the first rivet at the building's groundbreaking ceremony, a piece of political theater for which the waiting workers have little patience. On the site once stood a hotel, the demolition of which gives Briody pause during the self-congratulatory speeches:

> Briody is not surprised that none of the swells on stage mention the six men who died demolishing the old hotel. Not surprised in the least. He considers their ugly endings, the crushed and broken bodies spirited away like just more rubble, their names already forgotten. Their stories untold. He shifts his weight from foot to foot, is anxious to start work. His fellow workers watch with dull stares. They have no interest in the staged spectacle. They mutter and joke under their breath until one of the concrete crew makes a loud noise, like a ripe fart, and the superintendent swivels his fat head around and glares at them as if they were recalcitrant schoolboys. They fall silent. They want the work. The next stop is the breadline.

The tension in this paragraph is, to my eye, nicely restrained: impatience mixed with a downtrodden cynicism unique to Depression workers who are one step away from starvation. What is Briody's opinion of the ceremony? Kelly hardly needs to tell us; he simply lets Briody's passing regard for the dead workers who preceded him imply how he feels.

A short while later in the story, Kelly introduces another principle point-of-view character, Johnny Farrell, a lawyer and bribe collector for Mayor Jimmy Walker. Johnny is king of his world, but all is not right with his domain. Johnny's wife is from a rich and very proper family. She disdains his work and the people with whom he must associate. One Sunday morning they argue as his wife bundles their children off to her Episcopal church. After she departs, Johnny reflects on the differences in their upbringings:

> Farrell kissed the children goodbye and watched as Pamela shepherded them into the waiting car, insisting that they ride the four blocks to the Church of the Resurrection rather than walk because she liked to make an impression. He thought for a moment of his own childhood in the Bronx, how his mother used to drag them through the crowded neighborhood streets to St. Jerome's, all those immigrants seeing the church as a way to keep their past alive, and for a moment standing in his Fifth Avenue apartment so far from the warrens of his youth he could smell the incense and hear the Latin intonations and feel his mother's rough hand holding his. The woman had lived in fear. And

that fear had instilled in him a hunger, an ambition, and a need to never settle for anything, and now this is where that need had brought him—an elegant and spacious home among the city's elite where his own children were total strangers to him. He grabbed his coat and hat and headed out into the day.

What would you say this passage is about? Scene setting? No. It's about the different values of Pamela and Johnny Farrell, as well as Johnny's rueful realization that the fulfillment of his ambitions has a bitter side. Yet notice the period details that the author weaves in: the Church of the Resurrection, the Bronx, immigrants, long-gone Fifth Avenue mansions. I would say that Farrell's feelings about his family and childhood are intimately connected to New York City.

What does the setting of your current novel mean to the characters in it? How do you portray that meaning and make it active in the story? The techniques of doing so are some of the most powerful tools in the novelist's kit. Use them and you will not only give your novel a setting that lives, but also construct for your readers an entire world, the world of the story.

22

STRENGTHENING THE CONFLICT

How to Fuel Your Novel with Complications

Jack Smith

Conflict is the engine that makes the story run. It is essential to creating a strong character, one who is more than a portrait, one who becomes real by undergoing struggles and coming to some realization about self or world. This is what makes the character interesting—as well as the story. We would find it utterly boring to read a story where no conflict occurred, where everyone got along just fine, where no one lost her job, no one lost out in romance, everyone had absolutely everything they needed, no one ever got ill or died. Serious fiction, like life, includes many rug pullings. We may not want the grim, but we do want to experience fiction that deals honestly with humans and their condition, and clearly the lot of humans is not sheer pleasure or endless happiness, but pain as well.

You will surely be working with characterization as you deal with important aspects of conflict—the two elements are not separate but intricately entwined.

RAISING THE STAKES

Are the stakes high enough? What is the character's investment in his goal? First, the stakes need to be high enough that the reader cares. Secondly, they have to be believable, given everything we know about this character in these circumstances.

We can think of stakes in relation to one or more human needs and desires:

- **MATERIAL:** In Upton Sinclair's *The Jungle*, the protagonist, Jurgis Rudkus, works in horrible conditions at a meatpacking plant. The stakes are certainly high for this character—his basic survival is on the line. It may seem too obvious to point out that we have a different expression of material need in D.H. Lawrence's short story "The Rocking-Horse Winner." But I mention it only for contrast to emphasize that you must consider the makeup of your character, her circumstances, and so forth, in deciding the stakes. What's at stake must be firmly grounded in character. What is at stake in Lawrence's story? More and more money is required—an endless supply of it. The stakes may not seem as high as those in Sinclair's novel, but they are indeed very high because of the mother's desperate desire for money and social class. Without this desire we couldn't accept Paul riding to his death on the rocking horse.

- **EMOTIONAL:** Romantic love stories set the stakes high when characters are miserable in love: They must have their beloved or perish. But would a character kill for love—thinking that this is the only way to achieve what she wants? Certainly, the stakes are high enough here to generate reader interest, but now the burden falls on the writer to make sure this action is believable. In *A Wild Surge of Guilty Passion*, Ron Hansen makes us believe that Ruth Snyder is able to convince Judd Gray, driven by his lust for her, to kill her husband, whom she loathes.

- **PSYCHOLOGICAL:** A character may be vulnerable in terms of self-esteem and a sense of personal worth. In Alicia Erian's *Towelhead*, her young female protagonist, Jasira, finds no genuine love in either parent. She seeks an outlet for her sense of personal emptiness and engages in increasingly dangerous sexual rebellion. Clearly the stakes are high in this story: Will Jasira discover who she really is and steer a path toward self-affirming behavior? For readers, this issue matters, and Erian grounds her character's crisis of self in both character and circumstance.

- **INTELLECTUAL OR CULTURAL:** Why are the intellectual and cultural so important to this character? What would happen if he were deprived of intellectual stimulation, art, or culture? Thomas Hardy explores this question with great force in *Jude the Obscure*. For Jude Fawley, Christminster represents the august halls of learning and culture. Much is at stake. To enter the lofty fold, he devotes himself to study and to breaking free from his social class limitations as a stonemason, though in Hardy's naturalistic novel, fate has other plans for him.

- **SOCIAL:** For Madame Bovary, the need is both emotional and social. Steeped in sentimental novels and stuck in a marriage with a boring country doctor, Madame Bovary craves the excitement and social engagement of the grand balls. Her dull, provincial conditions are intolerable to her. She longs to be a gentlewoman. The stakes are truly high for her. It's a life-or-death proposition for Madame Bovary, and she will have nothing but this life she has sought out. When things go sour, she ultimately kills herself by ingesting arsenic.

When the stakes are high enough, the reader is interested in the character. Of course, readers expect struggle—and this is where a worthy antagonist comes in.

MATCHING THE PROTAGONIST WITH A WORTHY OPPONENT

In attempting to achieve what they want, or to avoid what they don't want, protagonists often struggle against antagonists—persons, groups, or whole systems.

What makes a worthy opponent? It's certainly not one who is easily defeated with little or no struggle. Readers expect an antagonist mighty enough to cause a rug pulling.

Antagonists are often single individuals with goals of their own that compete with the protagonist's goal. If the resolution is difficult, if antagonists relentlessly stand their ground, they are certainly worthy opponents. Several examples from literature come to mind, and they are all quite different. *The Scarlet Letter* has the arch-villain Roger Chillingworth, who sets out to avenge his lost honor and destroy Arthur Dimmesdale. *Daisy Miller* has Mrs. Walker, who shuns Daisy for her uncultured, unseemly behavior in Roman society. Whereas Chillingworth is a melodramatic figure of evil in Hawthorne's romance, Mrs. Walker is a much more realistic figure who is under the illusion that she is doing the right thing to ostracize Daisy from the Europeanized American community in Rome. Put another way, as an antagonist, she is more misguided than evil.

For the most part, we shouldn't think of an antagonist as "the villain" and the protagonist as "the hero." It's best to avoid such simplistic designations. Antagonists can, of course, be very bad people, but be careful not to turn them into clichés. Read your draft carefully for stereotypical treatment. If you find you've rigged things in favor of the protagonist by creating cardboard-character antagonists, look for ways to give them human dimensions. The antagonist doesn't have to be sympathetic, but your reader should be able to appreciate the workings of his mind (if he is a point-of-view character) or be fascinated by his actions (if he is presented from an omniscient viewpoint). If you make antagonists somewhat empathetic, your reader will appreciate the conflict between protagonist and antagonist a lot more. Don't draw the lines too narrowly between the two. Don't create a Roger Chillingworth.

The lines can certainly be blurred in a novel where two protagonists see each other as antagonists. This happens in T.C. Boyle's *When the Killing's Done*. In this novel, an animal rights activist goes head-to-head with an environmentalist. These two point-of-view characters are sufficiently developed, each presented sympathetically as worthy opponents in a battle not easily resolved. If either character was much less developed than the other, the writing would undoubtedly come off as preachy, as if the author sided with one character over the other. But Boyle avoids this. Through each protagonist's lens, we see the other as antagonist.

Antagonists can also be whole systems: social, economic, and political forces pitted against human beings. We find such examples in naturalistic fiction written by writers like Emile Zola, Theodore Dreiser, and Stephen Crane. In the worlds created by these writers, it's easy to see that these antagonists are worthy opponents. In Zola's *Germinal*, it's the well-entrenched capitalistic system that oppresses the poor, half-starved coal miners; in Dreiser's *Sister Carrie*, Chicago and New York, immense cities, determine the destiny of their inhabitants; in Crane's *The Red Badge of Courage*, the Civil War is a machine itself, much larger than any of the soldiers who fight in it.

If your novel deals with large societal forces like these, you need to decide what victory or defeat might possibly mean. Are you thinking like the naturalists, who hold that individuals have little or no power over such environmental forces, and that they tend to be pawns shaped and molded by forces much larger than themselves? Or are you thinking that individuals can mount a struggle regardless of the odds and achieve some kind of personal dignity? If characters have no power at all, they become merely pathetic. If they mount a valiant struggle and lose, we might see them more as tragic figures. The reader will probably find a tragic figure more sympathetic than a pathetic one—depending, of course, on one's philosophical orientation.

Though fiction involving struggles against such huge external forces isn't exactly popular today, it's possible that part of your novel might include a conflict that goes beyond individual relationship conflicts—probably not the same kind that Dreiser or Zola or Crane concerned themselves with, but perhaps a struggle against an irresponsible corporation (Pork Rite in my novel *Hog to Hog*), against local government (county government in Andre Dubus III's *House of Sand and Fog*), or—turning to a nineteenth-century classic—against a corrupt institution (charity school in Charlotte Brontë's *Jane Eyre*). It's important to decide how you will handle the struggle. The best way is to represent both sides as realistically as you can—assuming you're writing realism. Use individual antagonists to represent the larger societal institution that your protagonist is battling against, but give them enough human dimensions so they don't come off as melodramatic villains.

If you're writing satire, as I did for my novel, you still need to give your characters human dimensions, though satire is a form based on exaggeration and gross distortion. Even so, painting characters with a broad brush can put readers off.

BUILDING THE CONFLICT

Conflict enters the story in the form of a complication—a disturbance of an existing equilibrium. This complication can be something good, but only *apparently* good: It could be followed rather quickly by rug pulling. Consider the bag of money Moss finds in *No Country for Old Men*. That discovery is followed by quite the rug pulling. If the complication is something bad, it doesn't have to be monumentally bad. No one has to be maimed or killed. But, as we've already discussed, it does have to matter enough to your character for readers to get caught up in his apparent concern over it—whatever the impediment might be.

The conflict should be introduced early enough in the story that it has plenty of time to grow, or develop. In stories beginning with exposition, it may be introduced there. Otherwise, it could come out in an opening passage of narrative summary. It doesn't have to happen right out of the gate, but we do look for it fairly early. It might not appear to be that serious at first, but we suspect it must be in some way and that its seriousness will become apparent later. We should be hooked enough to want to read on to see how serious it becomes.

Conflict must be developed in the very fabric of the story. Once we know the conflict, we should feel it threading its way from scene to scene—or at least we must feel it looming, hovering over the world of your characters. But, as I've already suggested, this does not have to be a story with gripping conflict such as Richard Bausch's *In the Night Season*, in which killers arrive with an agenda. It can be a brewing marital conflict, as in T.C. Boyle's *The Inner Circle*, in which John Milk's relationship with his wife, Iris, is threatened by his involvement with the sex guru Alfred Kinsey. Whether John and Iris are arguing or breaking up, this conflict is sustained throughout the novel. It builds, and it undergoes different permutations.

As you revise, working to build and rebuild conflict, think of the different ways that conflict works: through speech and silence, through action and nonaction. Characters sometimes speak of it and share their thoughts with those they think they can trust, or they make mistakes and discuss their troubles with those they later realize they cannot trust.

Characters may remain silent, their troubles brewing in their minds. Internal conflict is essential in character-driven stories. But avoid long passages of exposition, unless these passages are particularly compelling. However you handle this, give a strong sense of interior engagement with perceived troubles.

Dramatic action is essential to heightening conflict. Characters must act and react. What should happen in a scene is determined by the nature of the conflict and the specific needs of the character or characters. Some very quiet stories do not include uproars and do not end with explosive showdowns, but still manage to have strong emotional impact. Note the conflict apparent in this excerpt from Man Martin's *Days of the Endless Corvette*, which won the 2008 Georgia Author of the Year Award for First Novel:

> Ellen had seen the doctor first thing in the morning, and it was a good job she had, because it gave her plenty of time to compose herself and dry her face before Earl came to get her. Now all she needed to do was to master herself to keep back the tears burning behind her eyes. Thinking he must have done something wrong—it's that frock coat, he told himself—Earl didn't say anything. And Ellen didn't say anything, and so the three of them rode home in silence.

We feel the tension, that third rider, but it's muted because the two characters say little. The style of the prose itself *feels* quiet.

Look for ways to shift the attention now and then away from the central conflict: scenes where characters are not speaking or acting out of concern for the major conflict, their attention apparently directed elsewhere. Such lulls in the storm can be purposeful. Often people do not speak of the big conflicts but pick at each other over little things. Characters might even approach the central conflict but draw back. Major conflicts are painful to deal with and often frustrating. This consternation can advance character and, perhaps unbeknownst to readers at this point, actually increase the conflict. Sometimes what is not said is more disturbing to stakeholders than what *is* said. Or perhaps this lull can be an opportunity to develop a subplot in your novel.

Furthermore, scenes dealing with minor conflicts can accomplish two basic things: They can broaden the main conflict of a novel in ways that may not become apparent until later, and, in the absence of this focus on the main conflict, they can create suspense. The reader will want to know what connections exist between these minor conflicts and the main one. And secondly, when will the main conflict surface again? We still feel the key conflict hovering in the air; we know it's not far off.

Another useful tool for building conflict is foreshadowing. Look for ways to hint at actions that will occur later in the story or novel—later chronologically, or later in the narrative, which could take the form of a flashback. Foreshadowing can appear in a scene or in the mind of a character. Drop hints along the way, teasing, creating more and more suspense. A character can start to make a statement and then drop it. Another character can make a veiled reference to it.

Conflict is also built by *echoes* of different kinds. Characters are reminded, or remind others, of past developments. Repetition creates emphasis. Together, foreshadowing and echoes knit the action together into a strand or plot thread.

MAKING CONFLICT SUBTLE AND COMPLEX

If you hammer home the conflict too bluntly to make sure that your reader gets it, you will lessen the impact of your fiction. It's best for conflicts to be subtle, and at times even perplexing, just as life is. We can't always say what it is that disturbs us about something. If it's a remark, is it what was said? Is it the way it was said? Is it something *underneath* what was said, some innuendo? In some cases, conflict is quite clear: a robbery at a bank, a physical assault, a messy divorce. But even in these cases, the reasons might vary and be very complex.

Consider Arthur Miller's *Death of a Salesman*, a classic play built around a number of complex conflicts. To oversimplify, we could say that Biff's conflict with Willy amounts to Willy's rigid expectations for his son. However, there are several other conflicts bundled into this larger, more obvious conflict: Biff's knowledge of Willy's cheating on Linda, Willy's ill treatment of Linda, Willy's living a lie and expecting Biff to do the same—and more. Conflicts between people are usually complex, and the more you represent this complexity in subtle ways (by suggestion rather than direct statement), the more you will intrigue your reader. If the conflict can be summed up too easily, it will seem too simple, too ordinary—and not worth the reader's attention or interest.

MAKING ABSTRACT CONFLICTS CONCRETE

An abstract idea is large in scope: war, poverty, salvation. John Bunyan's *Pilgrim's Progress* takes the abstract idea of salvation and makes it an arduous journey on foot. The abstract conflict—salvation versus damnation—is more important than anything concrete in the story. And yet the concrete does serve the purpose of making the abstract more real to the reader.

If your work tends to focus on certain abstract levels—ideas and themes—be sure to make these ideas concrete through dramatic event and intensity. The idea informing Shirley Jackson's short story "The Lottery" would surely not have the impact it does on the reader without the dramatic unfolding of the annual lottery.

RESOLVING THE CONFLICT BELIEVABLY

A conflict that is resolved too easily doesn't amount to much. The stakes can be high, but regardless of how high they are, and how worthy the antagonist, the conflict is suddenly over, and the character walks happily on. The reader, knowing life doesn't work that way, naturally feels cheated. This is all it came to? This is what I've spent my time for?

If John and Iris's marriage isn't going so well in *The Inner Circle*, T.C. Boyle doesn't cheat it by giving us a happy ending—they still face issues that are probably irresolvable. It's tempting to tie things up for your reader, to provide a happy ending. If you do this, make sure it's earned and not forced. Perhaps on the surface things are better, but not underneath. Some conflicts could still emerge later on, coming up through the floorboards—who knows when? An indefinite kind of ending will seem more believable to readers, unless they've lived a very sheltered life. But most people haven't.

Examine your draft, and note how you lead up to the ending. A strong ending provides closure, but it won't work if it feels engineered. To write the fitting ending for your novel may call for you to distance yourself from the work for a bit, and it may take several attempts. When the ending provides a sense of closure without shutting down all questions, you've nailed it.

Jack Smith has published three novels: *Being* (2016), *Icon* (2014), and *Hog to Hog*, which won the 2007 George Garrett Fiction Prize and was published by Texas Review Press in 2008. He has published stories in a number of literary magazines, including *Southern Review*, *North American Review*, *Texas Review*, *Xconnect*, *In Posse Review*, and *Night Train*. His reviews have appeared widely in such publications as *Ploughshares*, *Georgia Review*, *American Book Review*, *Prairie Schooner*, *Mid-American Review*, *Pleiades*, the *Missouri Review*, *Xconnect*, and *Environment* magazine. He has published a few dozen articles in both *Novel & Short Story Writer's Market* and *The Writer* magazine. His creative writing book, *Write and Revise for Publication: A Six-Month Plan for Crafting an Exceptional Novel and Other Works of Fiction*, was published in 2013 by Writer's Digest Books. His co-authored nonfiction environmental book titled *Killing Me Softly* was published by Monthly Review Press in 2002. Besides his writing, Smith was fiction editor of *The Green Hills Literary Lantern*, an online literary magazine published by Truman State University, for twenty-five years.

The Complete Handbook of Novel Writing

23

SEVEN TOOLS FOR TALK

Tinkering with Your Characters' Dialogue

James Scott Bell

My neighbor John loves to work on his hot rod. He's an automotive whiz and tells me he can hear when something is not quite right with the engine. He doesn't hesitate to pop the hood, grab his bag of tools, and start to tinker. He'll keep at it until the engine sounds just the way he wants it to.

That's not a bad way to think about dialogue. We can usually sense when it needs work. What fiction writers often lack, however, is a defined set of tools they can put to use on problem areas.

So here's a set—my seven favorite dialogue tools. Stick them in your writer's toolbox for those times you need to pop the hood and tinker with your characters' words.

1. LET IT FLOW

When you write the first draft of a scene, let the dialogue flow. Pour it out like cheap champagne. You'll make it sparkle later, but first you must get it down on paper. This technique will allow you to come up with lines you never would have thought of if you tried to get it right the first time.

In fact, you can often come up with a dynamic scene by writing the dialogue first. Record what your characters are arguing about, stewing over, revealing. Write it all as fast as you can. As you do, pay no attention to attributions (who said what). Just write the lines.

Once you get these on the page, you will have a good idea of what the scene is all about. And it may be something different than you anticipated, which is good. Now you can go back and write the narrative that goes with the scene, along with the normal speaker attributions and tags.

I have found this technique to be a wonderful cure for writer's fatigue. I do my best writing in the morning, but if I haven't hit my quota by the evening (when I'm usually tired), I just write some dialogue. Fast and furious. It flows and gets me into a scene.

With the juices pumping, I find I often write more than my quota. And even if I don't use all the dialogue I write, at least I got in some practice.

2. ACT IT OUT

Before going into writing, I spent some time in New York, pounding the pavement as an actor. While there, I took an acting class that included improvisation. Another member of the class was a Pulitzer Prize–winning playwright. When I asked him what he was doing there, he said improvisational work was a tremendous exercise for learning to write dialogue.

I found this to be true. But you don't have to actually join a class. You can improvise just as easily by doing a Woody Allen.

Remember the courtroom scene in Allen's movie *Bananas*? Allen is representing himself at the trial. He takes the witness stand and begins to cross-examine by asking a question, running into the witness box to answer, then jumping out again to ask another question.

I am suggesting you do the same thing (in the privacy of your own home, of course). Make up a scene between two characters in conflict. Then start an argument. Go back and forth, changing your actual physical location. Allow a slight pause as you switch, giving yourself time to come up with a response in each character's voice.

Another twist on this technique: Do a scene between two well-known actors. Draw from the entire history of movies and television. Pit Lucille Ball against Bela Lugosi, or have Oprah Winfrey argue with Bette Davis. Only you play all the parts. Let yourself go.

And if your local community college offers an improvisation course, give it a try. You might just meet a Pulitzer Prize winner.

3. SIDESTEP THE OBVIOUS

One of the most common mistakes aspiring writers make with dialogue is creating a simple back-and-forth exchange. Each line responds directly to the previous line, often repeating a word or phrase (an "echo"). It looks something like this:

The Complete Handbook of Novel Writing

> "Hello, Mary."
>> "Hi, Sylvia."
>> "My, that's a wonderful outfit you're wearing."
>> "Outfit? You mean this old thing?"
>> "Old thing! It looks practically new."
>> "It's not new, but thank you for saying so."

This sort of dialogue is "on the nose." There are no surprises, and the reader drifts along with little interest. While some direct response is fine, your dialogue will be stronger if you sidestep the obvious.

Consider the following:

> "Hello, Mary."
>> "Sylvia. I didn't see you."
>> "My, that's a wonderful outfit you're wearing."
>> "I need a drink."

I don't really know what is going on in this scene (incidentally, I've written only these four lines of dialogue). But I think you'll agree this exchange is immediately more interesting and suggestive of currents beneath the surface than the first example. I might even find the seeds of an entire story here.

You can also sidestep with a question:

> "Hello, Mary."
>> "Sylvia. I didn't see you."
>> "My, that's a wonderful outfit you're wearing."
>> "Where is he, Sylvia?"

Hmm. Who is "he"? And why should Sylvia know? The point is there are innumerable directions in which the sidestep technique can go. Experiment to find a path that works best for you. Look at a section of your dialogue, and change some direct responses into off-center retorts. Like the old magic trick ads used to say, "You'll be pleased and amazed."

4. CULTIVATE SILENCE

A powerful variation on the sidestep is silence. It is often the best choice, no matter what words you might come up with. Hemingway was a master at this. Consider this excerpt from his short story "Hills Like White Elephants." A man and a woman are having a drink at a train station in Spain. The man speaks:

"Should we have another drink?"

"All right."

The warm wind blew the bead curtain against the table.

"The beer's nice and cool," the man said.

"It's lovely," the girl said.

"It's really an awfully simple operation, Jig," the man said. "It's not really an operation at all."

The girl looked at the ground the table legs rested on.

"I know you wouldn't mind it, Jig. It's really not anything. It's just to let the air in."

The girl did not say anything.

In this story, the man is trying to convince the girl to have an abortion (a word that does not appear anywhere in the text). Her silence is reaction enough.

By using a combination of sidestep, silence, and action, Hemingway gets the point across through a brief, compelling exchange. He uses the same technique in this well-known scene between mother and son in the story "Soldier's Home":

"God has some work for every one to do," his mother said. "There can't be no idle hands in His Kingdom."

"I'm not in His Kingdom," Krebs said.

"We are all of us in His Kingdom."

Krebs felt embarrassed and resentful as always.

"I've worried about you so much, Harold," his mother went on. "I know the temptations you must have been exposed to. I know how weak men are. I know what your own dear grandfather, my own father, told us about the Civil War and I have prayed for you. I pray for you all day long, Harold."

Krebs looked at the bacon fat hardening on the plate.

Silence and bacon fat hardening. We don't need anything else to catch the mood of the scene. What are your characters feeling while exchanging dialogue? Try expressing it with the sound of silence.

5. POLISH A GEM

We've all had those moments when we wake up with the perfect response for a conversation that took place the night before. Wouldn't we all like to have those *bon mots* at a moment's notice?

Your characters can. That's part of the fun of being a fiction writer. I have a somewhat arbitrary rule—one gem per quarter. Divide your novel into fourths.

When you polish your dialogue, find those opportunities in each quarter to polish a gem.

And how do you do that? Like a diamond cutter, you take what is rough and tap at it until it is perfect. In the movie *The Godfather*, Moe Greene is angry that a young Michael Corleone is telling him what to do. He might have said, "I made my bones when you were in high school!" Instead, screenwriter Mario Puzo penned, "I made my bones when you were going out with cheerleaders!" (In his novel, Puzo wrote something a little racier). The point is you can take almost any line and find a more sparkling alternative.

Just remember to use these gems sparingly. The perfect comeback grows tiresome if it happens all the time.

6. EMPLOY CONFRONTATION

Many writers struggle with exposition in their novels. Often they heap it on in large chunks of straight narrative. Too much backstory—what happens before the novel opens—is especially troublesome. How can we give the essentials and avoid a mere information dump?

Use dialogue. First, create a tension-filled scene, usually between two characters. Get them arguing, confronting each other. Then have the information appear in the natural course of things. Here is the clunky way to do it:

> John Davenport was a doctor fleeing from a terrible past. He had been drummed out of the profession for bungling an operation while he was drunk.

Instead, place this backstory in a scene in which John is confronted by a patient who is aware of the doctor's past:

> "I know who you are," Charles said.
>> "You know nothing," John said.
>> "You're that doctor."
>> "If you don't mind I—"
>> "From Hopkins. You killed a woman because you were soused. Yeah, that's it."

And so forth. This is a much underused method that not only gives weight to your dialogue, but also increases the pace of your story.

7. DROP WORDS

This is a favorite technique of dialogue master Elmore Leonard. By excising a single word here and there, he creates a feeling of verisimilitude in his dialogue.

It sounds like real speech, though it is really nothing of the sort. All of Leonard's dialogue contributes to characterization and story.

Here is a standard exchange:

> "Your dog was killed?"
>> "Yes, run over by a car."
>> "What did you call it?"
>> "It was a she. I called her Tuffy."

This is the way Leonard did it in *Out of Sight*:

> "Your dog was killed?"
>> "Got run over by a car."
>> "What did you call it?"
>> "Was a she, name Tuffy."

The exchange sounds so natural, yet it's lean and meaningful. Notice how the dropped words create the feeling of real speech.

As with any technique, there's always a danger of overdoing it. Pick your spots and your characters with careful precision and focus, and your dialogue will thank you for it later.

Using tools is fun when you know what to do with them. I guess that's why John, my neighbor, is always whistling when he works on his car. You'll see results in your fiction—and have fun, too—by using these tools to make your dialogue sound just right.

Start tinkering.

24

CHOOSING THE BEST POV FOR YOUR STORY

How to Focus the Lens of Your Narrative

Nancy Kress

Because we lack telepathy, we are imprisoned in our own skulls. As Joseph Conrad wrote, "We live, as we dream, alone"—at least within our heads. The only thoughts, plans, dreams, and feelings we can directly experience are our own. It's because this one-viewpoint reality is hardwired in us that fiction is so fascinating. It lets us experience the world from inside someone else's head.

This is the definition of point of view: whose eyes we view the action through, whose head we're inside of, whose feelings we experience as that character feels them. As such, your choice of point-of-view character or characters is critical to your story. It will determine what you tell, how you tell it, and, often, even what the action means.

PROTAGONIST VERSUS POV CHARACTER

The protagonist of your story is the "star," the person we're most interested in, the one who takes engaging actions. Usually, but not inevitably, your protagonist will also be a POV character. Thus we see the events of John Grisham's best-selling *The King of Torts* through the eyes of its protagonist, Clay Carter, who is both the star and a POV character.

However, you can obtain some interesting effects by having your POV character be someone other than the protagonist. Two classics that do this are F. Scott Fitzgerald's *The Great Gatsby* and W. Somerset Maugham's *The Moon and Sixpence.*

Gatsby is told through the eyes of Nick Carraway, who is involved in the main action only peripherally, mostly as a standby friend and go-between. The real protagonists are the illicit lovers, Jay Gatsby and Daisy Buchanan, particularly Gatsby.

Maugham goes further yet. The protagonist of *The Moon and Sixpence* is Charles Strickland, who abandons his middle-class London existence to travel to the South Seas and become a painter. The unnamed narrator of the novel, the sole POV character, knows Strickland only slightly, as the friend of a friend. The narrator has several casual encounters with Strickland, but at no time does the narrator ever affect Strickland's life or Strickland affect the narrator's. Much of Strickland's later life is told to the narrator by other people, after the artist is dead.

The disadvantages of this convoluted structure are obvious: It lacks immediacy. Everything important that Strickland does, or that is done to him, occurs offstage. The narrator is told about events later, and he tells us about them. Maugham sacrifices a great deal of drama this way. So why did he do it?

Because separating your POV character from your protagonist also confers certain advantages:

- The POV character can continue the story after the protagonist dies, which both Strickland and Gatsby do in their respective novels. Maugham's POV character traces the fates of Strickland's widow, children, and paintings.
- The protagonist can be portrayed as much more secretive if he is not also a POV character. No one learns about Gatsby's real past until he is dead, and it's revealed that he has invented for himself a much more glamorous background than his actual one. Had Gatsby been a POV character, we would have known that from the very beginning, because we would have been "inside his head." Protagonists who are not also POV characters can preserve their mysteries. As Maugham's narrator says, "I felt that Strickland had kept his secrets to the grave."
- The POV character can make observations that would never occur to the protagonist. Carraway comes to see Buchanan as a careless lightweight and Gatsby as a touching idealist, views neither character (nor anyone else in the book) would have shared.

When considering your use of POV, first ask: *Will my protagonist and POV character(s) be the same? If not, do I have good reason for the split? Will I gain more than I lose?*

Once you know whether your protagonist will be a POV character, the next step is to determine who else will occupy that critical role.

POV CHARACTER SELECTION

It's a good idea, before you write anything at all, to consider all the choices for POV characters. The first choice to come to mind may not be the best pick.

Consider, for instance, Harper Lee's *To Kill a Mockingbird*, which takes place in pre–World War II Alabama. The main plotline concerns the framing of a black man, Tom Robinson, for the beating of a white woman, a crime he did not commit. His lawyer is the respected Atticus Finch, father of two children. Finch forces the identification of the true assailant, the victim's father, who then attempts revenge by attacking Finch's kids.

Lee could have told her story from any of these points of view. Instead, she embedded her main plot in a coming-of-age story and made her first-person narrator Finch's eight-year-old daughter, Scout. As a result, she ended up with a far different story than she would have if the POV character had been Atticus Finch, Robinson, or the true assailant. A better story? A worse one? No one can say; we haven't read any such alternate versions.

But certainly Scout is an effective choice. She meets the general criteria you should consider when choosing your POV character:

- **WHO WILL BE HURT BY THE ACTION?** Someone strongly affected emotionally usually makes the best POV character (although Maugham, as we have seen, chose to sacrifice emotional immediacy for other goals). Scout is the victim of attempted murder by the disgruntled woman beater and thus is in danger. Pick for your POV character someone with a strong stake in the outcome.
- **WHO CAN BE PRESENT AT THE CLIMAX?** In *To Kill a Mockingbird*, Scout is there. So is Nick Carraway in *The Great Gatsby*. Your POV character should be, too, or else we'll have to be told secondhand about the most important event of your story, thus distancing us from the action.
- **WHO GETS MOST OF THE GOOD SCENES?** We want to be present at those, too. Scout sneaks into the courtroom to witness her father's defense of Tom Robinson.
- **WHO WILL PROVIDE AN INTERESTING OUTLOOK ON THE STORY?** Scout brings to Lee's novel an innocent, fresh view of racism that no adult could. Carraway similarly views the action of *The Great Gatsby* from a more idealistic, simpler vantage point than do its other characters, who are mostly New York sophisticates. What kind of observations about life do you want to make in your novel? Who is fit to make them? Do you want that character as your "eyes" and "heart"?

- Whose head are you most interested in inhabiting during this story? Don't underestimate this criterion; it really is key.

DIFFERENT EYES, DIFFERENT STORY

You may think you already know who your POV character will be. Perhaps you're right. But take a few moments to imagine what your story might be like if you chose differently.

Let us suppose, for instance, that you are writing a novel about the abduction of a child. Major characters are the father, the mother, the child, the abductor, a suspicious-but-innocent neighbor, and the lead detective on the case. The child will be recovered, but the family will never be the same again. There are at least six potential novels here, all vastly different.

- If the mother or father (or both) is your viewpoint character, you will likely find yourself writing a novel of anguish (which might very well be your goal). These are good points of view if, for instance, the couple will eventually divorce, unable to incorporate the strain into an already fragile marriage. Perhaps one of them has an extramarital affair after the abduction. Perhaps one mounts an independent investigation. Perhaps one hires someone to murder the neighbor, who is then revealed—to the characters and to the reader—to be innocent.
- If the child is the POV character, you have a novel of bewilderment, fear, maybe rescue or escape. You will, of course, lose all scenes of the investigation and of parental interaction, because the kid won't see them. But you'll gain a lot of scenes between the abductor and abducted.
- If the neighbor is the POV character, you will have a novel of injustice. This could be quite interesting; stories of people wrongly accused always generate strong reader identification. Everyone loves to cheer for an innocent underdog.
- If the abductor is the POV character, you probably have a novel of either evil or madness. What is his motivation? Do you want to explore that? If so, he's your man.
- If the police officer or FBI agent is the POV character, you have a mystery novel. What's this character's stake in the conflict, beyond professional competence? Do you want to focus on how an investigation looks from the inside?

None of these POV choices is inherently better or worse than the others. It all depends on which suits the version of the story you want to tell. But if you don't

The Complete Handbook of Novel Writing

at least consider points of view other than the one that first occurs to you, you may be cutting yourself off from some very exciting possibilities.

Who among your assembled cast might be an interesting POV character with a more original outlook on the plot than your first choice? If you were not the writer but the reader, whose viewpoint might tell the most satisfying story?

CASTS OF THOUSANDS

How many points of view are you allowed? There is no one answer. Here's a rule of thumb: Have as few points of view as you can get away with and still tell the story you want to tell.

The reason for this is the aforementioned entrapment in our own skulls. We're used to experiencing reality from one POV. Each time you switch from one fictional viewpoint to another, readers must make a mental adjustment. If there are too many of these, the story feels increasingly fragmented and unreal.

On the other hand (there is always "another hand" in writing fiction), you may gain more than you lose. If you want to show how a romance feels to both parties, then you need two points of view. If one character simply cannot be present at every important scene you need to show, then you need more than one POV. You may need three, or even more, especially for a complicated or epic plot.

Figure out the fewest number of points of view you can have and still cover all major scenes and internal dialogues that your story requires. The point is to lessen the demands on the reader as much as possible so he can concentrate on the story and its implications rather than be distracted by trying to remember what that eighth POV character was doing the last time we saw her, 200 pages ago. Be aware that it can take awhile to cycle through eight points of view and do justice to each one, and that too many points of view can be hard on the reader.

Then choose the best way to tell that reader your story.

Nancy Kress is the author of thirty-three books, including twenty-six novels, four collections of short stories, and three books on writing. Her work has won six Nebulas, two Hugos, a Sturgeon, and the John W. Campbell Memorial Award. Her most recent works are the Nebula-winning *Yesterday's Kin* (Tachyon, 2014) and *The Best of Nancy Kress* (Subterranean, 2015). In addition to writing, Kress often teaches at various venues around the country and abroad; in 2008 she was the Picador visiting lecturer at the University of Leipzig. Kress lives in Seattle with her husband, writer Jack Skillingstead, and Cosette, the world's most spoiled toy poodle.

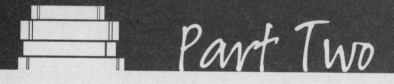

Part Two

THE WRITING PROCESS

BEST-SELLING ADVICE
Getting Started

" Get it down. Take chances. It may be bad, but it's the only way you can do anything really good."

—William Faulkner

"Know your literary tradition, savor it, steal from it, but when you sit down to write, forget about worshiping greatness and fetishizing masterpieces."

—Allegra Goodman

"Two questions form the foundation of all novels: 'What if?' and 'What next?' (A third question, 'What now?', is one the author asks himself every ten minutes or so; but it's more a cry than a question.) Every novel begins with the speculative question, What if X happened? That's how you start."

—Tom Clancy

"I think my stuff succeeds, in part, because of what it's about—a diagnosis by attempting the adventures oneself of universal American daydreams. Now, I'm not saying that any writer who decided to select that device or notion could have written a bestseller; you have to add ingredients that are very special, I agree, but I think I started out with a good pot to make the stew in.

—George Plimpton

"When I start on a book, I have been thinking about it and making occasional notes for some time—twenty years in the case of Imperial Earth, and ten years in the case of the novel I'm presently working on. So I have lots of theme, locale, subjects, and technical ideas. It's amazing how the subconscious self works on these things. I don't worry about long periods of not doing anything. I know my subconscious is busy."

—Arthur C. Clarke

"Beginning a novel is always hard. It feels like going nowhere. I always have to write at least one hundred pages that go into the trashcan before it finally begins to work. It's discouraging, but necessary to write those pages. I try to consider them pages -100 to zero of the novel."

—Barbara Kingsolver

"An outline is crucial. It saves so much time. When you write suspense, you have to know where you're going because you have to drop little hints along the way. With the outline, I always know where the story is going. So before I ever write, I prepare an outline of forty or fifty pages."

—John Grisham

"I do a great deal of research. I don't want anyone to say, 'That could not have happened.' It may be fiction, but it has to be true."

—Jacquelyn Mitchard

"Being goal-oriented instead of self-oriented is crucial. I know so many people who want to be writers. But let me tell you, they really don't want to be writers. They want to have been writers. They wish they had a book in print. They don't want to go through the work of getting the damn book out. There is a huge difference.

—James Michener

"I have a self-starter—published twenty million words—and have never received, needed or wanted a kick in the pants."

—Isaac Asimov

"Don't quit. It's very easy to quit during the first ten years. Nobody cares whether you write or not, and it's very hard to write when nobody cares one way or the other. You can't get fired if you don't write, and most of the time you don't get rewarded if you do. But don't quit.

—Andre Dubus III

25

WRITE LIKE POE

Reshape, Revise, and Reimagine Great Literary
Styles to Discover Your Own Voice

Mort Castle

While teachers urge beginning writers to find their own voices and critics praise established authors for their unique styles and sensibilities, I've experienced considerable success in borrowing other writers' voices and, ahem, emulating their literary techniques.

I've been faux Hemingway and fake O. Henry. I've donned the dark cloaks of twentieth-century horror masters H.P. Lovecraft and Robert Bloch. I've borrowed Samuel Pepys's parlance and Dr. Samuel Johnson's dictionary. And, it sometimes shames me to admit, I've made more money writing as (pseudo) Edgar Allan Poe than the tragic genius himself.

I've taken the concepts of these and other literati and added to them, extrapolated from them, or reshaped, revised, and reimagined them.

I've written pastiches.

So can you.

THE COPYCAT

The pastiche prose form openly mimes the content and mannerisms of another written work. It's a respectful, if often jocular, homage to the work that inspired it. (Its literary cousin is the parody, but that imitation subtly or savagely satirizes its source material.) The pastiche implicitly says, "I appreciate this author, the characters, and the fictive world … and my imitation is sincere flattery."

The affection for Sir Arthur Conan Doyle and his immortal Sherlock Holmes is evident in August Derleth's stories about brilliant, deerstalker-wearing Solar Pons of 7B Praed Street.

Bloch, Ramsey Campbell, Lin Carter, and many other fantasy and horror writers have provided us with their take on the "cosmic monstrosities" of Lovecraft's Cthulhu Mythos universe, often liberally borrowing from Lovecraft's pseudo-Gothic literary techniques. Philip José Farmer, a Tarzan devotee, has given us Lord Grandrith, a loin-clothed jungle Übermensch, as well as Doc Caliban, a pastiche clone of the pulp era's crime-busting Doc Savage, a character who also motivated mystery novelist Michael A. Black to create his own Doc Atlas.

Right off the bat, your pastiche should proclaim what it is and invite the reader in on your literary joke. The title of my novella "A Secret of the Heart," originally published in the anthology *Lovecraft's Legacy*, is plainly an allusion to "The Tell-Tale Heart."

Early in the story, I let the reader know that we're journeying into a Poe mindscape of madness by using the opening of "The Tell-Tale Heart" as my model:

> True! Nervous, very, very dreadfully nervous I had been and am; but why will you say that I am mad? ... I heard all things in the heaven and in the earth. I heard many things in hell. ... Hearken! and observe how healthily—how calmly I can tell you the whole story.

This opening, with its combination of "Who you callin' crazy?" "'I'm no wacko,' said the wacko," and "doth protest waaaaay too much," is associated with Poe by anyone who earned at least a C- in junior high English. Here's my rendering of the original in "A Secret of the Heart":

> Regard me! Madmen sweat and shake; they mutter to themselves and shout at delusional wraiths only they can apprehend. ... Madmen rage, they fume, one moment seeking to slyly cajole the listener to belief, then threatening him the next.
>
> Look into my eye to find therein not a glimmer of inner turmoil. ...

THE ELEMENTS OF STYLE

Authors' styles grow from the basic elements of prose: vocabulary, sentence length, structure, rhythm, narrative point of view, imagery, figures of speech, and much more. Style reflects a writer's line-by-line, moment-to-moment decisions about what to leave in or what to leave out, what tone to adopt and what mood to induce in the reader. Style is the summation of *how* a story is presented.

Naturally, you'll find it easier to craft a pastiche if the writer you are honoring or aping is a strong stylist. Many popular writers aren't considered stylists, and they seek what's termed a transparent style that focuses exclusively on plot. But the styles of such diverse writers as Nathaniel Hawthorne, Herman Melville, Franz Kafka, Gertrude Stein, J.D. Salinger, Norman Mailer, and William Styron are unquestionably distinct; a paragraph from any of these writers lets you know who you're reading, just as the opening notes of a pop song will quickly tell you if you're listening to Frank Sinatra, Tony Bennett, Barry Manilow, or Tom Waits.

And there are authors who have their own marked idiosyncrasies of style, which can easily be incorporated into your pastiche. Be ready to observe and use these little tricks.

For instance, in his National Book Award–winning novel *Cold Mountain*, Charles Frazier eschews the use of quotation marks instead employing en dashes to let us know we're getting a direct quote, like so:

> –That would be easy to toss into my story, Peter Pastiche said.
> –Oh? said Carmela Clone.

Yes. It's a device that promptly suggests the origin of my pastiche *Tepid Hill*.

When I wrote my Charles Bukowski pastiche (less-than-cleverly titled "Hank Crankowski"), published in 1976 in *Samisdat*, I tried for the author's borderline psychotic-deadpan fatalistic tone—and made good use of Bukowski's habit, in early works, of using only lowercase letters. Here, the protagonist of that story tells a would-be author the secret of crafting literature:

> *expose yourself to feel what wretches feel. get beat on the head by cops and get thrown in jail. get drunk and become a pacifist. ... crash an old chevrolet into a taco bell stand ... kick in a television set, howl at the moon, roar against the wind of being ... never use capital letters.*

SAY WHAT?

No matter how renowned authors may be for stylistic skills and original mannerisms, it is *what* they say, the subject matter and theme, that we come to associate as their personal territory. We pick up an Agatha Christie novel expecting a murder mystery with the emphasis on *mystery*, the clues there for us to discover (if we have "little gray cells" equal to those of her detectives, Hercule Poirot and Jane Marple). No rapacious extraterrestrial ever abducted Miss Crumbcake from the cozy village of Slothful-upon-Avon in a Christie novel, and we don't expect to read the story of the "Monocoled Prussian Assistant" in a collection of Flannery O'Connor's Southern Gothic tales. The forest primeval and its Native American, French, and English settlers—and Hawkeye!—belong to James Fenimore Cooper, just as the faraway galaxies and distant futures belong to the man who created them in the Foundation novels, Isaac Asimov. Elsewhere, dreamy and deceitful 1930s Los Angeles, its grifters and shysters and the lone PI following his own moral compass, is owned by Raymond Chandler.

Ernest Hemingway is credited with transforming the American prose style, but he's sometimes criticized for a "narrow" range of subject matter and theme: sports and war, machismo and violence. (In our politically correct times, I don't want to push that bright red button marked "bullfighting!")

I'm a card-carrying fan of Papa; I've read his collected short stories at least once a year for many years. When I was asked for a contribution to the anthology *Still Dead*, featuring stories set in the world of flesh-eating zombies inspired by George A. Romero's *Night of the Living Dead*, I saw an opportunity to do *my* Hemingway story.

I called the novella "The Old Man and the Dead." With that obvious allusion to *The Old Man and the Sea*, I told the reader what I was doing, and then I underscored it with these opening lines:

> In our time there was a man who wrote as well and truly as anyone ever did. He wrote about courage and endurance and sadness and war and bullfighting and boxing and men in love and men without women. He wrote about scars and wounds that never heal.

Later in the tale, I introduce the characters Adam Nichols (a young man not unlike Hemingway's Nick Adams); Jordan Roberts, who, like the American Robert Jordan in *For Whom the Bell Tolls*, is fighting for the Republic in the Spanish Civil War; and a tough female guerilla leader named ... Pilar.

Here's the final scene of the pastiche, my moment of memorial for a writer who has profoundly influenced me:

> It was early and he was the only one up ...
>
> He went to the front foyer. He liked the way the light struck the oak-paneled walls and the floor. It was like being in a museum or in a church. It was a well-lighted place and it felt clean and airy.

Carefully, he lowered the butt of the Boss shotgun to the floor. He leaned forward. The twin barrels were cold circles in the scarred tissue just above his eyebrows.

He tripped both triggers.

I know there are writers who have come to live in your mind. Your pastiche will be your way to acknowledge, learn from, and pay tribute to them. The passage above summarizes why I write in the style: It's my grateful tip of the hat to someone whose words mean so much to me.

Mort Castle has edited *All American Horror of the 21st Century* (Wicker Park Press) and the essential reference work *On Writing Horror* for the Horror Writers Association (Writer's Digest Books). For *Writer's Digest Annotated Classics: Dracula*, he provided the annotations. He is a three-time winner of the Bram Stoker Award, as well as the Black Quill Award, and has been a finalist for the Shirley Jackson and the International Horror Guild awards. Castle teaches creative writing at Columbia College Chicago and at conferences throughout the country.

26

BREAK THE BLOCKS TO CREATIVE FLOW

Techniques for Combating Writing Inertia

Jordan Rosenfeld

There is nothing as heady as the initial spark of an idea that flows into a rush of pure inspiration—it's a feeling both holy and euphoric. Who wouldn't be addicted to the thrill of writerly gush? But like all things, eventually that gush becomes a trickle and possibly even stops. If you're like me, that happens about two-thirds of the way through a project. I make it over the great muddle of the middle and then find myself stranded on the path, wondering if I can go on.

And as exhilarating as inspired flow can be, its opposite, writer's block, is incredibly demoralizing, even when it means different things to different people. Some of you may struggle to find inspiration or to finish work that's been hanging in limbo for a long time. You may think you don't have anything to say, or you may struggle with procrastination. But most of all, I find that creative block comes down to one of several elements I'll explore here.

Rather than calling it writer's block, I like to think of the state of being unable to produce material as *inertia*: a powerful force that keeps you from doing your work. I argue that inertia actually serves a purpose: to give you something to work against and to force you to set or shift goals, plunge deeper into the writing, or let something go. For something happens—dare I say "magic"?—when you focus your attention on overcoming an obstacle: Your work begins to move, grow, and expand, and has a much greater chance at success.

While I am more than familiar with inertia now, at age forty, I *rarely* experienced it in my twenties and only a few times in my thirties. Then I had a baby at age thirty-three. Before, I could always force myself to write when I wanted or needed to, but after my son's birth and during the exhausting months of caring for a newborn, I became intimately acquainted with inertia—not only in my physical body, which habitually collapsed onto the nearest piece of furniture whenever possible, but mentally as well. My mind also caved inward and away from work: Returning to the keyboard or the page seemed unbearably hard, an act I might never undertake again because I'd fallen so out of practice. Once inertia strikes with its powerful gravity, it's incredibly difficult to pull yourself free again. It's easy to consider writing, much less the pursuit of publishing, an exercise in futility. You lay your weary muse in the road, and the vultures begin to circle, taking her for dead.

But she's not dead. *You're* not dead. There's life in you, and your project, yet. But now you will have to provide yourself with the momentum formerly granted to you by the tailwinds of inspiration, deadline, or competition. This effort against inertia may come as a big adrenalized burst—forcing yourself into a day of writing—or it might be slow and steady progress, bits here and there.

It's hard to remember that your great ideas won't birth themselves. They may appear to you of their own mysterious volition, but they require you to finish the process of creation. If you find yourself stuck in the glue of inertia, it's time to take advantage of one or more of the following strategies.

ASSESS YOUR STAGE

The way I see it, there are only six main stages in writing and finishing a project. (Please understand that "revising" is often a stage that involves multiple drafts, but for our purposes I'll describe it as though it is one phase.)

1. outlining and plotting
2. writing the first draft
3. seeking feedback
4. revising
5. proofing
6. submitting to agents and/or editors, or self-publishing

Your block may stem from trying to do the work of a later stage when you haven't actually arrived at it yet. For instance, I know many writers who slow themselves down or even cut off their creative supply by trying to edit as they write. I always recommend refraining from revision during the drafting stage. Drafting is a wild process that requires room to roam and wander; if you try to crimp each thought right after you have it, you'll naturally stagnate.

Or you might find that your energy gets bound up in anxiety about the submitting stage. You worry about the competition, writing the perfect query, or how original your idea is—and the next thing you know, you've crimped off your creative stream. Be sure to take an honest look at the stage you're in before you trip yourself up by racing to a later one.

MAKE WRITING A PRIORITY

I know sometimes it seems hard, impossible even, to put writing first. But if you write first, before you do anything else, you'll carry that buoyant feeling around with you all day rather than the sludge of "I still haven't written." This doesn't necessarily mean to write "first thing in the morning" but at whatever time you set aside for writing. Make it the priority, and don't let anything else pull you away. If you think you don't have enough time, see the next tip.

TRY MICROWRITING

My friend Barbara turned me on to an idea called "micromovements," a concept that suggests that when you take things in small bites and give yourself credit for these little movements, rather than berating yourself for how you didn't do "everything," these small things add up and you're nicer to yourself in the process. So if all you can get done is a page, a sentence, a scene, that's more than you had before. And when you remove the pressure to do a specific set or amount, the muse has a funny way of taking hold of that single sentence or paragraph and running away with it.

SET A WORD COUNT GOAL

If you are, in fact, motivated by deadlines, then word count goals are elegant, simple, and time-tested. Set a minimal word count, and be amazed at how you're not only more likely to hit it but to exceed it. This is what has made National Novel Writing Month (NaNoWriMo) so wildly popular. The only thing writers must do to complete a 50,000-word novel draft in thirty days is use a daily word count goal to urge them on. Most writers I know who have successfully completed NaNoWriMo (myself included) found themselves writing more than the minimum (1,600 words or so) each day. But even a much smaller daily word count goal can help trick you into productivity without pressure. There's no need to be perfect—only prepared to write.

FIND AN ACCOUNTABILIBUDDY

When you're feeling the grip of inertia, you might need a writing friend—an accountabilibuddy—to keep you on task. Just like in your word count effort, you hold each other to some sort of standard and cheer and reward each other for getting it done. My accountabilibuddy sends me texts while I'm working and checks in with me about my goals. There's nothing like receiving a little cheerful pressure.

GET TO THE HEART

Sometimes inertia strikes because you don't want to explore or feel something that the work exposes. When it comes to writing, inertia is often a sign that you must go more deeply into the work, think in a wider direction, or cut something that isn't working. This is especially true if you're writing something personal (though most writing has a personal element, even fiction) and is one of the hardest aspects of writer's inertia to curb. This is when it's good to call on a supportive friend. And if talking to others doesn't work for you, then I recommend taking a step away and writing in a journal about the feelings that have created the claws of inertia. If nothing else, it's important to acknowledge that your inertia stems from a personal place so you can be aware of it.

CREATE CLIFF-HANGERS

One of the most effective techniques for finding your way back into material you've started is to leave off a writing session midsentence, paragraph, or scene. Creating these cliff-hangers has a way of jogging the brain into finishing that line of dialogue left unresolved or answered, or that scene about to culminate in a high point. It also takes away the burden of having to finish everything you write in one sitting.

FINISH THE UNFINISHED

Speaking of finishing, think for a second about your own unfinished projects: that roughly drafted NaNoWriMo novel, the short story you intended to send to that contest, the stack of essays you think might make a memoir. They may only physically live on your desk or your laptop, but you may not realize that they also live inside you, in all their impartial nature. They take up psychic residence in your mind, your heart; they're like the cluttered attic of your creative muse. And when the muse is weighed down with what hasn't been completed, it's harder for her to help you create new material.

"But what if it's crap?" the cranky voice in your head may ask.

Crap (i.e., raw, unpolished words, or words that detour from where you imagined they would go) never turns into creative gold until you finish it. It can't. And you won't ever find out if you're hung up on perfection. Sometimes starting a new project is a form of avoidance. From personal experience, I know that when I have to go deeper, tear something apart, or stretch into new territory, my urge to start a new project hits an all-time high. Finishing is doing the work.

More important, completion brings pride. I always feel a thrill of elation when I finish a draft, even when I know I'm still at an early stage of a project and that I have so much more distance to cover. Because without this draft I have nothing to revise, just a jumble of words in my brain.

Finishing also lets you see the merit and potential of an idea. Yes, some ideas will never reach an audience. But they almost always give birth to other ideas, new avenues. And you test and stretch your skills with every word you write, so something you did as an experiment will still pay off in your next project.

Finishing a project is a way of valuing yourself, your work, your words. It allows you to take *you* seriously. It lets you be true to your work. It's also one of the most important steps in building a long-lasting, sustainable writing practice that will give back to you during difficult times.

Finishing frees up head space and creative and emotional energy. Once you get the weight off your head, productivity has a funny way of returning. When you leave a project undone, it stays inside you, a squatter taking up unwanted residence. Finishing comes with an endorphin rush all its own. It's something you can check off that list and give yourself credit for.

MOVE IT

Physical movement is effective at shifting energy about 75 percent of the time without employing any other strategies. Thoughts and feelings have a way of getting pressed down too tightly into the cellar of the subconscious, trapped beneath the skin, and have the power to launch you into frustration, anxiety, and discouragement.

"Sweat is like WD-40 for your mind—it lubricates the rusty hinges of your brain and makes your thinking more fluid," says Christopher Bergland, author of *The Athlete's Way: Sweat and the Biology of Bliss.*

Here's the great news: You don't have to be an athlete to take advantage of exercise to stimulate your creativity. If you're blocked while sitting at the computer, simply break your focus. Get up, pace the room, do jumping jacks, or even just walk to another part of the house and take deep breaths. Or, if you're blocked but you have the creative urge, go for a walk or run. Many professional writers break up their workday by adding physical exercise. The list of famous authors who run is quite surprising and includes Joyce Carol Oates, Haruki Murakami, and Laurie Halse Anderson. Having a dog to walk, animals to feed, and children to tend to can often provide crucial break time. When you move your body, you engage the conscious part of your brain in the activity, which wedges open the door to the unconscious, where your creative magic hides.

MEDITATE

Meditation may seem like nothing more than sitting with your eyes closed while you battle to keep your thoughts from having a wrestling match in your head. But science has taken an interest in discovering what makes Buddhist monks in remote parts of Tibet calmer, less anxious, more focused, and able to withstand intense cold, heat, and other painful sensations. What is it about sitting still that has such a profound effect on our psyches?

Respected institutions, from the Mayo Clinic to Harvard University, have undertaken studies that reveal that even just a little bit of meditation, from five to fifteen minutes a day, can put your brain into the state most associated with clear, calm, and creative thinking. Not to mention that when you're feeling stuck creatively, sitting quietly without any intention or pressure allows access to the subconscious mind, where creative ideas are often stored.

DAYDREAM OR LET YOUR MIND WANDER

If meditation won't work for you in this moment—if you don't feel "ready" to calm down—try this time-tested, imagination-boosting method, practiced by kids all over the globe: daydreaming. It requires no tools, you can do it in any setting, and no one has to know what you're thinking. We spend so much time with our noses buried in computers that send constant streams of data into our minds; in just the decade or so since the birth of the smartphone, we rarely take a break from incoming information. Daydreaming is a form of letting your inner wisdom emerge without pressure. But don't take my word for it. Researcher and psychologist Scott Barry Kaufman co-authored a paper with Rebecca L. Miller called "Ode to Positive, Constructive Daydreaming" for *Scientific American*.

"Daydreaming is a way to 'dip into [your] inner stream of consciousness,' and personally reflect on the world and visualize the future," Kaufman says. "This sort of impromptu introspection can even help us to find the answers to life's big questions."

Try daydreaming about your characters and their stories, or about a theme or idea that's haunted you or compelled you to write. Don't give yourself any parameters or rules about writing what you dream up, but keep your notebook nearby just in case.

BEST-SELLING ADVICE
Rituals and Methods

"Exercise the writing muscle every day, even if it is only a letter, notes, a title list, a character sketch, a journal entry. Writers are like dancers, like athletes. Without that exercise, the muscles seize up."

—Jane Yolen

"Keep a small can of WD-40 on your desk—away from any open flames—to remind yourself that if you don't write daily, you will get rusty."

—George Singleton

"I try to write a certain amount each day, five days a week. A rule sometimes broken is better than no rule."

—Herman Wouk

"I think that the joy of writing a novel is the self-exploration that emerges and also that wonderful feeling of playing God with the characters. When I sit down at my writing desk, time seems to vanish. … I think the most important thing for a writer is to be locked in a study."

—Erica Jong

"I threw the thesaurus out years ago. I found that every time you look up a word, if you want some word and you can think of an approximately close synonym for it and look it up, you only get cliché usages. It's much better to use a big dictionary and look up derivations and definitions of various usages of a different word.

—James Jones

" I think writing verse is a great training for a writer. It teaches you to make your points and get your stuff clear, which is the great thing."

—P.G. Wodehouse

"When I really do not know what I am saying, or how to say it, I'll open these Pentels, these colored Japanese pens, on yellow lined paper, and I'll start off with very tentative colors, very light colors: orange, yellow, or tan. ... When my thoughts are more formulated, and I have a sharper sense of trying to say it, I'll go into heavier colors: blues, greens, and eventually into black. When I am writing in black, which is the final version, I have written that sentence maybe twelve or fifteen or eighteen times."

—Gay Talese

"I like to say there are three things that are required for success as a writer: talent, luck, discipline. ... [Discipline] is the one that you have to focus on controlling, and you just have to hope and trust in the other two."

—Michael Chabon

"If I'm at a dull party I'll invent some kind of game for myself and then pick someone to play it with so that I am, in effect, writing a scene. I'm supplying my half of the dialogue and hoping the other half comes up to standards. If it doesn't, I try to direct it that way."

—Evan Hunter

"The conclusion to be drawn is that I am happiest writing in small rooms. They make me feel comfortable and secure. And it took me years to figure out that I need to write in a corner. Like a small animal burrowing into its hole, I shift furniture around, and back myself into a cozy corner, with my back to the wall ... and then I can write.

—Danielle Steel

"I try to keep my space very, very contained, because I feel that inspiration and the spirits and the story and the characters live there for as long as I'm writing."

—Isabel Allende

"Write. Rewrite. When not writing or rewriting, read. I know of no shortcuts."

—Larry L. King

27

MINING FOR DIAMONDS

Strike It Rich with Research
Without Getting Buried Alive

David Corbett

Before becoming a novelist, I worked as a private investigator. My job required, among other things, that I knock on lots of doors and ask lots of questions of lots of strangers. Not all the people I approached reacted cheerfully. I was often yelled at, routinely cursed, frequently threatened, and once almost run over. (The man who tried to kill me, ironically, was a doctor.)

My job taught me the three key elements of any successful attempt to gather facts, and they've served me well in my fiction:

1. **PREPARE AND ORGANIZE.** Begin by developing a fundamental understanding of what you believe you need to learn. This means knowing enough about your basic story and its world, specifically the era and locale of its events and the action you foresee taking place, to have a working idea of the kinds of information and areas of inquiry you lack.
2. **REMAIN OPEN TO THE UNEXPECTED.** Once the research begins, keep an open mind (and eye and ear), taking note of unexpected revelations. Make sure the assumptions made during your initial preparation don't blind you to discoveries that lead in unforeseen and potentially valuable areas, even if they fundamentally change key elements of the story.
3. **REASSESS, ADAPT, AND FOLLOW UP.** Remain flexible yet disciplined. Always ask new questions shaped by what you've learned, to the point of rethinking the whole enterprise, without losing sight of the core inspiration that excited you in the beginning. This is a continual back-and-forth process of assimilation, reevaluation, and discrimination.

As you can imagine, these three guidelines are easier to state than to follow. But if you exhibit self-control and abide by them wisely, they really can help you know when you're straying into the fascinating but unnecessary.

CONSIDER THE ROLE OF FACT IN FICTION

The first question to answer in determining what to research isn't *what* but *why*. Consider for a moment this quote from Albert Camus: "Fiction is the lie through which we tell the truth." Dozens of great authors, from Ralph Waldo Emerson to Doris Lessing, have expressed similar notions. Which raises the question: If fiction is lying, why bother with facts at all? The answer lies in recognizing that, like magicians, storytellers create illusion. Though the purpose may indeed be to reveal a deeper truth, the fact remains that the focus of our effort is to *convincingly deceive*.

Research serves this purpose. Through credible detail, we establish a fictive world that convinces the reader it's worth her while to suspend disbelief and invest emotionally in our tale. The purpose of research, then, is to establish *authority*, not veracity. It's like misdirection in a magic act. By focusing my reader's gaze on *this* (the details I've supplied), I draw her attention away from *that* (the material I'm obliged to invent).

KNOW WHEN TO STEP AWAY

The peril of research lies in not recognizing its limited purpose and instead pursuing more information than necessary because it's just so darn fascinating. This is why so many novelists confess that the problem with research isn't digging in; it's digging out.

Worse, after so much investment, they feel obliged to shoehorn into the book all the neat stuff they've learned. Nothing stops a story in its tracks as effectively as a wall of needless information.

Research need not become an ever-descending mine shaft from which only the lucky return. All you need is enough information and detail to convince the reader you know your business. The degree of effort necessary to accomplish that end will depend on the sophistication of your audience. (Note: One should never underestimate the intelligence of readers.)

As a general rule of thumb, I try to nail down fundamental details that tell me how life is lived at the time and place of my story. That includes (but by no means is limited to) the following:

- **CLIMATE:** including standard precautions against the elements, from flood levees to parasols
- **CLOTHING:** from necessities to ornamentation, with an eye for the varieties of style within a given social or economic class and between classes
- **MANNER OF SPEECH:** with, again, an ear for variety (letters and newspaper accounts, if available, are invaluable—especially for historical settings—as is the simple act of listening if your story takes place in the present)
- **WORK:** such as who does what and why (this will dovetail with era and geography) and the physical details of that work, the wages, and the dangers
- **CLASS, RACE, SEX, AND POWER ARRANGEMENTS:** such as who feels free, who feels constrained or oppressed, who manages the money, who raises the children, how quickly the children reach adult status, who has leisure time, who inherits property, who cares for the sick, and who goes to war
- **ARCHITECTURE:** specifically the nature of the homes (and households) of the powerful, the powerless, and those in between
- **FOOD, MUSIC, ENTERTAINMENT:** the things that make daily life "lively"

You can see at a glance how this kind of research can easily get out of hand. Understanding your specific story needs permits you to exert some control. And yet wandering off in the dark for a bit may avail unforeseeable gems that automatically enhance your authority as storyteller, such as:

- the inviting honey color of certain varieties of whale oil used in lamps (as opposed to colorless kerosene, which replaced it)
- the class-tinged tension in the Old South between Methodism ("deeds not creeds") and Presbyterianism (which claimed salvation was predetermined and virtuous acts were irrelevant)
- the ethereal interpretation given to consumption (tuberculosis) before its contagious nature was discovered, especially among writers and poets such as Elizabeth Barrett Browning and Emily Brontë (it supposedly "purified the patient and edified her friends"[1])

---

1. Sheila M. Rothman, *Living in the Shadow of Death: Tuberculosis and the Social Experience of Illness in American History* (New York: Basic, 1994), page 16; as quoted in Gary L. Roberts, *Doc Holliday: The Life and Legend* (John Wiley & Sons, Inc., 2006), page 60.

Balancing the expected and commonplace with the surprising and unique creates the verisimilitude that perfects the illusion of truth.

DEFINE THE EDGES AND THE SHAPE OF THE UNIVERSE

The British novelist Tom Rob Smith follows what he calls a "four-month rule." He permits himself sixteen weeks of unlimited but intensely focused research before even considering putting fingers to keyboard in service of story. To make the most of that time, he also narrows his research to "best sources." To the greatest extent possible, he tries not to get caught up in scholarly debates that will require him to investigate everything from two (or more) opposing perspectives. For example, in researching *Child 44*, though there were sources on the Soviet Union that viewed the Stalin regime favorably, even triumphantly, he early on decided that this didn't serve his purposes, and he didn't waste time reading them.

Similarly, if you find in your research that scholarship has gone through stages of revisionism, you'll most likely want to use the latest sources available. For example, during the mid-1970s, research into nineteenth-century correspondence between women friends (and lovers) led many scholars to believe that women developed deep interpersonal bonds at least in part because their connections to brothers and fathers were emotionally wanting, to the point that it seemed as though men and women existed in mutually exclusive spheres.[2] But then Karen Lystra, a professor of American studies at Cal State University, discovered a treasure trove of correspondence between husbands and wives from this same period, archived at the Huntington Library in San Marino, California. These letters revealed profound intimacy between married couples, with spouses who often considered each other their closest, most trusted companion.[3]

The point is that knowledge, even of the past, isn't fixed. It's constantly evolving due to new discoveries and fresh interpretations. Not only that, but contemporary records are often wildly at odds. Newspapers from the 1800s often provide irreconcilable views of events due to the highly factional nature of reportage at the time. It may be true that newspapers are indeed "the first

---

2. See, for example, Carroll Smith-Rosenberg's seminal study, "The Female World of Love and Ritual: Relations Between Women in Nineteenth-Century America," *Signs: Journal of Women in Culture and Society*, 1975, Vol. 1, No. 1.
3. See *Searching the Heart: Women, Men, and Romantic Love in Nineteenth-Century America*, 1989, Oxford University Press.

The Complete Handbook of Novel Writing

draft of history," but this only underscores the necessity of further revision and correction.

There's also a creative way to address this fluidity of fact. The irreconcilable views of married life or Stalin's regime certainly represent a challenge in your research. You can choose one faction or the other to believe, or you can use these antagonistic opinions to provide conflict within your story. Tom Rob Smith may not have wasted time poring over pro-Stalin texts, but he understood the need to ground the Stalinist functionaries within his novel in the truth as they saw it.

However you establish the preliminary boundaries for your research, the need to keep an open mind about unforeseen discoveries remains one of the key elements of the work. These discoveries will not only provide details of daily life and animate conflicting perspectives, but they will also generate ideas for scenes and characters you did not anticipate at the outset. But this open-mindedness cannot be open-ended. Something like Tom Rob Smith's four-month rule is valuable because it forces you to begin writing.

Sometimes the time to stop researching and start writing is obvious—for example, when you realize you're encountering the same basic information, with only minor differences, over and over. That indicates you've learned enough. Now write. Another endpoint often comes when you gain a solid sense of what isn't or can't be known—authorities and sources are silent on a particular issue or fact. These omissions in the official record can actually open avenues of creative speculation and invention, which are natural starting points for stories.

But even if you don't encounter either of these natural transitional junctures—or set a time limit, or create some other cutoff—at some point you need to turn away from the research and toward the blank page. That said, nothing obligates you to curtail all research. In fact, you can continue to read and explore as you write your story—as long as the compulsion to learn doesn't dominate the need to meet your daily word count, become an inquisitive tic, or cause a block. You can always update details and scenes as you go along. Writing is rewriting. But you can't revise what you haven't written.

BEWARE OF FUSSING OVER THE FUSSY

Certain areas of expertise attract a devout, rabid, even unbalanced following. One ventures into the Civil War, for example, at some risk, since it forms such an area of intense obsession for many buffs and armchair experts. If writing within the framework of such a jealously guarded arena, it's sometimes best to read the best-available survey text or general history in order to avoid obvious errors, and then focus on some smaller, singularly focused, even idiosyncratic source for a more unique view on events.

In researching his brilliant novel *City of Thieves*—in which two prisoners face execution if they can't find a dozen eggs for a wedding cake—David Benioff relied not only on Harrison Salisbury's *The 900 Days*, the most authoritative text in English on the siege of Leningrad, but also acknowledged his debt to Curzio Malaparte's *Kaputt*, a "work of strange genius" that provided "a completely different perspective."

Even thoughtful precautions can prove fruitless, however. The crime writer G.M. Ford no longer refers to any weapon in a book as anything other than a "gun" because he wearied of the letters from handgun enthusiasts who insisted the sidearm he'd mentioned couldn't perform as described. "And never, *never* put a Harley-Davidson in a book," he added.

It's not just weapons and machinery that inspire such fierce reactions. A knowledgeable reader—a bookseller, no less—once confided to me that she stopped reading Dennis Lehane's *Mystic River* when a woman character used hot water to rid her husband's clothes of blood. "Any woman knows you use cold water," she said, admitting she put the book down at that point because the author "lost her." Fortunately, he didn't lose millions of others.

Worrying over such nitpicking is pointless. Do your best to get it right by using the most reliable sources you can: knowledgeable people you can interview, official documents and newspapers from the period and locale of the story, classic and canonical texts, biographies, letters, and, of course, the increasingly inescapable, if not always reliable, Internet. Then take the blame for all errors in your acknowledgments, and let go.

INTERVIEW AND OBSERVE

Earlier I mentioned my occasional encounters with hostility when trying to get people to talk to me as a private investigator—small surprise, given the fiercely contentious nature of the issues at stake. In general, however, I enjoyed the exact opposite reaction. If approached in a spirit of humility, respect, and curiosity, people tend to be very generous. We all like talking about what we know.

Often it's best to approach interview subjects with self-enforced parameters: "I have five quick questions." Once you sit down together, the information may flow freely, but take care to respect the interviewee's time. Do your homework, and separate the essential from the merely interesting.

Novelist Donna Levin wanted to visit the San Francisco coroner's office for a book she was writing, but she felt too shy to go alone. Knowing I was a PI (at the time), she asked if I'd come along. Her anxiety proved groundless. The staff member we met gave her a tour of the whole morgue and sat with her for several hours. This underscores a point I made at the beginning: It doesn't take bravado or cockiness to knock on a stranger's door—quite the contrary. Donna won over her interview subject with her thoughtfulness, intelligence, and self-effacing humor.

Experts also often lead to other experts with better, more precise information. For my novel set in El Salvador, *Blood of Paradise*, in which water rights were a key component of the story, I interviewed a hydrologist who had worked in-country. He introduced me, in turn, to another specialist who'd worked specifically on the issue of groundwater drawdown and well depletion in the region where my story took place. This gentleman also provided maps and reports of incredible value, along with anecdotes about battling the Kafkaesque local bureaucracy. His information not only gave me a bounty of great details; it also convinced me my original story idea wouldn't work. This meant a lot of rewriting, but it also spared me the embarrassment of getting it all wrong.

I traveled to El Salvador twice and employed guides from both an ecotourism company and a surfing outfit. They drove me around the country, identifying the prominent flora, fauna, beaches, and churches. We discussed local history, culture, and cuisine, and they even gave me pointers on *caliche* (Salvadoran slang). But the real find was Claire Marshall, a BBC reporter I met by chance on the beach at La Libertad. She introduced me to Carlos Vasquez, a deported former shot caller for Mara Salvatrucha in Los Angeles, now running an outreach group to help other gang members leave the life. We shared coffee in the Zona Rosa in the capital, and his insights on the *maras*, from both inside and outside perspectives, proved golden.

Such investments of time and money are not available to everyone—or necessary. The Internet, despite its faults, is a great source for preliminary information and can often direct you to people, documents, texts—and, most important, *images*—that can help you visualize and flesh out your story world. It's great to visit the locale of your book if possible, but take a cue from historical novelists: You can't visit medieval Ireland or ancient China or any other land in the past. Story worlds are conceived in the imagination and portrayed in words. Fortunately, both lie near at hand.

The same is true of in-person interviews—they're wonderful if possible, but phone or even e-mail contact is not only acceptable but often preferred for its less intrusive nature. Persistence may be required to get a response, but remember that you're searching for diamonds—if they were easy to come by, they wouldn't be so valuable.

The Complete Handbook of Novel Writing

28

MAP YOUR NOVEL WITH A REVERSE OUTLINE

Planning with the End in Mind

N.M. Kelby

We can all benefit from a sense of organization. I like to think of a novel outline as the bones of a story. As a child, your bones grow to the place where they'll support who you are meant to be on this planet. If your genes determine that you're tall, your bones will form that foundation, and your flesh will grow accordingly. As you grow older, you need calcium, and bones provide it to the point where they become brittle and can easily break.

This is the same with outlines. You need to create the basic framework for your story to grow on, but not so much that it takes away the energy from the work.

So where do you begin? Arthur Miller once said, "If I see an ending, I can work backward." So start with the end.

KNOW YOUR ENDING BEFORE YOU START

If you start with the end of the story, the ending won't be set in concrete; it can change. But starting with what you think is the end gives you a firm idea of where you are going when you begin a journey with 60,000 to 80,000 words in tow. And you'll need that. Once you decide on your ending, everything in the book will be shaped to arrive there. None of your characters should be superfluous, nor should your scenes. It's all about bones.

Of course, the most difficult part of writing any story, long or short, *is* ending it.

To write your ending, you have to ask yourself what action you want to set forth in the start. But be careful not to create a "purse-string" ending, with all the elements brought together in a tidy bundle. At the end of your story, you don't want to give readers the sense that they already know all there is to know. Give them a whisper and a dream, and send them on their way.

Once your ending is in place, you can weave your tale. Novelist Tony Earley always says, "A story is about a thing and another thing." So it's your job to plan your story so that you give your reader the satisfaction of getting closure from one "thing," the most obvious thing, but maintain the mystery of the other "thing."

A good example of this can be found in Sherman Alexie's "What You Pawn I Will Redeem," the short story about a homeless Spokane Indian's circular attempts to raise a thousand dollars to redeem his grandmother's powwow regalia from a pawnshop. The shop owner would like to give it back, but he paid a thousand dollars for it himself. So he gives the homeless man five dollars as seed money and twenty-four hours to raise the rest of the cash.

In the first paragraph, Alexie gives the reader notice and sets up the ending of his story:

> One day you have a home and the next you don't, but I'm not going to tell you my particular reasons for being homeless, because it's my secret story, and Indians have to work hard to keep secrets from hungry white folks.

The idea of a "secret story" is the key to the ending. While the protagonist does manage to earn money, he drinks, gambles, or gives it away. After twenty-four hours, the money has not been raised, but the pawnbroker gives him the regalia anyway. Here's the last paragraph of the story:

> Outside, I wrapped myself in my grandmother's regalia and breathed her in. I stepped off the sidewalk and into the intersection. Pedestrians stopped. Cars stopped. The city stopped. They all watched me dance with my grandmother. I was my grandmother, dancing.

Because the regalia is given back, the story does seem to tie itself up (that would be the first "thing"), but this really isn't about getting a stolen dress back. It's about the struggle to regain one's spirit—and that could be seen as the "secret" story (or the other thing) wrapped in this tall tale.

The ending that satisfies the reader, or ties things up, is never the real ending of the story. We discover that the grandmother's regalia is returned, and yet the story continues for a moment to put the act into context. Alexie leaves readers with a whisper and a dream, and sends them on their way.

OUTLINE YOUR STORY SIMPLY AND BRIEFLY

There is no set amount of pages in an outline because it all depends on how large a story you're going to tell. The story of *Harry Potter and the Order of the Phoenix* has thirty-eight chapters that spans 870 pages. Its table of contents provides an interesting look at the bones of an outline. It begins:

> One: Dudley Demented
> Two: A Peck of Owls
> Three: The Advance Guard

If you were J.K. Rowling and this was your outline, all you'd have to do is write a short summary paragraph after the title of each chapter. In the first chapter, you would tell us why Dudley is demented and make sure that there are bits in your description that set the action of the book in play. Then move on to the next chapter.

To build the bones of your own outline, begin by writing a short description of what happens in the last chapter, and then move to the first chapter. After that's done, divide the rest of Act One into as many chapters as it takes to properly introduce your protagonist and the conflict—the who, what, when and where of the tale.

Move on to Act Two, and, again, create as many chapters as it takes to explain the crisis, complications, and obstacles that present themselves on the protagonist's way to the climax. Make note of the emotional challenges he faces.

Once you've written the climax, it's time to create as many chapters as you'll need to lead to the final chapter.

Try not to get too fancy with the writing. When your agent pitches your outline, he's going to include fifty pages of your draft in the submission, so you don't need to show any style in the outline. Remember: This is all about bones.

GIVE YOUR STORY IDEA A LITMUS TEST

To see if you can turn your initial story idea into a novel, you have to decide if it has legs. Use this litmus test to find out.

First, answer these questions to the best of your ability. There are no wrong answers, but there *are* answers that inspire you to write. That's what you're looking for.

1. WHAT ABOUT THE IDEA DRAWS YOU IN? What's the most important element of it to you?

2. **WHO COULD THE PLAYERS BE?** Not just the people who inspired you to follow your idea, but the supporting characters. What types of people would be involved in the situation? Who are the protagonist's friends? Who are his enemies? Try to create a quick biography of each in which you explore their relationships to one another and to the protagonist. What do they sound like when they speak? Don't forget to add physical descriptions and aspirations, likes and dislikes.

3. **WHERE AND WHEN DOES THE STORY TAKE PLACE?** Keep in mind that you don't have to choose the setting where the incident that inspired you happened. Whatever you do, make the setting as concrete as possible. Every reader needs a sense of being grounded.

4. **WHAT ARE THE POSSIBILITIES FOR CONFLICT?** Don't just settle for what actually happened. Now that you have a chance to imagine this idea in a more fleshed-out manner, ask yourself what could happen given who the characters you've created are, in addition to where they are in the world of your story.

NOW write. This is the difficult part. Once you've decided the particulars of the story you want to tell, you need to just start writing it. Begin with what you think is the first chapter. Then write the next. Or just write a couple of chapters out of sequence. When you reach fifty pages, try to write your outline. If you can't do so, write some more and try again.

You're not looking for publishable pages; you're just looking to unlock the possibility of story and give yourself an understanding of the depth of the project.

CREATE A MODEL OUTLINE

Select a well-known novel from your shelf and create an outline for it. The story you choose should be similar in style or plot to your own work. After you're finished, do one for your own fiction. Compare the two. Look at how the acts work within the novel, paying special attention to how quickly the climax is reached, what the ending is, what the dénouement is, and how the protagonist was either changed or revealed. Examine your outline and decide whether you want to make revisions based on your observations of the published work.

29

CREATING A FLEXIBLE OUTLINE FOR ANY STORY

How to Go from Premise to Completed Draft

K.M. Weiland

Mention the word *outline* in a room full of writers, and you're sure to ignite a firestorm of passionate debate. Writers either love outlines, or they hate them. We either find them liberating, or we can't stand how confining they are.

My experience has been that more often than not, those who swear they dislike outlines are thinking of them in the wrong ways. Outlines are not meant to trap you into preset ideas or sap your creativity before you start the first draft. Outlines are also definitely *not* meant to be lifeless Roman-numeral lists.

To imbue your writing with the full power of outlining, you need to approach the process from a mind-set of flexibility and discovery. When you do this, you'll end up with a road map to storytelling success. Road maps show you the fastest and surest way to reach your destination, but they certainly don't prevent you from finding exciting off-road adventures and scenic drives along the way.

At their best, outlines can help you flesh out your most promising story ideas, avoid dead-end plot twists, and pursue proper structure. And the greatest part? They save you time and prevent frustration. Sketching out your plot and characters in your first draft can take months of trial and error. Figuring out those same elements in an outline requires a fraction of the time—and then allows you to let loose and have fun in your first draft.

Let's take a look at how to get the most out of the outlining process, beginning with the shaping of your premise and working all the way through to a complete list of scenes. (Note: Although this outlining method is one I use my-self and highly recommend, keep in mind that there is no right or wrong way to outline a story. The only requirement is that you find the groove that works for *you*. If you start outlining and begin to feel the technique isn't working for you, rather than denounce outlines entirely, consider how you might adjust the pro-cess to better suit your personality and creative style.)

1. CRAFT YOUR PREMISE

Your premise is the basic idea for your story. But it's not enough to just *have* an idea. "Guy saves girl in an intergalactic setting" is a premise, but it's also far too vague to offer much solid story guidance.

This is why your outline needs to begin with a tightly crafted premise sen-tence that can answer the following questions:

- **WHO IS THE PROTAGONIST?**
- **WHAT IS THE SITUATION?** What is the hero's personal condition at the beginning? How will that condition be changed, for better or worse, by the hero himself or by the antagonistic force?
- **WHAT IS THE PROTAGONIST'S OBJECTIVE?** At the beginning, what does the hero want? What moral (or immoral) choices will she have to make in her attempt to gain that objective?
- **WHO IS THE OPPONENT?** Who or what stands in the way of the hero achieving his objective?
- **WHAT'S THE DISASTER?** What misfortune will befall the hero as the result of her attempts to achieve her objective?
- **WHAT'S THE CONFLICT?** What conflict will result from the hero's reac-tion to the disaster? And what is the logical flow of cause and effect that will allow this conflict to continue throughout the story?

Once you've answered these questions, combine them into one or two sentences:

> Restless farm boy (**situation**) Luke Skywalker (**protagonist**) wants nothing more than to leave home and become a starfighter pilot so he can live up to the legacy of his mysterious father (**objective**). But when his aunt and uncle are murdered (**disaster**) after purchasing renegade droids, Luke must free the droids' beautiful owner and discover a way to stop (**conflict**) the evil Empire (**opponent**) and its apocalyptic Death Star.

2. ROUGHLY SKETCH SCENE IDEAS

Armed with a solid premise, you can now begin sketching your ideas for this story. Write a list of everything you already know about your story. You'll probably come to this step with a handful of scenes already in mind. Even if you have no idea how these scenes will play out in the story, go ahead and add them to the list. At this point, your primary goal is to remember and record every idea you've had in relation to this story.

Once you've finished, take a moment to review your list. Whenever you encounter an idea that raises questions, highlight it. If you don't know *why* your character is fighting a duel in one scene, highlight it. If you don't know *how* two scenes will connect, highlight them. If you can't picture the setting for one of the scenes, highlight that, too. By pausing to identify possible plot holes now, you'll save yourself a ton of rewriting later on.

Your next step is to address each of the highlighted portions, one by one. Write out your ideas and let your thoughts flow without censoring yourself. Because this is the most unstructured step of your outline, it's your best opportunity to unleash your creativity and plumb the depths of your story's potential. Ask yourself questions on the page. Talk to yourself without worrying about punctuation or spelling.

Every time you think you've come up with a good idea, take a moment to ask, "Will the reader expect this?" If the answer is yes, write a list of alternatives your readers won't expect.

3. INTERVIEW YOUR CHARACTERS

To craft a cast of characters that can help your plot reach its utmost potential, you'll need to discover crucial details about them, not necessarily at the beginning of their lives but at the beginning of the story.

To do this for your protagonist, work backward from the moment when he will become engaged in your plot (the "disaster" in your premise sentence). What events in your protagonist's life have led him to this moment? Did something in his past *cause* the disaster? What events have shaped him to make him respond to the disaster in the way he does? What unresolved issues from his past can further complicate the plot's spiral of events?

Once you have a basic idea of how your character will be invested in the main story, you can start unearthing the nitty-gritty details of his life with a character interview. You may choose to follow a preset list of questions (you can find a list of more than one hundred such questions in my book *Outlining Your Novel: Map Your Way to Success*), or you may have better luck with a "freehand interview" in which you ask your protagonist a series of questions and allow him to answer in his own words.

4. EXPLORE YOUR SETTINGS

Whether your setting is your childhood neighborhood or the seventh moon of Barsoom, you'll want to enter your first draft with a firm idea of where your prominent scenes take place.

Don't choose a setting just because it sounds cool or because you're familiar with it. Look for settings inherent to your plot. Can you change your story's primary locale without any significant alterations to the plot? If so, dig a little deeper to find a setting better suited to your plot, theme, and characters.

Based on the scenes you're already aware of, list the settings you think you'll need. Can you reduce this list by combining or eliminating settings? Nothing wrong with a sprawling story locale, but extraneous settings should be eliminated just as assiduously as unnecessary characters.

5. WRITE YOUR COMPLETE OUTLINE

You're finally ready to outline your story in full. This is where you will begin plotting in earnest. In Step Two, you solidified the big picture of your story by identifying the scenes you were already aware of and figuring out how they might fit together. Now, you will work through your story linearly, scene by scene, numbering each one as you go. Unlike the "sketches" in Step Two, in which your primary focus was on brainstorming and exploring possibilities, you will now be concentrating on molding your existing ideas into a solid structure.

How comprehensive you want to be is up to you. You may choose to write a single sentence for each scene ("Dana meets Joe at the café to discuss their impending nuptials"), or you may choose to flesh out more details ("Joe is sitting by himself in a booth when Dana arrives; Dana orders coffee and a muffin; they fight about the invitation list"). Either way, focus on identifying and strengthening the key components of each scene's structure. Who will be your narrating character? What is his goal? What obstacle will arise to obstruct that goal and create conflict? What will be the outcome, and how will your character react to the resulting dilemma? What decision will he reach that will fuel the next scene's goal?

Work to create a linear, well-structured plot with no gaps in the story (see the checklist at the end of this chapter). If you can get this foundation right in your outline, you'll later be free to apply all your focus and imagination to the first draft and bring your story to life.

As you mentally work through each scene, watch for lapses of logic or blank areas in how one event builds to another. Take the time to think through these potential problems so they won't trip you up later. If you get stuck, try jumping ahead to the next scene you know and then working backward. For instance, if you know where you want your characters to end up, but not how they'll get there, start at the ending point and then see if you can figure out what has to happen in the preceding events to make it plausible.

6. CONDENSE YOUR OUTLINE

Once you've finished your extended outline, you may want to condense the most pertinent points into an abbreviated version. Doing so allows you to weed out extraneous thoughts and summarize the entire outline into a scannable list for easier reference. Because your full outline may contain a fair amount of rambling and thinking out loud on the page, you're likely to end up with a *lot* of notes to review (I often have nearly three notebooks of material). Rather than wading through all of your notes every time you sit down to work on your first draft, you can save yourself time in the long run by doing a little organizing now.

You may choose to create your abbreviated outline in a Word document, write out your scenes on index cards, or use a software program such as the free Scrivener alternative yWriter.

7. PUT YOUR OUTLINE INTO ACTION

By now, you feel prepared and eager to get going on your first draft. Each time you sit down to work on your manuscript, begin by reviewing your outline. Read the notes for your current scene and the scene to follow. Before you start writing, work through any remaining potential problems in your head or on paper. If the time comes (and it *will* come) when you're struck with a better idea than what you had planned in your outline, don't hesitate to go off-road. These ventures into unknown territory can result in some of the most surprising and intriguing parts of your story.

An outline will offer you invaluable structure and guidance as you write your first draft, but never be afraid to explore new ideas as they occur. Remember: Your outline is a map that shows you the route to your destination, but that doesn't mean it is the *only* route.

CHECKLIST FOR STRUCTURING YOUR OUTLINE

- Identify the best hook with which to open your first chapter.
- Plan to introduce all prominent characters and settings within the first 25 percent of your book. Outline scenes in which you can bring these people and places onstage in a way that is both logical and interesting. Consider how to demonstrate what is at stake for your characters: What would they lose should they be defeated in the primary conflict?
- Note the first of four major plot points that will divide your book into approximate fourths. At the 25 percent mark, the first major plot point should shake up your character's normal world and force him into a series of reactions.
- Let your character's reactions lead to the midpoint. The second major plot point, at the 50 percent mark, will provoke a change in your character's attitude and response to the antagonistic force. From this moment on, he will start taking action on his own behalf instead of merely reacting to the conflict.
- Open your third act with a third major plot point that forces your character to a place of apparent defeat. Starting at about the 75 percent mark, he will have to rise from this moment, strengthened in his resolve to defeat the antagonistic force.
- Map out the climax. Give special care to this final part of your story. Aim to plot out scenes that will set up the action in unique ways and force your protagonist to dig down to his deepest self to defeat (or succumb to) the antagonist.

Historical and speculative novelist **K.M. Weiland** writes the award-winning blog Helping Writers Become Authors (helpingwritersbecomeauthors.com). She is the author of *Outlining Your Novel* and *Structuring Your Novel*.

30

PLANTSING

....

The Art of Plotting *and* Pantsing

————————

Jeff Somers

About fifteen years ago, I finally learned how to drive a stick shift. My whole life I'd wondered: Why would anyone choose to shift manually? It's like pushing the car uphill by yourself, Flintstone-style. But I'm glad I now know because, in the event of a zombie apocalypse, I can hijack and operate any available vehicle to make my escape.

Why are you reading about transmissions? Because they're surprisingly similar to the two types of methods writers use to produce novels.

Writing a novel is easy … said no writer ever. Sure, every year thousands of people write a rough draft of a short novel in thirty days during National Novel Writing Month, and plenty of literature's classics make it *look* easy. (Both *A Clockwork Orange* and *On the Road* were written in less than a month's time, for example.) But there are a plethora of ways a novel can go horribly, even hilariously awry—and the easiest hard thing to muck up is your plot.

Ideas are a baby step, but *plot* is a long haul. The difference between George R.R. Martin's A Song of Ice and Fire series and an elevator pitch that boils down to "the *Wars of the Roses* plus dragons" is a million words, two decades, and a sturdy, exciting, and well-constructed plot. As Martin once said in a *Rolling Stone* interview, "Ideas are cheap. I have more ideas now than I could ever write up. To my mind, it's the execution that is all-important."

ANIMAL INSTINCTS

Any writer can stumble into a failed plot. In fact, you probably should. It's part of the ongoing learning process that we writers engage in throughout our careers—

you can often learn more about the craft and process of writing from your failed manuscripts than from your successes. Stories or essays that pour painlessly from your fingers are exhilarating, sure, but that eerie sense that you're just a conduit for a supernatural muse doesn't necessarily instill confidence. It's tough to replicate a trick you didn't understand in the first place.

The most important aspect of a failed plot is the opportunity it offers to rise above *instinctive* writing and perform a literary autopsy—to discover your "writer's genetic code."

In many ways, writing is an instinctive act—which is to say our initial approach to style and plotting is "baked in." All writers, if they take an honest look, are better at some components of storytelling than others:

- Some writers can reel off big ideas for novels without effort but have trouble translating those concepts into 80,000 words.
- Some writers capture realistic-sounding dialogue without even trying but have difficulty efficiently moving their stories along.
- Some writers regularly craft gorgeous sentences but then struggle to populate scenes with interesting characters.

The most important aspect of your genetic code as a writer is your instinctual approach to plot, because if you can't create a compelling plot, the rest of the writing ultimately doesn't matter. And all writers instinctively fall into one of two categories: You're either a *plotter* or a *pantser*.

PLOTTING AND PANTSING

If you're a plotter, your approach to writing a novel is similar to a military campaign: You set up the logistics and supply lines in advance, and by the time your fingers actually touch the keyboard, you have the entire battle mapped out, blow-by-blow.

Pantsers, on the other hand, just start writing. They strap on a pirate costume, shout, "Avast!" and swing into the story with wild abandon.

Neither of these approaches is right or wrong. For a plotter, the idea of diving into a story without knowing where it leads is insanity. For a pantser, sitting down ahead of time and figuring out all the twists and turns sounds excruciatingly boring. And while arguments abound online and at writing conferences about which approach is the "better" one, I'd contend that it doesn't matter which approach you find a natural fit, really, because both have advantages and disadvantages.

Plotting: Pros and Cons

Plotters have one huge advantage: They know the whole story before they begin writing. They won't experience moments of day-drinking panic, when the story hits a wall and they realize they've written themselves into a tiny corner and now have to perform the world's most complex literary three-point turn to get out of it.

On the other hand, those lightning moments of sudden inspiration are hard to come by, and it's easy to ignore problems because your preplanned plot gives you a false sense of security. Sometimes plotting a novel ahead of time causes the resulting writing to feel mechanical, which can render scenes lifeless and make twists and turns feel like perfunctory stops along the way to the inevitable.

Pantsing: Pros and Cons

Pantsing a novel offers the opportunity for your subconscious to suddenly toss creative bombs into your story. This approach can make a plot feel brisk and naturalistic; the answers to creative questions are sometimes just as surprising to the author as they are to everyone else. Such freedom can make the *act* of writing as exhilarating as the act of reading.

On the other hand, those moments of genius aren't all that common—and if the "brilliant" twist you didn't plan for blows up other aspects of the story, it's not truly brilliant.

Because most writers naturally gravitate toward one approach over the other, they have a tendency to chalk up broken plots as the cost of doing business. A better approach is to stop writing instinctually—or, at least, to stop writing *entirely* on instinct. This involves taking the best aspects of each approach—plotting and pantsing—and using them both effectively as needed. The result? A hybrid approach we'll call *plantsing*.

THE HYBRID APPROACH

Plantsing combines the best aspects of both pantsing and plotting, and is a much more effective writing strategy because it moves you away from instinct and makes your writing mechanics more thoughtful and purposeful.

The cornerstone of plantsing is to always follow your instincts *at first*. If you tend to meticulously plot out your novels before writing a word, go for it! If you normally experience a fiery inspiration and then dive in and start writing immediately, do so. In fact, if your instinctual approach works and produces a completed novel with no serious problems, all the better.

Plantsing comes into play when you start to struggle. Whether you have a completely plotted story that now feels a bit stilted and unwieldy, or a novel that began with the thrill of a great idea but has cooled off in a sluggish middle, the trick is to not give up but rather to change tactics.

Mapping the Pantsed Wilderness

If you started pantsing your novel without a firm plan and you've suddenly lost the thread of your plot, stop grinding, go back to the beginning of your novel, and break down the plot you've already written. In other words, retroactively plot the story. When you reach your current point of progress, keep writing: Plot the next few steps until you feel like you know where you're going. Then switch back to pantsing mode. Repeat as necessary.

Jolting the Plotter's Muse

On the other hand, if your carefully structured plot starts to feel a little uninspired or not as cohesive as it first seemed, it's time to introduce some hot pantsing action. Go back to the last moment in your story that felt exciting, and just make something up. Forget your notes, forget your plan—forget your *plot*—and just pants it for a while. Even if what you write isn't great, it will lead you in directions that would have been hidden from view otherwise. When you feel like you can see where you're going again, plot out your new vision and proceed from there.

Plantsing is all about being flexible. The more tools and strategies you have when writing, the more likely it is you will end up with a pile of words that resembles a novel instead of, well, a pile of words.

PLANTSING IN REAL LIFE

You may be wondering if plantsing is just some sort of theoretical concept for me, or if it's an actual approach I take in my writing. It's the latter: I'm an inveterate pantser (ironically, despite a dislike for actually *wearing* pants), but my last few published novels have benefited from the plantsing approach.

Case Study: *Chum*

My novel *Chum* is a complex story of alcohol and murder. The book jumps around in time and revisits key moments from different perspectives, and each chapter is narrated by a different point-of-view character. Because I'm a pantser, I didn't know any of this when I started writing the book; all I had was an opening scene and a few characters.

By the time I figured out someone was going to die, the novel's time line was already a mess. I pantsed on, having a lot of fun, but when I finished the first draft I realized I had a problem: I couldn't decipher the order of events. And I was the *author*!

So I went back to the beginning and started plotting. I created a list of the chapters and a sublist of the major events. Then I started putting those events in order, using what *Doctor Who* would call "fixed points in time"—events that had to happen in a certain order and thus couldn't be moved—as anchors. This uncovered a wealth of inconsistencies and problems in the story. I had to delete scenes and even entire chapters—but I also found opportunities to replace them with much stronger material.

In the end, I plantsed my way to a story that retained its air of mystery and the fun of revelation, but also hung together tightly, and my agent sold the novel to Tyrus Books in 2013.

TAKEAWAYS:

- Plantsing can be applied at any stage—even after you've finished a draft.
- Sometimes what you're fixing isn't a lack of plot points but the *coherency* of those plot points.
- The difference between a near-miss manuscript and a published novel can be razor thin, and you need every possible advantage.

Case Study: *We Are Not Good People*

The original deal for this epic tale of grifter wizards and a magical apocalypse was for two novels as a duology. Then my publisher reconsidered the marketing and decided to combine both books into one volume titled *We Are Not Good People*. I was excited, but as I worked I became aware of a problem: I knew what the ending would be, but I couldn't see how to get there. At about the three-fourths mark, the plot got blurry.

So I got down to plantsing. I stopped trying to write my way through it (which wasn't working) and broke down the story into a series of scenes. I penciled in the ending that I envisioned, and then wrote down the major events (fixed points) that had to be in place to get there. Then I filled in each blank space until I had a clear path forward—a path I followed by going back to pantsing.

TAKEAWAYS:

- Life throws you curveballs. When a strategy isn't working—even if it always worked before—you have to accept the fact and try something different.
- Knowing the ending for a novel doesn't guarantee you know the path there, and plantsing can help reveal that path.
- With plantsing, you can switch back and forth between plotting and pantsing, following one approach when things are going smoothly, switching back when you run into trouble—and then switching *again* as the situation requires.

Ultimately, your approach to plotting, writing, revising, and even selling a novel is wholly your own. You might be a natural-born pantser or you might be a plotter down to your core, but both approaches go sideways from time to time, and knowing how to shift gears like a pro from one to the other might be the difference between finishing that novel or adding it to your list of abandoned projects.

Just like knowing how to drive a manual transmission may be the difference between surviving the zombie apocalypse and becoming zombie lunch.

PLOTTING FOR PANTSERS

You live for the moment, and every day is an adventure. Here's how to find your inner Hannibal Smith and learn to love when a plan comes together.

- Plotting can be overwhelming, so start with this strategy: If you're feeling stuck, simply make a list of events in your story. Leave blanks as needed, and then note any fixed points in time.
- Once you know how to get from your stopping point to the next fixed point, feel free to quit plotting and dive back into pantsing. Repeat the cycle as needed.
- Overplotting can be counterproductive for pantsers. Don't try to list every single event and line of dialogue. Leave yourself some blank space to pants your way through.
- When trying to figure out the next plot point, imagine you're the protagonist, and ask yourself what you would do (unless the answer is "take a nap").
- If you know where the plot needs to go, ask yourself *why* your characters get to that point. Then keep repeating that question, working backward to the point where it all fell apart.

The Complete Handbook of Novel Writing

PANTSING FOR PLOTTERS

The world of pure imagination is a scary place, and you prefer to have a plan. But plans can fail, and when they do, every good planner has a fallback. Here's how to painlessly make pantsing your backup.

- The unknown can be intimidating. The key to pantsing is to not worry about how it will all hang together. Just start writing.
- Know that it's not uncommon to throw away most, if not all, of what you write when pantsing—the approach often reveals your next plot point even if the words aren't usable.
- Be open to reworking the parts of your novel you've already written; sometimes pantsing suggests changes to plot points that you thought were locked in. Kill those darlings.
- Pantsing isn't magic. It's a technique, just like plotting. Allow yourself ample time to experiment in order to get results.
- If you really can't fathom pantsing your way through a manuscript, try pantsing in shorthand instead, as if you're writing a synopsis. In other words, don't write 30,000 words—just summarize what they might be. This makes it a lot faster and easier to test-drive different approaches and plot shapes.

Jeff Somers (www.jeffreysomers.com) was first sighted in Jersey City, New Jersey, after the destruction of a classified government installation in the early 1970s; the area in question is still too radioactive to go near. When asked about this, he will only say that he regrets nothing. He is the author of *Lifers*, the Avery Cates series from Orbit Books, *Chum* from Tyrus Books, and the Ustari Cycle from Pocket/Gallery, including *We Are Not Good People*.

31

ROUGH IT UP

··

Get Messy with Your First Draft
to Get to the Good Stuff

Elizabeth Sims

As Ernest Hemingway famously said, "The first draft of anything is shit." For years, I didn't understand. When I started writing fiction seriously, I kept trying to get it right the first time.

Every night after clocking out from my job in a bookstore, I'd sit at my favorite coffee shop with a yellow pad and the pens I collected from publishers' reps and carefully work on my first novel. I'd write my minimum 300-word requirement, staying inside the lines and squeezing out every word with great thought and deliberation. Grant me, at least, that I was disciplined: I counted my words, and if I got to 299, I wouldn't go back and add "very" to a sentence—I had to at least begin the next one.

By that method, I managed to produce quite a lot of pages. But guess what? My prose didn't consistently swing, sizzle, or startle. It took me a long time to figure out Hemingway's hidden meaning, and longer still to apply it. Over time, as I got rougher with my first drafts, my finished work got better and better.

BE HONEST

Why does a coherent first draft give birth to a stilted finished product? Because it means you haven't let it flow. You haven't given yourself permission to make mistakes because you haven't forgiven yourself for past ones. Admit it: Unless your throttle's wide open, you're not giving it everything you've got.

One day I realized that creativity in writing isn't a linear process, even though we read in a linear fashion and the words must go on the page one after the other; even though we must put our thoughts and words in order so the reader can make sense of them.

Writing, in fact, is the only art that is literally one-dimensional. If you can be gut-level honest with yourself, you've really got a shot at your readers. And the only way to find that honesty is to not overthink it.

For your writing to come alive—to be multidimensional—you must barter away some control. The rewards are worth it.

LEARN TO LOVE ANARCHY

Ignore sequence while writing your first draft. Beginning writers will often say, "I've got the basic story figured out, but I don't know how to present it so it hangs together. I'm never sure what should come next."

Nothing is as freeing as writing *what comes to mind next*, not necessarily *what must come next*. Transitions are unimportant. Hey, don't take my word for it—trust John Dos Passos, Patricia Highsmith, Mark Twain, and William Shakespeare. Exposition is always less important than you think it is. Just focus on what happens next.

Hemingway didn't mean, though, that if you begin with crap, dung, or merde, you'll end up with something far better without much effort. He also didn't mean that it's okay to start with a weak premise.

He meant that the first execution of your ideas must be as unfettered as possible. Which will result in—yes!—some crap: false starts, pretentiousness, clunky images, and clichés. Fine. Get them out now. They'll contaminate the good stuff only until you get around to your second draft.

GET LOOSE

Relax, physically and mentally. If, as I do, you write your first drafts longhand, consider your pen a paintbrush. Hold it relaxed in your hand and move it from your shoulder, instead of with your fingers. Your whole arm will move freely, and you'll pour out the words, as well as banish carpal tunnel syndrome all to hell.

Legibility is overrated. Remember that.

The common wisdom in writing workshops is that you shouldn't stop to revise. But let's be honest: That's unrealistic because sometimes you really do see another possibility right away, and you should be free to pursue it. I recommend overwriting as you go.

If, in a single moment, you think of two different ways of saying something, just write both, one after the other. Later you'll be able to decide which is better.

Write a box around a phrase; stack two competing adjectives atop each other; make notes in the margin. I use the margins for research notes such as "What's position of Sirius over L.A./August?"

Fresh sheets aren't just for motels. Use paper! I'm a big believer in using exactly the amount of natural resources you need, and no less. If you want to go off on a new tangent that's longer than a sentence, rip off your current page and start a fresh one. Never crowd a new thought into a crevice of the page you're on.

And for the love of God, don't wait for the new thought to fully form before you put it down. More often than not, as soon as you write the first shard of that new thought, it'll work itself to fullness as you write. And that's the magic we all live for, isn't it?

If you want to add a word or a block of text, don't stop at using carats to show an insert. Circle stuff, draw arrows, loop one piece of text into the middle of another. And keep going. If it's instantly obvious that one version of a word, sentence, or paragraph is better, strike out the bad one and go on without looking back.

If you compose on a keyboard, make the "return" button your best friend: Set off a new idea by hitting two carriage returns. Let your fingers splash on the keyboard. Let typos stand. Don't use the cut and paste functions while creating a first draft.

Note that I'm not telling you to write as fast as you possibly can, as in speed for speed's sake. No. Take time to pause and reflect. Then take whatever comes without judging it too much.

Why is it so important to suspend judgment when writing? Because that freedom opens you to the surprising stuff you never saw coming; stuff that makes you smile as you sit there in the coffee shop, your mug of joe cooling because you've forgotten to take a sip in fifteen solid minutes.

When beginning a writing session, new authors often feel that they must jump off to an excellent start, when all they really need is to start. In this, there's no difference between you and me.

Often I have to slog through crap to produce decent writing. But I never despair, having learned that if I just keep going, I'll get to someplace worthwhile.

FACE YOUR SECOND DRAFT

If you've practiced slovenliness with a liberal hand, you'll be delighted at how much fun your second draft will be. After I've got a chapter or two roughed out,

I go from my handwritten pages to my computer, where I edit and rewrite as I go, adding new text and omitting what—I can now clearly see—doesn't work.

Thus I establish the rough rhythm that works for me: a couple of days writing longhand, then a day at the old PC. Some authors work through their entire manuscript in longhand before sitting down to type, and that's dandy, too. Most beginning writers cling to every word they've written. But if you practice looseness and receptivity when writing your first draft, the day will come during revisions when you realize you have a surplus of good writing to sort through. You'll know joy.

I just took a spin through a couple of my old *Writers at Work* volumes (*The Paris Review* Interviews). Along with George Plimpton's interview of each famous author, the *Review* reproduces pages from their drafts.

I studied some of these:

- **CYNTHIA OZICK:** Her handwritten draft page is a beautiful mess, containing almost more strike-outs than unscathed text.
- **RALPH ELLISON:** He used a typewriter and then marked up his pages with a ruthless hand.
- **ERNEST HEMINGWAY:** His handwritten page from "The Battler" shows only one cross-out. However, between that and the published story, the passage shows subtle but significant differences.

During the course of writing six novels, I realized that the days when the truth shone brightest were the days my pen flowed the freest and messiest across the pages. And I was rewarded with longer and longer satisfactory passages.

It's paradoxical that giving up control rewards you with what you seek most: concise, insightful work.

32

TITLING YOUR STORY

....

Give Your Novel a Memorable, Inspired Title

—————————

Steve Almond

It happens every semester that I teach fiction, usually on the day we distribute stories for the first workshop. A student will raise her hand and offer the following caveat: "So I just wanted to, like, apologize for my story not having a title. I totally hate titles."

To which her classmates will inevitably respond with a chorus of amens about how much they, like, hate titles, too! To which I'll respond with a roar of anguished disbelief: "Are you *kidding* me? Guys, titles are the coolest part of the whole process! They're like the cherry on top of the sundae! They're the sign over the gate! A story without a title is like a doll without a head!" This statement hangs in the air for an uncomfortable moment. Then I launch into my lecture on titles, which I have titled: "Who Wants to Play With a Headless Doll? No One, That's Who."

I'm going to summarize that lecture here, and I'll restrain myself from threatening to flunk you. Instead, I'll entreat you (as I do my students) to think of titles not as a burden, but among the greatest opportunities writers are afforded.

A title should serve three purposes: an introduction to the story's crucial images and ideas, an initiation into the rhetorical pitch of the prose, and an inducement to keep reading. It's important to note that a title need not serve all of these purposes at once, but the best ones manage to nail this trifecta. Here are a few greats:

- *The Catcher in the Rye*: Salinger not only highlights the book's most striking image, but also underscores the preoccupation of his wry teenage hero—to save children from the corrupting artifice of adulthood. It's impossible not to be intrigued.

- *Pride and Prejudice*: This is an oddly formal title for this exquisite comedy of manners, but Jane Austen was determined to stress the serious themes bubbling beneath the drawing-room banter.
- *Lord of the Flies*: William Golding forces us to reckon with the most disturbing symbol in his novel of boys run amok—the pig's head that serves as a prophet of evil. The title makes fruitful allusion both to the Old Testament and King Lear. And bonus points for spawning an Iron Maiden song.

"Okay, fine," you're saying. "Those dudes make it look easy. That's why they're *famous*." Don't be fooled. Sometimes the right title comes to you in a flash. Other times, you have to struggle.

F. Scott Fitzgerald spent months fretting over the title of his great American novel. He considered a bunch of howlers: *Among Ashheaps and Millionaires* (precious), *The High-Bouncing Lover* (all wrong tonally), and, most famously, *Trimalchio in West Egg*, the reference being to a character from an obscure Roman novel. The book would still have been great, even saddled with such a pretentious name. But it would have lacked the tragic irony of Gatsby's self-mythification and the spirit of keen observation that Nick Carraway's narration brings to the book.

At the eleventh hour Fitzgerald reportedly tried to change the title to *Under the Red, White and Blue*. He wanted to pound home the book's connection to the American dream. But he went for something far too broad, a name that could have applied to any one of a hundred books. Thankfully, he failed.

Like any aspect of your fiction, a title should feel organic, not imposed. It should arise from the vernacular of the piece itself. Raymond Carver's short story "What We Talk About When We Talk About Love" doesn't just tell us what the story is about but *how* it's going to be told—in colloquial, prolix outbursts. The same can be said of Karl Iagnemma's wonderful short story "On the Nature of Human Romantic Interaction," the chronicle of a lovesick engineer. Or Lorrie Moore's short story "Which Is More Than I Can Say About Some People," which captures the oppressive chattiness of our heroine's mother.

I've chosen these exuberant titles to emphasize that there's no word limit on titles. I'm not suggesting that longer titles are better, only that there's no prevailing orthodoxy.

But titular mistakes are easy to make. Don't name your story after a character. This is a failure of imagination. It tells us nothing we don't already know. Don't recycle the last line of the story. It's like hitting the same nail twice. A title should do original work on behalf of the piece. Don't use obvious or clever puns. If you write a story about a couple who can't conceive a child, please don't call it *Fruitless* or *Womb Without a View* or, worst of all, *Grin and Barren It*. Finally, don't quote William Shakespeare or the Bible. How many tepid short stories titled *Brief Candle* or *Let There Be Light* have I read? Too many.

Of course, rules were made to be broken.

How did William Faulkner get away with *The Sound and the Fury*? Well, for one thing, he was Faulkner. (It helps to be Faulkner.) But the quote he lifts from Macbeth's famous soliloquy travels to the heart of his novel, which is a "tale told by an idiot," about the loss of dignity and the futility of life.

Or consider Vladimir Nabokov's *Lolita*. Why does it work? Because the book is about how Humbert Humbert transforms his stepdaughter into a fetish object. The chief indicator of his obsessive love is the lurid-sounding name he gives her, the one he rolls around his mouth like a morsel.

So where do great titles come from? For the most part, they're right under your nose. I tell students to consider details or even snatches of dialogue that jump out at them and resonate.

Several years ago, for instance, I had a brilliant student named Ellen Litman. She turned in a story about a family of Russian immigrants newly arrived in America. Her original title was something like "How to Survive in America." But as we went over the piece in class, we kept returning to a scene in which the narrator's father, set adrift in a huge American grocery store, clutches a chicken "like it was the last chicken in America." This image seemed to encapsulate the story: its blend of black humor and pathos, of bewilderment and neediness and courage. Not only did the story get a new name, but (at Ellen's instigation) it became the title of her wonderful debut novel, *The Last Chicken in America*.

Another student looked to dialogue as a source of inspiration. She came up with the title *Look Who Decided to Show Her Face*, which captured the tough feel of the working-class milieu she was writing about, but also the tentative self-examination of her heroine.

Part of what keeps writers from finding strong titles is embarrassment. They may be ready to write a story, but they're not ready to name the thing or openly woo readers. They view titles as a form of advertising for a product they don't quite believe in yet.

Well, folks, titles are a form of advertising. (Think about it: What makes you turn to a particular story when you read a magazine's table of contents?)

That's not an invitation to histrionics; it's an exhortation. The search for a title should be a means of interrogating your story, trying to discern the heart of the thing you've created. It's a promise you're making to the reader.

If you can't come up with a title, or find yourself relying on the gambits cited above, it might be that you simply need a loudmouth like me to enable you. But it may also be that your story or novel isn't ready for the world yet. I'm convinced that the right title is like the right romantic pairing: You'll know when you've found it, even (and especially) when it forces you deeper into life's mysteries.

FIND THE PERFECT TITLE

- Take a look at your most recent work. Underline the phrases that resonate the most. Test-drive them as titles. Do any of them change the way you envision the story?
- Make a list of your favorite novels and short stories. Consider how the titles operate in each case. What work are they doing? What promises do they make?
- Consider what expectations, in terms of plot, theme, and tone, the following titles provoke: The Day I Became a Virgin; Blue Falls; First Month, Last Month, and Security; Sacrifice Fly; Sylvia Plath Is My Love Goddess
- Gather any old stories you have lying around, particularly ones that employ puns, famous allusions, or character names. Now burn them. Kidding! Don't burn them. Think about how you might retitle them.

Steve Almond spent seven years as a newspaper reporter in Texas and Florida before writing his first book, the story collection *My Life in Heavy Metal*. His nonfiction book *Candyfreak* was a *New York Times* bestseller. His short fiction has been included in *The Best American Short Stories* and Pushcart Prize anthologies, and his collection *God Bless America* won the Paterson Prize for Fiction. He is most recently the author of the *New York Times* bestseller *Against Football*. Almond writes commentary and journalism regularly for *The New York Times Magazine* and *The Boston Globe*. A former sports reporter and play-by-play man, Almond lives outside Boston with his wife and three children.

BEST-SELLING ADVICE
Revision and Editing

" My own experience is that once a story has been written, one has to cross out the beginning and the end. It is there that we authors do most of our lying."

—Anton Chekhov

"Half my life is an act of revision."

—John Irving

"If it sounds like writing, I rewrite it. Or, if proper usage gets in the way, it may have to go. I can't allow what we learned in English composition to disrupt the sound and rhythm of the narrative."

—Elmore Leonard

"I do not rewrite unless I am absolutely sure that I can express the material better if I do rewrite it."

—William Faulkner

"I almost always write everything the way it comes out, except I tend much more to take things out rather than put things in. It's out of a desire to really show what's going on at all times, how things smell and look, as well as from the knowledge that I don't want to push things too quickly through to climax; if I do, it won't mean anything. Everything has to be earned, and it takes a lot of work to earn.

—Peter Straub

" If you're writing for a magazine or a newspaper, then you're a guest. It's as if you're a guest violinist in some great conductor's orchestra. You play to his rhythm, to his audience. You're invited in and he edits you and tells you what he wants. On the other hand, when you're writing a book, the only reason you're writing it is to say it your own way, in your own words, and tell the story the way you see it."

—Teddy White

"... Falsely straining yourself to put something into a book where it doesn't really belong, it's not doing anybody any favors. And the reader can tell."

—Margaret Atwood

"I'm a tremendous rewriter; I never think anything is good enough. I'm always rephrasing jokes, changing lines, and then I hate everything. *The Girl Most Likely To* was rewritten seven times, and the first time I saw it I literally went out and threw up! How's that for liking yourself?"

—Joan Rivers

"When your story is ready for rewrite, cut it to the bone. Get rid of every ounce of excess fat. This is going to hurt; revising a story down to the bare essentials is always a little like murdering children, but it must be done.

—Stephen King

33

THE GEYSER APPROACH TO REVISION

··

How to Keep Your Inspiration Flowing During the Editing Phase

James Scott Bell

In Mexico there's a popular tourist stop called La Bufadora. It's billed as the world's biggest blowhole. The tide rolls into an underwater cave, and pressure blasts a huge geyser to the surface. Then the water subsides until the next surge.

Oohs and ahhs abound.

No two eruptions are alike. Sometimes the geyser is big and splashy, other times it's more subdued.

The quiet parts are pretty much the same, though, as we wait until the next surge, anxious to see what it'll be like.

This oceanic performance is a good picture of what the writing life should feel like. Outbursts of creativity—sometimes big, sometimes little, producing oohs and ahhs of discovery—followed by a mellow assessment of what you've got.

One mistake authors make, however, is to turn off the geyser of imagination completely during those quiet revision periods. Methodical analysis takes over, and there's very little spontaneous spray.

TAKE ADVANTAGE OF LOW TIDE

You've finished your first draft of a novel or short story. You've written hot. Now you're ready to revise cool with the help of creative spurts.

I advocate that you wait at least two weeks before you do a first read-through of a draft (in hard copy). Then go through it as fast as possible, as if you were a reader, resisting the urge to tweak anything just yet.

Once that's done, plan by jotting some notes to yourself on the biggest issues you saw.

Did the overall story make sense? Is there enough at stake in the plot? Did the characters jump off the page? Are there obvious dull parts?

And so on.

Make a list of those issues, and prioritize them. This is the analytical half of your brain taking charge. Let it. It has been waiting a long time to help you with all that fun you had writing the story.

Now you can plan your revisions accordingly. As you go through the draft, looking to cut and add, be ready to turn on La Bufadora.

INVITE THE FLOW TO RETURN

As Ray Bradbury said, don't rewrite—relive. Your fiction is about creating emotion in the reader, and you can't do that well without feeling it yourself.

If you did your job right when you were writing the first draft, you opened a vein many times. You didn't just write the story—you *felt* it. Then, as you were assessing your first draft, it was necessary to achieve distance from your work, to let your quiet, analytical side take over as you decided what needed to be done. But now, to do the best revision possible, you need to recapture the feeling you had while writing your draft in the first place.

One way to do this is through music. Find several pieces that move you to feelings consistent with your book. Movie soundtracks are an especially fertile option. Compile a playlist of songs that evoke the mood—or, better yet, a medley of the various moods—you hope to convey in your story, and use it as background each time you sit down to self-edit.

For example, if the scene I'm working on is one of great heart and emotion, I have songs from one of my favorite movies, *The Best Years of Our Lives*, at the ready. I've found the haunting strains of the *To Kill a Mockingbird* soundtrack equally effective at these times. But when, as is often the case, I'm working on a suspenseful section, I favor a slew of scores I've compiled from Alfred Hitchcock films and other thrillers.

Music reaches a part of your mind that usually remains inactive when analyzing. So wake it up and put it to work with tunes.

Another way to recapture the feel of your book is to create a visual representation. Some writers I know compile a collage of pictures on a big board using downloaded images or clippings from magazines. One look at this creates a feeling, and the feeling translates to the page.

Experiment with various ways to relive your manuscript. It was alive as you wrote it. Keep it running around as you revise.

CHANNEL THE POWER AS IT BUILDS

In the old railroad days, a stoker would shovel coal into the engine fire to keep it burning hot. There are a number of ways to get fresh heat into your revisions. One of the best is to analyze each scene in your manuscript and determine if it's strong or weak. A strong scene will have the following:

- a single point of view
- a clear objective for the character
- opposition (conflict) to the objective
- a struggle that is felt emotionally by the POV character
- an outcome that forces the reader to read on

A weak scene will usually manifest itself by lacking one or more of these elements.

Once you've made a list of strong and weak scenes (with complete honesty!), you have decisions to make. Start with the weakest scene and cut it—even if you think you can't do without it.

How's that feel? Painful? Don't worry, your book is better off without that scene. Now move on to the next weak scene. Should you cut that, too?

If it's too much for you, and you want to keep it, then stoke the fire: Find the heart of your scene and heat it up.

Every scene should have a heart, the moment that gives it a reason to exist. For example, say you've got a scene in which Dirk walks into his supervisor's office to ask for a raise. The first draft of the scene includes discussion of work, Dirk's satisfaction with his job, and the supervisor's challenges with the division.

Is any of this material dull? Cut it.

Then comes the heart of the scene:

> Dirk cleared his throat. "Sir, the main reason I came in was, well, I really was hoping I could get a raise. You see, my wife is expecting, and there are challenges, as I'm sure you're aware. Plus, I've been here over a year now."
>
> "I understand, Dirk," Roger said. "But I'm afraid I have some distressing news."
>
> "Distressing?"

"You see, the word has come from upstairs that everyone is going to have to increase their productivity by 25 percent. Those that don't will be eased out."

"Oh my," Dirk said. "Well, I guess that's that."

"Sorry, Dirk."

"It's okay."

What can we do to fire this up?

First, look at the moments just before and just after the heart of the scene. How can you ratchet up the emotional intensity? Feel it. Feel it with the character.

Now, how can you increase the conflict in the encounter? Close your eyes and relive the scene in the movie theater of your imagination. What actions can the characters take that push the conflict further?

> Dirk cleared his throat. His palms were sweating and his heart kicked his chest. He was sure Roger could hear it beating, like he was some Salvation Army drummer parading outside the office.
>
> This was ridiculous. He had to ask. They needed the money. With the baby on the way, he just had to get this raise.
>
> "Sir, the main reason I came in is, well, I really was hoping I could get a raise. You see, my wife is expecting and there are--"
>
> "You think I care about your home life?" Roger said. "This is a business. If you can't hack it--"
>
> "I didn't say I couldn't hack it."
>
> "Anything else?"
>
> "I mean, I've been here over a year now."
>
> "Hand me a violin. Look, you might as well know. The word from upstairs is that everyone is going to have to increase productivity by 25 percent. If you don't, you hit the bricks."
>
> Dirk tried to say something, but his mouth was too dry. His tongue lay there like a tree sloth. He started to shake. He looked for something to stab Roger with.

Fire. Keep looking for it and feeling it.

LET THE GEYSER LOOSE

Sometimes you find areas in your book that need expansion. You might require more description or a deeper exploration of an emotion. Maybe you need to stretch the tension in a scene.

Wherever you need to add or spice up material, channel La Bufadora by overwriting. Gush out the words this way:

1. Identify the place where you need to add or rework prose. Mark it with a notation, such as a letter or number in the margin, that will uniquely identify this scene.
2. Open a new document, or take out a fresh page. At the top, put the same notation to show that this file corresponds to the place marked in your manuscript.
3. Now write for five to ten minutes without stopping, concentrating only on creating as much new material as you can. Overwrite.

Let's say I'm writing a hard-boiled detective story with a private investigator as the narrator. He's come to an apartment building in L.A. to question the manager about a woman who's gone missing. Here's the original scene I'd flagged for a rework:

> I knocked on the door. A moment later it opened, and a man filled it. A very large man.
> "Yeah?" he said in a deep, scratchy voice.
> "I'm looking for a woman named Song Li," I said. "She used to live here."
> He gave me a hard look. "Who are you?"

Now, in rewriting this particular section, I've decided I want to focus on the description of the man. So on a clean page, I overwrite for a few minutes without stopping and let my imagination go where it wants to:

> He was a large man, a big man, a blimp-sized guy in a T-shirt that cried for mercy against his massive gut, and shoulders that seemed like roof beams and eyes the exact shape of pizza ovens, or manhole covers or truck tires. He could've doubled for Rhode Island or cast a shadow across the city at sunrise. Lay him on his back and float him, and you could take a party to Catalina on him. I'm talking big, and massive and enormous and all those things.

And so on. The great thing is that intentionally overwriting brings up all manner of surprises, most of which you'll not use. But from the pile you'll pull out a gem that you will want to keep. It might be only one line or word, but that's enough.

In this case, for some reason, I like the Rhode Island reference, and comparing the eyes to pizza ovens (I'm not sure the latter is perfectly logical, but it's fresh, at least to me). So my scene would now begin:

> I knocked on the door. A moment later it opened, and a man filled it. He could have doubled for Rhode Island. His eyes were the size of pizza ovens.

In this way, the geyser approach can lead to revisions that are much stronger than text you might have reworked while editing in your original document, from an analytical frame of mind.

USE THE BEST OF BOTH TIDES

Your main job as a writer is to transport the reader to a fictional world, as in a dream. Enable the suspension of disbelief by creating a story world that is every bit as vivid as the one we all inhabit. In shaping your manuscript into something that accomplishes all this and more, embrace the ebb and flow of a revision process that maximizes both creative surges and quiet analysis. Start with these two methods that use the best of both tides to your manuscript's advantage.

Deepen Details

A crucial part of the revision process involves making sure all your details are as strong as they possibly can be, that no word is underutilized or wasted.

Take, for instance, this paragraph of vanilla backstory:

> Some time after his father's death, Bobby fell in love with a bike in a store window. He hinted to his mother about the bike in every way he knew, and finally pointed it out to her one night when they were walking home from the movies.

That's fine as far as it goes. It's not going to hurt anybody. But look how much more alive and real it sounds when Stephen King does it in *Hearts in Atlantis*:

> Eight years after his father's death, Bobby fell violently in love with the 26-inch Schwinn in the window of the Harwich Western Auto. He hinted to his mother about the Schwinn in every way he knew, and finally pointed it out to her one night when they were walking home from the movies (the show had been *The Dark at the Top of the Stairs*, which Bobby didn't much understand but liked anyway, especially the part where Dorothy McGuire flopped back in a chair and showed off her long legs).

Note the specificity about the timing of his father's death, the kind of bike, the name of the store. And then King not only mentions the name of the movie but also a particular scene that got to Bobby and thus characterizes him a bit, too.

It's this feeling of richness that King adds to the prose that makes his fiction seem more substantial than many other works in the same genre.

To achieve this, you can use a combination of the overwriting exercise from the previous section, and your analytical brain via research. For example, if you're writing about a car from 1988, do some research on popular makes and models, get details from websites or experts, and then layer in those details in a natural way.

And always be on the lookout for another kind of detail—the telling kind.

Find the Telling Detail

A telling detail is a single descriptive element—a gesture, an image, an action— that contains a universe of meaning. Such details can illuminate, instantly, a character, setting, or theme.

In Thomas Harris's *The Silence of the Lambs*, FBI trainee Clarice Starling has been dispatched by the head of the behavioral unit, Jack Crawford, to interview the notorious killer Hannibal Lecter.

Lecter, in his cell, asks to see her credentials. The orderly slips in Starling's laminated ID card. Lecter looks it over, then:

> "A trainee? It says 'trainee.' Jack Crawford sent a *trainee* to interview me?" He tapped the card against his small white teeth and breathed in its smell.

The tapping of the teeth is a telling detail, relating of course to their use in eating people such as census takers. Also, the smallness of the teeth gives off a feral vibe, adding to the menace.

But it's the smelling of the card that really hits home. It tells of Lecter's longing for a previous life, on the outside. It is a whiff of freedom.

Not only that, it signals his strange power to get to know people intimately without really knowing them at all. It's creepy, touching, and dangerous all at once.

In Raymond Carver's story "Will You Please Be Quiet, Please?" a husband and wife are having an intense conversation in the kitchen. The wife is reluctantly going over details of what happened at a party years ago, when another man took her for a ride in his car and kissed her. Observe the husband's reaction as he listens:

> He moved all his attention into one of the tiny black coaches in the tablecloth. Four tiny white prancing horses pulled each one of the black coaches and the figure driving the horses had his arms up and wore a tall hat, and suitcases

were strapped down atop the coach, and what looked like a kerosene lamp hung from the side, and if he were listening at all it was from inside the black coach.

What is going on in the husband is revealed completely in the images and in how he relates to them. There is no need for Carver to *tell* us how the husband feels.

That's the power of telling details.

How do you find them? Follow these four steps:

1. Identify a highly charged moment in your book.
2. Make a list of possible actions, gestures, or setting descriptions that might further reflect upon the scene to make it even stronger.
3. Let the geyser loose, and list at least twenty to twenty-five possibilities, as fast as you can. Remember: The best way to get good ideas is to come up with lots of options and then choose the ones you want to use.
4. Write a long paragraph incorporating the best details from your list, and then edit the text until it's lean and potent. The telling detail works best when it is subtle and does all the work by itself.

And that's how you get the best of both worlds of your brain. Use the powerful ebb and flow of La Bufadora as you revise, and your fiction may well make a splash.

34

YOUR REVISION CHECKLIST

Removing the Guesswork from the Process

Josip Novakovich

In the revision stage, you strive to make your writing coherent, clear, and effective. Out of chaos, a fully developed story gradually emerges. Clumsy sentences become graceful; clichés become wit; muddled action becomes drama. If you wonder how to sound original, the answer is revise and revise. Even if you think your stories don't work, you can make them work—if you revise well.

As you revise, don't fear changing your text radically in search of its best possible shape. And certainly don't hesitate to get rid of whatever does not work. On the other hand, don't rush to throw things away. Give yourself time, and if in a week you still think that something you've written doesn't work and can't be made useful, get rid of it. Sometimes, what appears weak one day may appear fine the next.

So that you don't have to fumble in the garbage among banana peels and cockroaches (though cockroaches come from a noble literary lineage), save an early draft. If you cut too much, you can restore. That knowledge should help you freely look at your text. See it again. Look at what fits and what doesn't. If something is pretty but does not connect to the rest of the text, cut it.

Remember that all parts of your story must work before it can fly, so make sure that each part is the best it can be. This checklist will guide you through the process.

PLOT

- Does enough happen in your story? Something must. The event doesn't need to be big, but it must be dramatic and significant.

- Is the story structured around a conflict? Can you state the conflict in a sentence or two? What is the struggle about? This is your theme. The theme should not be separate from the conflict.
- Do you introduce the conflict soon enough—preferably as a crisis in the first few pages? Do you sustain the conflict long enough, through most of your story?
- Is the conflict carried to its logical conclusion? Does the ending make sense in light of the beginning?
- Can you identify the key event and its climax? This should be the turning point. You've reached the peak, and now things will inevitably slide, faster and faster, to a conclusion. Earlier, there were options, but now the protagonist's choice has become clear.
- Does your story give enough information on the causes of the main event? Although the advice remains "show; don't tell," whenever you *can't* show readers enough, *tell* them, summarize, fill them in. After all, you're the storyteller. Whatever happens in the story must make sense.
- Do you present readers with the right sequence of events (scenes and summaries) so that the story has the cogency of a good argument?
- Do you avoid a stock plot? Try to steer clear of plots too often encountered in commercial novels—for example, the detective investigating a murder is the murderer.
- Is your plot easy to follow? Even if it's a mystery, what happens during the investigation should be easy to follow.

CHARACTER

- Who are the protagonists? Antagonists? In general, you should have at least two characters engaged in some kind of action or tension. One character reminiscing and laughing out loud at his thoughts or smiling at ashtrays doesn't offer enough dialectical potential for a story.
- Are the main characters well developed (round)? If not, give them sufficient complexity—desires, obstacles, weaknesses, strengths.
- Are there flat characters? Perhaps they don't need to be round, but on the other hand, don't let them become stereotypes.
- Can you see the basic motivations—desires and fears—of the main characters?
- Do the characters encounter obstacles? Are the obstacles sufficiently tough?
- Does your main character change or come to some crucial insight over the course of the story?

SETTING

- Is the setting appropriate (and authentic) for your story? If your story's set in Austin, Texas, make sure there's no subway system. If it's Venus, make sure there are no people living in forests.
- Does your setting work in synergy with characters and plot? The setting should deepen your characterization and ground your plot. Realistically drawn landscapes and cityscapes increase believability, even in fantasy stories.
- Have you given us the setting gradually, together with the characters and the action, or have you dumped it all in a long chunk in the beginning or middle?
- Have you used the setting for special effects (foreshadowing, mood expression, beautiful images, change of pace)?

POV

- From whose POV is the story told? Would it be better from another character's POV?
- Is the POV consistent? If it shifts, is there a good reason for it to do so?
- Does your POV shift midsentence? Midparagraph? Even in the omniscient POV, you might do better to sort out POVs by paragraphs.
- In the omniscient POV, do you enter too many of your characters' heads? Generally, limit yourself to the main ones. The minor ones can remain external.
- Do you use interior monologues to your advantage? If there's a crisis point in which your POV character is alone, waiting, you might deliver an interior monologue to heighten suspense and clarify motives.
- Do you use stream of consciousness where you can? If there's a crisis point in which your POV character is injured or disoriented, you might switch to stream of consciousness to reflect the crisis and to change the narrative pace.
- Whom does the narrator of your story address? Is there an ostensible audience, such as "Gentle Reader," "Dear President," "Mimi"? Is the audience used consistently?
- As the author, whom are you addressing? An imaginary person, or friend, or nobody? Who do you think will read your story? Children, adults, punks, U.S. Marines, Connecticut tax evaders?
- Are there authorial intrusions? Are they warranted? In the omniscient POV, they're fair game; in other POVs, they may be distracting.

The Complete Handbook of Novel Writing

VOICE, ATTITUDE, AND HUMOR

- What voices are heard in your story? Naturally, each character should have a distinct voice, different from the author's in most cases, unless the narrative is a piece of overt autobiography. (In the narrative part, is the voice clear enough?)
- Do you joke at inappropriate moments—for example, at the peak of a tragic action? Are your jokes in poor taste? Some characters may joke under stress; it's all right to reproduce that, but make sure the authorial humor does not undermine the tension.
- Do you strain too hard for sentimental effects? Any *rivers of tears*? Above all, especially in the third-person POV narrative, don't tell that what happened was *devastatingly sad*, unless you're parodying sentimental writing.

TIMING

- Does your story start at the right moment? Does it start too early, before the main action—or too late? Identify your first crisis moment, and open with it. A strong swimmer jumps far into the pool rather than swim from the very edge of it; the better you write, the further into the story you'll be able to jump.
- Does your story end at the right moment? Find the point when things have begun to fall into place, and cut the action; ending here implies that they will continue to do so.
- Is the chronology—and the grammar that indicates it—clear? If you frequently backtrack in time, try using the present tense for your *now* action so you can use the simple past tense, rather than past perfect, for your *then* action.

  - Check your story's tenses. Within a chapter, unless there is a flashback or a fast-forward, the tense should remain the same and shouldn't switch within a sentence.
  - Keep the sequence of motions chronological, from first to last. A sentence should not ordinarily read like this: "After he lies on a sofa, upon walking in the room, he breathes out his anxiety." Readers strain to straighten out the sequence of actions here. The same holds true of paragraphs. Keep going forward, except when there are memories or flashbacks. But

even then, once you switch into the past to explain what had happened, lay it out as chronologically as possible.

- If you've used flashbacks or memories, did you need to? Could you tell the story from the first event to the last without backtracking and without losing the cogency of your story as an argument? This is a difficult choice. Sometimes you must go with the shape of the argument rather than with the linearity of time. It's best if you can accomplish both.
- Has the story been paced well? Don't bore the reader, but don't run out of plot too fast, either. Make sure that you've done enough showing to give body to any telling you may have done.

DIALOGUE AND SCENE

- Is the dialogue natural? Do your characters sound like real people rather than technical books?
- Do your characters sound different from the general narrative and from each other? Go through the dialogue, line by line, and give signature expressions to a character, making sure that the other characters don't use the same ones, except when being sarcastic to each other.
- Is your dialogue complex enough? Combine small scenes into big ones so that they portray characters, advance the plot, and raise tension.
- Do you have enough dialogue in proportion to the narrative? There's no set rule, but at least some parts of your story should be written in dialogue, unless you're writing a "man against nature" tale or some other type of story in which dialogue might not appear. And despite the current trend in favor of dialogue, your fiction should include description, summary, and other sorts of narrative—for the change of pace, transitions, and quick information.
- Is the story told mostly as a nonscenic narrative? If so, your story will sound like an essay. Decide where the action is, and stage it.
- Are the scenes compounded ("Mondays she would pray") or are they specific ("One Monday she prayed")? Compounded scenes work well to introduce the main event, but the main event must take place as a fully developed, specific scene. Your story or novel should contain a larger proportion of specific scenes than of compounded scenes and background exposition.
- Are the right scenes dramatized and the right ones summarized? Usually, your key event should be fully dramatized (though you should skip greetings

The Complete Handbook of Novel Writing

and other tedious exchanges, unless they can show something important). Some supporting scenes can be summarized, others dramatized. Transitions between various events are usually summarized.

- Do you have too many similar scenes? Are there ten quarrels? Maybe two will do; make each one unique. If you write three similar scenes to show a pattern, distill them to one, and tell us that the dramatic action is part of a pattern.
- Are your dramatic scenes long enough? If not, expand them.
- Are the dramatic scenes suspenseful enough? Though they must be fairly long, they also must be quickly paced. Achieving this balance can be difficult. Raise the tension of the conflict, and point toward the resolution, which should make sense of it all.

DESCRIPTION AND DICTION

- Do you *show* enough? The most important story moments must be shown in scenes.
- But do you also *tell* enough? You need not show absolutely everything. Sometimes it's all right to tell, for the sake of pacing the narrative. Some crucial points can be both told and shown; if you tell them, show them also.
- Do you describe characters in a fresh way? No chiseled features, sky-blue eyes, pearly white teeth.
- Do you genuinely describe settings? No ominous train stations, squalid quarters, posh offices.
- Do you have enough dynamic descriptions incorporated into the action?
- Are there enough metaphors? Too many? Do they work? Do they create a parallel text? Is the parallel text something you want? For example, if all of your metaphors concern various beasts devouring each other, are you sure you want this Hobbesian dimension in your story—and is this killing (and feeding) frenzy what your story is about? If you have a tame romance with such metaphors, you have a choice: Either get rid of bestial metaphors and resort to botany (although flowers have been overused in this context), or listen to your metaphors. They may suggest a major plot change. The romance might turn into a struggle and become all the more interesting. In other words, metaphors may bring out the full potential of a story. If you listen to them, your story might grow into a larger one.
- Are the descriptions effective? Do they engage readers' senses? Or are some senses atrophied? Why? In most cases, if your sentences do not make readers see (or hear, touch, smell, or taste), cross them out. Leave what you can perceive.

When you've successfully answered all of the questions in this checklist and have made all the necessary revision changes, you're still not quite finished: You've got to polish. As James Baldwin put it, "Most of the rewrite is cleaning." Polishing can turn out to be a lot of work. You want each sentence to be sharp, and each word to count.

Jerzy Kosinski said, "Every word is there for a reason, and if not, I cross it out. I rarely allow myself to use English in an unchecked, spontaneous way. I always have a sense of trembling—but so does a compass, after all. I cut adjectives, adverbs, and every word which is there just to make an effect."

Below is a mechanical checklist to hone your own prose.

THE POLISH

- Check your spelling.
- Keep your misspellings to a minimum. Do you misspell for any kind of effect—stuttering, dialect, shouting? You can indicate outside the dialogue that something is said with a Southern drawl—or, better, you can rely on syntax and word choice to give flavor to your voice.
- Check your paragraphs. Are they fully developed? Journalistic practices aside, your paragraphs should contain more than one sentence, except in dialogue or when you're conferring special emphasis.
- Punctuate conventionally. Write in complete sentences, not comma splices or sentence fragments, except now and then for special effect. Unless you're experimenting, use conventional grammar. The less attention your use of punctuation attracts to itself, the more attention will remain on your story.
- Make sure your sentences are not monotonous. Vary sentence length and structure. Alternating simple and complex sentences establishes a pleasing rhythm and avoids choppiness and monotony.
- Don't let each sentence travel. In long sentences, it's easy to lose track of the subject and the object. Be sure that each pronoun has a clear antecedent.
- Make sure you are *clear*. Sometimes you must weed out the passive voice and abstract vocabulary to achieve clarity.
- Is the language weak? Too many adjectives and adverbs? Passives? Clichés? On the other hand, can you find strikingly fresh usages, *le mot juste*?
- Make sure your sentences are direct. Scrutinize your use of prepositional phrases—especially *of* and *in* constructions. "The paint on the table in the kitchen" becomes "the kitchen table's paint" to speed up the prose.

- Get rid of repetitions. Some repetitions are not immediately visible; they are redundant and superfluous expressions, such as "She came to a complete stop." *Complete* is superfluous. If the stop is incomplete, it's not a stop. If in a ten-line paragraph you use *love* or *response* (or any other words, other than articles and helping verbs) more than three times, eliminate them, unless they're essential. Find synonyms. For *response*, perhaps *reaction* could do.
- Delete all unnecessary modifiers in dialogue tags. For example: "'Will you please please go home?' he said beseechingly." *Beseechingly* wastes time; it's clear from the sentence that a plea is going on. "He beseeched" might be an improvement, but since "he said" does not commit redundancy, you should prefer it.
- Omit all unnecessary indications of who's speaking. On the other hand, is it always clear who is speaking? Whenever in doubt, indicate the speaker and use *said*.

Josip Novakovich is the author of a novel, five story collections, and two collections of narrative essays, and has been anthologized in *Best American Poetry, Pushcart Prize,* and *O. Henry Prize Stories.* He currently teaches at Concordia University in Montreal. He has received the Whiting Writer's Award, Guggenheim Fellowship, and two National Endowment for the Arts Fellowships, and was a finalist for the Man Booker International Prize in 2013.

35

THE GREAT REVISION PYRAMID

How to Tackle Revisions Layer by Layer

Gabriela Pereira

Nonwriters believe revision is something you do in an afternoon, manuscript and red pen in hand. They picture this as a cosmetic process, choosing one word over another, or transplanting a paragraph to a different page. They think once that first draft is written, the book is practically finished.

They're wrong.

Writers know better. They know that a jumbled draft can be even more terrifying than a blank page. They know that there is a lot more to revision than a few red marks on the manuscript. And they know that the first draft is simply the raw material that they must shape, carve, and polish into a masterful story.

Revision is work. It's not nearly as much fun as writing with abandon, with all the adrenaline that comes from drafting a story for the first time. Revision requires perseverance. It's no wonder that so many writers get stuck in a dangerous cycle of producing one first draft after another, but never following through to the finish line.

No writer wants to send out mediocre work. We all want to put our best foot forward, but the process of cleaning up a manuscript can get confusing. It's hard to see a middle ground between marking up your book line by line and doing a complete rewrite. It's also hard to know what to fix in revision, and even harder to know when that process is finished.

Fear not. There is a solution. It's called Layered Revision.

Layered Revision is inspired by psychologist Abraham Maslow's hierarchy of needs. Maslow theorized that humans pursued the higher needs (e.g., satisfaction) only after the more basic ones (e.g., survival) were met. This concept translates poignantly to revision. You need to address your book's most fundamental needs first, before turning your attention to less crucial aspects of the revision process.

Many writers try to juggle everything at once when they revise. They go through the manuscript looking at all the different aspects of their story side by side. They work to improve character development and story structure, all the while being distracted by weaknesses in their setting, dialogue, and theme. This process can become so overwhelming that it's not uncommon to give up, in spite of all the countless hours that have already been expended in crafting that rough (by definition) draft.

With Layered Revision, on the other hand, you make several passes through your manuscript, but each time you focus on only one key element. You might zero in on your protagonist in one pass, your villain in the next, then plot or worldbuilding in a later round. This layered approach means that each individual pass goes much faster than if you were to try to revise everything at once. The work feels more doable, one step at a time. And it's more effective, too, because you are more likely to spot problems—and fix them—when your attention is focused systematically.

Just as Maslow's hierarchy places basic needs at the base of his pyramid and higher-order needs up top, you want to address the fundamental elements of a story first, because changes to these areas will have a broader impact on your manuscript. You also want to resist the urge to make small, superficial changes early on; since you might end up deleting entire chapters later, that work could go to waste. Start at the bottom of the revision pyramid and work your way up.

The beauty of Layered Revision is that not only will you avoid unnecessarily reworking pages that will end up on the cutting room floor, but your editing process will go faster with each subsequent layer. As you strengthen your story at each level of the pyramid, you will also solve problems further up because you have addressed the root cause behind those problems. Finally, with each pass through your manuscript, you will feel more confident and motivated, making you less likely to give up and more likely to finish your revisions—all the way to a polished final draft.

Let's look at the pyramid layer by layer.

LAYER 5:
COSMETICS
GRAMMAR,
PUNCTUATION,
SPELLING, AND
WORD CHOICE

LAYER 4:
THE SCENES
WORLDBUILDING, DESCRIPTION,
DIALOGUE, AND THEME

LAYER 3:
THE STORY
PLOT AND STRUCTURE

LAYER 2:
THE CHARACTERS
PROTAGONIST AND SUPPORTING CAST

LAYER 1:
THE NARRATION
VOICE AND POINT OF VIEW

LAYER 1: THE NARRATION

Narration—the way you choose to tell your story—includes the point of view of your story, as well as the voice of your narrator. This is one of the most important decisions a writer makes in drafting a story, and often you make it without even realizing it. In most cases, the process of writing draft zero forces you to home in on your voice and POV as you test out different approaches and make adjustments as you write.

Sometimes, though, that almost inevitable experimentation with finding your narrator's voice can leave your first draft's narration or POV feeling scattered and unfocused.

The first step of any revision, of course, is to reread your work and make some overall notes on what you do and don't think is working in the story as it stands. Once you have decided which type of narration you want, you will likely need to "reboot" the scenes that depart from that style or POV so that everything is consistent. Read over each scene in question, and then set the original aside and rewrite it from memory in the newly defined voice or POV. When you write a scene from memory, your brain holds on to the parts that work but lets go of the rest. This allows you to give that scene a fresh voice—as opposed to tweaking or tinkering with the writing until you break it.

Altering voice and POV might seem minor compared to revisiting characters or changing plot points. Don't be fooled. Narration is, in fact, the most important component of your story, because it affects *how the reader experiences it*. In reworking the narration, you are refocusing the reader's lens for viewing your story, and that can have a domino effect on all other elements of your book.

LAYER 2: THE CHARACTERS

The next layer in this revision process is character—the heart and soul of your story. Your characters give your readers someone to root for (or against), and they give your story meaning. Without characters, a book is nothing more than a series of random events. Characters make us care about the events of your story; they make those events matter.

By now you should know your protagonist almost as well as you know yourself. In crafting the first draft, you likely answered the three central questions that drive main characters: *What does this character want, and to what lengths will he go to get it? What obstacles stand in the way, and what is at stake if the protagonist fails? How will the protagonist change in the pursuit of this desire?* In the course of putting that journey onto the page, you've spent hundreds of pages with this person. You've watched him struggle, and you've watched him overcome against all odds. You know his strengths and, yes, his flaws, too. Still, no matter how well you think you know your protagonist, sometimes when you finally look over your work and see him anew on the page, suddenly he feels ... flat. Unmotivated, even, though you know the motivations are there. When this happens, I recommend using what I call the "sandbox" technique.

Take your character out of the story and put her in a different situation. If your story takes place in her hometown, send her on a road trip. If the story takes place during the school year, transport her to a summer's day. The key is to remove your character from her comfort zone or the "normal" world of your story, to experiment and write a few scenes that take place in a different context.

Open a blank document or grab a clean page; label it "sandbox." Here, you can play and make a mess. The reason for this approach is twofold: First, you're more likely to discover something new about your protagonist by seeing him in an unfamiliar environment. Second—and more important—when you experiment with your character in sandbox mode, whatever you do stays in the sandbox (unless and until, of course, you decide you want to take it out and apply it to your story). When you test things out in the sandbox, you eliminate the risk of accidentally breaking anything in your manuscript. This technique gives you the freedom to see how far you can take your character, but also offers a safety net. My experience has been that you're more likely to have breakthroughs in the sandbox than when playing neatly within the confines of your story. And when you return to your completed draft with those breakthroughs in hand, suddenly ways to bring your character more vividly to life will become clear.

Of course, revision isn't confined to your protagonist. One of the big challenges with supporting characters is to portray enough depth that they resonate with readers, but not so much that they steal the show. Naturally, we want our supporting cast to feel fleshed out instead of one-dimensional. All characters, if we have developed them well, believe they are the heroes of their own lives. As you revise, however, remember that the primary function of each supporting character is to *support* the development of the protagonist.

Ask yourself what necessary role each character plays in the story. If two or more serve the same function, consider eliminating one or merging them together. Then watch out for characters who behave or sound the same. You don't want your supporting players to blur together in the reader's mind.

If, in spite of your best efforts, you find that your characters still sound similar on the page, I recommend a process called "method writing." Like method acting—where an actor steps into a character's skin and "becomes" that character—you need to get inside the mind of the character you want to understand. Imagine you *are* that character. Feel what he feels, see what he sees, think what he thinks. Write a few paragraphs or pages from that character's POV. Once you have truly stepped into that character's mind-set, the rest will fall into place.

LAYER 3: THE STORY

The next level is the story. By this point you should have a firm grasp on who your characters are and what motivates them, and these insights will drive the events of the story forward.

When it comes to plot, all you have to remember is $3 + 2 = 1$. No, we are not bending the rules of mathematics. In traditional story structure—from picture books to grand epics—you have three acts and two crucial decisions made by the protagonist. These decisions fall at the end of Act One and Act Two, respectively. Together, the acts and decisions yield a universal story that has been used ever since humans began telling stories in the first place.

One of the biggest mistakes writers make in revision is tackling plot and story structure too early in the process. They go through their mental list of plot elements, filling them in like they're painting by numbers. Inciting incident? Check. Point of no return? Check. Denouement? Check.

The danger with this approach is that it forgets that *characters* are the driving force in your story. When you fixate on a rigid plot structure, you leave character by the wayside. But your story exists *because* of decisions your character makes.

Whenever I see a writer struggling to plug up holes in the plot, that's usually a telltale sign that something is amiss on a more fundamental level, usually with the characters. The best plots are often the simplest ones, so if you find yourself overcomplicating things to make the story work, that may be a sign that you need to step back to the character layer and get a better handle on who your players are and what motivates them.

If your characters are sound and the plot still isn't working, try this: Regardless of whether or not you drew up an outline before you wrote your first draft, extract an outline now from the manuscript you have written. Do it scene by scene; for each one list which characters are present, what happens, and why that scene is important. The latter is critical, because if you can't think of a good reason for including a particular scene in your story, it may be redundant or extraneous. Breaking down your story in this way can help you see more clearly where you still need to revise to give the plot cohesiveness and strength, with a logical flow and high notes that hit in all the right places.

LAYER 4: THE SCENES

Now it's time to look even more closely at those scenes, one at a time, and zero in on elements such as worldbuilding, description, dialogue, and theme.

First, examine the world of your story. Does it feel real, or do you throw a lot of information at the reader but fail to show the world in action? Remember also that depending on the POV you have chosen, your narrator's state of mind may affect your description of that world. If a character is terrified and fearing for her life, she will see the world around her with a much darker perspective than if she's giddy with puppy love. This is another reason why understanding your voice, POV, and characters early in the revision process can help you with description and worldbuilding later on.

Next, it's time to look at the dialogue driving your scenes. There are two keys to strong dialogue: understanding your characters, and recognizing that written dialogue is not real-life dialogue. By this stage of the revision, you should instinctively know how each character speaks. In any scenes where those conversations aren't coming easily, return to the "method writing" technique from Layer Two. If your dialogue still doesn't ring true, often you need to tighten what's being said. Remember that in reality people hem and haw, talk in circles, and take forever to get to the point—but none of that works on the page. Trim your dialogue to the barest minimum that still captures the essence of each scene.

That minimalist approach will serve you well with other elements at this layer, too. When it comes to making your scenes sing, keep your reader on a need-to-know basis. Give the least amount of information necessary to understand what's happening. We've all had the old adage "show; don't tell" hammered into our brains, and so often our response is to overload our scenes with useless details. Instead, show just enough to keep your reader "in the know," and elsewhere, use exposition—the "tell" part of the equation—to cut to the point. A well-crafted scene should be like a house of cards: If you remove one piece, the whole thing comes crashing down.

Finally, when it comes to theme, by this point you likely have a good idea of what your theme is and how it fits into your story. Now it's simply a question of making sure that every scene you've written relates to that overall theme. You don't have to wallop your reader over the head with it, but if you find a scene that has no relation to your theme whatsoever, that's a hint that you might have a bit more work to do.

When this layer is complete, and only then, is it time to tackle Layer Five: proofreading and editing at line level. We've reached the top of the pyramid.

ACCIDENT-FREE FINAL DRAFTS

Whether you write something that comes out beautifully or make a mess of your manuscript, the last thing you want is to have done it by accident. After all, you don't want to leave your story in shambles if there's still room to make it better, and if you wrote something that works well, you want to understand how you did it so you can do it again in the future.

The purpose of Layered Revision isn't to follow a set of rules or check items off a list. Your goal is to write the best book possible. In the end, this is *your* book, and you get to decide what to eliminate and what to keep. These should be active choices, not decisions by default. Every character, every scene, every word in your story should be there because you intended it. Know the rules so when you break them, you do it on purpose and do it with panache.

Gabriela Pereira is a writer, teacher, and self-proclaimed word nerd who wants to challenge the status quo of higher education. As the founder and instigator of DIY MFA, her mission is to empower writers to take an entrepreneurial approach to their education and professional growth. Gabriela earned her MFA in creative writing from The New School and teaches at national conferences, at local workshops, and online. She is the author of *DIY MFA: Write with Focus, Read with Purpose, Build Your Community*, and is also the host of *DIY MFA Radio*, a popular podcast where she interviews best-selling authors and offers short audio master classes. To join the word nerd community, go to DIYMFA.com/join.

Part Three

EXPLORING
NOVEL GENRES

36

LITERARY LUST VERSUS COMMERCIAL CASH

Earning Respect *and* an Income

Jodi Picoult

I remember the moment I crossed over to the Dark Side.

It was after I'd published my second book at a big New York publisher that had a reputation for publishing classics or works that would one day *become* classics. As with most literary contracts, they had the right of first refusal on my next novel.

"Well," they said after they read it, "we'll publish it if no one else wants to."

Not exactly a ringing endorsement.

My agent took the manuscript to a publishing house that, philosophically, was diametrically opposed to my current one. It was known for its domination of *The New York Times* bestseller list, with so many brand-name authors under its roof that I was convinced my agent's exercise was futile.

The editors offered me a two-book deal. They wanted to pay me ten times what I'd made before. There was only one catch: Could I cut out some of that Native American stuff in the novel and beef up the Hollywood scenes?

I was too excited that a publishing company wanted the kind of stories I wrote to realize that, well, they actually *didn't*. They wanted to groom me to join their highly profitable stable of writers, turning out bestsellers and beach reads. All I had to do was agree that, from that moment on, I was going to be a commercial writer.

The difference between a commercial writer and a literary writer is, at first sight, painfully clear. Literary writers get clout. They get reviews in *The New York Times*. They win National Book Awards. Their stories haunt you, change the way you think about the world, are destined to be part of college curricula. These authors teach at prestigious universities. When they do readings, it's at a place like Carnegie Hall. Their print runs are in the tens of thousands, and they don't make gobs of money, but that doesn't matter, because a literary writer is "above" mundane things like that.

By contrast, a commercial writer's books *sell*. They're given marketing and advertising budgets. They don't get reviewed in *The New York Times* but have big, splashy full-page ads inside, and they grace the peaks of its bestseller list. Commercial books are the ones you trip over when you walk into a bookstore, stacked in enormous displays. They're the stories you can't put down at night and can't remember in detail after you've read them. Their print runs are in the hundreds of thousands; their advances are dissected in "Publishers Lunch" reports.

As a beginning writer, I'd labored under the misconception that I could surely be both literary and commercial at the same time. Why couldn't I write books that changed the world … and still make enough money to pay my mortgage? Did those two criteria have to be mutually exclusive?

Yes, but not for the reasons you'd think. At some point in your career, you'll be forced to choose either the commercial path or the literary one. You can start by straddling the two, but eventually, as they veer apart, you're going to tumble onto one side or another. And—here's the big stunner—what makes a writer literary or commercial has far less to do with her writing than it does with marketing. We live in a publishing world that's made up of bottom lines, which means every book must have a target audience. Whereas literary fiction is made up of masters with oeuvres, commercial fiction is comprised of genres. It makes sense for a publisher to pitch a writer as the new James Patterson—it tells bookstore owners that mystery lovers will buy the book. The same goes for romance novels, family dramas, and horror. When you label a commercial writer by her genre, you've already sold her.

Interestingly, the distinctions are arbitrary. For years, half of my books were shelved in the mystery section; the other half were shelved in literature. There was no salient plot difference between the books in either category; they'd just been pitched to two different corporate buyers by my publisher. Although many people compare my writing to Anita Shreve's, she's considered literary by the chain stores, whereas I'm commercial, because, again, we're pitched to two different buyers. My mentor from the creative writing program at Princeton University, Mary Morris, writes books that I can't put down and is (along with Sue

Miller, Anne Tyler, and Alice Hoffman) one of the finest detailers of human relationships, but because she's a literary writer she isn't as well known as they are.

Or, in other words, it's not that you won't find literary writers enjoyable. It's just that you won't *find* them, period. Part of the marketing strategy for commercial fiction involves co-op advertising at chains and box stores—namely, a contract between the store and the publisher to pay for the spot where a book is placed (much like at a supermarket when Cheerios pays for the end-of-aisle display for a week). Commercial fiction is far more likely to be in the front of a store than literary fiction, which will be tucked into the side shelves—and therefore is less likely to be an impulse purchase.

All writers wish for commercial success. But at what price? If you sell your soul to the devil of profitability, you have to be able to look in the mirror every day and say, without flinching, that you're a commercial fiction writer. You have to be aware that your books may not have the lasting power of a literary novelist's. Naturally, no one plans to be a hack when they set out to write the Great American Novel; yet digestible reads are the ones that sell best. If you ask me, the trick is to be a commercial writer—but don't sell out. Write for a wide audience, but don't compromise what you write.

I'm living proof that you can have your literary cake and eat it commercially, too. Although I get letters all the time from fans who say things like, "I read only mystery/romance/courtroom drama, and you're my favorite mystery/romance/courtroom drama writer!" I really am none of those things—and all of them. My books are a combination of commercial genres, and I have no inclination or intention to narrow it down.

Frankly, I don't care what genre a reader thinks my book is, as long as it gets him to pick it up. Does this make my books a harder sell for my poor beleaguered publisher? You bet. It may be the reason it took me twelve years to be an overnight commercial success. But it also has allowed me to defy the logic of the literary/commercial split: My genre has become the very lack of one.

Because readers have become accustomed to me not writing the same book twice, my publisher expects me to do something new every time, which gives me the freedom to try new things and to use fiction to explore moral and social conundrums—a trait more commonly associated with the literary writer. And, in one of the greatest ironies of my career, I've heard of new commercial novelists being pitched as the next Jodi Picoult.

I admit that when I dove headfirst into the sea of commercial fiction, I made mistakes. When that publisher asked me to "pump up the Hollywood," I did. In retrospect, I wish I hadn't. I was too naïve to stick up for my writing; to understand that a commercial novel could still be resonant and relevant; that I didn't have to dumb it down to the masses. See, here's what the publishers *won't* tell you: You don't have to write to the lowest common denominator if you're a commercial author. You can up the ante; your readers will rise to the occasion.

When you reach that junction—and you have to pick the literary high road or the crowded commercial one—remember that you're standing in front of a mirage. Let the business folks at the publishing company slap a label on you, but write what you want and need to write. The label can't dictate what's between the covers; that's up to you.

And for those compatriots who choose to join me on the commercial side of fiction, take heart in our forbearers: William Shakespeare was a commercial hack who cranked out his plays on deadline. Charles Dickens was paid by the word and was wildly popular with the masses. By the same token, Ian McEwan and Joan Didion and Philip Roth have all enjoyed crossover success as huge literary bestsellers. Maybe that means what's commercial today might be literary tomorrow, or vice versa. Or maybe—just maybe—it means that when you're talking about good writing, there simply are no divisions.

Jodi Picoult is the *New York Times* best-selling author of twenty-four novels, including *My Sister's Keeper, Nineteen Minutes, Between the Lines, The Storyteller,* and, most recently, *Small Great Things.*

37

UNDERSTANDING THE ELEMENTS OF LITERARY FICTION

How to Incorporate Style, Symbolism, and Characterization

Jack Smith

For a fictional work to be classified as "literary," it must have the capacity to resonate with readers on several different levels. To put it another way, it must be layered and multifaceted in meaning: There is much more at hand than the story you're "seeing" and following on the page—it contains levels that go fathoms beyond plot and characterization.

So, how do you pull that off? Well, it's not just about artful language, as many think—but that's a great place to start.

STYLE AND RESTRAINT

While prose style alone doesn't definitively separate literary fiction from other forms of writing, it is true that literary fiction has an element of stylistic restraint that at least *some* other fiction does not possess. Instead of the occasional *bathos*, or overly sentimental prose, the reader discovers *pathos*—emotion with an intellectual component. Instead of over-the-top writing, the reader finds finely controlled language.

When it comes to the literary genre, remember these characteristic traits:

THE LANGUAGE IN LITERARY FICTION IS NOT SENTIMENTAL. Consider this passage:

> Her grandmother was a woman of great strength and inner beauty, so full of life, so willing to give her all, that it just made your heart ache to think she was now gone.

Let's assume the sentimentality in this passage is authorial exuberance rather than an attempt to capture the nature of the narrator's character. To achieve a more literary style, you would tone down such a passage, strip it of its excess, avoid *overtelling*, and let your prose breathe on its own and speak for itself in a more formal style:

> Her grandmother was a woman of great strength and inner beauty. She had, it seemed, a natural alacrity for living, a ready openness to experience and to personal accomplishment—undoubtedly, she would be missed.

The phrases "natural alacrity for living," "ready openness to experience," and "undoubtedly, she would be missed" lend a more reserved tone to this passage while maintaining the sentiment the author wanted to convey. It's not that emotion isn't important in literary fiction—certainly readers want to connect with characters on an emotional level. But you don't need sentimental prose to convey sentiment. In literary fiction, less is typically more.

DESCRIPTIVE LITERARY LANGUAGE DOESN'T HAVE TO BE FLORID. Rather, it escapes purple prose with the use of apt similes, metaphors, and analogies for states of being, actions, thoughts, and emotions. Consider this simile:

> He just loved life! Life to him was like a NASA space launch into brave, new, wonderful worlds.

Would you agree that it seems overblown to describe one's life prospects as a launchpad to the great wonders of celestial achievement? That line might work as satire or burlesque of innocence, grandiose imagining or gross naïveté, but otherwise, a reader would consider this simply florid writing on the part of a gushy writer.

For contrast, note the originality of this description from Elizabeth Strout's Pulitzer Prize–winning literary novel-in-stories, *Olive Kitteridge*:

> But at this stage of the game, she is not about to abandon the comfort of food, and that means right now she probably looks like a fat, dozing seal wrapped in some kind of gauze bandage.

Olive Kitteridge is a heavyset woman; she willingly acknowledges it. Given her character, then, the imagery—"like a fat, dozing seal wrapped in some kind of gauze bandage"—is apt. It's not overdone, but it does take risks and provoke thought. Note the further similes and imagery as Strout continues:

> But the mind, or the heart, she didn't know which one it was, but it was slower these days, not catching up, and she felt like a big, fat field mouse scrambling to get up on a ball that was right in front of her turning faster and faster, and she couldn't get her scratchy frantic limbs up onto it.

Olive's weight and sense of ineptitude are brought to life through this prose, making the passage provocative, energetic, and believable.

Finely tuned figurative prose rich with similes, metaphors, and analogies is a great element of polished literary fiction—but it goes beyond the aesthetic level. Such language can suggest abstract and universal ideas, which can contribute greatly to thematic development and levels of meaning in a work.

AVOIDING SENTIMENTALITY

Rewrite the following passage so that the reader *feels* the intended emotion— and so that it doesn't read as if the writer is attempting to engineer an emotional response by relying on sentimental, clichéd language.

> He felt so horribly miserable. Right now, if you asked him, he'd say there wasn't a thing in the world to live for. His wife didn't love him, his kids hated him, and he just felt like dying—just turning his face to the wall. And why not? The world was a horrible place!

SYMBOLISM

Now we move to the real core-dividing line between literary and genre fiction: the fact that literary works transcend the surface levels of plot, character, and setting. Literary fiction must allow for, or lend itself to, interpretation of human experience, establishing a vision (if not a particular worldview) of what it means to be human. Themes and ideas may include insights into topics such as these:

- what makes people tick (psychology)
- the nature of humans in groups, society, and culture (history and sociology)
- the meaning of human life (philosophy, religion)
- the nature of fair play and moral action (ethics)

Think of the historical and cultural frameworks in Amy Tan's writing, the philosophical ideas in Thomas Mann's, or the moral choices in Tim O'Brien's. Literary works can also include such themes as the nature of personal identity, art versus life, appearance versus reality, and mercy versus justice.

So, how do you develop such themes?

BRAINSTORM SYMBOLISM ON THE MACRO SCALE. Plot is the literal level of a work, but it can go beyond the action of the story to a more abstract level—the thematic level. In Melville's *Moby-Dick*, Ahab's monomaniacal pursuit of the white whale symbolizes an attempt to destroy the very essence of metaphysical evil. Other literary works could have quite different plots but share this same basic theme.

Characters can also be symbolic. Madame Bovary stands in for women seduced and corrupted by romantic literature. But again, different characters in novels with quite different plots could suggest this same theme. A setting can serve as a symbol as well. The Mississippi River becomes a symbol of freedom in *The Adventures of Huckleberry Finn*, and the psychiatric facility in Ken Kesey's *One Flew over the Cuckoo's Nest* becomes symbolic of an oppressive world that crushes those who are perceived as different.

To summarize, a plot can suggest ideas that transcend the particulars of the basic story itself, a character can come to stand for an entire type of individual, and a setting can take on meanings far beyond the items in the room. So think about your story in a big-picture sense. Brainstorm symbolism in your work, and then begin to flesh out how your story might bring that to life.

USE SYMBOLISM ON THE MINOR SCALE. What do particular actions mean in light of other actions occurring in the work? When Jay Gatsby flings his beautiful new shirts about, what does this mean? Does this action echo other actions as well as themes or ideas suggested before—or perhaps foreshadow actions or ideas to follow? Yes to both: It echoes, in a small way, the conspicuous display of wealth we've seen so far in Gatsby's huge mansion and in the lavish parties he throws. It foreshadows the sterility of such wealth by novel's end. As a scene, then, it's richly symbolic of the value placed on material things in this culture of privilege and money.

Are certain passages of dialogue also suggestive in some way? When Gatsby says of Daisy, "Her voice is full of money," what does this mean in light of everything that occurs in the novel? Think of it this way: Money is plenitude in Daisy's voice—in her soul. In an age when the American Dream equals money and conspicuous consumption, Daisy requires vast riches to meet the requirements of her romantic attention. Gatsby's few, well-chosen words about Daisy crystallize the rampant materialism of the age. Fitzgerald's novel, like other works of literary fiction, demonstrates how certain actions and passages of dialogue knit together the larger meanings of the work. Perhaps not all, but many, scenes in a literary novel might require the reader to "put things together" by seeing and understanding the symbolic and suggestive possibilities. This is another hallmark of literary fiction. Passages in the work can be open to multiple readings and be intellectually enriching for the reader.

Consider this example, which employs the power of figurative language as a means to achieve those powerful literary depths, from Ian McEwan's *Atonement*:

> She would soothe the household, which seemed to her, from the sickly dimness of the bedroom, like a troubled and sparsely populated continent from whose forested vastness competing elements made claims and counter-claims upon her restless attention.

In this woman's fertile imagination, the household is more than the mansion with its various members and guests to attend to: It's a terrestrial landscape—troubled and needful. In this novel, one sees that in spite of the civilized, orderly, aristocratic house setting, human impulses and errors do indeed produce serious trouble. This one simile inspires further reflection on the nature of order versus chaos.

POINT OF VIEW AND CHARACTER

To make larger insights possible, you must choose the point-of-view character that allows for the greatest capacity to introduce several levels of meaning. While your point-of-view character doesn't need to possess sophisticated intelligence and cultural breeding, you do need to choose a character who will provide the greatest range and depth of ideas to readers. This can be handled in one of several possible ways in a story, including:

1. **A PROTAGONIST WHO COMES TO SEE LIFE IN MORE COMPLEX TERMS.** Your character must be dynamic, able to grow in knowledge of self and world. Consider how Huck Finn decides at the end of his novel to strike out for the territory; he's had enough civilization to last him a lifetime.

2. **A CHARACTER WHO COMES TO POSSESS SOME SPECIFIC KNOWL-EDGE—BUT NOT AS MUCH AS THE READER DOES.** Expatriate Frederick Winterbourne, of Henry James's *Daisy Miller*, realizes at novella's end that he misjudged Daisy. While he dismissed the American woman before for her

wildness and apparent immorality, after her unexpected death he receives a note from her that makes him realize that she was in fact quite innocent. However, Winterbourne, rather than experiencing a true transformation of character, returns quickly to his life in Europe, and James even states that he is having an affair with a "very clever foreign lady" whom we once again believe will reshape his thoughts on European propriety. Readers can assume that Winterbourne has not profoundly changed, and that he will make the same mistake yet again regarding his opinions of American innocence. By novella's end, we feel we know more about Winterbourne and his tendencies than perhaps he himself does.

3. **A CHARACTER WHO LEARNS VERY LITTLE—AND LEAVES THE MATTER OF LEARNING TO THE READER.** One might imagine that Herman Melville's Billy Budd learns only a fraction, if anything, in the course of his eponymous novella—but the reader discovers the quintessential nature of evil. Turning to drama, how much does Willy Loman of *Death of a Salesman* learn? That Biff loves him—but he rejects any knowledge that would liberate him from his destructive dreams.

Ask yourself this: Which character in your novel would give you the greatest potential to explore—dramatically—the complex nature of lived experience, of the possibilities for meaning and value? Which character would provide the lens that would help you mine the deepest depths of human experience?

EXPERIMENTAL APPROACHES

Literary work need not be experimental, but certainly experimental work is usually literary. If it's done *well*, that is. Failed experimental writing is just bad writing. Of course, the same can certainly be said of work that attempts to be literary but fails because it comes off as pretentious or affected instead.

Experimental fiction is a risk. The risk is certainly worth it if the experimental techniques accomplish an overall purpose and are not just there for the sake of it. Basically, experimentation is centered on narrative technique, or the manner of telling the story. This may be loosely termed *style*.

It is clearly experimental to write a novel with, say, a first-person omniscient author, a character who assumes knowledge of any and all characters in the work. And it's tough to pull off. Yet Vladimir Nabokov does it in *Pnin*, and Russell Banks does it in *Affliction*. To succeed at such an endeavor, you must, in some way, make the reader believe that the *I*-narrator can enter into the consciousness of one or more other characters. Or the *I*-narrator must at least imaginatively enter into these other characters' minds and report actions outside the *I*-narrator's ken in believable and compelling ways. Certainly both Nabokov and Banks do so.

There are, of course, a host of other experimental techniques at your disposal—too numerous to mention here.

A strong suggestion: Learn the standard narrative techniques first, and then break with them only as needed as a means of developing your literary novel to its fullest potential.

PUTTING IT TOGETHER

In literary fiction we may know everything that has occurred action- and plot-wise, but now we must decide what it all means. How do all the ideas we've encountered add up? In the case of so-called popular fiction, once we can state the basic plot and the characters, we often know the story in its entirety. This is not to say that almost any work of fiction might not stand as a microcosm for a larger framework, the macrocosm. A thriller, for instance, might suggest the vulnerability of humans in a world filled with dangerous, perhaps psychopathic, killers. Yet the degree of suggestiveness is much greater in literary fiction. While the literal level of the novel is important, successful literary fiction hinges on whether there is more at hand, meaning-wise, than what appears on the surface.

38

WORLD CREATION IN SCIENCE FICTION

Establishing the Rules for Hyperspace, Time Travel, and More

Orson Scott Card

World creation sounds like a marvelous free-for-all, in which you come up with all kinds of ideas; ask, "Why?" and "How?" and "What result?" a lot; and when there's a really big pile of good stuff, you sit down and write.

I wish it were that easy. But that big pile of neat ideas is just that—a pile, shapeless, chaotic. Before you can tell a meaningful story, you have to hone and sharpen your understanding of the world, and that begins with the fundamental rules, the natural laws.

Remember: Because speculative fiction always differs from the knowable world, the reader is uncertain about what can and can't happen in the story until the writer has spelled out the rules. And you, as a writer, can't be certain of anything until you know the rules as well.

RULES OF STARFLIGHT

Take space travel, for instance. Why would a story need space travel at all?

One reason might be simply that you want a landscape completely different from Earth. Another might be that you want your story to take place in a developing society, a frontier that is so far away from settled places that your characters can't call for help and expect it to come anytime soon.

But let's say your reason is even more basic. Your story centers on an alien society that you have thoroughly developed. The aliens live in an environment that is pretty much Earthlike, so that either species can live in the other's habitat. But the aliens are strange enough that there's no way they could have evolved on Earth. So you have to put them on another planet.

Other planets in our solar system just won't do. Despite speculation in earlier years, the Voyager II photographs seem to confirm that not only is there no planet or moon remotely suitable for Earthlike life, there isn't much chance of any kind of life at all. So your aliens are going to have to inhabit a planet in another star system.

Why must you decide all these things, when your story begins after the voyage is over? First, because the characters who did the traveling—human or alien—have just finished the voyage, and their relationship with each other and their attitude toward this new world and toward authorities on the old one will be largely shaped by what the voyage back entails.

If another ship can't come for months, if the whole voyage was at risk of death and some did die, and if there's only a sixty-forty chance of getting back home alive, then the voyagers will be determined to survive on the new planet, and will be grimly aware that if they don't make things work, their lives may end. They also won't take faraway authorities on their home planet half so seriously.

But if they reached the planet by taking a six-hour flight, and traffic between this world and the home planet will be easy and frequent, they have much less at stake, and their attitude will be far more casual. Furthermore, homeworld authorities will be much more involved, and reinforcements or replacements will be easy to obtain.

Why must you establish clearly what the rules of space travel are? So that the reader understands why the characters are getting so upset—or why they're not getting terribly upset—when things go wrong. So that the reader knows just what's at stake.

And—not a trivial consideration—so that the experienced science fiction reader will recognize your proper use of a standard device and feel confident that the story is being written by somebody who knows how this is done. Even if you plan to rebel and use nonstandard devices, you still must address the same issues; the effect on the reader is still reassuring.

THE PROBLEM OF INTERSTELLAR FLIGHT

The problem of interstellar flight is twofold: the speed of light, and the ratio of fuel mass to fuel energy.

Let's look at the speed of light first. According to Einstein's theory, light-speed is the absolute ceiling on the speed of any motion in the universe. Nothing can go faster than light. Furthermore, anything that actually goes the speed of light becomes energy. So you can't get from one star system to another any faster than a bit more than one year per light-year of distance between them. To get from Earth to a star system thirty light-years away would take, say, thirty-one years. Your human characters, who were in their twenties when they left, are now in their fifties.

What are the strategies for getting around the lightspeed barrier?

Hyperspace

Though this goes by many different names, the idea is as old as the 1940s at least, and there's really no reason to make up a new term, since if hyperspace is ever found to exist it will almost certainly be called hyperspace (just like when robots were finally created, they were called robots because science fiction writers had been calling artificial mechanical men by that name ever since Czech writer Karl Capek coined the term in his play *RUR* back in the 1930s). You can call it hyperspace—in fact, you probably *should* call it hyperspace, since most of your readers will be familiar with that term and will recognize it instantly.

Hyperspace is based on the idea that space, which seems three-dimensional to us, is really four-dimensional (or more!); and that in another dimension, our space is folded and curved so that locations that seem far apart to us are really quite close together, provided you can find a way to get out of our three-dimensional space, pass through hyper-dimensional space, and then come back out at the point you desire.

This passage through hyperspace is usually called "the jump," and there are many different rules associated with it. Isaac Asimov wrote a robot story in which the jump to hyperspace caused human beings to temporarily cease to exist, a sort of mini-death that drove a robot pilot mad as it was trying to take humans through the jump.

Timothy Zahn's "Cascade Point" and other stories set in that same universe propose that at the moment of the jump, there is an infinite array of possible points of emergence, in most of which you die; but since you only remember the jumps you survive, you're never aware of the universes in which you are dead.

Other versions of hyperspace require you to be near a large star in order to make the jump, or to be a safe distance away from a large gravity source, or the jump gets distorted. In some stories, Heinlein allows an infinite number of possible jumps, with your emergence depending on the elaborately careful calculations of your velocity and trajectory leading to the jump. Others, like Frederik Pohl with his Heechee novels, have written stories allowing only a limited number of gateways through space, each leading consistently to its own destination—which, until all the gateways are mapped, might as easily be an inhabited world or the edge of a black hole.

And some versions of hyperspace don't even require a spaceship. They place "doorways" or "gates" or "tunnels" on or near a planet's surface, and if you simply walk though the right spot, going in the correct direction, you end up on—or near—the surface of another planet!

Another version of this, often used by Larry Niven, is that such doorways are not natural but are machines that create passages through hyperspace. And in one variation of this, hyperspace isn't used at all. You get into a device that looks a bit like an old-fashioned phone booth, it analyzes your body, breaks it down into its constituent parts, and then transmits an image of it at lightspeed to a booth on another planet (or elsewhere on Earth) that carefully reconstructs you. In either case, booths can send you only to other booths, so that somebody has to make the long journey to other planets at sub-lightspeed first in order to assemble the booth that will allow others to follow them instantaneously.

The advantage of hyperspace in all its variations is that it allows relatively quick, cheap passage between worlds. How quick and how cheap is up to you. Think of it as being like voyages between the New World and the Old World. In 1550, the voyage was uncertain; some passengers and crew on every voyage died before they reached land, and some ships disappeared without a trace. By the mid-1800s, the voyage was much faster and death far less likely, though the trip was still miserable. In the age of steam, there were still wrecks and losses, but the voyage was cut down to a week or two. Today, it can take only a few hours. You can have starflight using hyperspace that functions at any one of these danger levels. It's as safe and fast as the Concorde—or it's as dangerous and slow and uncertain as a caravel navigating with a quadrant and an unreliable clock.

Generation Ships

You've decided you don't want to use hyperspace, either because it strikes you as nonsense science or because you don't want all that coming and going on your new planet. Another alternative is to send a ship at sub-lightspeed and let the voyage take as long as it takes.

Without getting into the science of it (primarily because I don't understand it in any kind of detail myself), the problem with sub-light voyages is that they take a long time. And you have to carry all your fuel with you. The good news is that you can coast most of the way—there's little friction in space, and once you reach a certain speed, you should continue traveling at that speed in the same direction until something happens to turn you or slow you down. So most of the voyage needs no fuel at all.

The bad news is that your fuel is part of the mass that your fuel has to lift. There comes a point when the fuel needed to further accelerate will add enough weight that you either can't lift it or can't design a sturdy enough ship to hold it. Furthermore, because it takes just as much fuel to slow you down at the end of your voyage, you have to save exactly half your fuel for the slowdown, plus any fuel required for maneuvering into orbit. That means that the fuel must be able to accelerate more than twice its own mass. Worse yet, if there isn't any more fuel at your destination, you're either not coming home again or you're going to have to carry more than four times the fuel needed to accelerate you to your traveling speed.

So that you don't waste fuel trying to lift a huge ship out of the gravity well of a planet like Earth, such ships are usually assumed to have been built out in space and launched from a point as far as possible from the Sun. Thus, when they arrive at the new world, they put their huge ship into orbit and use landing vehicles or launches or (nowadays) shuttles to get down to the planet's surface.

Using the technology I've just described, you'll be lucky to get to 10 percent of lightspeed. That's pretty fast—about sixty-seven million miles an hour—but at that rate, it will take your ship more than three hundred years to get to a star system thirty light-years away. And that doesn't even allow for acceleration time!

That's why such ships are called "generation ships." Assuming that the ship is a completely self-contained environment, with plants to constantly refresh the atmosphere and grow food, a whole human society lives aboard the ship. People are born, grow old, and die, and the elements of their bodies are processed and returned to the ecosystem within the ship. This idea has been well explored in many stories—particularly stories about ships where the people have forgotten their origin, forgotten even that the ship is a ship—but it has a lot of life left in it.

The problem with this (besides the fact that a completely self-contained ecosystem would be almost impossible to create) is that none of the people who reach the new world have any direct memories of their home planet. Their whole history for generations has been inside a ship—why would they even want to go out onto a planet's surface? The fact of living inside a ship for so long is so powerful that it almost takes over the story. If your story is about that, like Rebecca Brown Ore's brilliant debut story, "Projectile Weapons and Wild Alien Water," then that's fine—but if your story is about something else, a generation ship is hard to get over.

Cryo-Travel

Another alternative is to have the crew travel for all those years in a state of suspended animation—either frozen or otherwise kept viable until the ship itself, or a skeleton crew, wakens the sleepers at the voyage's end. This has the advantage of not requiring living space and supplies for so many people for so many years, and it still achieves the result of making frequent voyages between the new world and the home planet unthinkable—or at least impractical.

The drawback is that if suspended animation is possible at all in your future universe, then you have to let it be used for anything it's needed for. Characters who get sick or critically injured or even killed must be rushed back to the ship and popped into a suspended animation chamber until a cure or repair can be worked out. Also, there are bound to be people who try to abuse the system to prolong their lives beyond the normal span of years. You can't have a technology exist for one purpose and then ignore it for another—not unless you want to earn the scorn of your more critical and vocal readers.

A variation on cryo-travel is to send colony ships that contain no human beings at all but rather frozen human embryos; when the ship's computer determines that the starship has reached a habitable planet, some of the embryos are revived and raised to adulthood by computers or robots inside the ship. They come to the new planet as virtually new creations, having known neither parents nor any human society except the one they form. Obviously, this is a one-way trip with no hope of later visits or help from the home planet, since no one on the home world will know whether the colony ship happened to find a habitable planet, let alone where.

Ramdrives

Long before the personal computer culture taught us to use the term *RAM drive* for a virtual disk in volatile memory, science fiction readers were introduced to the ramscoop stardrive, or ramdrive, that solved part of the fuel problem. Instead of carrying enough fuel to handle all of a ship's acceleration, a ramship would use conventional fuel to get up to a certain speed, then deploy a huge network, like a funnel, in front of it to scoop up the loose matter that is everywhere in space. This matter would then be used as fuel so that acceleration could continue without having to carry all the fuel along.

There are theoretical problems—the efficient use of the loose interstellar "dust," some structure for the net that isn't so heavy that the matter it collects can't provide enough energy to accelerate it, the fact that at velocities far below lightspeed the interstellar dust stops being harmless and starts being extremely dangerous and explosive debris that harms any ship traveling that fast. But the ramdrive is fun and semiplausible, and it allows you to have a starship that isn't the size of your average asteroid.

Time Dilation

Time dilation space travel is a sort of middle path. With this set of rules, your starship can travel at a speed so close to the speed of light (say, 99.999 percent of lightspeed) that, while you don't turn into pure energy, you get from point A to point B at almost the speed of light. Relativity theory suggests that time aboard an object traveling at that speed would be compressed, so that while an outside observer might think thirty years had passed, people on the ship would only have lived through a few hours or days or weeks.

This allows you to get people from world to world without generation ships or cryo-travel. The travelers who reach the new planet have clear memories of their home world. But they won't be particularly eager to get back because, while to them it has only been a few weeks since they left home, back there it has been thirty years. Anybody they left behind has aged a whole generation or died. For all intents and purposes, it's still a one-way voyage—but one that allows the travelers to arrive with their society intact, relatively unchanged by the voyage.

Still, the characters will have been cut off from anyone they knew and loved. This suggests that either the travelers will be going through some degree of grief or they will have had no close friends or family on their previous world; in either case, this will have a lot to do with how you characterize them.

And feign ignorance about the fact that, when traveling at such a high percentage of lightspeed, space dust would strike them like intense gamma radiation. Just say that they use a half-mile-thick layer of crushed asteroid as shielding, or that they have a force field that shields them from the radiation. Or don't say anything at all—time dilation stories are such a staple in science fiction that you really don't have to apologize for them anymore.

The Ansible

I first ran across this variation on time dilation in the works of Ursula K. Le Guin and found it one of the most useful devices in space travel. In essence, the ansible is a device that allows you to communicate instantaneously, regardless of distance. Thus travelers can go on one-way time dilation voyages, yet still report to and receive instructions from people on the home planet.

This is enormously convenient if you want to have a fairly unified interstellar society and yet don't want people hopping from planet to planet the way some people commute by air from Boston to New York. A space voyage remains an irrevocable decision, cutting you off from everyone you leave behind, yet the whole interstellar society can share literature, politics, news—anything can be transmitted by ansible. It's as if the Pilgrims could have communicated with England by radio but still had to do all their traveling in small, dangerous, unhealthy wooden ships.

As science, of course, this is pure nonsense—yet it is so useful that many of us have used some variation on it. After all, we're not trying to predict the future, only to tell a story in a strange place!

Warp Speed

I haven't even touched on the silliest of space travel rules—the one used in the *Star Trek* universe, where the speed of light is no more a barrier than the speed of sound, and you only have to persuade Scotty in the engine room to really step on the gas to get to four, eight, ten times the speed of light. This sort of stardrive shows such contempt for science that it's best to reserve it for light adventures or comic stories—or, of course, *Star Trek* novelizations.

In fact, unless you're actually writing a *Star Trek* novel (which means you must already have a contract with the publisher licensed by Paramount Pictures) or are deliberately trying to be funny, never refer to "warp speed" in your fiction. It's not only bad science; it also pegs you instantly as a writer who knows science fiction only through *Star Trek*. Beware of anything that makes non-Trekkie readers think of *Star Trek*. That's the equivalent of applying for a position as a physics professor with a résumé that lists your training as "Watched every episode of *Mr. Wizard*." You may actually know something, but it'll be hard to get anyone to take you seriously long enough to find out.

WHAT THE RULES CAN DO FOR YOU

All this attention to space travel, and your story doesn't have a single scene aboard a ship! Do you really have to go through all this?

Yes—in your head, or perhaps in your outline. Just enough time to make your decisions about the rules and then ensure that your whole story doesn't violate them. But your reader doesn't have to go through all that with you. Once you've decided that you're using a difficult, dangerous hyperspace where the emergence points can shift by parsecs without warning, then all you have to do is drop some reference into the story—perhaps a single sentence, like this:

> It was a perfect flight, which is to say that they didn't emerge from the jump through hyperspace in the middle of a star or heading straight for an asteroid, and even though everybody puked for days after the jump, nobody died of it.

That's it. That's all. No more discussion about the mechanics of starflight. But your readers will understand why none of the travelers are eager to leave the planet, and why it'll be quite a while before another ship comes. And now, with the rules established, you're free to do things like have your viewpoint character think of someone else this way:

> Back at Moonbase, Annie had thought Booker looked pretty good, thought he might be worth getting to know a little better. But after the hyperjump she had had to clean up his vomit while he whimpered and cried in the corner. He didn't emerge from his hysteria till they were in orbit around Rainbird. Annie knew that Booker couldn't help it, that a lot of people reacted that way to the jump, but then, she couldn't help it, either, that it was impossible to respect him anymore after that.

Maybe this relationship will be important in your story; maybe it won't. But if you didn't know that people puke a lot after the hyperspace jump, if you hadn't worked out the rules in advance, then you couldn't have given Annie this memory and this aspect to her relationship with Booker. The rules you establish don't limit you; they open up possibilities.

Know the rules, and the rules will make you free.

TIME TRAVEL

You have to go through the same process with time travel. Without going into the same detail, let me just list some of the possible variations on time travel.

1. If you go back in time, you can make any changes you want in the past and you'll continue to exist, because the very act of traveling in time takes you outside timestream and removes you from the effects of changes in history. (See Asimov's *The End of Eternity*.)

2. If you go back in time, you can make changes that destroy your own society—so time travel is a closely guarded secret, and those who travel in time are only the most skilled and trusted people. Perhaps they are sent to rescue great works of art that have been lost for centuries. Or perhaps, as in John Varley's classic "Air Raid" (published under the pseudonym Herb Boehm), these time travelers rescue people from airplanes that are about to crash or ships that are about to go down with no survivors, and then force these healthy people to colonize planets and save humanity from extinction in a hideously polluted future.

3. If you go back in time far enough, any changes you make won't have major effects in your own time, because history has a kind of inertia and tends to get itself back on track. So if you kill Napoleon as a baby, France still has an early nineteenth-century empire and a protracted war with England, and by 1900 everything is right back where it would have been.

4. If you go back in time, you are only able to make changes that have no long-term effects, since any universe in which you change your own future could not exist.

5. When you go back in time, you're invisible and unable to affect anything. But you can watch—so there's quite a tourist business.

6. Time travel consists of going back into the mind of somebody living in the past, seeing events through his eyes. He doesn't know you're there. (But, in Carter Scholz's brilliant short story "The Ninth Symphony of Ludwig von Beethoven and Other Lost Songs," the presence of time-traveling observers in Beethoven's mind drove him mad and eventually killed him, stopping him from writing his greatest works. The time travelers never realized what they were doing, however, because with history altered, they "knew" that Beethoven had never written any such symphonies after all.)

7. Time travel consists of going back into your own mind at an earlier stage in your life, able to observe but not to act. Or, in a variation, you can act, but then your youthful self will have no memory of what you did while your future self was in control. I used that one in a love story called "Clap Hands and Sing."

8. Time travel consists of observation only, like watching a hologram or a movie. You aren't actually there, and perhaps you aren't altogether sure that what you're seeing is the real past. Maybe it's never the same way twice! (I actually don't remember seeing a story about that—feel free to use that set of rules and see what develops.)

9. Your body remains inside the time-travel device, but a semi-real body is assembled for you in the past; your consciousness remains with that simulacrum until it dies or fades, whereupon you wake up and emerge from the machine. In a story called "Closing the Timelid," I had a group of thrill seekers using such a machine to go through repeated deaths by making their simulacra commit suicide.

Do you get the idea? Each one of these sets of rules opens up a whole new range of story possibilities—and trust me, there are hundreds of variations that nobody's tried yet and that have many, many stories left in them.

Orson Scott Card is the author of the novels *Ender's Game*, *Ender's Shadow*, and *Speaker for the Dead*, which are widely read by adults and younger readers, and are increasingly used in schools. His most recent series, the young adult Pathfinder series (*Pathfinder*, *Ruins*, *Visitors*) and the fantasy Mithermages series (*Lost Gate*, *Gate Thief*, *Gatefather*) are taking readers in new directions. Besides these and other science fiction novels, Card writes contemporary fantasy, historical novels, the American frontier fantasy series The Tales of Alvin Maker, poetry, and many plays and scripts.

The Complete Handbook of Novel Writing

39

WHAT "HIGH CONCEPT" MEANS IN ANY GENRE

Gauging How (and Where) Your Work Fits In

Jeff Lyons

You're ready to begin the process of pitching your book to prospective literary agents or publishers. You begin combing through market listings, thinking it will be a simple matter of finding those who accept work in your genre—but time and again, you discover submission guidelines expressing a preference for "high-concept" stories. Your brow furrows. *High concept? What the heck does that mean?* Your confusion turns to frustration, and maybe even panic, because no one on your wish list defines this popular *term d'art*. They simply declare that it is what they want a story to be, it is what they prefer, indeed, it is the Holy Grail for submission success. But how are you to succeed when you don't even understand what they're asking for?

You're not as out of the loop as you may feel. The truth is that many of the very gatekeepers who use the term *high concept* aren't much clearer about what it means than you are. Take the simpler buzzword *concept*, for starters. If you were to ask a random selection of agents or editors to define it, you'd likely get as many definitions as people responding to your question:

- "It's your story's hook."
- "It's what's fun about your story."
- "It's your story in a single image."
- "It's your story's heart."
- "It's your story as a movie one-sheet."
- "It's the essence of your premise."

… and so on.

Similarly, there is no consensus on the true definition of *high concept*. So how can you as a writer deliver what these markets want, when they can't even define the thing they're asking for?

High concept exists on a continuum of expression; it is not a single, definable attribute. Think of it as a collection of qualities that once identified can help you pinpoint the height of the concept present in your story. In my twenty-plus years consulting with novelists, screenwriters, and nonfiction authors, I have identified seven common traits in stories, across all genres, that most industry pros seem to agree signify a high concept.

SEVEN QUALITIES OF HIGH-CONCEPT STORIES

1. high level of entertainment value
2. high degree of originality
3. born from a "what if" question
4. highly visual
5. clear emotional focus
6. inclusion of some truly unique element
7. mass audience appeal (to a broad general audience or a large niche market)

Most stories do not possess all seven qualities. Because high concept develops along a continuum, a high-concept story may be strongly identifiable by two of the qualities, or may more vaguely possess five of these traits. The more of them you can identify in your story, the higher the concept. Having just one quality out of seven does not necessarily mean that you don't have a high-concept idea; it just means that your story's potential to appeal to "high-concept" markets (or to gatekeepers who specify that they are seeking high-concept work) might be softer than other stories that possess multiple qualities from the list. When the idea of high concept is put in the context of these seven qualities, it becomes easier to see how commercially appealing books have a clear line of demarcation. That line is the high concept.

With that in mind, let's look more closely at each of these qualities to get a better idea of what they mean.

1. HIGH LEVEL OF ENTERTAINMENT VALUE: Defining "entertainment value" is like trying to define pornography; it's in the eye of the beholder. Here's where you may need to get some outside advice, because you might not be the best judge of how your own work is perceived by others. Ask a trusted reader to explain, as best he can, what is purely entertaining about your idea or story. Get a second opinion, and a third, and a fourth. This can be invaluable feedback, provided that you recruit people willing to tell you the truth and not what they think you want to hear.

2. HIGH DEGREE OF ORIGINALITY: People often use the term interchangeably with words such as *fresh*, *new*, or *innovative*—but what does it really mean to be *original*? Think of originality as approach-centric. Your story's idea may be centered in a familiar context, but your approach to that idea comes from an unexpected angle. For example, Mary Shelley's *Frankenstein* took a familiar idea—evil monster terrorizes humans—and added an original take: The monster and humans switch moral ground, and the humans terrorize the monster. Originality is more about finding new ways to present the familiar than it is about inventing something that's entirely unlike anything that's ever been done before (a nearly impossible feat).

3. BORN FROM A "WHAT IF" QUESTION: What if dinosaurs were cloned (*Jurassic Park*, Michael Crichton)? What if women stopped giving birth (*The Children of Men*, P.D. James)? What if Martians invaded the earth (*The War of the Worlds*, H.G. Wells)? High-concept stories often begin with a "what if" scenario, and then the hook becomes clear. What's the hook, you ask? That part of the concept that grabs the reader by the scruff of the collar and doesn't let go.

4. HIGHLY VISUAL: High-concept stories have a visual quality about them that is palpable. When you read or hear about a high-concept story, your mind starts conjuring images and you can *see* the story unfold. High-concept books tend to make for great film adaptations, and this is why. Books with cinematic imagery are almost always high-concept stories.

5. CLEAR EMOTIONAL FOCUS: As with imagery, high-concept stories spark emotion, but not just any emotion. Usually it's a primal emotional response: fear, joy, hate, love, rage. There is no wishy-washy emotional engagement of the reader. The involvement is strong, immediate, and intense.

6. INCLUSION OF SOME TRULY UNIQUE ELEMENT: Whereas originality is about a fresh approach or perspective, uniqueness is about being one of a kind, incomparable. In high-concept books, this can often take the form of a unique physical execution of prose formatting or book design. Take, for example, Clive Barker's *Abarat: Absolute Midnight*. The book includes more than 125 full-color illustrations, giving the work a hybrid prose/graphic novel character. Being unique transcends originality.

7. MASS AUDIENCE APPEAL: High-concept stories, even if easily categorized by a certain genre (romance, science fiction, horror, etc.), appeal to an audience beyond the narrow confines of that genre's readers or fans. The target market is broad, diverse, and large. High-concept stories are often those that become popular, even trendy, because they possess the potential for crossover appeal, or even for being dually categorized on mainstream/popular shelves in bookstores. For example, high-concept mysteries might appeal to people who don't typically think of themselves as mystery buffs. High-concept memoirs might appeal to readers who don't typically enjoy personal accounts.

It's important to remember that this list of high-concept qualities is not some sliding scale of good or bad, or an attempt to judge your work as worthy or unworthy of submission—quite the contrary. Your submission will be considered based on many factors, and in fact, there are plenty of good agents and publishers who don't specify a preference for high-concept work in their guidelines. This list simply presents an effective tool for helping you to know with confidence that you are positioning your writing appropriately, with the right potential representatives, in the right markets. In a submissions process that can often feel like a guessing game, understanding what high concept means, and honestly assessing how closely your work fits that description, can eliminate much of that guesswork and set you up for submission success.

HIGH-CONCEPT TITLES ACROSS POPULAR GENRES

These novels each possess several of the "Seven Qualities of High-Concept Stories"—and you'll likely recognize them by their mainstream appeal regardless of whether or not you typically visit these sections of the bookstore. All are well worth studying as examples of how seasoned authors use high-concept material to lead them to the bestseller lists.

HORROR

- *Abraham Lincoln: Vampire Hunter* by Seth Grahame-Smith
- *Abarat: Absolute Midnight* by Clive Barker
- *World War Z* by Max Brooks

YOUNG ADULT

- *Mockingjay* by Suzanne Collins

- *Confessions of a Murder Suspect* by James Patterson and Maxine Paetro
- *Beautiful Creatures* by Kami Garcia and Margaret Stohl

ROMANCE

- *Safe Haven* by Nicholas Sparks
- *Fifty Shades of Grey* by E.L. James
- *Love in a Nutshell* by Janet Evanovich and Dorien Kelly

SCIENCE FICTION/FANTASY

- *A Memory of Light* by Robert Jordan and Brandon Sanderson
- *A Dance With Dragons* by George R.R. Martin
- *Ever After* by Kim Harrison

THRILLER/SUSPENSE

- *Gone Girl* by Gillian Flynn
- *Suspect* by Robert Crais
- *Catch Me* by Lisa Gardner

Jeff Lyons is a published author, screenwriter, editor, and story development consultant with more than twenty-five years' experience in the film, television, and publishing industries. He has worked with thousands of novelists, nonfiction authors, and screenwriters, helping them build and tell better stories. Jeff has written on the craft of storytelling for *Writer's Digest*, *Script Magazine*, *The Writer*, and *Writing Magazine*. His book, *Anatomy of a Premise Line: How to Master Premise and Story Development for Writing Success*, is the only book devoted solely to the topic of story and premise development for novelists, screenwriters, and creative nonfiction authors. His other book, *Rapid Story Development: How to Use the Enneagram-Story Connection to Become a Master Storyteller*, will be published by Focal Press in late 2017.

40

WRITE THIS, NOT THAT

....

Key Ingredients for a Satisfying Mystery

Elizabeth Sims

Just as eating a balanced diet requires an endless series of good choices, so does writing a successful mystery. And just like anyone else, we authors are constantly tempted by junk. It's true: When crafting a story or chapter, you can opt for the cheap, first-thing-to-hand alternative, or you can push yourself toward something that may be less convenient but that will ultimately be more fulfilling for both you and your readers.

Think of it this way: As an author, you're feeding your readers. Those readers come to a mystery hungry for certain elements, and they expect to feel satisfied at the end. They don't want formulaic, predictable stories that are the equivalent of fast food; they want substance, flavor, verve, and originality. If you want to keep them coming back for seconds, you need to nourish them with quality prose, cooked up with skill and caring.

Here's how to make smart choices in your writing (with apologies to the *Eat This, Not That* diet book) when it comes to the five key ingredients readers expect from a juicy mystery.

1. COINCIDENCES

WRITE THIS: A COINCIDENCE THAT ARISES ORGANICALLY FROM A SOLID PLOT.

EXAMPLE: In Richard Condon's *The Manchurian Candidate*, a crucial plot point is protagonist Ben Marco finding out that he isn't the only member of his platoon having strange recurrent nightmares about garden club ladies who morph into Communist officers. This is key because it's the first evidence that the soldiers have been brainwashed. Condon crafted the story so that Marco learns of another soldier's dreams when his platoon leader, Raymond Shaw, mentions a letter he received from the soldier. Better still, when Shaw reveals the key information in the letter, he does so without realizing its significance. The reader puts two and two together, right along with Marco—and is completely hooked. If Marco had just happened to meet another nightmare sufferer somehow, readers may have had a hard time suspending their disbelief.

NOT THAT: A CONTRIVED COINCIDENCE THAT HAS NOTHING TO DO WITH WHAT CAME BEFORE.

A prime example is the off-duty detective who just happens to be walking past the abandoned warehouse at the precise moment the villain starts torturing the abducted coed.

HOW TO DO IT: Mystery writers are constantly tempted to solve a plot problem by putting in a coincidence. After all, mysteries tend to have complex plots, and complex plots are challenging to write.

Fortunately, readers love coincidences—provided they work. Life is full of real ones, so to turn your back on them in your writing would be to reject a reasonable plotting technique. The key is to generate realistic coincidences rather than contrived ones that will leave readers rolling their eyes. So how do you do it?

You'll find that organic coincidences will suggest themselves if you populate your story with enough strong, varied characters. Let's say you have a damsel in distress—that coed in the warehouse, bound and gagged by the bad guy. You need this exciting scene; your plot relies on her survival. Some of your most interesting possibilities hinge on the characters themselves. Take the bad guy, for instance. What if there's more than one? What if one of them is holding a secret grudge against the leader? Can you see where this could go?

Or, rather than drawing on your villains, say you want a hero to stop by and bust up the party. Make this more than a ploy to get your damsel out of trouble: Make it a real subplot that twines throughout the story.

For example, perhaps the building has been scheduled for an inspection. The inspector knows the building is a blight and has been fighting with the mayor to get it torn down; the bad guy knows the building is a perfect hideout. The plots about the inspector and the bad guy (who, let's say, were best friends in high school but haven't met in years) can be parallel and separate, with the building being the piece in common. This way, you can make both characters converge on the scene at the same time, resulting in a natural coincidence. Written just so, the arrival of the building inspector with the bolt cutters will make readers slap their foreheads and go, "Oh, *yeah,* the building inspection! Oh boy, what's gonna happen next?"

2. DYNAMIC DESCRIPTIONS

WRITE THIS: A DESCRIPTION BASED IN UNCONVENTIONAL COMPARISON.

EXAMPLE: "More cop cars pulled up, more cops came in, until it looked like they'd been spread on with a knife." (This is from my first novel, *Holy Hell.*)

NOT THAT: A DESCRIPTION YOU'VE READ A DOZEN TIMES: "THE PLACE WAS CRAWLING WITH COPS."

I almost think I became a crime fiction author so I could write books without using the sentence, "The place was crawling with cops," thus proving it can be done.

HOW TO DO IT: I believe many aspiring mystery writers fall into clichéd descriptions because of the genre's deep roots in pulp, work-for-hire, and cheap magazines. These outlets served, it must be admitted, less-than-discriminating audiences. (The Twinkie eaters of mystery readers, metaphorically.) Today's mystery readers demand better.

Constantly be on the lookout for clichés in your writing. Welcome the occurrence of a cliché in your rough draft, because now you've got an opportunity to show off!

I learned from best-selling author Betty MacDonald (*The Egg and I,* among other golden oldies) to compare people with nonhuman entities, and nonhuman entities with people. She wrote things like, "As evening fell, the mountain settled her skirts over the forest." That's a great technique, a terrific cliché buster.

Let's say you're describing a man who storms into a room, and you just wrote, "He was like a bull in a china shop." You stop in horror, hand to your mouth with the realization: *I have just written a cliché.*

Brainstorm other comparisons as well as other contexts for your description. What if he was like a garbage truck with no brakes? What if he was like a ballplayer driven insane by the worst call he'd ever seen? What if (simply describing what he does) he tears off his shirt, and the sound of the popping buttons is like a burst from an Uzi?

The Complete Handbook of Novel Writing

3. FALSE CLUES

WRITE THIS: A RED HERRING THAT'S BUILT INTO THE PLOT FROM THE GET-GO.

EXAMPLE: Agatha Christie did it beautifully in her famous short story "The Witness for the Prosecution," which later became a classic Billy Wilder film. The protagonist, Leonard Vole, is on trial for murder. He's a sympathetic character, and you find yourself rooting for him from the beginning. The evidence against him is circumstantial but heavy; even his wife testifies against him.

The wife is the red herring. She appears to be trying to send him to jail; she says she hates him and presents marvelous evidence for the prosecution. You begin to focus on her, wondering, *Gosh, what's her angle?* Dame Agatha stokes your high suspicion. All of a sudden, however, Mrs. Vole's testimony is discredited, and Vole goes free. *Aha*, you think, *I was right: She had it in for him!*

But then (spoiler alert!), in a wonderful twisted ending, the wife reveals that she'd been working for that result all along; she herself provided the discrediting evidence, knowing the jury would be more easily manipulated that way. We learn that Vole had indeed committed the murder. Because our attention had been drawn to the wife, the heart-clutching moment when we learn of Vole's guilt is the stuff mystery readers long for.

NOT THAT: A FALSE CLUE THAT'S ISOLATED.

In too many amateur mysteries, we get red herrings like a creepy next-door neighbor who turns out to be a good guy. You know you're being cheaply manipulated when you realize the neighbor has nothing to do with the plot; he appears solely to frighten us from time to time.

HOW TO DO IT: Mystery writers are always in need of red herrings to shake readers off the scent. A terrific test for these false clues is to ask yourself: "If I removed this clue from the story, would I have to change anything else to accommodate the cut?" If the answer is no, you've got some work to do.

Let's say you've got multiple suspects in your murder mystery. One is the proverbial creepy next-door neighbor who someone reports having heard arguing with the victim the night of the crime (of course, he'll later be revealed to be innocent). This is a typical false clue to plant; readers have seen it before. So why not expand the clue to give it some deeper roots? You might make the argument part of a long-running feud, one that's now taken up by the victim's family members, who have shown up for the funeral. Suddenly this isn't an isolated clue but a part of the story.

You might also further consider the neighbor character himself. What if he is revealed to have been the victim's first husband? Did he kill her out of jealousy? Or did he rent the house next door so that he could protect her because he loved her so truly? Characterizations like this can turn an ordinary red herring into a satisfying subplot.

4. ACTION-PACKED DIALOGUE

WRITE THIS: DIALOGUE THAT ARISES FROM ACTION, EMOTION, OR NECESSITY.

EXAMPLE: One of my favorite Sir Arthur Conan Doyle stories is the Sherlock Holmes novel *The Valley of Fear*, which is packed with textbook dialogue. Here's the character Jack McMurdo responding with calculated disbelief to a workingman's offhanded comment that a gang called the Scowrers is a murderous bunch. Thus he goads the man into giving him specifics:

> The young man [McMurdo] stared. "Why, I am a member of that order myself."
>
> "You! I would never had had you in my house if I had known it …"
>
> "What's wrong with the order? It's for charity and good fellowship. The rules say so."
>
> "Maybe in some places. Not here!"
>
> "What is it here?"
>
> "It's a murder society, that's vat it is."
>
> McMurdo laughed incredulously. "How can you prove that?" he asked.
>
> "Prove it! Are there not fifty murders to prove it? Vat about Milman and Van Shorst, and the Nicholson family. … Prove it! Is there a man or a voman in this valley vat does not know it?" …
>
> "That's just gossip—I want proof!" said McMurdo.
>
> "If you live here long enough, you vill get your proof."

Not only does this passage give McMurdo the information he's looking for, it also advances the story in a natural way.

NOT THAT: DIALOGUE IN WHICH ONE CHARACTER TELLS ANOTHER SOMETHING THEY BOTH ALREADY KNOW, JUST SO THE READER CAN KNOW IT AS WELL.

We've all read stuff like this:

HERO: "Hurry! We've got to move fast!"

SIDEKICK: "How come?"

HERO: "Because we've got to sabotage that convoy!"

SIDEKICK: "You mean the one that's carrying forty thousand gallons of deadly radioactive bacteria straight toward the vulnerable entry point in the New York City water system?"

HERO: "Exactly! Yes!"

Ludicrous, no?

HOW TO DO IT: Weak dialogue in mystery can often be pinned on the easy habit of telling too much too soon. Did you notice that in the former example, McMurdo learns a lot (and tells a lot about himself) simply from the way he *reacts* to something the other man said? Having a character make friends with another for a specific purpose can work well; the reader can pick up on the manipulation and enjoy it.

Masterful writers have long known that emotion is a great dialogue engine. When a character is outraged, or dying to get laid, or seeking pity or admiration, that's when she might let something slip, or unleash a whole tirade, which can trigger explosive action, be it a counter-tirade from another character, violence, flight, you name it.

You can engineer a juicy hunk of dialogue by writing down the result you want, then setting up a convincing sequence of events for the characters to reach that point. Expect dialogue to be a springboard for your characters.

And finally, here's a rule of thumb I've found transformative: *When in doubt, cut the talk.*

5. CHARACTER MOTIVATIONS

WRITE THIS: CHARACTERS MOTIVATED BY ALMOST UNBEARABLE FORCES.

EXAMPLE: In "The Monkey's Paw" by W.W. Jacobs, one of the most perfect short stories ever written—and one of the scariest—maternal grief is the reason Mrs. White interferes with fate and meddles with the terrible three-wish charm.

After receiving this supposedly magic paw and wishing upon it for two hundred pounds sterling, she and her husband come into the money, but they are horrified to get it as compensation for the death of their son Herbert, who is mangled to death at work. Mrs. White, deep in grief, begs her husband to wish upon the paw for their son to be alive again. He reluctantly does so. But he had seen what was left of Herbert—who has been in his grave for a week—and now something is pounding at the front door, and there's one more wish left in the paw.

NOT THAT: CHARACTER MOTIVATION THAT BOILS DOWN TO ... NOT ENOUGH.

"So exactly why is this character risking his marriage, his children, and his career as a doctor by serially murdering mafia chieftains?" I once asked a student in a mentoring session.

"Um, see, he wants to keep the streets safe."

Wanting to help strangers may be a plausible motivation for lying, but not for murder.

HOW TO DO IT: Making your characters take drastic risks is good, but this works only if their motivations are rock solid. In fact, the biggest favor a good agent or editor or writing group will do for you is challenge your character motivations. Internal motivation can work, but external motivation is better.

For example, it's conceivable a cop or a P.I. could risk his life to find the truth because he loves the truth—but if the truth involves finding out why his partner was murdered in cold blood, as Sam Spade felt driven to do in Dashiell Hammett's *The Maltese Falcon*, now you've got something.

Do like Hammett did: Combine motivating factors. Not simply love, not simply money, but love *and* money. Hate and glory. Envy and shame. Sex and loss.

The possibilities are limitless. And, as with so many of the healthy writing choices I've listed here, you'll find substantial combinations to be much more satisfying than quick and easy fixes. Feed your readers with them well, and they'll keep coming back for more.

41

THE STUFF SERIES ARE MADE OF

How to Keep Readers Riveted from Book to Book

Karen S. Wiesner

"The disease of writing is dangerous and contagious," Abelard famously said to Heloise. So, too, can a book series become a relentless obsession: It's why readers follow series devotedly to the last, why writers write them for years on end, and why publishers contract them in spades. In our trend-driven world, series are hotter than ever.

But if writing a novel can seem overwhelming, the idea of creating a whole series of them can be exponentially more so. Whether you've been pondering starting a series from page 1, or you've finished a book and don't want to let the characters go, there are plenty of simple things you can implement now to lay a strong foundation for what's to come.

TIES

If a series doesn't have a "tie" that connects each book, it can hardly be called a series. Ties can be any (or even all) of the following:

- a recurring character or couple (think Aloysius Pendergast in Douglas Preston and Lincoln Child's Pendergast series, or J.D. Robb's Eve and Roarke from the In Death series)
- a central group of characters (George R.R. Martin's A Song of Ice and Fire, Kate Jacobs's Friday Night Knitting Club)
- a plot or premise (Robin Cook's Jack Stapleton medical mysteries, Dan Brown's treasure hunts starring Robert Langdon)

- a setting (Harry Potter's Hogwarts School of Witchcraft and Wizardry, Twilight's Forks, Washington)

Series can be open-ended—in which each book stands on its own, and the series could continue indefinitely (Langdon)—or closed, in which an underlying plot continues in each book and resolves in the last (Harry Potter).

What connects the books in a series should be evident from Book One. Ensuring this kind of continuity requires advance planning, starting as early as possible.

STORY ARCS AND SERIES ARCS

Every work of fiction, series or otherwise, has a contained storyline. That story arc is introduced, developed, and concluded within each individual book. Series books often have a series arc as well: a long-term plot thread that is introduced in the first book; developed, expanded, and/or alluded to in some way in each subsequent book; and resolved only in the final installment of the series.

Series arcs can be prominent or can be more subtly defined. The series arc is generally separate from each individual story arc, though they must fit together seamlessly in each book to provide logical progression throughout the series. For example, in *Harry Potter and the Sorcerer's Stone,* the story arc is the Sorcerer's Stone plotline. The series arc, in the most simplified terms, is good overcoming evil among this set group of characters in the fantasy world of the series. The series arc runs progressively and cohesively beneath the individual story arcs in all the successive books.

Unless a series is completely open-ended, it is imperative that you pay off promises made early in your series arc in the concluding book. You've presented a nagging situation in the first book that must be settled satisfactorily in the last. Without that, readers who have invested time, money, and passion will feel cheated. If, in the course of Brandon Mull's Fablehaven Series, Kendra and Seth didn't defeat the evil threatening the Fablehaven preserve and stop the plague that could have led to a hoard of imprisoned demons escaping into the world, Mull would have left his fans crying foul because he broke the pledge of a satisfactory resolution implied in the first book.

Take the time to map out your series arc as much as you can up front, so you can work through that premise from the start and ensure you'll reward readers at the finish.

C-S-P SERIES POTENTIAL

Readers fall in love with characters, settings, and plots. They want conflict but don't want you to hurt their heroes. They want something different but don't want things to change. But a character, setting, or plot that doesn't evolve doesn't remain lifelike and eventually becomes boring.

Series characters, settings, and plots should have longevity and intriguing potential that continues to grow, never stagnating or waning, throughout the course of a series. While none of these should ever have a radical transplant from one book to the next, it's crucial that they're affected by changes. Consider the three *P*s that make characters (and just as certainly settings and plots) three-dimensional:

1. **PERSONALITY:** always multifaceted, with strengths and weaknesses, and capable of growing—being molded, deeply delved, and stretched
2. **PROBLEMS:** combining light and dark, good and evil, simple and complex—not necessarily in equal parts
3. **PURPOSE:** evolving goals and motivations broad enough to introduce new and unpredictable themes throughout the series, but narrow enough to maintain focus in each individual story

If you don't introduce something new for series characters, settings, and plots in each book, your readers will lose motivation to read all the way to the end.

To plant seeds for future growth in your series, nurture your C-S-P (Character-Setting-Plot) potential by establishing "plants" in early books that can be cultivated at any time during the life of the series to expand on one or all three of these components. Naturally, the sooner you incorporate these, the more believable they'll be when it's time to fully develop them.

In Dan Brown's novels, for example, Robert Langdon frequently mentions the Mickey Mouse watch he wears—not something most grown men would be caught dead in. It was a gift from his parents on his ninth birthday, and it's rife with sentimental value. Considering that his plots involve racing against the clock, the significance of this object is heightened.

The watch becomes pivotal when Langdon is thrust in a tank of breathable oxygenated liquid in *The Lost Symbol* (Book Three). If that were the first time it was mentioned, the story's believability would have been drowned as a consequence. But Brown planted the item early enough in Book One—during an appropriate time for passive reflection—that its later role in life-or-death action scenes doesn't feel contrived or overly convenient to the plot.

Most authors include numerous "plants" in the first book in a series without even realizing it. That's good news for you if your first book is already well under way. But that doesn't mean you shouldn't deliberately insert them. When developing your C-S-P series potential, write free-form summaries for the following questions. Don't worry if you can't come up with much right away; simply use these as a jumping-off point as the series progresses, assuming that these seeds may be planted (and left mostly unexplored) in the early books for development in later titles:

- How can you outfit all series characters, even minor ones, with heroic traits and habits in addition to flaws and vices that can lead to natural growth as well as interesting plots and subplots?
- How can you give them occupations, hobbies, interests, and idiosyncrasies that might be gradually developed?
- What relationships and potential enemies or villains can you add to expand the potential for subplots, characters, or ongoing conflicts or rivalries that might play a bigger role in a later book?
- What lessons, backstory, or experiences can be hinted at for later revelation and development that may lead to suspenseful plots or emotional crises?
- What life conditions, challenges, trials, grudges, grief, betrayals, threats, heartaches, or obsessions can characters face that may lead to compelling situations throughout the series? (Think romance, marriage, divorce, parents or children, illness, medical ailment, or death.)
- What locations can you set the series and individual books in to expand characters and plots?
- What world, regional, or local events, holidays, important dates, or disasters (natural or man-made) can provide a catalyst?
- What quest—fortuitous, cursed, or anywhere in between—can be undertaken?
- What item or object might become the basis for plot, setting, or character development?

Always leave plenty of plants unexplored to give your series longevity and your characters and storylines flexibility. In the early books in the Pendergast series, it was revealed that the protagonist's wife had been killed years earlier. Superficial details about this death were alluded to but kept sparse and flexible enough that, when the authors moved into their Helen Trilogy quite a few books later, they could easily mold this event any way they needed to and maintain believability. Had they locked down specific details early on, the trilogy might never have seen the light of day.

Hints and allusions are essential when implementing C-S-P potential. In real life, no one walks around with a list to show others of the people they know, the places they've been, or the things they've done. These are shared a little at a time. In the same way, from one book to the next, explore the facets of C-S-P slowly. If you give too much detail too soon, you may find it hard to change or adapt when the time comes to use a plant.

Remember: If no one wants to see more of these characters, settings, and plots over the long haul, the series is doomed. Always spin established facts on their axis so the reader will have a new, emotional, and unexpected journey in each story. Every offering must be *at least* as exciting as the one before. These are the ingredients that bring readers back for more.

ORGANIZATION OF DETAILS

The best way to learn how *not* to write a series is to do so with no organization whatsoever. You'll likely miss countless opportunities to plant and grow seeds for C-S-P series potential, be forced to backtrack to clear up issues that arise, and maybe even write yourself into a corner.

While some authors may be capable of outlining every book in a series before writing a word, that's not possible for everyone. Maybe the only way for you to figure out where you're going with your series is to complete the first book, then set it aside while you think about what might lie ahead: Which characters will take the lead? What story will be told, and which conflicts will arise? What seeds can you go back and plant in the first manuscript to prepare readers for the next installments? Even if you're not much of a planner, try answering the C-S-P potential questions as much as you can. Never underestimate the value of the key story (and series!) questions percolating in your mind.

How much preplanning you do is up to you, but at minimum I recommend you at least attempt to build on your C-S-P potential by writing summary blurbs for the series and its individual books. Just see how far you can get. Play with them, and don't expect perfection the first time. You can work with them more as your series progresses.

For a series blurb, you're not focusing on individual stories but on the gist of what the series *as a whole* is about. If the series blurb is done well enough, it'll accurately reflect what every book in the series is about in a concise, intriguing summary. Remember your series ties while you're working; they'll help you figure out what your series arc should be. In no more than four sentences, define your series arc by using "leads to" logic (note that the components don't have to be in order, nor is a resolution required since you may not want to defuse the intrigue or tension):

Introduction ⋙ Change ⋙ Conflicts ⋙ Choices ⋙ Crisis ⋙ Resolutions

Here's an example from my Incognito series:

> The Network is the world's most covert organization. Having unchallenged authority and skill to disable criminals, the Network takes over where regular law enforcement leaves off in the mission for absolute justice (**Introduction**). The price: men and women who have sacrificed their personal identities (**Choices**) to live in the shadows (**Change**) and uphold justice for all (**Conflicts**)—no matter the cost (**Crisis**).

Next, try blurbing the individual stories you foresee comprising the series. It's all right if you've only gotten as far as brainstorming one or two books. Start with what you have, and add to your brainstorm as more comes to you. Even if you don't think you know enough to get started planning this way, you'll likely find that the process of putting your ideas into words helps your concepts multiply.

Focus on which characters will take the lead in individual stories and what each story arc (conflict) will be. Write free-form summaries covering the who, what, where, when, and why of each story. Then try creating a more compelling blurb using this equation (if you have more than one main character, do this for each):

> (**Name of Character**) wants (**Goal to Be Achieved**) because (**Motivation for Acting**), but faces (**Conflict Standing in the Way**).

As before, you can mix up the order of the components. Here's the story blurb from *Dark Approach*, the twelfth book in my Incognito series:

> Network operatives and lovers Lucy Carlton and Vic Leventhal (**Names of Characters**) have spent years living in the shadows, the property of the covert organization they gave their loyalty to in the lofty pursuit of justice for all (**Motivation for Acting**). Disillusioned, they're now determined to live their lives on their own terms. When the Network's archenemy secretly approaches the two about defecting—freedom for information that will disable the Network (**Goal to Be Achieved**)—the couple must choose between love and loyalty. In the process, they jeopardize the Network's anonymity ... and its very existence (**Conflict Standing in the Way**).

Blurbing in this way will help you develop your series—and get you excited about writing it.

The appeal of writing a series is obvious: You don't have to leave behind characters, places, or premises you've grown to love when you finish a single book. While each story should stand on its own, remember that no series book should feel quite complete without the others since readers will be emotionally invested in your story even more than they would with a stand-alone novel. Keep the above factors at the forefront as you work, and you'll keep your series satisfying for your fans—and for you.

Karen Wiesner is an accomplished author with 117 titles published in the past eighteen years, which have been nominated or won 134 awards, and has thirty-nine more releases contracted, spanning many genres and formats. Karen's books cover such genres as women's fiction, romance, mystery/police procedural/cozy, suspense, paranormal, futuristic, fantasy, Gothic, inspirational, thriller, horror, chick-lit, and action/adventure. She also writes children's books, poetry, and writing reference titles such as her bestseller, *First Draft in 30 Days*, as well as *Cohesive Story Building* and *Writing the Fiction Series*. For more information about Karen's fiction and series, consult her official companion guide, *The World of Author Karen Wiesner: A Compendium of Fiction*, or visit her website at www.karenwiesner.com. Karen also enjoys designing websites, graphics, and cover art.

42

WRITING INVESTIGATION

Clues, Red Herrings, and Misdirection

Hallie Ephron

Investigation is the meat and potatoes of a mystery novel. The sleuth talks to people, does research, snoops around, and makes observations. Facts emerge. Maybe an eyewitness gives an account of what he saw. A wife has unexplained bruises on her face. The brother of a victim avoids eye contact with his questioner. A will leaves a millionaire's estate to an obscure charity. A bloody knife is found in a laundry bin. A love letter is discovered tucked into last week's newspaper.

Some of this evidence will turn out to be clues that eventually identify the villain. Others are red herrings—evidence that misdirects the reader and leads to false conclusions. On top of that, some of the information your sleuth gathers will turn out to be nothing more than the irrelevant minutiae of everyday life, inserted into scenes to give a sense of realism and to camouflage the clues.

INVESTIGATING: OBSERVING AND INTERROGATING

A sleuth's investigation centers on two main activities: observing and asking questions. If your sleuth is a professional detective or a police officer, then investigating might include examining the crime scene, questioning witnesses, staking out suspects, pulling rap sheets, checking DMV records, and going undercover. If your sleuth is a medical examiner, we're talking autopsies and X-rays, analysis of stomach contents and DNA. If your character is an amateur sleuth, he's going to sneak around, ask a lot of questions, and cozy up to the police.

How your sleuth investigates should reflect his skills and personality. Here is an example from one of Peter Robinson's DCI Banks mystery novels, *Friend of the Devil*. DCI Banks observes the crime scene:

> "Looks like we have manual strangulation to me, unless there are hidden causes," Burns said, stooping and carefully lifting a strand of blond hair, gesturing toward the dark bruising under her chin and ear.
>
> From what Banks could see, she was young, no older than his own daughter Tracy. She was wearing a green top and a white miniskirt with a broad pink plastic belt covered in silver glitter. The skirt had been hitched up even higher than it was already to expose her upper thighs. The body looked posed.

Banks is a pro. He's unemotional and analytical in his observations, even though the victim is the same age as his daughter. His years of experience have shown him what dead bodies look like, so he knows when one seems "posed."

Whether your sleuth schmoozes over tea with the victim's neighbor, makes telephone calls to witnesses, formally interrogates a suspect, or huddles with colleagues to discuss blood spatter, he or she asks questions and gets answers. Talk, talk, talk. It can get pretty boring if all you're doing is conveying information. So create a dynamic between the characters during the Q&A to hold the reader's interest. Interrogation becomes interesting when the relationship between the characters has an electrical charge, some inner dynamic, as in this passage in which DCI Banks interrogates a suspect later in *Friend of the Devil*:

> "Never mind the bollocks, Mr. Austin," said Banks. "You told DC Jackman that you weren't having an affair with Hayley Daniels. Information has come to light that indicates you were lying. What do you have to say about that?"
>
> "What information? I resent your implication."
>
> "Is it true or not that you were having an affair with Hayley Daniels?"
>
> Austin looked at Winsome, then back at Banks. Finally he compressed his lips, bellowed up his cheeks and let the air out slowly. "All right," he said. "Hayley and I had been seeing one another for two months. We started about a month or so after my wife left. Which means, strictly speaking, that whatever Hayley and I had, it wasn't an affair."
>
> "Semantics," said Banks. "Teacher shagging student. What do you call it?"
>
> "It wasn't that," said Austin. "You make it sound so sordid. We were in love."
>
> "Excuse me while I reach for a bucket."
>
> "Inspector! The woman I love has been murdered. The least you can do is show some respect."

"How old are you, Malcolm?"

"Fifty-one."

"And Hayley Daniels was nineteen."

With his word choice (*bollocks, shagging*) and attitude (*"Excuse me while I reach for a bucket."*), Banks shows his working-class roots and his disdain for Malcolm Austin. He's not at all impressed with this man's pedigree as a teacher, and he doesn't suffer fools. His disgust with this man who seduced a young woman is more than professional; it's personal—the victim reminds Banks of his own daughter.

Notice how Robinson uses body language as subtext, conveying to the reader a character's emotions without spelling it out, letting the reader do the work of interpreting: *Austin looked at Winsome, then back at Banks. Finally he compressed his lips, bellowed up his cheeks and let the air out slowly.*

That physical description, inserted in the middle of spare back-and-forth dialogue, highlights a tipping point—a transition between Austin's insistence that he wasn't having an affair with the victim and his confession that he was. Instead of rushing past this key moment, Robinson opens it up, slowing the reader down and drawing attention to the shift by inserting a physical description between the lines of dialogue.

Look for tipping points in your novel where the emotional balance shifts or a revelation comes to light. Open those tipping points by slowing down the narrative, but don't bang your reader over the head with them or spoon-feed conclusions. Often you can let the reader interpret what it means.

Blending Clues and Red Herrings

A clue can be just about anything:

- an object the sleuth discovers (a bloody glove)
- the way a character behaves (he keeps his hands in his pockets)
- a revealing gesture (a woman straightens her boss's collar)
- what someone says ("Julia Dalrymple deserved to die.")
- what someone wears (a locket stolen from the victim)
- an item that doesn't fit with the way the person presents himself or his history (a suspect's fingerprint is lifted from a room the suspect says she was never in)

Here are some techniques that enable you to play fair and, at the same time, keep the reader guessing:

- **EMPHASIZE THE UNIMPORTANT; DEEMPHASIZE THE CLUE.** The reader should see the clue but not recognize its significance. For example, the sleuth investigates the value and provenance of a stolen painting and pays little attention to the identity of the woman who sat for the portrait.
- **ESTABLISH A CLUE BEFORE THE READER CAN GRASP ITS SIGNIFICANCE.** Introduce the key information before the reader understands the context it fits into. For example, the sleuth strolls by a character spraying her rose bushes before discovering that a neighbor was poisoned by a common herbicide.
- **HAVE YOUR SLEUTH MISINTERPRET THE MEANING OF A CLUE.** Your sleuth misinterprets evidence that takes the investigation to a dead end. For example, the victim is found in a room with the window open. The sleuth thinks that's how the killer escaped and goes looking for a witness who saw someone climbing out of the house. In fact, the window was opened to let out telltale fumes.
- **HAVE THE CLUE TURN OUT TO BE SOMETHING THAT SHOULD BE THERE BUT *ISN'T*.** The sleuth painstakingly elucidates what happened, failing to notice what should have happened but didn't. The most famous example is from the Sherlock Holmes story "Silver Blaze." Holmes deduces there could not have been an intruder because the dog didn't bark.
- **SCATTER PIECES OF THE CLUE IN DIFFERENT PLACES AND MIX UP THE LOGICAL ORDER.** Challenge your reader by revealing only part of a clue at a time. For instance, the sleuth might find a canary cage with a broken door in the basement, along with other detritus; later the sleuth has a "Wait a minute!" realization when he discovers the dead canary with its neck wrung.
- **HIDE THE CLUE IN PLAIN SIGHT.** Tuck the clue among so many other possible clues that it doesn't stand out. For example, the murder weapon, a nylon stocking, might be neatly laundered and folded in the victim's lingerie drawer. Or the sleuth focuses on the water bottle, unopened mail, pine needles, and gas station receipt on the floor of the victim's car and fails to recognize the significance of a telephone number written in the margin of the map.
- **DRAW ATTENTION ELSEWHERE.** Have multiple plausible alternatives vying for the reader's attention. For example, the sleuth knows patients are being poisoned. He focuses on a doctor who gives injections and fails to notice the medic who administers oxygen.
- **CREATE A TIME PROBLEM.** Manipulate time to your own advantage. For example, suppose the prime suspect has an alibi for the time of the murder. Later the sleuth discovers that the time of the alibi or the time of death is wrong.

- **PLACE THE REAL CLUE RIGHT BEFORE A FALSE ONE.** People tend to remember what was presented to them last. For example, your sleuth notices that the stove doesn't light properly and immediately after that discovers an empty prescription bottle, marked with the label "Poison," stuffed in the trash. Readers (and your sleuth) are more likely to remember the hidden bottle than the malfunctioning stove that preceded it.
- **CAMOUFLAGE A CLUE WITH ACTION.** If you show the reader a clue, insert some extraneous action at the same time to distract attention. For example, your sleuth gets mugged while reading a flyer posted on a lamppost; the mugging turns out to be irrelevant, but the flyer contains an important clue.

PLAYING FAIR

In a mystery novel, it's considered bad form to flat-out withhold information that the narrator knows. It can be infuriating when an author withholds, even temporarily, some important piece of information that the point-of-view character knows.

Here's an example:

> Sharon's cell phone rang.
>
> "Sorry," she told Bob. "This could be important."
>
> She flipped the phone open and pressed it to her ear. "Hello?"
>
> Sharon recognized the caller's voice, the last person she'd expect to call her after all that had happened. "What's up?" she said, trying not to sound surprised.
>
> "You need to know this—" the caller began.
>
> As Sharon listened, she found herself pressing against the car door, trying to insert a few extra inches between herself and Bob. Bob was eyeing her closely, and his unconcerned look suddenly seemed no more than a thin veneer.

The chapter ends, and the reader doesn't discover for twenty pages the identity of the caller or what troubling information that person imparted. Never mind that we've been hanging out in Sharon's head for the last hundred pages and she's been blabbing everything she sees, hears, feels, and thinks. Now, all of a sudden, she plays coy with this critical tidbit.

The reader and the sleuth should realize the identity of the culprit at about the same time. Authors succumb to the temptation of withholding information the narrator knows in an effort to create suspense. When they do, they cheat the story and exasperate readers. I know, I know, mystery authors get away with this shtick all the time, but it's a cheap trick. Here's my advice: Don't succumb.

This is why guilty narrators are problematic in a mystery. They know too much. But plenty of mystery writers have managed to pull off a villainous narrator, keeping the character's identity hidden without enraging their readers. For example, Peter Clement's *The Inquisitor* is written from the point of view of a particularly chilling villain who gets his jollies bringing terminal patients near death:

> "Can you hear me?" I whispered, holding back on the plunger of my syringe.
>
> "Yes." Her eyes remained shut.
>
> I leaned over and brought my mouth to her ear. "Any more pain?"
>
> "No. It's gone."
>
> "Do you see anything?"
>
> "Only blackness." Her whispers rasped against the back of her throat.
>
> "Look harder! Now tell me what's there." I swallowed to keep from gagging. Her breath stank.
>
> "You're not my doctor."
>
> "No, I'm replacing him tonight."

Notice that by writing this passage in first person, Clement not only conceals the villain's identity but also the villain's gender. This subterfuge leaves the author free to cast suspicion on both male and female characters.

But it's cheating to spend chapter after chapter in a character's head, only to reveal in a final climactic scene that she's been hiding one small detail: She did it. You might get away with it if the character is an *unreliable narrator* who can't remember (she has amnesia), doesn't realize (she's delusional, naïve, simpleminded, or bamboozled), or can't admit even to herself that she's guilty.

CONFUSION: INTEREST KILLER

Your goal is to misdirect but never to confuse. Lead the reader down a series of perfectly logical primrose paths—your reader must always feel grounded, even if the story is veering onto a false path. Set too many different possible scenarios spinning at once, or overwhelm your reader with a cacophony of clues, red herrings, and background noise, and your baffled reader will get frustrated and set the book aside—permanently.

As you write, keep track of the different scenarios and of the clues that implicate and exonerate each suspect. Also, be sure to track who knows what and when they know it—particularly if you're writing from multiple viewpoints. If you're confused, your reader is sure to be.

COINCIDENCE: CREDIBILITY KILLER

All of us are tempted, from time to time, to insert a coincidence into a storyline. Wouldn't it be cool, you say to yourself, to have a character run into the twin sister she never knew she had in a hall of mirrors at a county fair? Dramatic, yes. Credible, no.

Never mind that Agatha Christie wrote a story that turns on a similar coincidence: A man runs into his unknown twin brother coming out of a drugstore; the evil twin then commits a murder and implicates his brother. Never mind that you once read a newspaper article about separated twins who ran into each other in a supermarket. Life is full of bizarre coincidences. You can't put a coincidence like that in a mystery novel today and expect your work to be taken seriously.

Coincidence is most likely to creep in when you maneuver your character into position for the sake of your plot. Maybe your character needs to find out when and where a crime is going to occur, so you have him coincidentally find that information in a letter someone drops on the sidewalk. Or maybe your character needs to find a buried clue, so you give her the inexplicable urge to plant petunias and dig in just the right spot. Or maybe your character needs to know the scheme two characters are hatching, so he happens to pick up the phone extension and overhears them planning.

It's much more satisfying if you come up with logical ways to maneuver your character into position to find the clues and red herrings your plot requires. Repeat after me: *Thou shalt not resort to coincidence, intuition, clairvoyance, or divine intervention.* In a mystery, logic rules and credibility is paramount.

If you do put coincidence in your story, at least have your point-of-view character comment on the absurdity of the coincidence. While it's not the most elegant solution, at least it will keep the reader from dismissing you as a hack.

Hallie Ephron is the *New York Times* best-selling author of suspense and mystery novels. Her novels have been called "deliciously creepy" (*Publishers Weekly*), "gripping" (*The Boston Globe*), and "snaky and unsettling" (*Seattle Times*). She is a four-time finalist for the Mary Higgins Clark Award, recognizing excellence in suspense. Her novel *Never Tell a Lie* was turned into a movie for the Lifetime Movie Network. She wrote an On Crime book review column for *The Boston Globe* for more than ten years and won the Ellen Nehr Award for Excellence in Mystery Reviewing. The first edition of her book *Writing and Selling Your Mystery Novel* was an Edgar Award finalist, and a revised and expanded edition was released in December 2016. Hallie is a popular speaker and teaches writing at conferences, nationally and internationally.

43

BLURRED LINES

....

How to Write and Sell a Cross-Genre Novel

Michelle Richmond

For as long as any of us can remember, the term *genre fiction* has referred to work that fits neatly into a single prescribed category: science fiction, romance, mystery, fantasy, horror, historical, etc. But take a close look at any bookshelf today, and you might be surprised to see how much the lines between genre fiction and mainstream fiction—and even between certain traditionally compartmentalized genres—are blurring.

M.J. Rose, best-selling novelist and founder of AuthorBuzz, knows what it means to defy genre conventions. While some of her novels are easily categorized, others combine elements from such varied genres as romance, paranormal, and mystery. And while that might sound like watering down a story, it's actually been lifting her work to the top. In March 2012, Rose's *The Book of Lost Fragrances* simultaneously made both Amazon's Best Books of the Month in the science fiction/fantasy category and *Publishers Weekly*'s Top Ten Mysteries and Thrillers rankings.

Books like Rose's demonstrate the potential of quality cross-genre fiction to reach exponentially more readers by appealing to multiple audiences. They also show how much the publishing landscape is changing. "For years," Rose says, "publishers told my agent that they loved my work but didn't know how to market such cross-genre fiction."

These concerns were very real in the brick-and-mortar marketplace. "Fiction in different genres is packaged and marketed differently and shelved on different bookstore shelves … so cross-genre fiction wouldn't be the *easiest* way to start a career," explains veteran literary agent Elizabeth Pomada. But today, thanks in large part to the rise of online booksellers and the accessibility of digital publishing (and self-publishing), there's plenty of room on the virtual shelf for books that defy easy categorization. "[Suddenly, we are living] in a bottom-up culture in which readers, not publishing conglomerates, are the gatekeepers," Pomada says.

My own career has been a twelve-year lesson in crossing genres. My first novel blended elements of erotica, political fiction, and murder mystery; was set in China and the Deep South; and addressed an impending environmental disaster. The agents I queried questioned how the book would be positioned. Was this a coming-of-age story? A mystery? A political or environmental cautionary tale? Was it too racy for mainstream readers? I never quite pinned down the genre (or genres) in my pitch—and I never found an agent, either. I'd all but given up on the novel when I connected with a small publisher that had an interest in Southern writers (I'm from Alabama). When *Dream of the Blue Room* was published with MacAdam/Cage in 2003, reviewers didn't know what to make of it. "There's a lot going on in this book," a reviewer for the *San Francisco Chronicle* wrote. In hindsight, I see that I was trying to juggle too many balls.

I had the feeling that what I'd been missing was a sense of urgency and focus, so with my second novel, I decided to have a child character go missing on page one. Delving into suspense was a huge departure from my comfort zone, but it felt good to put my characters in a situation I (and they) couldn't walk away from. Fortunately, by that time I'd met my agent, Valerie Borchardt, who encouraged me to write what I most wanted to write; as a result, the story also became a meditation on memory—something that allowed me to indulge my meandering nature and my affinity for more literary prose.

With strategic, targeted marketing to both women's fiction and mystery readers, my second novel, *The Year of Fog*, did indeed reach a much larger audience than my previous work, even hitting *The New York Times* bestseller list. With the release of my next book—which combined an ancient mathematical puzzle, a historical perspective on coffee, and a decades-old murder—the *Daily Mail* dubbed me "mistress of the kind of literary mystery that packs the punch of a fine thriller, but with added insight and wisdom." As someone who'd never much contemplated being mistress of anything, I was happily surprised.

THREE KEYS TO WRITING THE CROSS-GENRE NOVEL

My own cross-genre success happened almost by accident, but only after the trial and error of my first novel. I've since learned that a more focused approach is the most direct route to crafting the kind of manuscript that will draw the attention of agents, publishers, and readers.

You don't have to look far to find authors having wild success with focused cross-genre approaches. Take Charlaine Harris's best-selling Southern Vampire Mysteries, featuring telepathic waitress Sookie Stackhouse. The series, which from the outset included a well-defined and consistent blend of paranormal elements, romance, and mystery, was so marketable it transcended book form and spawned the popular HBO series *True Blood*.

Then there's bestseller-list staple Sandra Brown, author of dozens of romantic suspense novels, including *The Alibi*, *The Crush*, and *Low Pressure*. Her titles are so equally successful in both genres that Brown has received both the Romance Writers of America Lifetime Achievement Award and the International Thriller Writers' top designation of ThrillerMaster.

Successful novels that have done what you'd like your own work to accomplish can be wonderful learning tools. Here are some other strategies to keep in mind as you shape your cross-genre story:

RECOGNIZE YOUR PRIMARY GENRE—AND USE IT AS YOUR COMPASS.
Examine the fundamental core of any cross-genre story, and you'll likely find that one primary genre drives the plot. It's important to recognize this in your own work and pay homage to that genre's time-honored traditions: A murder mystery should have red herrings, a romance heroine should face obstacles to true love, and a political thriller needs a villain who stands in the way of your protagonist's search for justice.

Let that genre guide you from page one. Brown's romantic thriller *Lethal* begins with a mother and her young daughter being held at gunpoint in their home; from the first chapter, the reader is confronted with the sense of imminent danger that propels the novel forward.

Let your primary genre give your story structure, and you'll have a strong foundation upon which to build. From there, layer on fundamental aspects of at least two (but no more than three) genres in a way that gives fair, if not equal, time to each.

DRAW ON YOUR STRENGTHS AS A WRITER, REGARDLESS OF GENRE.
Julianna Baggott is the best-selling author of more than twenty books that run the gamut from young adult fiction to poetry. Two of her recent novels, *Pure* and *Fuse*, are part of a futuristic YA trilogy that has also drawn a devoted following among adult science fiction fans—not surprising, given that she began her career writing fiction for adult readers. Baggott encourages writers to take what they know from the genre in which they feel most comfortable and find a way to use

it to their advantage in anything they write. "Each genre has its own demands," she says, "[but] the lessons learned in one are often transferable to another."

By relying on what comes naturally to you even as you venture into something new, you'll be more likely to find a cross-section of genres that is inherent to the story at hand rather than forced by any preconceived ideas of what the story should be. "I find it a huge advantage to take what the world hands you—that raw material—and ask what form it most desires," Baggott says.

Pomada agrees. "Write what you love, and write it with an eye toward entertaining your reader," she says. "The essential virtue of salable prose is that it keeps readers turning the pages. If writers can do that, they can write anything."

CREATE CHARACTERS THAT DEFY GENRE CONVENTIONS. Genre fiction is often criticized for being formulaic and short on character. As you write, keep asking yourself: If you were to extract your main character from the novel and set her down in an entirely different situation, would the reader still care what happens to her? If not, you have more work to do.

Holly Goddard Jones's debut novel, *The Next Time You See Me*, is literary suspense that opens with a time-honored mystery setup: the discovery of a body. But as the story progresses, the way in which each character reacts to his own suffering—an emotion-driven hallmark of literary fiction—turns out to be every bit as important to the story as uncovering the identity of the killer. Ryan McNear, the believably flawed protagonist of Ransom Stephens's scientific legal thriller *The God Patent*, isn't just a physicist who has patented man's soul; he is also a man on the run who is reeling from the loss of his family.

PITCHING YOUR CROSS-GENRE NOVEL

Agents and publishers want to know how a novel will fit into an existing niche, but they also want to know how it's different from what's already on the market. Instead of giving in to the urge to say, "I don't want to be labeled," consider labels a way to make your book more marketable.

NAME THE PRIMARY GENRE AND ONE OR TWO ADDITIONAL GENRES IN YOUR PITCH. Don't throw too many labels into the mix. No agent is likely to embrace a "Western romantic thriller with elements of science fiction and fantasy." If you can, distill your genres into one adjective (the secondary genre) plus a noun (the primary genre): *historical thriller, science fiction drama, romantic fantasy*. The more specific your description, the more confident your pitch will sound.

PLAY UP THE WAYS IN WHICH YOUR CROSS-GENRE APPROACH WILL BROADEN YOUR TARGET AUDIENCE. In her pitch for *French Lessons*, Ellen Sussman capitalized on the intersection of two genres: suspense and romance. Her pitch, she says, went something like this: "This novel will appeal to readers who love a literary page-turner, as well as those who are looking for a steamy romance." An agent wants to know you've thought about your audience.

EMPHASIZE THE STORY IN RELATION TO THE GENRE. "When pitching a genre-blurring novel, talk about the world of the novel and the characters who endure within it," Baggott advises. *Pure* features a young female protagonist, Pressia, facing off against a lawless society and a powerful group that wants her dead; the genre is futuristic YA, but the draw is Pressia herself, the emotional center of the story.

Consider M.J. Rose's pitch for her genre-bender *The Seduction of Victor H.*: "In 1853, Victor Hugo began a series of secret séances in an effort to reach his dead daughter. He wrote transcripts of those séances and claimed to have reached Jesus, Dante, Shakespeare, and dozens more spirits, including someone he called the Shadow of the Sepulcher, known to us by another name: Lucifer. What if one set of transcripts was hidden because they were too controversial? What if a modern-day woman finds them, and they put her life in jeopardy? Celtic legends, the Isle of Jersey, reincarnation, perfume—all come together in my first ghost story."

Notice how Rose mentions the cross-genre elements of her novel—historical figures with religious subtext—in one juicy paragraph that begins and ends with emphasis on her primary genre: paranormal.

Michelle Richmond is the author of six books, including *Golden State* and *The New York Times* bestseller *The Year of Fog*. Her latest story collection, *Hum*, received the Catherine Doctorow Innovative Fiction Prize. A native of Mobile, Alabama, she lives in Northern California with her husband and son.

44

LOVE GONE WRONG

Five Common Flaws in Romance Novels

Leigh Michaels

If you sense that something is wrong with your romance work-in-progress, you can likely blame one of the five following problems: (1) inadequate conflict, (2) unrealistic or unsympathetic characters, (3) unclear relationship motivation, (4) straying focus, or, simply, (5) lackluster writing. As an award-winning romance novelist who continues to lead writing workshops in the genre, I have encountered one or more of these issues in every unsuccessful romance novel I've ever read. Here is how to diagnose—and treat—these ailments in your own manuscript.

1. INADEQUATE CONFLICT

A story about two people who are doing little more than fighting against their overwhelming attraction to each other is unlikely to bear the weight of a 250-page novel.

Real conflict involves important issues. What's at stake? What do both characters want that only one of them can have? Or what do they both want so badly that they must work together to get it?

Authentic conflict has at least two realistic, believable, sympathetic sides—positions that reasonable human beings could logically take. If you (and your readers) can't convincingly argue from either point of view, then your conflict is likely one-sided and flat.

When you have genuine conflict, your characters will have plenty to talk about. When you don't, they may argue until doomsday, but their conversations will be superficial and won't lead anywhere.

Symptoms of inadequate conflict include:

- **CHARACTERS WHO ARGUE BUT DON'T TALK TO EACH OTHER.** If simply explaining their positions would have solved the problem in the very first chapter, then the couple is only having a misunderstanding, not a true conflict.
- **ONE-SIDED CONFLICTS.** If one of your characters is trying to save the rainforest and the other takes glee in burning it to the ground, it's hard to be sympathetic to the latter character.
- **CIRCULAR ARGUMENTS.** The characters argue the same points again and again without making progress toward a solution. If the conflict is genuine, a real discussion will develop and the characters will gradually modify their points of view as they explain their positions.
- **LOW STAKES.** The issue doesn't seem important enough to warrant a story. A difference of opinion between two teachers about how to run a classroom, or a quarrel between parents about whether their daughter should wear short shorts, isn't likely to keep readers up at night.

2. UNREALISTIC OR UNSYMPATHETIC CHARACTERS

If during their first meeting your hero and heroine act as if they've hated each other for years, then they're not believable. If they behave badly toward each other throughout the novel without clearly justifiable reason, then they're not sympathetic. If they show nothing but distaste for each other throughout the entire book but fall into each other's arms on the last page, then their chances of lasting happiness are unconvincing.

Symptoms of unrealistic or unsympathetic characters may include:

- **A HEROINE YOU WOULDN'T WANT TO BEFRIEND.** If she isn't someone you'd want to hang out with, odds are your readers won't, either. *You* may know that deep down your heroine is a sweetheart—but if she spends all of chapter one shrieking at her mother, readers will see only her unpleasant side.
- **A HERO YOU WOULDN'T WANT TO BE MARRIED TO.** Your main man has to be more than a handsome, sexy shell to have lasting appeal. If he's angry, can readers empathize with his emotions? Does the bad boy have a secret sensitive side, or is he so dangerous that a sensible woman would run?
- **CHARACTERS WHO ARE OUT OF BALANCE.** If the hero is aggressive and the heroine is weak, or if the heroine is pushy and the hero is passive, the story is apt to trail off. In a good pairing, the hero and heroine will be roughly equal in strength and assertiveness.

- **TOO MUCH TELLING.** If the characters are not realistic or relatable, it will be difficult to bring them to life—and thus make you more susceptible to just writing about them rather than showing them interact.
- **UNMOTIVATED OPPOSITION.** The hero should not try to prevent the heroine from getting what she wants (or vice versa) simply to be nasty. Readers will find both characters more sympathetic if there is a good reason for their opposition.
- **TOO MUCH INTERNALIZING.** This occurs when readers hear all about a character's thoughts—more than they want to—but don't have any reason to care.

3. UNCLEAR RELATIONSHIP MOTIVATION

This particular problem occurs when there isn't any major factor keeping the main characters in the current relationship situation. For instance, if a man dislikes a woman (even though he thinks she has a great body) and she detests him (even though he's quite a hunk), there isn't anything preventing either character from walking away. What makes it necessary for them to stay in contact long enough to discover that their attraction to each other is really love? If you can't state in one sentence the reason your hero and heroine need each other, that reason needs redefining.

Symptoms of unclear motivation include:

- **A HERO AND HEROINE WHO HAVE LITTLE TO SAY TO EACH OTHER.** If their conversations contain no substance, maybe they need more reasons to talk in the first place.
- **CHARACTERS WHO ARE MOTIVATED TO OPPOSE EACH OTHER BY PETTY IRRITATION RATHER THAN REAL DISAGREEMENT.** Are they just sniping at each other instead of discussing a substantial problem? If so, there may be no reason for them to be together.
- **A HERO AND HEROINE WHO ARE OFTEN SEPARATED PHYSICALLY.** When they're not together, there's no interaction—perhaps because they don't have enough reason to spend time with each other.

4. STRAYING FOCUS

If the romance isn't at the heart of the book, your readers in this genre will be disappointed. The other parts of the novel—the mystery of the missing money, the child in need, the subplot involving secondary characters—are sometimes

The Complete Handbook of Novel Writing

more fun and are often easier to write than the immediate interaction between the main characters.

But readers want to see a developing relationship—fondness, trust, attraction—between the hero and heroine. The rest of the story, important though it is, should serve as the background for the romance.

Symptoms of straying focus include:

- **EXCESS OF PLOTS.** Too many events or subplots means less time for the developing relationship.
- **TOO MANY PEOPLE ONSTAGE.** If the hero and heroine aren't alone together, it's more difficult for their feelings to develop. Even in a packed auditorium you can isolate your two main characters. Move them off to a corner, or let them carry on a whispered private exchange while surrounded by other people.
- **SCENES THAT VEER OFF TRACK.** Side issues become more important than the main story, and everybody—author, characters, and readers—forgets the point of the scene. Or the backstory of secondary characters distracts readers from the main story.
- **INTERFERENCE BY OTHER CHARACTERS.** Whether the interference is intended to create trouble between the hero and heroine or to bring them together, it takes the focus off the main relationship. The hero and heroine should solve their own problems.

5. LACKLUSTER WRITING

You haven't put words on the page in a spellbinding way. Perhaps you're summarizing the story instead of showing the complete narrative arc. Or sentences may be unclear, forcing readers to deduce or interpret what you mean. You may depict the action in the wrong order, confusing readers. Or maybe you're showing only part of the scene, leaving out details necessary for readers' understanding.

Symptoms of lackluster writing include:

- **SLOW STARTS.** Chapter one might consist of the heroine reflecting on her past and what has brought her to this stage in her life. If you start with action instead, you give readers a reason to care about the character; then they'll sit still to hear about the roots of the problem.
- **PEACEFUL ENDINGS.** Chapters or scenes that end with the heroine drifting off to sleep without a care are wonderful places for readers to do the same.

- **RUSHED DRAMATIC ACTION.** Watch out for words and phrases such as *later, after a few hours, when she'd had time to think it over,* and other indications that readers are being told rather than shown what happened.
- **LOW EMOTIONAL LEVELS.** When the story events and characters are not emotionally compelling, readers find it difficult to care whether the hero and heroine get what they want.
- **WANDERING VIEWPOINTS.** The point of view shifts back and forth for no good reason, or it's difficult to even figure out who the viewpoint character is.
- **FILLER DIALOGUE.** Instead of relaying important information, the dialogue focuses on everyday detail—lots of instances of *hello* and *goodbye* and *How do you like your coffee?*
- **POOR GRAMMAR, SPELLING, WORD USAGE, OR MECHANICS.** Anything that takes readers' attention off the story and forces them to figure out what the author meant makes it easier for them to put down the book.

You owe it to yourself—and your readers—to make your novel the best it can be. By sharpening the conflict, crafting realistic characters and relationships, honing the focus of your narrative, and adhering to the tenets of strong storytelling, you give yourself a fighting chance to earn a place on your readers' "favorites" shelf.

PUT THEIR LOVE TO THE TEST

Use these probing questions to spot areas in your own romance novel-in-progress where you've lost the thread of your story, revealed too much too soon, or left out crucial information or steps in the development of the plot or relationship.

- What do readers know about the main character by the end of chapter one? What do readers not know but want to? What unnecessary information can you cut?
- What forces the hero and heroine to stay in the situation? If being around each other makes them unhappy, why doesn't one of them just leave?
- What keeps the hero and heroine apart? Could their disagreement be solved if they sat down for a heart-to-heart?
- Is the conflict personal? Sympathetic? Important to the characters and readers? Can readers picture themselves or someone they love caught up in a similar difficulty?
- Is the disagreement between the main characters strong enough to keep them apart despite their obvious attraction?

- Do readers get to savor the excitement? Listen to the arguments? Watch the action? Or is the dramatic potential of the story summarized?
- Does each scene and each chapter end at a point of interest, where readers will find it difficult to stop reading?
- Of the total number of pages in the manuscript, how many show the hero and heroine interacting together? How many show them in the same room but not interacting?
- What is the longest time (in page count) that the hero and heroine are separated?
- Do readers see a relationship developing between the hero and heroine? How much time do they spend kissing, flirting, making love? Fighting? Just talking? Do the hero and heroine get cozy too quickly?
- Is sexual tension maintained throughout the story? When do the readers see attraction between the characters? Is the sexual tension diminished or increased by the love scenes?

Leigh Michaels is the author of more than one hundred books, including contemporary romance novels, historical romance novels, and nonfiction books. More than 35 million copies of her romance novels have been published. Six of her books have been finalists for Best Traditional Romance novel in the RITA contest sponsored by Romance Writers of America. She has received two Reviewer's Choice awards from *Romantic Times* (RT Book Reviews). She is the author of *On Writing Romance*, published by Writer's Digest Books; *Creating Romantic Characters*; and *Writing Between the Sexes*.

45

BETWEEN THE SHEETS

How to Write Compelling Love Scenes

Deborah Halverson

Writing a sex scene that's truly sensual and emotionally satisfying for readers requires just as much attention to craft as any other scene in your story. But before you start writing about your characters' romps in the sheets, you should ask yourself how explicit you want your story to be. What are you comfortable reading and writing? You might feel that you have to go into explicit detail in order to satisfy your audience, but that's simply not the case (unless you're writing strict erotica). If a PG-13 rating is more your style, there are plenty of readers for you, and there are plenty of ways for you to tell a sensuous story that pleases your audience without making anyone uncomfortable.

At least for women, sexual satisfaction depends a lot on what goes on inside their heads. As long as you keep the romance factor high, your sensual tension taut, and your focus on the immediate emotions, you don't have to describe the act in intimate detail. Forcing yourself to write beyond your comfort zone is just asking for ham-handedness—you'll likely drop in stock phrases and move through the scene quickly rather than linger as the lovers explore each others' bodies and emotions. Your discomfort will show.

If you're comfortable writing more explicit content—and if your chosen romance subgenre aligns with readers' expectations—proceed boldly, even as you challenge yourself to think creatively about describing the action. Even explicit content needs nuance and elements particular to your characters so that it doesn't feel as if you could pull the scene out of this book and drop it into another without anyone noticing the seams.

You also need to consider the novel as a whole. Does explicit detail fit the tone of the rest of the story? Will it feel like an organic part of this storyline, or will it feel out of step with the rest of the narrative or with the characters themselves? For example, if you are describing a character's first time being intimate, it would make sense to include a plethora of physical details and sensations as the character focuses on each new touch. In contrast, if your characters are bold about expressing themselves, they're going to be bold in bed, so stronger words and descriptions would feel organic to that cast. Let your story, circumstances, and character personalities help you reach your decision regarding explicitness.

Once you have a feel for the degree of detail you want in any given love scene, use the following strategies for writing a satisfying tryst that feels as though it could be in only your specific story, featuring your specific characters:

LAY THE FOUNDATION. Great buildup begets great sex. Suddenly throwing in a sex scene without proper lead-in puts too much burden on the scene to rev itself up from nothing, making it feel forced, unearned, and schlocky. Adhere to the mantra, "Story first, then sex." If you build your characters' relationship and desires, then the love scene will come along organically.

BE SENSUAL, NOT MECHANICAL. Instead of focusing solely on actions, write about things that trigger readers' senses and make them feel as if they're in that moment of passion. Write about the setting, the crackle of the fire in the hearth, or the thrum of the waves on the sand. Write about the scent of the character's hair, the amorous lick of the cool breeze on her skin. Write about the curtained room with just that one shaft of moonlight penetrating the darkness.

Sensory detail offers you opportunities to work in contraception, since many writers want to address that but don't want it to break the mood. Write the sound of a drawer opening, the flash of a wrapper, the nod of her head. No awkward "Did you bring protection?" dialogue needed. You have the power to suggest things by invoking sounds, scents, sensations, and textures. Mine that power. There's certainly a time and place for direct, deliberate actions like thrusting and kissing, but surround those with sensual elements that put readers in that moment.

BRING THEIR ISSUES TO BED. Write about what's going on in the point-of-view character's head. Does she have trust issues? Write about her desire to drop the wall with this man in bed. Consider how this moment of intimacy fulfills her needs at this time—or doesn't. Also, it's easy to see how issues from childhood or previous interactions with members of the opposite sex can play into one's comfort between the sheets—but remember that anything can come to bed with us. Is stress about a big decision weighing on your character? She'll bring that tenseness to the scene. Is he distracted by problems with co-workers? Is she jazzed about scoring a coveted internship or vanquishing some kind of mortal enemy? That'll be a part of the sexual dynamic, too. If it can stir up your character's brain or heart, it can hinder or help her libido.

WHAT'S THE DIFFERENCE?

Because a romantic relationship is so different from a friendship, it calls for a different mind-set on your part. You will need to focus on your lovers' differences, on their distinct contributions to the relationship, and on the reasons you've romantically linked them in the first place.

Here's the scenario: Your couple is having a fight about a canceled date. Each character must make an accusation, and each character must concede something; that way, we get the full breadth of an argument, from accusation to resolution. This fight should be about more than the cancellation—use subtext to convey the underlying conflict.

Use these three phrases:

"You always ..."

"You don't understand ..."

"I didn't know that."

When you're done, consider what you learned about each character's needs in this fight. How can you incorporate these insights into the most intimate moments between them?

TAKE YOUR TIME. Even fast and furious intimacy should be indulged on the page. Readers want satisfaction from the scene, not to see you tick off a box, so give the moment its full pay. If you feel an urge to rush through it, that may be your red flag that you're just hitting a plot marker, not building deep characters and working on the internal arc. Use these strategies to make the love scene fun for you to write and possibly even to discover things about your characters' relationship you never knew, sparking your excitement about the scene. Make the scene about more than the lovemaking so that you'll invest as much importance in it as you do any scene that you know is actively pushing your protagonist through her arc.

USE YOUR WRITER'S TOOLBOX, NOT YOUR THESAURUS. Writing an interesting scene is not about switching up the lingo to avoid repeating the same word, or using words that feel vulgar or awkward to you because you want the scene to be "hot." Consulting a thesaurus for every variation of an action or a body part will result in awkwardness that won't do anything to enrich the scene. Your love scene deserves the same careful crafting and variety that you give to any other scene. Avoid cliché phrasing and predictable similes. Respect your audience's ability to hear strong and precise words rather than get cutesy with euphemisms. "Her secret garden" is the stuff of cliché legend—leave it there. If your character is one who would be comfortable talking dirty in bed, then by all means let the banter fly. If that doesn't suit your characters, don't be afraid to leave out the strong words. Have your character reassure the other person with gentle words and sentiments that deliver an emotional wallop: "It was always you."

Alternatively, you can have them talk in playful teases or try to talk but be unable in the face of their desire:

> "That blouse …" He groans as she slowly unbuttons her shirt, her fingers pausing halfway to gently push away his reaching hand.
>
> She shakes her head. "Patience." Her fingers move to the next button.

That example uses teasing dialogue—it concentrates on a shirt rather than a body part, and it isn't likely to punch anyone's vulgarity buttons. By using a prop to focus readers on very precise details and anatomical regions, it manages to lead the mind toward other very specific actions and regions without saying so explicitly. And it lingers, building sexual tension.

When writing your love scene, combine these strategies to create a rich reader experience that evokes all the senses. Include opinions and judgments that show emotions are being engaged and baggage is being dealt with or denied. Remember that the scene is about your *characters* and their feelings and thoughts—not just the action and the dialogue.

Deborah Halverson is the award-winning author of *Writing New Adult Fiction* and *Writing Young Adult Fiction for Dummies*, as well as the teen novels *Big Mouth* and *Honk If You Hate Me* and several books for struggling readers and children. Formerly an editor at Harcourt Children's Books and now a freelancer specializing in new adult fiction, teen and tween fiction, and picture books, Deborah has been working with authors—bestsellers, veterans, debut, and aspiring—for over twenty years. She is also the founder of the popular writers' advice site DearEditor.com and serves on the advisory board for the UC San Diego Extension "Children's Book Writing and Illustrating" certificate program. Find out more at www.DeborahHalverson.com.

46

KNOW YOUR YOUNG AUDIENCE

How to Write for Middle-Grade and
Young Adult Readers

Mary Kole

To write riveting fiction for middle-grade (MG) or young adult (YA) readers, you must be willing to take a long, thoughtful hike in their shoes. What issues and plots will resonate with middle-graders? What themes and characters will keep teens glued to your pages? What genres are particularly popular, and what pitfalls should you avoid? To make your story authentic and relatable, you'll need to figure out what makes your readers tick: what they think, how they feel, and what they consider most important.

INSIDE THE MIND OF YOUR MG READER

When you're an MG reader (age eight to twelve), you live in a world of contrasts:

- You want to be loyal to your family, but you also start to crave independence from them.
- You want to define yourself as an individual, but you also want to fit in with friends and social groups at school.
- You feel that pull to *go*—grow up, make big choices, be unique—but also the pull to *stay*—be a kid, be safe, have things decided for you when the going gets tough.

When you're this age, you're finding a place in the world without straying too far from the comforts of childhood. Then puberty hits, and the boys and girls who used to have "cooties" in elementary school are suddenly alluring. Your body betrays you by growing up and changing. Not only are your emotions and hormones a mess, but everything else seems to slide into confusion, too. During this time, you start to make tough choices and wrong choices, and to pay the consequences of your actions and decisions.

Friendships that were forged over a mutual love of applesauce in kindergarten start to get complicated. Parents and heroes you've trusted unconditionally turn out to be imperfect. Things you thought about yourself, others, and the world turn out to be different or untrue.

Remember that tweens are focused on themselves, but they're also thinking about how others perceive them. Gone is the innocent freedom of being a kid. In its place is the awkward feeling that they're being watched and judged and doing everything wrong. (Middle-graders also start giving their parents this kind of close scrutiny and become perpetually embarrassed.) But on the positive side, they're discovering a lot of new aspects to life.

Use this information, for example, by having your descriptions reflect the freshness of tween-age existence. How does your character interact sensorially with the world? How does she smell, taste, touch, and hear things? Come middle school, kids have a lot of new experiences for the first time. How does this change your story's voice?

Checking for "Content"

Things get complex at this point in a child's life, but MG is not nearly as edgy as YA, nor should you feel the pressure to make it edgy *at all*. There can be *some* edgy material (what I like to call "content"), though you should avoid strong language and sex.

The edgier you make your MG, the more resistance you will meet, especially in more conservative households and school districts. An editor might warn you away from content, too, because he's thinking about your overall sales potential and marketability.

If you really want to explore a darker shade with your MG story, give the edgiest issue to a secondary character. For example, in a YA book, your main character might be an alcoholic or involved in a violent relationship. In MG, you can still cover these things, but you'll usually use the lens of a secondary character, such as a distant mother or an abusive uncle.

If a romance figures prominently in your story, it should be tender and innocent, such as the ones in Jenny Han's *Shug* or Eva Ibbotson's *The Dragonfly Pool*.

Romance is, at this point, becoming more of a preoccupation for your readers (it will almost completely overtake them by the time they reach young adulthood), but there is typically no room for something sexually graphic or gratuitous in MG.

For examples of how crushes are handled in the MG realm, let's look at a small excerpt from Newbery Medal–winning *When You Reach Me* by Rebecca Stead. Here, Miranda's crush, Colin, decides to kiss her:

> Colin stood there, holding his skateboard in front of him like a shield, looking not exactly like himself.

The kiss is mentioned after this, but Stead does not go into detail.

In Danette Haworth's *Violet Raines Almost Got Struck by Lightning*, Violet simply notices a neighborhood boy in a new way. There's an awkward Truth or Dare kiss in another scene, but this is about the extent of the romance:

> His eyes burn with their full power. God Almighty, it's like I never seen his eyes before.

While it's important to acknowledge budding romantic feelings and urges in your MG audience, it's best not to get too explicit.

Using Your Insights

Understanding the reader allows you to play with theme and give your stories larger resonance. In the examples we mentioned earlier, the authors incorporate age-appropriate concerns into their stories. These characters' experiences and emotional turning points directly speak to the MG experience. Such revelations, when incorporated organically and subtly into the manuscript, will really strike a chord.

To go back to Haworth's Violet from *Violet Raines Almost Got Struck by Lightning*, we see her contemplating old mementos in a quieter moment:

> Even when you outgrow your childish things, someone saves them for you. Someone who loves you does that so you don't forget who you are.

This moment perfectly captures the in-between feeling of being a preteen, that time when childhood is still fresh and tangible in the mind.

Blue Balliett's *Chasing Vermeer* is a gripping MG mystery. Calder, one of the three protagonists, is thinking about the importance of a priceless Vermeer painting that has gone missing:

> Art, for [Calder], was—something puzzling. Yes. Something that gave his mind a new idea to spin around. Something that gave him a fresh way of seeing things each time he looked at it.

This directly reflects the newness of life for preteens.

Finally, there's a reason that the MG category is sometimes called "coming of age." Nobody in my library captures that feeling more than Mississippi Beaumont (or Mibs, for short), the protagonist of Ingrid Law's MG smash hit *Savvy*. The book is about a family of quirky characters, each with a special magical power, or "savvy." When she gets her savvy, Mibs considers the bigger picture:

> I realized that I had just turned into a teenager myself, and there were changes coming in my life that didn't have anything to do with my savvy.

There's also:

> Things in my life were changing faster than I could keep up with.

I love arming writers with these ideas about the MG mind-set because, I hope, they will inspire you to create something thematically rich that speaks directly and urgently to your audience.

INSIDE THE MIND OF YOUR YA READER

There's something crucial that I want you to remember about YA (age thirteen to eighteen), and that's the all-consuming nature of being a teenager. It's that sense of possibility. That feeling of your heart welling so big it could explode. It used to happen for me when I was driving around my hometown, late at night, in my wizard-purple Ford Taurus (before the hip redesign, thank you very much) and the perfect song would come on the radio. Everything felt so big and so important in that moment, like all the parts of the universe had finally—yet fleetingly—clicked into place.

Remember the electricity of adolescence? You experience your first love, your first heartbreak, your first truly selfless act, your first betrayal, your first seriously bad decision, your first moment of profound pride, the first time you're a hero. The milestones space out as we age, but when you're a teenager, they all happen in very close proximity to one another.

The decisions you're making during young adulthood can seem as if they will have ramifications *forever*. You feel by turns invincible and vulnerable, inconsequential and permanent. All of these experiences are happening for the very first time, and you're packed into a group with hundreds of other teens who feel exactly the same way (though they hardly ever let on). So you're also isolated and craving community, which is why you search for a book that feels like it's written just for you.

It's, in a word, *intense*.

I like to quote a YA-before-it-was-YA novel, *The Perks of Being a Wallflower* by Stephen Chbosky, which was published in 1999 for the adult market (my, how times have changed). In one scene, his teen characters go through a tunnel and emerge into a beautiful view of city lights. The narrator, Charlie, says:

> And in that moment, I swear we were infinite.

Conveying Romance and Darkness

Teens feel everything very intensely, and two things in particular: an interest in romance and an attraction to darkness. If you've been in the teen section of a bookstore recently, you'll know what I mean. It seems as if every cover greets you with the same combination of a pouting girl, a brooding boy, and the colors purple and black.

The paranormal and dystopian genres are such forces in the marketplace that I'm dedicating this entire section to explaining them. First, the discouraging fact: These genres are on the wane, so I wouldn't dive into them right now if I were you. A lot of publishers aren't signing many new projects in these veins.

A lot of readers and writers (and yes, editors and agents) are getting tired of these genres and wondering why they took off with such velocity in the first place. When I think about the teen reader mind-set, the reasons become clear.

Romantic relationships are a huge obsession for teens. Most teens, however, lack real-life romantic experience. Teen boys inviting you over to play Xbox and teen girls texting through dinner dates at The Cheesecake Factory must leave a lot to be desired. Since there aren't many dashing Edward Cullens willing to die on the fangs of vampires for today's teen girls, these hungry readers turn to fiction to flesh out their rich fantasy lives.

Teens also don't often feel empowered. Their lives can seem like endless cycles of classes, test prep, sports, and volunteer work, and the message they hear is: If you get off this track, fail the SATs, or don't get into the right college, then the rest of your life is in jeopardy. They feel trapped and helpless. Most want control, so the kick-butt aspect of paranormal (vampire slaying, zombie battles, etc.) is attractive.

Finally, teens are exploring the dark side of their personalities around the time they hit fourteen or fifteen. They get interested in suicide and serial killers and other darker shades of humanity. Death-related worlds and characters help them explore that through fiction. One of the biggest hits of the last decade is Jay Asher's *Thirteen Reasons Why*, a book about one girl's suicide and the reasons behind it.

Some teens start to see the darker underbelly of life during high school—a friend starts cutting herself, someone gets pregnant, a classmate dies—and they use fiction to explore these issues in a safe way. The trend toward dystopian fiction is an extension of this and a way of dealing with the anxieties of living in a world full of economic depression, war, and social inequality.

When you think about your teen readers, keep the above in mind. Whether or not your romance is paranormal, know that your (mostly female, in most genres) audience craves stories about crushes and relationships. Even if your story doesn't have a darker shade to it, acknowledge that your readers are dealing with a complex world where everything isn't always unicorns and rainbows.

I would not counsel you to include stock paranormal elements in your manuscript—vampires, werewolves, fallen angels, demons, mermaids, Greek mythology, zombies—because of overcrowding on the shelves and general fatigue. If you simply *have* to do paranormal, find a unique twist or uncover an underutilized mythology or creature. For example, Laini Taylor's *The Daughter of Smoke and Bone* offers a fantastic and fresh take on angels.

If you can, do try to include some kind of love interest. You don't have to write an all-out romance, but you'll be missing a huge potential selling point if you don't acknowledge this part of your readers' lives. The romantic element in your story can range from an unrequited crush to falling deeply in love.

Incorporating Themes and Big Ideas

When you understand the teen mind-set and can place yourself in your target readers' experience, you're that much more likely to write a book that resonates with them on a deeper thematic level.

Let's go back to the shelves for a look at how YA writers have incorporated theme into their teen characters' narratives. First up is McLean from blockbuster novelist Sarah Dessen's *What Happened to Goodbye*. She moves around the country with her restaurant consultant father, trying on new names and personalities in each town. As she lands in a new spot, she contemplates her predicament:

> Sure, it was always jarring, up and leaving everything again. But it all came
> down to how you looked at it. Think earth-shattering, life-ruining change,

and you're done. But cast it as a do-over, a chance to reinvent and begin again, and it's all good. We were in Lakeview. It was early January. I could be anyone from here.

Teens often feel as if their identities aren't quite fixed yet, as if they could rip themselves up and start all over again if they wanted to. Honor that and see if you can incorporate it thematically.

Next up is master of the teen mind-set John Green and his book *Paper Towns*. In it, an earnest teen boy, Quentin, (Q for short), falls for a hipster named Margo Roth Spiegelman, a teen so disillusioned with her suburban life that she runs away. Being a stand-up (lovesick) guy, Q spends the rest of the book trying to save Margo from herself.

A lot of teens see the world or society and want to change it. Here, Margo speaks about her claustrophobic Florida town:

> All those paper people living in their paper houses, burning the future to stay warm. All the paper kids drinking beer some bum bought for them at the paper convenience store. Everyone demented with the mania of owning things. All the things paper-thin and paper-frail. And all the people, too. I've lived here for eighteen years and I have never once in my life come across anyone who cares about anything that matters.

And here's Q trying to put himself into Margo's Converse All Stars a little later in the story:

> And all at once I knew how Margo Roth Spiegelman felt when she wasn't being Margo Roth Spiegelman: she felt empty. She felt the unscaleable wall surrounding her.

These teens see the world and interpret it intensely. They feel deep longing and pain and love and searching. Understanding these qualities about adolescence will make your literature for these readers richer and deeper.

Mary Kole was a literary agent for six years with the Andrea Brown Literary Agency and Movable Type Management. She is the founder of kidlit.com and the author of *Writing Irresistible Kidlit* (Writer's Digest Books). She offers freelance editing and consulting services to writers of all levels at marykole.com.

The Complete Handbook of Novel Writing

47

MAKING MAGIC

···

How to Enchant Readers with Magic Realism

Kristin Bair O'Keeffe

Ever since I started writing as a kid, unusual things have happened in my well-grounded stories. A man named Harold sprouted a flower on his head. A line of seemingly nonsensical text became a secret code ("Tulips are on sale in Kanaga-wa—the place."). A tree grew in a girl's innards after her father fed her a cherry stone. A rabble of butterflies inspired a lusty softening of the heart. And in my latest novel, *The Art of Floating*, it's not quite clear whether a mysterious man who just walked out of the sea is alien, fish, or lost soul.

Early on, friends and family dubbed my work "the odd stuff Kristin writes," and it wasn't until a literature class in college that I realized there was a name for it—magic realism—and that an honorable lineage of writers had been writing such "odd stuff" for years. Brilliant authors like Gabriel García Márquez, whose *One Hundred Years of Solitude* introduced the world to the fictional town of Macondo and generations of the Buendía family, whose lives are touched again and again by unusual and magical occurrences; Audrey Niffenegger, whose much more recent *The Time Traveler's Wife* makes you believe in the possibility of tumbling through time, as well as extraordinary love; the venerable Toni Morrison, who summoned the ghost of Sethe's child in *Beloved*; and Japanese author Haruki Murakami, whose *1Q84* commingles two representations of the same world so adeptly that you end up saying, "Wait, wait, back up! What is real here?" for more than a thousand pages.

ORIGIN

German art critic Franz Roh coined the term *magical realism* in a 1925 essay and subsequent art book *Nach Expressionismus: Magischer Realismus: Prob-*

leme der neuesten europäischen Malerei (*After Expressionism: Magical Realism: Problems of the newest European painting*). While he initially used the term to describe an artistic shift from abstraction to figural representation, the meaning grew muddy and controversial, and, soon after, the term fell out of fashion in the art world—as things tend to do. Sometime in the 1960s, when literary folks needed an appropriate descriptor for *One Hundred Years of Solitude*, the term *magic realism* was resurrected and reshaped by the literary community. "How else," they likely argued over whiskey and beer, "can we describe a novel that so stunningly straddles the magical and the realistic—a novel in which Remedios the Beauty ascends into the sky while folding a sheet, and Melquíades, the gypsy, dies not once but twice?"

In this case, the term stuck. But what *magic realism* really is, what defines the genre, and just who the heck's work gets to be categorized as *magically realistic* has become one of the hottest debates in the literary community. Highbrow purists with fists in the air argue that only Latin American authors write authentic literature in this genre. Hybrids argue that magic realism crosses all borders and boundaries, and that it's more about the characteristics of the story than the place from which the author hails.

Because this debate tends to get bloody depending on the parties involved, I advise writers drawn to this magnificent genre to steer clear of the whole damn conversation and accept that, while magic realism may (or may not) have been birthed in Latin America, it has evolved and migrated. Stick to the writing and the ongoing development of your craft. After all, while the debate rages on, writers continue to create intoxicating stories that fall into the magically realistic genre. Just take a look at Sarah Addison Allen's *The Girl Who Chased the Moon* and Eowyn Ivey's *The Snow Child*.

MAGICAL REALISM: WHAT IT IS (AND ISN'T)

Once again, a magically realistic story is one that is deeply grounded in a realistic place and situation but in which odd, unusual, and magical events occur. While reading such a tale, you may never be 100 percent sure what is real and what is not. It's a bit like looking at one of those images that occasionally trends on Facebook in which the first time you glance at the image you see a sheep, but if you stare and let your eyes go soft, you see an alien.

Glance: sheep.

Stare and soften: alien.

The complete image is made up of the two smaller images, but they're so artistically blended that you're never truly sure what you "should" see. And, in fact, there is no image that you "should" see because the story—if well crafted—is a perfectly balanced combination of the two.

One thing that writers do need to keep in mind—and one thing over which critics do not draw blood—is that magic realism is not the same as science fiction or fantasy. While these three genres share certain qualities, they differ greatly. In science fiction and fantasy, the line between what is real and what is magical or mystical is clear and distinct; in magic realism, it's fuzzy. In science fiction and fantasy, new worlds are often created; in magic realism, it's the same old world with interesting nuances. Science fiction and fantasy are often escapist; magic realism rarely is. And in science fiction and fantasy, rational explanations are provided for unusual occurrences. Do not expect an explanation in a magically realistic story. Things just *are*.

NUTS AND BOLTS

Before you set out to write your magically realistic tale, consider the nuts and bolts of the genre.

- **PLACE:** A realistic sense of place will help move your story forward and facilitate magical occurrences. In the first chapter of *The Time Traveler's Wife*, Niffenegger introduces us to the unique features of Chicago's Newberry Library. Eventually, we learn that Henry is petrified of landing in the library's "cage" when tumbling through time because it has no exit. It's the perfect setup.
- **FANTASTICAL ELEMENTS:** In a magically realistic story, characters can levitate, implode, move objects with their minds, travel through time, speak languages they never were taught to speak, and much more. As long as you weave your carefully chosen fantastical elements into the realistic fabric of your story, anything goes.
- **HABITS, BELIEFS, AND QUIRKS:** Use your characters' habits, beliefs, and quirks to instigate or heighten the magical elements in your story. The fact that Clare Abshire, in *The Time Traveler's Wife*, is a paper artist becomes more integrated with Henry's time travel as the story progresses. In *1Q84*, Aomame's antisocial, über-efficient ways play right into the development of the plot. Keep in mind that figuring out which habits, beliefs, and quirks best lend themselves to your story takes time and many drafts. Don't rush it.

- **TONE:** Magically realistic stories are told without astonishment. Narrators don't run around yelling, "Oh, my god! I can't believe a ghost just sat down to dinner with us!" If a woman drifts away or a man travels through time or a woman climbs down a staircase from a highway and enters a different reality, the narrator shares that information in the same tone she'd use to inform you she was out of ketchup.
- **NARRATOR'S AUTHORITY AND RETICENCE:** Your narrator is the big boss who isn't interested in explaining things to readers. If a ghost sits down for dinner or a mysterious taxi driver points someone to a questionable stairwell, the narrator is not going to lean forward, give a wink, and whisper, "Here's how it works …" This would shatter readers' trust in the characters'—and the world's—credibility.
- **TIME:** In many magically realistic stories, time is fluid and cyclical, not rigid and linear. Now, then, the distant future, the distant past, yesterday, today, tomorrow—it's all fair game. *One Hundred Years of Solitude*, for example, opens with a flashback that stretches all the way to a time when "[t]he world was so recent that many things lacked names, and in order to indicate them it was necessary to point." But in some stories, like Aimee Bender's *The Particular Sadness of Lemon Cake*, time is persistent and unidirectional. Make good use of this great flexibility with time. Decide which is best for your story, and then run with it.
- **RULES AND REGULATIONS:** Every establishment is governed by specific rules and regulations—towns, churches, governments, parks, schools, sales forces, families, friendships, marriages, genders, etc. In a magically realistic story, you can manipulate those rules. For example, in Japan during rush hour on a highway, a woman would never get out of a car, take off her shoes, and walk to a staircase reserved for emergency workers. In *1Q84*, Aomame does just that. As the writer, you must know the rules of the reality you present; only then can you allow characters to break those rules and see what gets stirred up.
- **HYBRIDITY:** Multiple planes of reality are common in magically realistic stories. In *1Q84*, two versions of the realistic world exist at the same time, and in *The Time Traveler's Wife*, present-day Henry often time travels to a period in which a younger or older Henry exists. Thus, often there are two Henrys present. Such hybridity allows you, the writer, an opportunity to reveal a deeper truth about the world that you wouldn't have if you represented just one reality.

MAGIC REALISM: A READING LIST

- *One Hundred Years of Solitude* by Gabriel García Márquez
- *The Time Traveler's Wife* by Audrey Niffenegger
- *Beloved* by Toni Morrison
- *1Q84* by Haruki Murakami
- *The Girl Who Chased the Moon* by Sarah Addison Allen
- *The Particular Sadness of Lemon Cake* by Aimee Bender
- *The Snow Child* by Eowyn Ivey
- *Life of Pi* by Yann Martel
- *Song of Solomon* by Toni Morrison
- *The House of the Spirits* by Isabel Allende
- *Like Water for Chocolate* by Laura Esquivel
- *The Master and Margarita* by Mikhail Bulgakov
- *The Tiger's Wife* by Téa Obreht
- *The Museum of Extraordinary Things* by Alice Hoffman
- *The Ocean at the End of the Lane* by Neil Gaiman
- *Swamplandia!* by Karen Russell
- *Life After Life* by Kate Atkinson
- *The Night Circus* by Erin Morgenstern

MAGICAL IDEAS

Ever since I began writing, I've been a collector. Not of things—shells, stamps, figurines, stuffed monkeys, autographs, etc.—but of possibilities. Odd happenings and images from around the world and in my dreams that could—and often do—make their way into my writing. While many might be considered mundane observances, paired with the right character in the right situation, I know they'll make terrifically fantastic occurrences.

In recent years, these possibilities have included a giant eyeball that washed up on a beach in Florida; thousands of rotten pigs floating down the Huangpu River in Shanghai; an Arctic flower that was regenerated after thirty-two thousand years of dormancy in a squirrel's burrow; 7,700 people who were sterilized against their will between 1933 and 1977 as an experiment in genetic engineering; a man who sells the moon; the death of the world's tallest woman in China's Anhui province; a house with ladders between floors that I dream about every few months; and many more.

Although sometimes I'm tempted to save every odd, quirky bit that comes my way, I've trained myself to save only those snippets that cause a thump somewhere in my soul. Those are the bits that stick ... the pieces that resonate with me as an artist.

If collecting possibilities doesn't come naturally to you, here are three sure-fire ways to happen upon interesting stuff:

1. Mine your dreams, and if you don't remember your own, mine your spouse's, child's, or friend's dreams. I'm lucky enough to have, and have always had, intense, detailed dreams that feed directly into my writing, but I'm not above poaching those my daughter or a good friend tell me about.
2. Follow headlines. Newspaper, Internet, and magazine headlines feature all kinds of kooky things happening in the world. Use them. And don't stick closely to the publications you read all the time. Check out publications you never read, including grocery store tabloids.
3. Listen in on conversations—to the two women gossiping in the fitting room next to you, to the father and son at the dentist's office, to the taxi driver talking to his dispatcher on the radio, to the endless number of phone conversations going on at airports, and so on.

When something does resonate with you, be sure to record and store it. If you don't, you'll lose track and forget all about it. How and where you record and store your possibilities will depend on your organizational style. As an Evernote devotee, I save everything that piques my interest to a folder in my Evernote account labeled "Possibilities." I've also been journaling since I was eight and blogging since 2006. When I'm deep into a novel, I'm constantly pulling out old journals, rereading past blog entries, and, yes, accessing my "Possibilities" folder.

WORLDBUILDING

Your first hurdle will likely be figuring out how to let your readers know that they're reading a magically realistic story. Different authors handle this in different ways. In the first pages of *1Q84*, the taxi driver tells Aomame, "[P]lease remember: things are not what they seem." And while he is talking directly to her, he's also talking to readers. In *The Time Traveler's Wife*, Clare and Henry simply talk about Henry's time travel capability as if it's the most normal thing on earth.

Once you've handled that hurdle, resist the urge to plunk in fantastical elements. Instead, imbue. The less you jar readers from the streamline of the story, the more trust they will place in you. The last thing you want as a writer is for your reader to get to a fantastical element, feel like it's a fake, and say, "No way. That could never happen."

As you set off on this journey to write a magically realistic story, the most important question you must ask yourself is not "How do I introduce magic into this story?" or "Can my setting support surrealistic elements?" but instead "What is possible in this world?" You must be able to imagine something happening in the world beyond what most people see. To this end, I encourage you to look under the rug, listen beneath the sound of the wave, peer beyond the solid figure that blots out the sun, and ask yourself again and again, "What is possible in this world?"

Then pick up your pen.

Kristin Bair O'Keeffe is the author of the novels *The Art of Floating* and *Thirsty*, as well as essays about China, bears, adoption, off-the-plot expats, and more. Her work has appeared in numerous magazines and journals, including *The Manifest-Station*, *Flyway: Journal of Writing and Environment*, *The Gettysburg Review*, *The Baltimore Review*, *The Christian Science Monitor*, *Poets & Writers Magazine*, *Writer's Digest*, and other publications. As a writing instructor, her peripatetic nature has landed her in classrooms and conferences around the world. A native Pittsburgher, Kristin now lives north of Boston with her husband and two kiddos. Follow her on Twitter and Instagram: @kbairokeeffe.

Part Four

FINDING AND CULTIVATING A MARKET FOR YOUR WORK

BEST-SELLING ADVICE
Publishing

" To gain your own voice, you have to forget about having it heard."

—Allen Ginsberg

"The most important thing is you can't write what you wouldn't read for pleasure. It's a mistake to analyze the market thinking you can write whatever is hot. You can't say you're going to write romance when you don't even like it. You need to write what you would read if you expect anybody else to read it.

And you have to be driven. You have to have the three Ds: drive, discipline and desire. If you're missing any one of those three, you can have all the talent in the world, but it's going to be really hard to get anything done."

—Nora Roberts

"Inevitably, you react to your own work—you like it, you don't like it, you think it's interesting or boring—and it is difficult to accept that those reactions may be unreliable. In my experience, they are. I mistrust either wild enthusiasm or deep depression. I have had the best success with material that I was sort of neutral about; I didn't think it was the greatest thing in the world, nor did I think it was bad; I liked it, but not too much."

—Michael Crichton

"One of my agents used to say to me, 'Mack, you shouldn't submit anything anywhere unless you [would] read it aloud to them.' "

—MacKinlay Kantor

" I would advise anyone who aspires to a writing career that before developing his talent he would be wise to develop a thick hide."

—Harper Lee

"If you have the story, editors will use it. I agree it's hard. You're battling a system. But it's fun to do battle with systems."

—Bob Woodward

"Publishers want to take chances on books that will draw a clamor and some legitimate publicity. They want to publish controversial books. That their reasons are mercenary and yours may be lofty should not deter you."

—Harlan Ellison

"It's wise to plan early on where you'd like to go, do serious self-analysis to determine what you want from a writing career. ... When I began, I thought I'd be comfortable as a straight genre writer. I just kept switching genres as my interests grew. I've since been fortunate that—with a great deal of effort—I've been able to break the chains of genre labeling, and do larger and more complex books. But it's difficult, and few people who develop straight genre reputations ever escape them."

—Dean Koontz

"There's really a shortage of good freelance writers. ... There are a lot of talented people who are very erratic, so either they don't turn it in or they turn it in and it's rotten; it's amazing. Somebody who's even maybe not all that terrific but who is dependable, who will turn in a publishable piece more or less on time, can really do very well.

—Gloria Steinem

> There's no mystique about the writing business, although many people consider me blasphemous when I say that. Whatever else my books are, they're also products, and I regard and treat them as such. To create something you want to sell, you first study and research the market, then you develop the product to the best of your ability. What happens next? You market it.

—Clive Cussler

48

BASICS OF A SOLID THREE-PARAGRAPH QUERY

How to Pitch Your Novel Like a Pro

Ann Rittenberg

Like many independent literary agencies, mine is small, with only two full-time people, one part-time person, and no more than fifty active clients at any given time. Yet even we receive at least fifty query letters every week. Potentially, we could replace our entire client list—which has been more than twenty years in the making—every week of the year. And at the end of each year, we've read, processed, answered, thrown away, cried over, winced at, yawned over, or gotten excited about nearly three thousand letters about as-yet-unpublished books. That number doesn't include the e-mail queries—which we officially don't accept but which nevertheless come in at the rate of twenty or more a week.

Out of those three thousand pleas, nearly 75 percent are about novels. And out of those, at least 90 percent are about first novels. That brings the number of queries about first novels to about two thousand every year. And in a recent year, I accepted as a client one new novelist out of those two thousand. That's not 2 percent, or 1 percent, or even one-half of a percent. That's one-tenth of one-half of a percent.

Reading statistics like those must be thoroughly discouraging. Statistics are, after all, often discouraging: The number of people who apply to certain schools versus the number who get in is always a discouraging number. Our chances of winning a million-dollar-plus lottery are also discouraging, but many of us still buy tickets. So let's look at those numbers another way: 80 percent of those query letters about first novels never should have been sent.

That's right—a full 80 percent of the letters I read pitching first novels never should have been sent to me, or to any agent or editor. Either the writers were not ready to be published and their books were not ready to be agented, or they misdirected the query letter by writing to me about the kind of book I don't represent.

So, if we subtract 80 percent from the two thousand first-novel query letters I (and many of my colleagues) see every year, we come up with a grand total of four hundred. Four hundred letters a year is only about eight per week. I would happily read to their end eight letters a week about first novels. Yet if I still take on only one writer of those four hundred, I have taken on one-quarter of a percent of the writers who write to me about their first novels. It's still a small percentage, but 1/400th is considerably better than 1/2000th. (Try reading that sentence out loud, and you'll see one reason why.)

So, with that in mind, let's make sure you have the tools you need to write a query letter that sets you apart from the pack—a letter that should definitely be sent.

QUERY LETTER BASICS

A good query letter, like the best writing, has urgency and clarity. It's not dull, but it attends to the business at hand without fuss. It is, of course, a sales pitch directed with passion, belief, and enthusiasm to someone likely to buy the product being pitched. You're trying to find a reader for your book. And because every editor and agent is first a reader, you're going to write this letter to the reader who is most likely to want to read your book.

Let's start with the basics. For instance, you've probably figured out that an effective query letter:

- doesn't state the obvious—if it does, agents will think your book is all "telling," no "showing."
- is never longer than one page—if it is, agents will think your book is overwritten.
- is not about you—if it is, agents will think your book will be too navel-gazing to invite the reader in.
- never sounds generic—if it does, agents will think your book won't have a unique or appealing voice.
- makes the book sound interesting—if it doesn't, agents will know the book isn't.

So what does a good query letter look like? Well, here's a letter that got my attention:

> Dear Ms. Rittenberg,
>
> I am seeking representation. I have won a few awards for fiction and poetry. My novel, THE CLEARING [later titled *A Certain Slant of Light*], is a supernatural love story told from the point of view of a young woman who has been dead 130 years. She's haunting a high school English teacher when one of the boys in his class sees her. No one has seen her since her death. When the two of them fall in love, the fact that he is in a body and she is not presents the first of their problems.
>
> Please let me know if you would be interested in reading part or all of THE CLEARING. I have enclosed an SASE. Thank you, and I look forward to hearing from you.

Although the author, Laura Whitcomb, began the letter by saying something that might not have been strictly necessary, she said it with admirable brevity. I didn't have time to stop in the middle of the opening sentence. Before I knew it, I had read the whole letter and written the word *yes* at the bottom. (If you could see the pile of rejected query letters in my office every week, you would see how the *no* is always written at the top of the letters. That's because I didn't reach the end.) Laura's letter wasn't written with fireworks, but it didn't need to be, because the story as she described it briefly needed no embellishment. And she had enough confidence in her story to let the description be.

Let's break it down paragraph by paragraph and see how all the pieces fit together.

THE FIRST PARAGRAPH: YOUR HOOK

The first paragraph of your query letter should skip the throat clearing—or at least keep the opening pleasantries to a bare minimum—and get quickly to the one-line description. In that sentence you'll give the title of the novel and insert the genre if appropriate. Here's the first line of a letter I saw several years ago:

> [Title] is a coming-of-age novel about two young women trying to survive their first year of college and find their own identities.

To tell you the truth, that sentence would have been enough to describe the book, but the author went on for four more sentences in an attempt to make the novel sound dramatic. If she had taken out those four additional sentences, she would have had a serviceable description of the novel. However, she probably also would have had to face the fact that her novel was not inherently dramatic enough to interest agents and editors in a competitive marketplace. It didn't have a hook. Somewhere within herself, she knew this, and that's why she added the four sentences.

Look again at Laura's letter:

> My novel, THE CLEARING, is a supernatural love story told from the point of view of a young woman who has been dead 130 years.

The genre, the title, and the hook are in one sentence. Laura added a few more sentences to flesh out the basic idea, but she didn't go on too long, and, more important, she left the reader with a cliff-hanger by saying:

> When the two of them fall in love, the fact that he is in a body and she is not presents the first of their problems.

Your hook should be your novel's distinguishing feature. A distinguishing feature can be something imaginative in the plot—the way Laura's book was a love story featuring a heroine who'd been dead for 130 years—or it can be sheer good writing. It can be something unique about the book or about the way you describe the book. But if the one-liner doesn't make anyone sit up and take notice, all the additional plot description in the world isn't going to help.

Your letter should not describe your book at length, should not drag the reader all the way through the plot, and should not give away the ending. A real mood killer is to use an overworked notion like redemption or a clichéd description—such as "It's about the human condition"—when describing your book. Stick to the concrete. It's easy to see why someone might think that a one-line description is the same thing as a summary, but it's not.

THE SECOND PARAGRAPH: YOUR BIO

In your second paragraph, give some brief and pertinent biographical information. Writing courses, publications, and awards are good to mention. But more than a sentence summing up minor publications and writing study is not so good.

Remember—the immediate task of the query letter is to get an agent or editor interested in reading your novel. It's not to showcase what an interesting, fabulous, credentialed, or kooky person you are. That will come later, when your agent needs to sell you as well as your book. But for now, you need to come across as professional, serious, dedicated, and confident.

Anything you say about yourself should somehow, briefly and brilliantly, make us think we want to read your book. All Laura said of herself was, "I have won a few awards for fiction and poetry." Because she couldn't claim to have won the Pulitzer, hadn't invented nuclear fusion, wasn't married to someone famous, and, more to the point, had never published a book, there was no point in giving a long résumé of her achievements.

Many query writers insert a sentence beginning, "Although I am an unpublished writer ..." Doing so simultaneously states the obvious (you're writing about your first novel, after all) and dwells negatively on you—on what you haven't done. Remember that the query letter is looking to the future. The future is when someone is going to read your novel, and your job is to convince us that we will be that future someone. Say no more than one or two things:

- I received my MFA from the Columbia Writing Program, where my novel was awarded the Prize for Singular Fabulousness.
- I've worked as a taxi driver and a mail carrier while writing and publishing short fiction in literary journals.

THE THIRD (AND FINAL) PARAGRAPH: YOUR CONCLUSION

Your third paragraph should be the sign-off paragraph. Wrap up the letter with a word or two about having enclosed an SASE and looking forward to a response, and sign off. Don't drag it out. Don't give your vacation schedule with your spouse's cell phone number. If you've used a letterhead with your address, e-mail address, and telephone number, or inserted that information in a business-letter-appropriate fashion, anyone who wants to track you down will find you. So stop talking, finish the letter with a complimentary closing, and hit "Save." Then prepare yourself for the next step: researching agents to find the right one for your book.

TEN QUERY LETTER NO-NOS

10. Letters that have typos in the first sentence.
9. Letters that start with a nugget of wisdom: "Every step we take in life moves us in a direction."
8. Letters with faint or very small type. You can assume that just about everyone in publishing suffers from eyestrain.
7. Letters longer than one page.

6. Letters with overcomplicated directions for replying: "I'm going to Tortolla for the next three weeks. If you need to reach me, please call my cell number. Don't leave a message at my home number because I won't get it until I return." A simple street or e-mail address will do.
5. Photocopied letters with no salutation.
4. Letters that start, "I know how busy you are, so I'll get straight to the point and not take up too much of your valuable time." By writing this, you've already taken up a full sentence of my valuable time.
3. Letters with grandiose claims: "My novel will appeal to women, and because there are 150 million women in the United States, it will sell 150 million copies."
2. Letters that say, "I've worked very hard on this novel." Does that fact alone make it a good novel?
1. And the number one query letter no-no: "I have written a fiction novel." When an agent sees this sentence in a query letter, he quickly draws the conclusion that a writer who doesn't know that a novel is, by definition, a work of fiction is a writer who isn't ready to be published.

Ann Rittenberg, president of her own literary agency (www.rittlit.com), has worked in publishing for more than thirty years. She is the co-author, with Laura Whitcomb, of *Your First Novel* (Writer's Digest Books). Ann lives in lower Manhattan with her husband and very literate Papillon.

49

YOUR GUIDE TO AN EFFECTIVE NOVEL SYNOPSIS

Summarize Your Story in a Compelling Way

Chuck Sambuchino and the
Editors of Writer's Digest

Before you submit your novel to an agent or publisher, there are things you need to do. First and foremost, you must finish the work. If you contact an agent and she likes your idea, she will ask to see some or all of the manuscript. You don't want to have to tell her it won't be finished for another six months. If your novel is complete and polished, it's time to write your query and synopsis. After that, you're ready to test the agent and editor waters.

How you submit your novel package will depend on each agent or publisher's specified submission guidelines. You'll find that some want only a query letter; others request a query letter and the complete manuscript; some prefer a query letter plus three sample chapters and a synopsis; and still others request a query letter, a few sample chapters, an outline, and a synopsis. All want an SASE (self-addressed, stamped envelope) with adequate postage, unless they request an electronic submission. To determine what you need to submit, visit the agent's or publisher's website for guidelines, or consult a current edition of a market resource such as *Novel & Short Story Writer's Market*, *Writer's Market*, or *Guide to Literary Agents*. These sources have submission specifications that come straight from the editors and agents, telling you just what to send, how to send it, and when to anticipate a response.

Be prepared to send at least a query letter, a synopsis, and three consecutive sample chapters. These are the most important—and most requested—parts of your novel package. You may not need to send them all in the same submission package, but you probably will need to use each of them at one time or another, so prepare everything before you start submitting. Here, we'll focus on what writers often find the most difficult component of their novel submission package: the synopsis.

DEFINING THE SYNOPSIS

The synopsis supplies key information about your novel (plot, theme, characterization, setting), while also showing how these coalesce to form the big picture. It quickly tells what your novel is about without making the editor or agent read the novel in its entirety.

There are no hard-and-fast rules about the synopsis. In fact, there's conflicting advice about the typical length of a synopsis. Most editors and agents agree, though: The shorter, the better.

When writing your synopsis, focus on the essential parts of your story, and try not to include sections of dialogue unless you think they're absolutely necessary. (It's okay to inject a few strong quotes from your characters, but keep them brief.) Finally, even though the synopsis is only a condensed version of your novel, it must seem complete.

Keep events in the same order as they happen in the novel (but don't break them down into individual chapters). Remember that your synopsis should have a beginning, a middle, and an ending (yes, you must tell how the novel ends to round out your synopsis).

That's what's required of a synopsis: You need to be concise, compelling, and complete, all at the same time.

CRAFTING TWO SYNOPSES

Because there is no definitive length to a synopsis, it's recommended you have two versions: a long synopsis and a short synopsis.

There used to be a fairly universal system regarding synopses. For every thirty-five or so pages of your manuscript, you would have one page of synopsis explanation, up to a maximum of eight pages. So if your book was 245 pages, double-spaced, your synopsis would be approximately seven pages. This was fairly standard and allowed writers a decent amount of space to explain their story. You should write a synopsis following these guidelines first. This will be your long synopsis.

The problem is that during the past several years, agents have started to get busier and busier, and now they want to hear your story now-now-now. Many agents today request synopses of no more than two pages. Some even say one page, but two pages is generally acceptable. To be ready to submit to these agents, you'll also need to draft a new, more concise synopsis—the short synopsis.

So once you've written both, which do you submit? If you think your short synopsis is tight and effective, always use that. However, if you think the long synopsis is actually more effective, then you will sometimes submit one and sometimes submit the other. If an agent requests two pages max, send only the short one. If she says simply, "Send a synopsis," and you feel your longer synopsis is superior, submit the long one. If you're writing plot-heavy fiction, such as thrillers and mysteries, you might really benefit from submitting a longer, more thorough synopsis.

Your best bet on knowing what to submit is to follow the guidelines of the agency or publisher in question.

FORMATTING YOUR ELECTRONIC SUBMISSION

Some editors or agents might ask you to submit your synopsis via e-mail. The editor or agent can provide you with specific formatting guidelines indicating how she wants it sent and the type of files she prefers.

If an agent or editor does request an electronic submission, keep the following four points in mind:

1. Follow the same formatting specs you would for a paper synopsis submission.
2. When sending your synopsis via e-mail, put the name of your novel in the subject line (but don't use all caps—it's just obnoxious).
3. Send the synopsis as an attachment to your e-mail unless the editor or agent requests otherwise.
4. Include a cover letter in the body of your e-mail. Your cover page and table of contents should go in the file along with the synopsis.

YOUR ESSENTIAL SYNOPSIS CHECKLIST

FORMATTING SPECS

- Use a 1-inch margin on all sides; justify the left margin only.
- Put your name and contact information on the top-left corner of the first page.
- Type the novel's genre, word count, and the word *Synopsis* in the top-right corner of the first page.
- Don't number the first page.

- Put the novel's title, centered and in all caps, about one-third of the way down the page.
- Begin the synopsis text four lines below the title.
- The text throughout the synopsis should be double-spaced (unless you plan to keep it to one or two pages, in which case single-spaced is okay).
- Use all caps the first time you introduce a character.
- After the first page, use a header on every page that contains your last name, your novel's title in all caps, and the word "Synopsis," like so: Name/TITLE/Synopsis.
- After the first page, number the pages in the top-right corner on the same line as the header.
- The first line of text on each page after the first page should be three lines below the header.

OTHER DOS AND DON'TS

- **DO** keep in mind that this is a sales pitch. Make it a short, fast, and exciting read.
- **DO** establish a hook at the beginning of the synopsis. Introduce your lead character and set up a key conflict.
- **DO** remember to always introduce your most important character first.
- **DO** provide details about each of your central characters (age, gender, marital status, profession, etc.), but don't do this for every character—only the primary ones.
- **DO** include the characters' motivations and emotions.
- **DO** highlight pivotal plot points.
- **DO** reveal your novel's ending.
- **DON'T** go into detail about what happens; just tell the reader what happens as concisely as you can.
- **DON'T** inject long sections of dialogue.
- **DO** write in the third person, present tense, even if your novel is written in a different point of view.

Chuck Sambuchino (chucksambuchino.com) is an editor, best-selling humor book author, and authority on how to get published. He works for Writer's Digest Books and edits *Guide to Literary Agents*. His Guide to Literary Agents Blog (guidetoliterary agents.com/blog)—all about agents, submissions, and platform—is one of the largest blogs in publishing. He is the author of the humor books *How to Survive a Garden Gnome Attack*; *Red Dog, Blue Dog*; and *When Clowns Attack*. In addition, Chuck has also written three writing-related titles: *Formatting and Submitting Your Manuscript 3rd Edition, Create Your Writer Platform*, and *Get a Literary Agent*.

50

STRAW INTO GOLD

Transform Rejection into a Plan of Action

Wendy Burt-Thomas

As much as you'd probably like to burn your rejection letters or mold them into little voodoo dolls of the editors who sent them, don't. There's a lot to be learned from the responses (yes, even those that arrive with nothing more than a standard check box of reasons the piece wasn't accepted).

Think of your rejections as reactions from first dates: Some will be very general ("Sorry, I'm just not that into you"), some will offer minimal feedback ("You talked nonstop about your ex; I don't think you're ready for a new relationship"), and some will offer detailed information to help you improve for your next attempt ("You were charming and attractive, and we had a lot in common, but I just don't date smokers").

While it might be hard to swallow, the feedback provided in these letters could be your best hope of improving your work—query, proposal, and/or manuscript—and eventually getting published. Be grateful for it. Most editors are so busy sorting through their slush piles (in addition to all their other work) that they don't have time to offer advice. So when they make time to do so, it could be either because they believe your work has potential or because your approach is so far off the mark that they're trying to help you correct your mistakes. Either way, they wouldn't respond if they weren't trying to help.

So, what are some of the specific types of responses you might get, and what can you glean from them?

First, the responses that could have been avoided if you'd done your homework before submitting:

- "No simultaneous submissions."
- "Not our genre."
- "Too long."

- "Too short."
- "No unagented submissions."
- "Not right for our audience."
- "No e-mail queries."
- "Query only" (i.e., don't send a proposal, manuscript, or synopsis).
- "No anthropomorphic characters."

Lesson learned. Now, here are the responses that you may not have been able to predict.

"NOT OUR STYLE/VOICE/TONE."

TRANSLATION: This could mean that the writing or idea was good but the publisher doesn't print books like yours.

YOUR NEXT MOVE: Try another publishing house.

"WE NO LONGER ACCEPT THIS GENRE."

TRANSLATION: The publishing house has found that it can profit more from other genres. That doesn't mean your genre isn't profitable; it's just not for them.

YOUR NEXT MOVE: Try another publisher that recently printed a book in your genre.

"WE AREN'T ACCEPTING NEW CLIENTS AT THIS TIME."

TRANSLATION: The literary agency could be overwhelmed with clients, in the process of restructuring, or even about to fold.

YOUR NEXT MOVE: Try another agency.

"THIS TOPIC HAS BEEN DONE TO DEATH."

TRANSLATION: The editor may not be saying that her publisher in particular has covered this topic in numerous books, but rather that several publishing houses have printed books similar to yours recently and the market is saturated.

YOUR NEXT MOVE: Find a fresh angle to your story to avoid getting this response from other publishers.

"I REALLY LIKE YOUR PROTAGONIST, BUT I JUST CAN'T GET ON BOARD TO REPRESENT YOU."

TRANSLATION: You're great at developing characters, but other areas (like plot, motivation, dialogue, or conflict) are still lacking or weak.

YOUR NEXT MOVE: Ask a professional editor with expertise in your genre to give you feedback on your strongest and weakest areas. You may also want to consider taking a class (or attending workshops at a writing conference) specific to your genre.

"NUMEROUS GRAMMATICAL ERRORS."

TRANSLATION: You either didn't proofread and spell-check your piece, or your grammar skills are lacking (or both).

YOUR NEXT MOVE: Paying someone to proof your work will help with the initial step. But if you're going to write another book or do your own press releases, you'll need to take a few English classes and invest in a copy of Strunk & White's *The Elements of Style*.

"THE BOOK DIDN'T QUITE LIVE UP TO MY EXPECTATIONS."

TRANSLATION: "The first few sample chapters you sent were great; that's why I requested more. But the book lost its appeal the more I read."

YOUR NEXT MOVE: Revisit your story and see where it might be going off track. Does it change focus? Does the action slow down? Do the main characters lose their charm or do something that no longer makes them believable? Don't be afraid to cut any words that aren't working.

"I RECOMMEND YOU READ OTHER AUTHORS IN YOUR GENRE."

TRANSLATION: Your work was mediocre or did not adhere to the conventions of the genre in which you are writing, and you need to learn about basic narrative elements like plot, structure, motivation, characters, etc.

YOUR NEXT MOVE: Read several classic and contemporary books in your genre and take a writing class before heading back to revise your manuscript. Then join a critique group or attend a writers conference where you can get feedback from an industry professional. Don't submit your book to any other publishers until someone knowledgeable about your genre has "approved" your piece. And no, your mom doesn't count.

"THIS ISN'T QUITE RIGHT FOR US, BUT HAVE YOU TRIED CONTACTING [INSERT NAME OF AGENT OR ACQUISITIONS EDITOR]? THIS MIGHT BE A GOOD MATCH FOR THEM."

TRANSLATION: "This is a good, solid piece of writing. We can't publish it, but it's good enough that I'm willing to put myself out on a limb to give you a referral to another publishing house. I want them to call and thank me when they make money from your book."

YOUR NEXT MOVE: Contact the acquisitions editor at the second publishing house and tell her who referred you. Ask if you can e-mail your query/synopsis/proposal/manuscript immediately. Write the first editor a nice thank-you note and keep him updated in the process.

"YOU MAY WANT TO CONSIDER SELF-PUBLISHING."

TRANSLATION: Unfortunately, this may mean that in this editor's opinion, there is nothing that can be done to salvage this book. You need to take writing classes, hire an editor, join a critique group, attend every writing conference in your area over the next three years, and then start from scratch. But it may also mean that your topic or audience is so niche that it's not commercially viable. The editor may be able to tell that this story means a lot to you, but she also knows enough about the industry to see that the book may not appeal to larger audiences.

YOUR NEXT MOVE: In case of the first scenario, ask your mom to tell you how great you are. In the second, start researching self-publishing options if you're determined to see your story in print.

Wendy Burt-Thomas is the author of more than one thousand published articles, reviews, essays, and short stories. Her work has appeared in such publications as newyorktimes.com, MSNBC.com, *The Writer*, *Family Circle*, and many others. She is the author of *Oh, Solo Mia!: The Hip Chick's Guide to Fun for One*, *Work It, Girl!: 101 Tips for the Hip Working Chick*, and *The Writer's Digest Guide to Query Letters*.

51

AUTHOR PLATFORM 2.0

The Next Steps to Successful Self-Promotion

Jane Friedman

You've been through the drill already. You know about establishing your own website, being active on social media, plus networking up and down the food chain. You've heard all the advice about building your online and off-line presence—and perhaps you've landed a book deal because of your strong platform.

But platform building is a career-long activity. It doesn't stop once your website goes live or after you land a book deal. In fact, your continued career growth depends on extending your reach and uncovering new opportunities. So what's next?

I'll break it down into three categories:

1. Optimize your online presence.
2. Make your relationships matter.
3. Diversify your content.

OPTIMIZE YOUR ONLINE PRESENCE

First things first. You need your own domain (e.g., janefriedman.com is the domain I own), and you should be self-hosted. If you're still working off Blogger or Wordpress.com, then you won't be able to implement all of my advice due to the limitations of having your site owned or hosted by someone else.

Once you truly own your site, hire a professional website designer to customize the look and feel to best convey your personality or brand. If you don't yet have a grasp on what your "personality" is, then hold off on a site revamp until you do. Or you might start simple by getting a professionally designed header that's unique to your site.

Website and Blog Must-Haves

Here's a checklist of things you should implement aside from a customized design.

- Readers should be able to subscribe to your blog posts via e-mail or RSS. You should be able to track the number of people who are signing up and see when they are doing so.
- Customize the e-mails sent to anyone who subscribes to your blog posts. This can be done if you use Feedburner (free service) or MailChimp (free up to 2,000 names). Each e-mail that your readers receive should have the same look and feel as your website or whatever branding you typically use. You should also be able to see how many people open these e-mails and what they click on.
- If you do not actively blog, start an e-mail newsletter and post the sign-up form on your site. This way you can stay in touch with people who express interest in your news and updates. Again, MailChimp is a free e-mail newsletter delivery service for up to 2,000 names. You should also have e-newsletter sign-up forms with you at speaking engagements.
- Install Google Analytics, which offers valuable data on who visits your site, when they visit, what content they look at, how long they stay, etc.
- Add social sharing buttons to your site and each post so people can easily share your content on Facebook, Google, etc. This functionality might have to be manually added if you have a self-hosted site.

Review Your Metrics

As I hope you noticed, many of the above items relate to metrics and measurement. Advance platform building requires that you study your numbers. Especially think about the following:

- **HOW DO PEOPLE FIND YOUR SITE?** For example, if you're dumping a lot of energy into Twitter to drive traffic to your blog posts, but very few people visit your site from Twitter, that means your strategy is not working, and you might need to course correct.
- **WHAT CONTENT IS THE MOST POPULAR ON YOUR SITE?** This is like a neon sign, telling you what your readers want. Whatever it is, consider how you can build on it, repurpose it, or expand it.
- **WHAT CAUSES A SPIKE IN TRAFFIC, FOLLOWERS, OR SUBSCRIBERS?** When you achieve spikes, you've done something right. How can you repeat the success?

- **WHAT'S EXTENDING YOUR REACH?** Most days, you're probably talking to the same crowd you were yesterday. But every so often, you'll be opened up to a new audience—and from that you can find new and loyal readers. Identify activities that have a broad ripple effect and make you heard beyond your existing circles. (In Google Analytics, this would mean tracking how new visitors find you.)

Advanced Social Media Monitoring and Involvement

Just about everyone by now has a Facebook profile or page, a LinkedIn profile, a Twitter account, etc. But static profiles can only do so much for you. Social media becomes more valuable when you decide how to interact and how to facilitate valuable discussion among your followers. Here are a few areas to consider:

- **IMPLEMENT AN ADVANCED COMMENTING SYSTEM.** Sometimes the most valuable part of a blog is having a comments section where people can contribute and interact with each other. But this usually means actively filtering the good comments from the bad. Using a robust system like Disqus or Livefyre (and paying for access to their filtering tools) can help you develop a quality discussion area that rewards the most thoughtful contributors.
- **ADD A FORUM OR DISCUSSION BOARD.** Very popular bloggers, who may have hundreds of comments on a post, will often add a forum or discussion board so their community can interact in an extended way. If your site is Wordpress-based, plug-ins can help you add a forum to your site in one step. Or you can consider using a private Facebook group or Ning (www. ning.com) as the base for your community.
- **USE HOOTSUITE TO BE STRATEGIC WITH YOUR SOCIAL MEDIA UP-DATES.** HootSuite is a free Web-based software that helps you schedule updates primarily for Twitter but also for other sites. It also helps you analyze the effectiveness of your tweets (e.g, it can tell you how many people clicked on a link you tweeted).
- **USE PAPER.LI (FREE SERVICE) TO AUTOMATICALLY CURATE THE BEST DAILY TWEETS, UPDATES, AND POSTS ON WHATEVER SUBJECT YOU'RE AN EXPERT ON—BASED ON THE PEOPLE OR ORGANIZATIONS YOU FOLLOW AND TRUST.** Sometimes curating is one of the best services you can provide for your community—not only do you provide valuable content, but you help people understand *who else* provides valuable content!

A final word about social media: Everyone knows about the usual suspects (Facebook, Twitter, Google Plus). Make sure you're not missing a more niche, devoted community on your topic. For example, All About Romance (www.likesbooks. com) is a very popular site for readers and authors of romance.

MAKE YOUR RELATIONSHIPS MATTER

The key components to platform are the relationships you have and grow. Often when you see a successful author, only the *visible* aspects of his or her online presence or content are apparent. What you can't see are all of the relationship-building and behind-the-scenes conversations that contribute to a more impactful and amplified reach.

Am I saying you have to know big-name people to have a successful platform? No! Do you need to build relationships with successful or authoritative people (or organizations/businesses) in your community? Yes. Here's how to amplify your efforts.

Make a List of Who's Interacting with You the Most

Regardless of where it's happening (on your site or on social media), take note of who is reading, commenting on, or sharing your content. These are people who already pay attention, like what you're doing, and are receptive to further interaction.

If you're ignoring these people, then you're missing an opportunity to develop a more valuable relationship (which will likely lead to new ones), as well as reward and empower those you're already engaged with.

What does "rewarding" and "empowering" look like? You might drop a personal note, offer an e-book or product for free, or involve them somehow in your online content. You might have a special newsletter for them. Do what makes sense—there are many ways to employ this principle. Christina Katz, who teaches classes to writers, creates "Dream Teams" of writers who are selected from previous students. It's a great idea that rewards both Christina and the students she coaches.

Make a List of Your Mentors and How You Can Help Them

You should have a list (or wish list!) of mentors. If not, develop one. We all know of people who are doing something we dream about doing or who operate a few steps beyond where we're currently at.

If you're not already closely following your mentors on their most active channels of communication (blog, Twitter, Facebook, etc.), then start. Begin commenting, sharing, and being a visible fan of what they do. Then consider other ways you can develop the relationship; e.g., interview them on your blog or review their book. But most of all, brainstorm how you can serve them.

If you engage mentors in an intelligent way (not in a needy "look at me" sort of way), then you may develop a more meaningful relationship when they reach out to acknowledge your efforts. But be careful: Do not approach this as something you're going to "get something" out of, or it will backfire.

Do watch for opportunities that mentors will inevitably offer (e.g., "I'm looking for someone to help moderate my community. Who wants to help?"). I once helped an author arrange a book event when he stopped in Cincinnati, and that helped solidify a relationship that had only been virtual up until that point.

Finally, don't forget a time-honored way to cozy up to mentors: offer a guest post for their blog. Just make sure that what you contribute is of the highest quality possible—a higher quality than what you'd demand for your own site. If you bring a mentor considerable traffic, you'll earn her attention and esteem.

Look for Partnerships with Peers

Who is attempting to reach the same audience as you? Don't see them as competitors. Instead, align with them to do bigger and better things. You can see examples of partnership everywhere in the writing community, such as:

- Writer Unboxed website
- Jungle Red Writers blog
- The Kill Zone blog

We all have different strengths. Banding together is an excellent method for extending your platform in ways you can't manage on your own. When presented with opportunities to collaborate, say yes whenever you'll be exposed to a new audience or have a chance to diversify your online presence.

Stay Alert to Your Influencers and Who You Influence

There are many ways to identify important people in your community, but if you're not sure where to start, try the following:

- **BLOG ROLLS:** Find just one blog that you know is influential. See who they're linking to and recommending. Identify sites that seem to be on everyone's "best of" list—or try searching for "best blogs" plus your niche.
- **KLOUT:** This social media tool attempts to measure people's authority online by assigning a score. It will summarize who you influence and who you are influenced by.

- **DISQUS:** If you use the Disqus commenting system, it will identify the most active commenters on your site.

DIVERSIFY YOUR CONTENT

Writers can easily fall into the trap of thinking only about new *written* content. It's a shame, because by repurposing existing content into new mediums, you can open yourself up to entirely new audiences.

For example, I have a friend who has a long solo commute by car, plus he walks his dogs while listening to his iPod. Nearly all of his media consumption is podcast driven. He rarely reads because his lifestyle doesn't support it. That means that if he can't get his content in audio form, he won't buy it.

Envision a day in the life of your readers. Are they likely to be using mobile devices? Tablets? (Guess what: Google Analytics tells you the percentage of mobile and tablet visits to your site!) Do your readers like to watch videos on YouTube? Do they buy e-books? Are they on Twitter?

If you adapt your content to different mediums, you will uncover a new audience who didn't know you existed. While not all content is fit for adaptation, brainstorm a list of all the content you currently own rights to, and think of ways it could be repurposed or redistributed.

A popular repurposing project for longtime bloggers is to compile and edit a compilation of best blog posts and make it available as an e-book (free or paid). Some bloggers will even do that with a handful of blog posts that can serve as a beginner or introductory guide to a specific topic. How about offering a sampler of your work in e-book or PDF form?

Some forms or mediums you might want to explore:

- creating podcasts and distributing them through your own site (or via iTunes)
- creating videocasts and distributing them through YouTube or Vimeo (did you know that YouTube is now the number two search engine?)
- creating tips or lessons in e-mail newsletter form
- creating PDFs (free or paid) and using Scribd to help distribute
- creating online tutorials or offering critiques through tools such as Google Hangouts, Google Docs, and/or Screencast.com
- creating slide presentations and distributing them through SlideShare

The only limit is your imagination!

HOUSEKEEPING

On a final note, I'd like to share a few housekeeping tips that can help boost your image and authority online. While they may seem trivial, they go a long way in making a good impression and spreading the word about what you do.

- Get professional headshots that accurately convey your brand or personality—what people know you and love you for.
- For your social media profiles, completely fill out *all* fields and maximize the functionality. This is important for search and discoverability. For instance, on LinkedIn, add keywords that cover all of your skill sets, pipe in your Twitter account and blog posts, and give complete descriptions of all positions you've held. On Google Plus, list all the sites that you're a contributor for. On Facebook, allow people to subscribe to your public updates even if they aren't your friends.
- Gather updated testimonials and blurbs, and use them on your site and/or your social media profiles if appropriate.

However you decide to tackle the next stage of your platform development, ensure consistency. Whether it's your website, e-newsletter, Facebook profile, business cards, or letterhead, be consistent in the look and feel of your materials and in the message you send. Unless you are appealing to different audiences with different needs, broadcast a unified message no matter where and how people find you. Believe me—it doesn't get boring. Instead, it helps people remember who you are and what you stand for.

Jane Friedman has twenty years of experience in the publishing industry, with expertise in digital media strategy for authors and publishers. She's the co-founder and editor of *The Hot Sheet* (hotsheetpub.com) the essential publishing-industry newsletter for authors, and is the former publisher of Writer's Digest. She has been interviewed and featured by NPR, PBS, *The Washington Post*, the National Press Club, and many other outlets.

The Complete Handbook of Novel Writing

52

GOING PUBLIC

How to Ace Readings, Signings,
Interviews, and More

Elizabeth Sims

It was a dark and stormy night in Northern California. I was in a large bookstore to read from my debut novel, *Holy Hell*, and this was my very first author event. Only four people had shown up, but I felt triumphant that it wasn't zero.

In honor of the occasion, I'd brought a box of fine chocolates to share. My small audience sat comfortably and paid attention as I spoke. At the end there were no questions, but everybody came up for an extra chocolate.

One person told me she'd enjoyed my reading. I tried to hand her a book, desperate to make at least one sale, saying, "Wouldn't you like to get one? I'd be glad to sign it for you."

"Oh, no," she said. The others were drifting away. "Goodnight, Ed!" she called. "Goodnight, Jerome!" The woman turned back to me. "See, we're all homeless, and we come in here to warm up. We can't buy anything."

"Oh," I said, then stammered the only thing I could think of: "Well, would you like to take the rest of the chocolates?"

"Yes, thank you." She took the box and left.

A low point to start from? Perhaps.

Since then, I've given a book and bus fare to a guy who attended one of my readings, showed up for an appearance in 104-degree heat to find that the air-conditioning had broken (zero attendance there), and been snubbed by store clerks who perceived my mystery series as beneath them.

Fortunately, I've also enjoyed well-attended events and built lasting relationships with many booksellers and readers who appreciate my work—and tell their friends.

Having worked as both a bookstore manager and a media spokesperson before becoming an author, I've experienced the business from several angles. The main lesson: Your public persona as an author is not about you. Really. It's about your work and your audience. And all you need is a little preparation to serve them both well. Let's look at the most common scenarios you'll face.

BOOKSTORE APPEARANCES

The standard venue for a public appearance by an author is still the bookstore. Here's how to ensure each event you do is a successful one.

KNOW THAT YOU'LL BE JUDGED BY YOUR OWN COVER. It might not be fair, but people accord greater respect to those who dress in good clothes. Show up in an outfit you'd wear to accept a literary prize. Be fastidious about your grooming (and breath). Look sharp, and you'll feel sharp.

ARRIVE EARLY. Introduce yourself to the manager, and get squared away. You will have phoned or e-mailed weeks in advance to make sure they've stocked your books. (Always double-check all logistics—date and time, book inventory—even if you're published by a traditional house with someone assigned to make arrangements for you.) Check out the physical space, and set up your stuff (a good pen for signing, bookmarks or other giveaways, sign-up sheet to join your e-mail list, water bottle, throat lozenges). Find out where the bathroom is.

Typically, you won't have much room to work with. It's reasonable to expect—and nicely ask for, if need be—eight to ten chairs, a table, and a little space for them. If nothing's set up, say, "Okay if I just pitch in and help?" Then drag chairs over, hunt down your books, and make a good time of it.

Avoid demanding more from the bookstore unless you're a major or especially charismatic author. I remember one big-name author telling me quite frankly on the phone before his event, "I'm an alcoholic, and I'm going to need a bottle of scotch and a glass within easy reach, or things won't go well." Given that we expected to sell several hundred copies of his books, I gladly ran to the liquor store.

Unless you're that guy, bring your own liquor. Better still, unless you're that guy, show up sober and tidy.

BE CHARMING NO MATTER WHAT HAPPENS. Realize that you are an entertainer and will be judged by how well you amuse and accommodate. When introduced to bookstore staff, look them in the eye, say their name twice, and then call them by name evermore. (It helps to picture a person's name engraved across her forehead.) Most mortals get upset when things go wrong; you can elevate yourself to special status by reacting with good humor to any mishap, such as a fire alarm getting pulled or the coffee machine breaking down.

TAKE COMMAND OF THE CLOCK. Here is a good way to manage your time for a one-hour appearance:

- **FIVE MINUTES:** Introduction, thank-you for coming, thanks to the host, invitation to sign up for your e-mail list. (Note: Be prepared to introduce yourself if no one is on hand to do it.)
- **TEN TO FIFTEEN MINUTES:** Read, with intro or commentary.
- **TEN TO FIFTEEN MINUTES:** Talk about your book and yourself.
- **TEN TO FIFTEEN MINUTES:** Q&A, thanks to audience and host.
- **TEN TO FIFTEEN MINUTES:** Sign books, kibitz, wrap up, and go.

READ WELL, LIVELY, AND LITTLE. Audiences like to hear a short anecdote as to how your book came about. Then, a couple of passages totaling ten to fifteen minutes work well as an appetizer to entice your listeners to buy the book.

For fiction, avoid passages with long descriptions and/or lots of dialogue (imagine the task of trying to alter your tone or pitch for each different voice). An effective reading shows your protagonist engaged in some action and reveals a bit of his personality or motivation at the same time. Unless you're starting at the very beginning, provide some context: "Okay, Officer Rodriguez has just gotten dumped by his girlfriend, but he doesn't know how his luck is about to change. We pick up with him as he's called to investigate a suspicious smell coming from the apartment next door."

Ideally, do a practice run in front of someone (or someones) who can provide constructive criticism. Vary your voice tones, put your emphasis in different places, vary your loudness and softness, use gestures. Also, it's okay to pause for effect. (This is a good time to look up and make eye contact with someone in the audience.)

It has become the fashion for authors reading aloud to laugh, or barely suppress laughter, at the witty places. Do not stoop to this. If your work is funny, reading it with straight earnestness will make them laugh. A well-timed pause can make all the difference. Take my word for it.

KEEP THEM LISTENING. When you finish reading, it's okay to say a few things about your writing process and how you came to be an author, but mostly your attendees want to hear why they should spend their hard-earned money on your book. They want to know how it will change their life or make them think in a new way.

Based on that, a good way to give a successful little talk is simply to tell anecdotes. How did you come up with the characters and their foibles? In all genres, audiences love to hear stories about the research you did for your book. I've held rooms spellbound as I relayed how my friend, a surgeon, educated me in how it feels and sounds to set a broken bone.

ALWAYS TAKE QUESTIONS AT THE END. Do this *before* you offer to sign books. Be generous in answering, and let one question lead to another.

If things are slow, I might jump-start the situation by pulling out a few cards and saying brightly, "As it happens, I brought a few questions from the old mailbag just in case!" Of course these are of my own devising, and the crazier the better: I've "asked" myself about rabbits, golf, revenge, theatrical makeup, arson, and more, all of it relevant in some way to one of my books.

Enjoy your audience; let them see you having fun. If someone starts to monopolize the Q&A, just smile and say, "Let's you and I get together after I've wrapped up, okay?"

ADAPT YOUR TALK TO YOUR AUDIENCE. All these tips work great whether you've got an audience of twelve or 120. But the number one question I'm asked about bookstore appearances is this: What if nobody (or almost nobody) comes? It's a valid concern—we've all been there. But knowing how to handle it can set you apart.

If your census is between one and four, I suggest you forsake the lecture format, make a circle of the chairs, and just have a conversation. Forgo the awkwardness of standing in front of the room, and put your audience at ease. Often other customers will be drawn in. You can still talk about your book and even read, but keep it loose and informal. The point is to bond with your listeners. Ask them what they're reading, what they're hungry for, whether they love only happy endings, even what they like to drink while reading.

If the worst happens and nobody turns out, chat up the staff. If they're busy, stay out of their way, but if there's downtime, ask them things. Booksellers are a fount of information. "Which book or author has most affected you?" "What books are getting your customers excited these days?" "Do you see any trends in the [fill-in-the-blank] genre?"

You can also sell books by roaming the store. Hold a copy of your book, walk around, smile, and introduce yourself as "today's author." Tell them something nice a reviewer has said, then say, "Here, take a look!"

SIGN PROPERLY. When it's time to sign books, say, "Now I'll be glad to personalize a book for—well, everybody!" Take your position behind your table, make eye contact with one and all, get the spelling of each name right, and sign the title page (not inside the cover or on a flyleaf).

CONFERENCES AND EVENTS

Writers tend to be horrible at schmoozing. That's because of a mistaken idea that they're supposed to "get something" out of other people, which feels awkward and uncomfortable. In fact, good schmoozing is about *engaging* with people.

You can get comfortable by realizing that everybody wants to be liked. It's magic when you take the initiative to make a friendly comment, smile, ask people about themselves, and pay attention to what they say. Enjoy people. Try to put everyone at ease, but stop short of being totally ingratiating. Do this by not hogging the spotlight. Listen with alert kindness. One of the best schmoozers I've ever seen made a point of introducing people to one another at events, always with some little connecting comment: "Do you know Dmitri? He teaches at the college!" She flitted around throwing people together all over the place, and everybody loved her.

When doing an event with multiple authors (always a great idea), be hearty and be happy to see them. A golden open-ended question is, "What are you working on now?"

It's a good rule of thumb to follow etiquette rules you might have been taught about polite conversation at dinner parties. Just as you wouldn't assume everybody around you shares your religion, do not assume they share your political slant. Don't be afraid to be yourself, but keep conversation topics in the neutral zone (unless, of course, your book or platform is related to a specific position or opinion).

MEDIA INTERVIEWS

Writers sometimes get featured in print, on the Web, on TV and radio. A useful and efficient way to prepare for these opportunities—while simultaneously creating an effective promotional tool you'll use again and again—is to start by interviewing yourself, in writing. Think of the things you're most likely to be asked, and write your answers out in basic Q&A form: *What led you to write this book? Why is your book important?* And so on.

You can then post this in a Q&A section on your website and even use choice responses in press releases and other promo materials.

And, having thought through these questions and more in advance, you'll find that you're now prepared for most any interview. Having a microphone in front of your face makes most people's adrenaline spike, so knowing what you want to say will help you stay calm. Speak slowly, and you'll sound normal.

The key to nailing an interview is to realize that the interviewer, who is usually at best vaguely familiar with you or your book, will be glad if you take his questions and run with them. Tell what *you* would like the world to know about your book, using the anecdotes you've worked up already. That way, the outcome of the interview is in your control, regardless of how lackluster the questions may be. It's not unusual for an author who is featured in a local newspaper to get a call from a radio producer who spotted the article. Or for a writer who gives an entertaining talk on a popular podcast to be invited to appear on TV. Taking the time to prepare and grant a good interview will likely pay off tenfold as one opportunity leads to another.

GUEST BLOGGING AND BLOG TOURS

Whether you're invited to contribute to an existing blog or you're actively organizing a promotional "blog tour" of your own (or just looking to expand your online platform), writing guest posts is a fun way to engage with potential readers. Ask the blog host what she's looking for, and accommodate as best you can. If the content is all up to you, consider your target audience's point of view: What might they find interesting, amusing, even salacious? (A little gossip goes a long way—remember my bit about the writer and the scotch?) You might include a short excerpt from your book or write up anecdotes just as you'd tell them in an interview.

Let your social network know when your post goes live, making sure to appreciatively acknowledge your host. It's good form to check back on your post, especially the day of and the day after. Reply graciously to all comments, keeping the conversation going.

FOLLOW-THROUGH

Write a thank-you note for every appearance. For physical events, handwrite a note, address it to "The Management and Staff of XYZ Bookstore (or Library)," and let them know how much you appreciated their time and trouble. If you were a guest for an interview or blog, write an e-mail saying the same. Aside from the fact that it's the decent thing to do, a thank-you might help you get invited back.

Every chance for a writer to interact with the public is a special opportunity. By understanding the bigger picture, and by preparing yourself to maximize your impact and handle whatever happens with grace, you will stand the best chance of making a terrific impression, selling books, and creating good karma.

53

REVISE YOUR PATH TO PUBLICATION

Assessing Your Current Trajectory
and Adjusting for the Best Outcome

Jane Friedman

Don't you wish someone could tell you how close you are to getting published? Don't you wish someone could say, "If you just keep at it for three more years, you're certain to make it!"?

Or, even if it would be heartbreaking, wouldn't it be nice to be told that you're wasting your time, so that you could move on, try another tack, or simply write what brings you personal pleasure, with no other aim in mind?

I've counseled thousands of writers over the years, and even if it's not possible for me to read their work, I can usually say something definitive about what their next steps should be. I often see when they're wasting their time.

No matter where you are on your own publishing path, it's smart to periodically take stock of where you're headed and revise as necessary. Here are some steps you can take to do just that.

RECOGNIZING STEPS THAT AREN'T MOVING YOU FORWARD

Let's start with five common time-wasting behaviors. You may be guilty of one or more. Most writers have been guilty of the first.

Time-Waster 1: Submitting Manuscripts That Aren't Your Best Work

Let's be honest. We all secretly hope that some editor or agent will read our work, drop everything, and call us to say: *This is a work of genius! YOU are a genius!*

Few writers give up on this dream entirely, but to increase the chances of this happening, you have to give each manuscript *everything* you've got, with nothing held back. Too many writers save their best effort for some future work, as if they were going to run out of good material.

You can't operate like that.

Every single piece of greatness must go into your current project. Be confident that your creative well is going to be refilled. Make your book better than you ever thought possible—that's what it needs to compete. It can't be good. "Good" gets rejected. Your work has to be the best.

How do you know when it's ready, when it's your best? I like how *Guide to Literary Agents* editor Chuck Sambuchino typically answers this question at writing conferences: "If you think the story has a problem, it does—and any story with a problem is not ready."

It's common for a new writer who doesn't know any better to send off his manuscript without realizing how much work is left to do. But experienced writers are usually most guilty of sending out work that is not ready. Stop wasting your time.

Time-Waster 2: Self-Publishing When No One Is Listening

There are many reasons writers choose to self-publish, but the most common is the inability to land an agent or a traditional publisher.

Fortunately, it's more viable than ever for a writer to be successful *without* a traditional publisher or agent, primarily due to the rise of e-books and e-readers. However, when writers chase self-publishing as an alternative to traditional publishing, they often have a nasty surprise in store: No one is listening. They don't have an audience.

Bowker estimated that in 2009, more than 760,000 new titles were "nontraditionally" published, which included print-on-demand and self-published work. How many new titles were traditionally published? About 288,000. And none of these numbers take into account the growing number of writers releasing their work in electronic-only editions.

If your goal is to bring your work successfully to the marketplace, it's a waste of time to self-publish that work—in *any* format—if you haven't yet cultivated an audience for it or can't market and promote it effectively through your network. Doing so will not likely harm your career in the long run, but it won't move it forward, either.

Time-Waster 3: Publishing Your Work Digitally When Your Audience Wants Print

E-books have become the darlings of the self-publishing world, and for good reason. They're easy to create, require little investment, and can reach an international market overnight. They also allow you to experiment, to have a direct line to a readership, and to see what effectively grows that readership.

But it won't do you a bit of good if your audience is still devoted to print. If you don't know what format your readers prefer, then find out before you waste your time developing a product no one will read or buy.

Rework this maxim as needed for your particular audience (e.g., don't focus on producing print if your readers favor digital).

Time-Waster 4: Looking for Major Publication of Regional or Niche Work

Every year agents receive thousands of submissions for work that does not have national appeal and does not deserve shelf space at every chain bookstore in the country. (And that's typically why you get an agent: to sell your work to the big publishers, which specialize in national distribution and marketing.)

As a writer, one of the most difficult tasks you face is gaining sufficient distance from your work to understand how a publishing professional would view the market for it, or to determine if there's a commercial *angle* to be exploited. You have to view your work not as something precious to you but as a product to be positioned and sold. That means pitching your work only to the most appropriate publishing houses, even if they're in your own backyard rather than New York City.

SIGNS YOU'RE GETTING CLOSER TO PUBLICATION

- You start receiving personalized, "encouraging" rejections.
- Agents or editors reject the manuscript you submitted but ask you to send your next work. (They can see that you're on the verge of producing something great.)
- Your mentor (or published author friend) tells you to contact his agent, without you asking for a referral.
- An agent or editor proactively contacts you because she spotted your quality writing somewhere online or in print.

Time-Waster 5: Focusing on Publishing When You Should Be Writing

Some writers are far too concerned with queries, agents, marketing, or conference going, instead of first producing the best work possible.

Don't get me wrong—for some types of nonfiction, it's *essential* to have a platform in place before you write the book. The fact that nonfiction authors don't typically write the full manuscript until after acceptance of their proposal (with the exception of memoir and creative nonfiction) is indicative of how much platform means to their publication.

But for everyone else (those of us who are *not* selling a book based solely on the proposal), it's best not to get consumed with finding an agent until you're a writer ready for publication.

And now we come to that tricky matter again. How do you know it's *that* time? Let's dig a little deeper.

EVALUATING YOUR PLACE ON THE PUBLICATION PATH

Whenever I sit down for a critique session with a writer, I ask three questions early on: How long have you been working on this manuscript, and who has seen it? Is this the first manuscript you've ever completed? And finally: How long have you been actively writing?

These questions help me evaluate where the writer might be on the publication path. Here are a few generalizations I can often make:

- Most first manuscript attempts are not publishable, even after revision, yet they are necessary and vital for a writer's growth. A writer who's just finished her first manuscript probably doesn't realize this and will likely take the rejection process very hard. Some writers can't move past this rejection. You've probably heard experts advise that you should always start working on the next manuscript rather than wait to publish the first. That's because you need to move on and not get stuck on publishing your first attempt.
- A writer who has been working on the same manuscript for years and years—and has written *nothing else*—might have a motivation problem. There isn't

usually much valuable learning going on when someone tinkers with the same pages over a decade.

- Writers who have been actively writing for many years, have produced multiple full-length manuscripts, and have one or two trusted critique partners (or mentors) are often well positioned for publication. They probably know their strengths and weaknesses, and have a structured revision process. Many such people require only luck to meet preparedness.

- Writers who have extensive experience in one medium and then attempt to tackle another (e.g., journalists tackling the novel) may overestimate their abilities to produce a publishable manuscript on the first try. That doesn't mean their effort won't be good, but it might not be *good enough*. Fortunately, any writer with professional experience will probably approach the process with a professional mind-set, a good network of contacts to help him understand next steps, and a range of tools to overcome the challenges.

Notice I have not mentioned talent. I have not mentioned creative writing classes or degrees. I have not mentioned online presence. These factors are usually less relevant in determining how close you are to publishing a book-length work.

The two things that *are* relevant:

1. HOW MUCH TIME YOU'VE PUT INTO WRITING. I agree with Malcolm Gladwell's ten-thousand-hour rule in *Outliers*: The key to success in any field is, to a large extent, a matter of practicing a specific task for a total of around ten thousand hours.

2. WHETHER YOU'RE READING ENOUGH TO UNDERSTAND WHERE YOU ARE ON THE SPECTRUM OF QUALITY. In his series on storytelling (available on YouTube), Ira Glass says:

> The first couple years that you're making stuff, what you're making isn't so good. It's not that great. It's trying to be good, it has ambitions, but it's not that good. But your taste, the thing that got you into the game, your taste is still killer. Your taste is good enough that you can tell that what you're making is kind of a disappointment to you. You can tell that it's still sort of crappy. A lot of people never get past that phase. A lot of people at that point quit. ... Most everybody I know who does interesting creative work, they went through a phase of years where they had really good taste [and] they could tell that what they were making wasn't as good as they wanted it to be.

If you can't perceive the gap—or if you haven't gone through the "phase"—you probably aren't reading enough. How do you develop good taste? You read. How do you understand what quality work is? You read. What's the best way to improve your skills aside from writing more? You read. You write, and you read, and you begin to close the gap between the quality you *want* to achieve, and the quality you *can* achieve.

In short: You've got to produce a lot of crap before you can produce something publishable.

KNOWING WHEN IT'S TIME TO CHANGE COURSE

I used to believe that great work would eventually get noticed—you know, that old theory that quality bubbles to the top?

I don't believe that any more.

Great work is overlooked every day, for a million reasons. Business concerns outweigh artistic concerns. Some people are just perpetually unlucky.

To avoid beating your head against the wall, here are some questions that can help you understand when and how to change course.

1. IS YOUR WORK COMMERCIALLY VIABLE? Indicators will eventually surface if your work isn't suited for commercial publication. You'll hear things like "Your work is too quirky or eccentric." "It has narrow appeal." "It's experimental." "It doesn't fit the model." Or possibly, "It's too intellectual, too demanding." These are signs that you may need to consider self-publishing—which will also require you to find the niche audience you appeal to.

2. ARE READERS RESPONDING TO SOMETHING YOU DIDN'T EXPECT? I see this happen all the time: A writer is working on a manuscript that no one seems interested in but has fabulous success on some side project. Perhaps you really want to push your memoir, but everyone loves the humorous tip series on your blog. Sometimes it's better to pursue what's working, and what people express interest in, especially if you take enjoyment in it. Use it as a stepping-stone to other things, if necessary.

3. ARE YOU GETTING BITTER? You can't play poor, victimized writer and expect to get published. As it is in romantic relationships, pursuing an agent or editor with an air of desperation, or with an Eeyore complex, will not endear you to them. Embittered writers carry a huge sign with them that screams, "I'm unhappy, and I'm going to make you unhappy, too."

If you find yourself demonizing people in the publishing industry, taking rejections very personally, feeling as if you're owed something, and/or complaining whenever you get together with other writers, it's time to find the refresh button. Return to what made you feel joy and excitement about writing in the first place. Perhaps you've been focusing too much on getting published, and you've forgotten to cherish the other aspects. Which brings me to the overall theory of how you should, at various stages of your career, revisit and revise your publication strategy.

REVISING YOUR PUBLISHING PLAN

No matter how the publishing world changes, consider these three timeless factors as you make decisions about your next steps forward.

1. WHAT MAKES YOU HAPPY: This is the reason you got into writing in the first place. Even if you put this on the back burner in order to advance other aspects of your writing and publishing career, don't leave it out of the equation for very long. Otherwise your efforts can come off as mechanistic or uninspired, and you'll eventually burn out.

2. WHAT EARNS YOU MONEY: Not everyone cares about earning money from writing—and I believe that anyone in it for the coin should find some other field—but as you gain experience, the choices you make in this regard become more important. The more professional you become, the more you have to pay attention to what brings the most return on your investment of time and energy.

3. WHAT REACHES READERS OR GROWS YOUR AUDIENCE: Growing readership is just as valuable as earning money. It's like putting a bit of money in the bank and making an investment that pays off as time passes. Sometimes you'll want to make trade-offs that involve earning less money in order to grow readership, because it invests in your future. (E.g., for a time you might focus on building a blog or a site, rather than writing for print publication, to grow a more direct line to your fans.)

It is rare that every piece of writing you do, or every opportunity presented, can involve *all three* elements at once. Commonly you can get two of the three. Sometimes you'll pursue certain projects with only one of these factors in play. You get to decide based on your priorities at any given point in time.

At the very beginning of this chapter, I suggested that it might be nice if someone could tell us if we're wasting our time trying to get published.

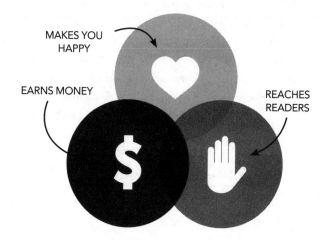

MAKES YOU
HAPPY

EARNS MONEY

REACHES
READERS

Here's a little piece of hope: If your immediate thought was, *I couldn't stop writing even if someone told me to give up*, then you're much closer to publication than someone who is easily discouraged. The battle is far more psychological than you might think. Those who can't be dissuaded are more likely to reach their goals, regardless of the path they ultimately choose.

54

DISSECTING THE SELF-PUBLISHING CONTRACT

Five Key Issues for Authors

Aimee Bissonette

Self-publishing can be a huge undertaking. There are so many issues to weigh. Different self-publishing service providers have different strengths, and it can be hard to know which to use. Is your book primarily text or images? Do you plan to publish your book as an e-book, in print, or both? Do you need assistance with the entire self-publishing process, or are you able to do some of the work yourself?

All of these are important considerations—but they aren't the only ones. The contract terms offered by the providers you are considering are important as well. Provider contracts (often referred to as "Terms of Use" by online providers) vary widely, and some are fairer than others. Authors need to protect their creative works and their investment in the self-publishing process. Understanding the terms that govern the author/provider relationship is essential.

The following are five key contract issues for authors evaluating self-publishing providers.

1. RIGHTS OWNERSHIP

Who "owns" the book and who controls its distribution and sale are key issues in all publishing contracts. Provider contracts should clearly state that the author is the sole owner of the text of the self-published book. In addition, the author should own the book design, cover art, and formatting of the self-published book—even when these are created by the provider. Plainly said, self-publishing should mean that you, the author, own 100 percent of the rights to your book.

Instead of talking in terms of ownership, a provider's contract language should discuss licensing of rights. The contract should enumerate the rights licensed: most commonly, the right to print, publish, distribute, and sell the book. The author may also license the right to convert the book to one or more e-book formats and the right to house an electronic copy of the book on the provider's server.

The provider's contract should state whether the licenses are "exclusive" or "nonexclusive." If an author grants an exclusive license to a provider, the provider is the only person or entity that may exercise that right while the contract is in place. The licensed right may not even be exercised by the author during that time, so authors should be careful about granting exclusive licenses. Exclusive licenses are appropriate when a provider agrees to significant obligations beyond merely publishing and selling (e.g., warehousing, order fulfillment, marketing, publicity, catalog, and website presence) but then only if the contract is easily terminated by the author.

Licensed rights should be limited only to those that are necessary for the provider to fulfill the self-publishing services, and the length of time those licenses remain in place should also be limited (licenses should either be for a specific period of time or terminable at will by the author). Some provider contracts require authors to grant very expansive licenses that allow the provider tremendous control. These providers also may try to include "out of print" clauses, noncompete clauses, and option clauses in their contracts—none of which are appropriate in a self-publishing scenario. Steer clear of these providers.

2. DESIGN SERVICES

Self-publishing providers offer a range of packages and services. Authors engage these providers for their expertise in editing and design, as well as distribution and e-book conversion. It is important to compare and contrast these offerings to determine exactly what the various providers include in terms of cover art, interior design, fonts, placement of bar codes, and so on.

Provider contracts should be clear about the services offered and when additional fees will be charged. For instance, the contract should state whether an author must pay additional fees for revisions of the designs created, and whether the provider will refund an author's money should the provider and the author fail to see eye to eye on production issues.

When evaluating the many additional services offered by various providers (and the attendant fees), authors should consider what, if anything, they can do themselves. There is no need to buy what you don't need. For instance, many providers will procure ISBNs as part of their services. Because it is expensive for an individual to purchase a single ISBN, it may make sense for the author to have the provider do so, unless the author intends to issue the self-published book in multiple formats or editions. (Each version and format of a book requires a separate ISBN. If you anticipate that you will be issuing the book in multiple formats, or reissuing your book in the future through someone other than your current provider, you may be better off purchasing a block of ten ISBNs.)

By comparison, copyright registration is easily done online and requires payment of a nominal filing fee to the U.S. Copyright Office (the current fee is $35). Registering your copyright yourself is preferable to paying your provider a marked-up fee to do so.

As noted above, ownership issues can arise with regard to design aspects of self-published books. Authors who engage providers to design and format their books are encouraged to look for contract language along the lines of "Author owns 100 percent of the book cover, design, and layout." If authors supply their own images for their self-published books, they must first clear the rights to use those images.

Authors own the rights to images they create themselves (e.g., photos they take), but they are not free to use images pulled from the Internet without first obtaining permission. Even stock images obtained via Internet or subscription services are subject to restrictions. Authors must abide by the licensing terms and pay the appropriate fees to such services before including images on or in their self-published books.

If an author retains a freelancer (an independent contractor) to provide cover art or other book design services, an agreement between the author and the freelancer that specifically states, in writing, that the freelancer's work is a "work for hire" under U.S. Copyright law and that the freelancer makes no claim of ownership in the author's book should be drawn up. This allows the author to use the book's cover and design aspects in other ways as well, for example, on the author's website, in print materials, and on social media.

3. HOW THE MONEY FLOWS

Providers take different approaches to pricing. Some dictate pricing and royalty terms, while others allow authors to set their own retail price, author discount, and wholesale price (although sometimes this is subject to a minimum dollar amount to ensure the provider can cover its administrative and credit card costs). Authors should seek arrangements that provide them with 100 percent of book royalties after deduction of production costs and third-party service provider costs.

When it comes to tracking and getting paid for sales, self-publishing service providers offer an advantage over traditional publishers. Several offer easily accessible sales information online and pay royalties on a monthly or quarterly basis, as opposed to the annual or semiannual payments provided by traditional publishers.

Compare provider contracts based on how providers track sales, how frequently they pay royalties, and the manner in which they pay. Many providers set up author accounts and establish a threshold amount, above which funds are made available for electronic transfer. (If an author prefers a physical check, a processing fee may be charged.) Look for contract language that establishes definite parameters and procedures for payment and provides a mechanism by which authors can track sales and, thus, judge the accuracy of payments made.

With regard to payments, be aware that, as with traditional publishers, providers will declare the right to withhold payments as an offset against any money the author owes the provider (e.g., payment for services, returns, refunds, customer credits). Providers will withhold payments if a claim is made against an author for copyright infringement, defamation, or other violation of a third party's rights. Some providers will also withhold payments for a period of time after termination of the contract (e.g., Amazon will hold funds for three months), so they are sure to have funds on hand to process refunds, credits, and returns that accrue after the contract has ended.

Lastly, authors are responsible for paying income tax on the revenue they derive from book sales. Most providers will require, at a minimum, that you provide them with a Social Security or Tax Identification number so they may fulfill their reporting obligations to the taxing authorities.

4. ENDING THE RELATIONSHIP

Self-publishing is changing rapidly. The services offered by providers this year may be radically different from those offered in years to come. For that reason, it is important to have flexibility when it comes to terminating a contract with a provider. Ideally, an author should be able to terminate a provider contract (or, in legal terms, "rescind" the author's grant of rights) at any time. Provider contracts may require advance notice of termination, but such notice should not exceed thirty days.

Most provider contracts allow for immediate termination, followed by a short period within which the provider may alert third-party sellers and fulfill sales pending at the time of termination. Authors who have purchased additional services from their providers (e.g., inclusion in an online or print catalog, premium distribution services) may have separate contracts for those services and may need to take additional steps to terminate them.

Be aware that providers also have termination rights. Many providers include contract language that allows the provider to suspend an author's access to its services, particularly if an author engages in illegal or unethical behavior, or otherwise violates the rights of others. Authors are counseled to keep backup copies of their books and other content as protection in the unlikely event they are denied access to their providers' services.

5. RESOLVING DISPUTES

As with any business relationship, the possibility exists for a dispute between authors and providers. Sometimes these disputes are about money, which highlights the importance of reviewing and auditing royalty statements, as mentioned above. Sometimes the disputes occur before publication and are resolved by a refund of some or all of the author's money. Regardless of the dispute, provider contracts will include dispute resolution provisions, which generally benefit the provider.

Some provider contracts set a discrete, and usually short (e.g., six to twelve months), period of time within which an author may bring a claim against the provider for breach of contract. Authors are contractually bound by these time periods, even if state law provides a longer period of time within which a claim may be brought.

Providers also often include language that limits the issues on which an author may base a claim, or that limits the author's recovery to only unpaid royalties, or that requires the author to use arbitration rather than the courts to resolve disputes. These dispute resolution provisions are not likely to be negotiable, but because they dictate how and when an author may bring legal claims against a provider, they should not be disregarded.

THE SMART CONSUMER'S APPROACH

In conclusion, there are a multitude of issues for authors to consider when evaluating self-publishing provider contracts. The issues outlined above are particularly important, however, because they affect an author's ability to control the self-published work. There are many reputable providers whose contracts offer even-handed terms.

In comparing provider contracts, trust your gut. Ask yourself if the contract seems fair. Is it written in easy-to-understand language? Are you able to negotiate any terms (or, at least, choose from a variety of packages)?

Be a smart consumer. Talk to others who have used the self-publishing provider you are considering. And, above all, review contract terms so you can minimize the risk of problems and maximize all the possible benefits.

Aimee Bissonette earned her bachelor's degree from Colorado State University and her law degree from the University of Minnesota Law School. She has worked as an occupational therapist, teacher, lawyer, and small-business owner. In her legal practice, she works with numerous children's book authors and illustrators. In addition to her books for children, Aimee has published a book for K–12 teachers and administrators on the legal issues associated with technology in the schools. She lives with her husband, family, and dogs in Minneapolis, Minnesota.

55

FAILURE TO LAUNCH

Why Good Novels Fail to Sell

Donald Maass

You'll never meet an author who admits to publishing a "failed" novel. You will, though, encounter authors in bars and on blogs who will loudly tell you what's wrong with the book industry. They'll chronicle in detail how their titles languished on the shelves because their publishers screwed up and failed *them*.

But accept blame? No way. If sales were disappointing or an option was dropped, it's the fault of weak "support," a lousy cover, awful back-panel copy, bad timing, distribution mistakes, lack of subsidiary rights sales, or a host of other common publishing woes.

How can it be the author's fault? After all, he wrote a book that was *good enough*. It was published. It met the standard—one that sometimes seems impossibly high. Any poor performance was therefore not the author's doing but someone else's, right?

But if that's true, then why do some novels become successful *in spite of* the sting of small deals, minimal press runs, little promotion, forgettable covers, bland copy, distribution snafus, and the absence of movie deals or translation sales?

Take timing and distribution troubles, for instance. In a September 2012 interview in *Writer's Digest* magazine, British author Chris Cleave related that due to a terrorist attack in London on the publication day of his first novel, *Incendiary*—which happened to be about a terrorist attack in London—the book was yanked from bookshop shelves after only about ninety minutes on sale. Talk about disasters! Yet that book later found its audience and was successful, even becoming a feature film. Cleave went on to write the mega-sellers *Little Bee* and *Gold*.

And what about awful covers? Do you remember what was on the covers of *Mystic River* or *Empire Falls*? I didn't think so. It didn't matter. In fact, think about any great novel you read in the last decade and ask yourself this: Was the reason you bought or loved that novel the flap copy, the Italian edition, the movie option, the author's Twitter feed, or the news of her honking big advance? Probably not.

I'm not saying that the industry is perfect or that authors can't increase their sales with smart self-promotion. (Although my experience has been that the boost is typically smaller than evangelists would like you to believe.) If you want to distract yourself with those issues, go ahead. I won't stop you. But you'll be missing a critical point.

As a literary agent who's helped guide fiction careers for more than thirty years, here's what I've learned: Runaway success comes from great fiction, period. The publishing industry may help or hinder but cannot stop a powerful story from being powerful. Conversely, the book business cannot magically transform an adequate novel into a great one.

You may not like every bestseller (*Fifty Shades of Grey*, anyone?), but if a book is selling well then it's doing things right for many readers. By the same token, less commercially successful novels are not doing enough of those things, even if they were good enough to get into print.

What are those critical factors, then? Let's take a look at some of the most common.

CULPRIT 1: TIMID VOICES

Great novels not only draw us in immediately but also command our attention. They not only hold our interest but also hold us rapt. They cast a spell. A snappy premise and meaty plot can hook us and keep us reading but cannot by themselves work that magic. It takes something extra: voice.

What is voice, anyway? Narrative style? Character diction? A set of subject matter or a singular setting? All of the above? Pinning it down can be difficult, but start with this: We primarily experience stories through point-of-view characters.

To put it differently, voice in a novel is not the author's thoughts or vocabulary but the sum total of what her characters observe, think, feel, and express in their own unique ways.

First-person narrators automatically have a voice, but that doesn't necessarily mean it's strong. Victims, whiners, and passive daughters often have weak voices. On the flip side, snappy narrators who fire off zingers every page or so don't always leave a lasting impression, either. Have you ever met a government-issue alpha male or central-casting kick-ass heroine whose name you forgot as soon as you turned the final page? Then you know what I mean.

Lorrie Moore's best-selling literary novel *A Gate at the Stairs* is the coming-of-age story of Tassie Keltjin, a twenty-year-old student and daughter of a potato farmer. As the novel opens, Tassie is on a term break and needs money. She is looking for babysitting jobs.

> I was looking in December for work that would begin at the start of the January term. I'd finished my exams and was answering ads from the student job board, ones for "childcare provider." I liked children—I did!—or rather, I liked them OK. They were sometimes interesting.

Tassie is about as ordinary as characters get. She's a student. She needs a job. She has no odd talent, paranormal ability, or backstory secret. The only reason we're compelled to read about her is her voice, her take on things. Her take on herself is wry. She's a future babysitter trying to talk herself into liking kids. That wry voice makes her engaging enough to lure us forward into the rest of her tragicomic story.

Third-person narrators are a step removed from the reader, true enough, but when their inner experiences are both vivid and different, then their voices can become strong. It's not just language. It's not only getting into a character's head. It's how you use both of those things to create a strong voice.

Erin Morgenstern's best-selling literary fantasy *The Night Circus* is a three-ring carnival of voice that's all the more remarkable for using not only the third person but the often icy present tense. Open her novel at random and see. Here's Lefèvre, the circus manager, practicing knife throwing by aiming at the byline of a reviewer in a newspaper clipping:

> The sentence that holds his name is the particular one that has incensed M. Lefèvre to the point of knife throwing. A single sentence that reads thusly: "M. Chandresh Christophe Lefèvre continues to push the boundaries of the modern stage, dazzling his audiences with spectacle that is almost transcendent."
>
> Most theatrical producers would likely be flattered by such a remark. They would clip the article for a scrapbook of reviews, quote it for references and referrals.
>
> But not this particular theatrical producer. No, M. Chandresh Christophe Lefèvre instead focuses on that penultimate word. Almost. *Almost.*

How often do you use the words *thusly* and *penultimate* in your fiction? Not often? That's okay. I'm not saying that stuffy diction is the way to craft a strong voice. But in this case, it makes the repressed anger and obsessive perfectionism of M. Chandresh Christophe Lefèvre wonderfully distinctive.

STRENGTHEN THAT HARD-TO-DEFINE VOICE:

- What's your protagonist's initial view of the main story problem? Evolve that understanding in three steps. How is it different at the end? Put each stage on the page.
- What's your protagonist's opening opinion of a secondary character, the story's locale, or era? Open with that … then change it by the end.
- Pick anything ordinary in the world of your story: for example, a vehicle, a sport, or a topic of public debate. Give your protagonist a fanatic view. Write his rant. Add. (It's pure voice.)

CULPRIT 2: UNTESTED CHARACTERS

If voice comes from a character's way of looking at the world, a character's continuing grip on the reader comes from what she does, why she does it, and who she is. It's not enough for your characters to simply have actions, motives, and principles. Those drivers can be weak, or they can be strong.

Let's start with actions. The weakest action is inaction. You'd think this is obvious; yet many scenes, indeed whole novels (yes, even published ones), can pass without a character actually doing something. Reacting, observing, and bearing what is hard or painful are not actions. Running away is active, technically speaking, but it isn't as strong as facing up, confronting, and fighting.

More compelling are actions that show spine, take courage, spring from high principles, or bring characters face-to-face with their deepest fears. Strongest of all are self-sacrifice, forgiveness, and other actions that demonstrate growth, grace, and love.

What about motives? In life our motives are many, deep, and intertwined. Unfortunately, in many novels characters are motivated in ways that are single-minded and simplistic. Generic motives make for cartoonish characters.

You can observe such motives in some genre novels. Detectives have codes, romance heroines seek love, and fantasy heroes fight evil. Is that bad? No. Codes, yearning for love, and fighting evil are good—but as characters' lone motives they're also generic.

What makes characters' motivations genuinely gripping, then? There's a hierarchy. Mixed motives make characters real. Conflicting motives make characters complex. Most gripping of all are motives that reveal to us characters' innermost cores. We're shaped by our hurts. When a character's hurts are unique and specific, what propels them on their journeys—motivates them—paradoxically becomes universal.

Think of it this way: The deeper you dig into what drives your protagonist, the more readers will be able to connect.

What about principles? They are the rules we live by and the beliefs we hold. These, too, can be weak or strong. Generic principles are common and obvious. *Do unto others* is a fine but commonplace rule for living. Compelling principles are personal, a twist on what's familiar. *Build a bridge to everyone you meet— then walk across it*, is somewhat more personal. That's especially true if the protagonist who lives by that rule is a bridge inspector.

When actions, motives, and principles come together, the effect can be profound. Jamie Ford's longtime bestseller *Hotel on the Corner of Bitter and Sweet* is set largely in Seattle in 1942. It's the story of Henry Lee, a sixth-grade Chinese-American boy who falls in love with Keiko Okabe, a Japanese-American girl in his class. When Keiko and her family are removed to an internment camp, Henry is distraught. That would be enough for many literary novels. The romantic tragedy has happened. The political point is made.

But Ford has his protagonist *do something*: Henry gets a job as a kitchen assistant to the school cook who has been contracted to feed the prisoners at the internment camp. He goes looking for Keiko.

> Another language barrier Henry ran into was within Camp Harmony. Just seeing a Chinese kid standing on an apple crate behind the serving counter was strange enough. But the more he questioned those who came through his chow line about the Okabes, the more frustrated he became. Few cared, and those who did never seemed to understand. Still, like a lost ship occasionally sending out an SOS, Henry kept peppering those he served with questions.
>
> "Okabes? Does anyone know the Okabes?"

Henry's search poignantly shows the strength of his character. He rejects his father (who tries to force a Chinese Nationalist identity on Henry), ignores social prejudice, and defies the odds. His actions, motives, and principles are high, more so because he's only a kid.

PUT YOUR PROTAGONIST TO THE TEST:

- What's the biggest thing your protagonist could possibly do, but can't? By the end of the story, have her do it.
- The story problem bugs your protagonist like it bugs no one else. The real reason hearkens back to something from childhood—what? Build that into a dramatic, character-defining backstory event. Let it underlie every scene, but reveal what happened only late in the story.
- In what way are your protagonist's operating principles unlike anyone else's? Boil them down to one precept. Drop that in early, and then depict, challenge, and deepen that axiom at least three times by the story's end.

CULPRIT 3: OVERLY INTERIOR OR EXTERIOR STORIES

You're the god of your story world. So there's no reason not to play god with your story.

Certain story patterns are pretty much guaranteed to lead to fiction of underwhelming force. That's often true of novels built on delay, suffering, and being stuck. Even plot-heavy yarns can leave us yawning. Stupendous plot turns don't necessarily have a stupendous effect.

Quiet authors need to create a disturbance in church. At the other end of the spectrum, razzle-dazzle storytellers need to recognize that a burst of flash powder doesn't cause the audience to feel deeply. More simply, interior stories need more dramatic outward events; by the same token, dramatic outward events need to create a more devastating interior impact.

If you shy away from that cheap gimmick called "plot," I applaud your integrity—but try focusing on the inner state of your main character at any given moment and finding a way to externalize it. Make something happen. If, conversely, you focus on keeping your pages turning at a mile a minute, good for you—but try sending your protagonist on a mission not just to save the world but also to save himself.

In a practical sense, playing god with your story means making your characters do bigger things and, conversely, *feel* bigger things when they experience something small.

Earlier I mentioned *Fifty Shades of Grey*. It's hard to find anyone who thinks this mainstream erotica is especially well written; yet its blockbuster status suggests that millions nevertheless find it easy to surrender to it. Why is that, then?

The novel's heroine, student Anastasia Steele, falls under the spell of a man with a dark sexual side, entrepreneur Christian Grey. Anastasia at first resists his magnetic appeal. The slow breakdown of that resistance generates the tension in the novel's early chapters. It's an internal tension, though, and to work it must infuse every routine encounter.

In an early scene Grey comes into the hardware store where Anastasia works and buys cable ties, masking tape, and rope. Anastasia renders polite customer service, but inside is intrigued, confused, and quivering. When he leaves, she narrates her feelings in this passage:

> *Okay, I like him.* There, I've admitted it to myself. I cannot hide from my feelings anymore. I've never felt like this before. I find him attractive, very attractive. But it's a lost cause, I know, and I sigh with bittersweet regret. It was just a coincidence, his coming here. But still, I can admire him from afar, surely. No harm can come of that.

While the prose may not be the most artful ever written, notice in this passage the push-pull of Anastasia's feelings. She submits to her attraction but immediately rejects it. She dismisses his visit to the hardware store as a fluke. (Really? Masking tape?) Her decision to admire him from afar is an amusing piece of foreshadowing. Most significantly, her response to Grey's hardware shopping is overly large, as if a godlike master has dropped into a humble hardware store from on high—which for Anastasia is true.

PLAY GOD WITH YOUR STORY:

- Your character is stymied, suffering, and stuck. She phones a crisis hotline. You answer. You're trained to convince callers to get help. What should your protagonist do? Make her do it … then make it fail.
- Your action hero races ahead at top speed. Throw up a roadblock. Force a one-hour delay. During that hour, ask your hero the following: Why are you racing? Why does it matter? You're racing but also running from—what? Write it down. Fold it in. There's time to deepen your character.
- Rain a punishment on your protagonist, and simultaneously test his inner conviction. What's the hardest possible test for him? Add it. What's being tested? Make that clear.

A MEASURE OF SUCCESS

If there are no pink slips for published authors, how do you know you've "failed"? The fact is that there is no failure per se; there are only disappointing sales, dropped options, unreturned calls, panic, and anger. A bruised self-image is painful.

Recovery starts with examining first how you define success. If it's by *selling a lot of copies*, then you're setting yourself up for failure, because you'll always lose to the heavy hitters like Harlan Coben. Indeed, I've found that focusing on selling a lot of copies is almost a guarantee that you won't.

Likewise, blaming the publishing industry for your disappointment will not heal or strengthen you. It's a mental trap. Book publishing is a big industry. It's dominated by a handful of big conglomerates that put out roughly six thousand new works of fiction every year. Things are bound to go wrong.

While the industry isn't without blame, the fact is that you can't change the business. You can only change your writing.

When you make it to that happy place called *published*, remember that as a writer you have the same strengths and weaknesses that you did before. Your strengths have grown strong enough to get you over the first hurdle; your weaknesses have lessened enough that they didn't stop you from jumping over the bar. But you still have growing to do.

If you encounter disappointments in your publishing career, don't despair. That happens to pretty much every author. The trick is not to simmer but to learn. Learn what? How to become a more powerful storyteller.

The good news is that when you do, industry flaws become less bothersome. In fact, you'll run into fewer of them and finally none at all. Your books will succeed—not because you've beat the odds but because you've become a great novelist.

56

BEST OF BOTH WORLDS

Cultivating Success as a Hybrid Author

Chuck Wendig

At our last house, the lawn died. One day it was green and lush. A week later a brown circle appeared in the grass. Another week went by, and the whole yard suffered a withering demise, as if we'd angered the lawn goddesses and grass gods, as if our garden gnomes and lawn mower hymns were not enough.

At our current home, the lawn isn't so much a *lawn* as it is a *mighty gathering of weeds*. Hardly a blade of grass in the bunch. It's hearty and hale. Drought doesn't bother it. Disease can't kill it. It's so green, you might call it "emerald." Mow it over, it looks like any other lawn.

A lesson in the power of polyculture over monoculture.

Monocultures don't exist on their own. We create them. And they don't work well. Plant one thing over a single field—corn, soy, whatever—and it becomes vulnerable to disease and pests. Diversify planting across a single field, however, and resistance to pests and diseases rises sharply.

Diversity means survival. That's true in agriculture. It's true in our stock portfolios. It's true on our dinner plates.

And it's true in publishing. Survival as a writer means embracing diversity from the beginning. And that means thinking of yourself as a "hybrid" author.

PUBLISHING OPTIONS: PROS AND CONS

A "hybrid" author sounds like one who was grown in a lab. Some mutant of Stephen King and E.L. James breaking free of its enclosure, terrorizing Manhattan with deviant prose.

Thankfully, it's a whole lot nicer than that.

A hybrid author is one who refuses to accept that there exists One True Way up the Publishing Mountain and who embraces *all* available methods of getting his or her work out there. The hybrid author takes a varied approach, utilizing the traditional system of publishing *and* acting as an *author-publisher* (a term I prefer to *self-publisher* because it signals the dual nature of the role you now inhabit).

Any form of publishing comes with benefits and disadvantages, and it's important to know these ahead of time.

For the traditional system of publishing, the pluses include the following:

- You receive money earned up front (an advance).
- You get professional quality control (editing, design).
- You have theoretical access to big marketing efforts.
- You have likelier access to ancillary rights (film, TV, foreign).
- You have a better chance of being reviewed in mainstream media
- You have a better chance of being distributed to bookstores.
- The money flows *to* you (you don't pay production costs).

And here are the minuses:

- It can be difficult to get projects that lack measurable commercial appeal through the gatekeepers (editors, agents).
- Publishing is glacially slow.
- Sometimes the marketing support never materializes and is left largely to the author.
- Physical space on bookstore shelves is dwindling.
- It's a risk-averse environment.
- The system does not adapt quickly to change.
- Contracts can occasionally be restrictive.

Being an author-publisher has its own panoply of ups and downs. Here are the pluses:

- You retain creative control.
- A greater percentage of money (about 50–70 percent) remains with you.
- You become part of a strong community full of resources.
- Some genres do gangbusters in this space (romance, military, science fiction).
- It's faster than traditional publishing.
- New options and distribution platforms are appearing all the time.
- You retain all rights.

- You can adapt faster to change.
- You can take greater calculated risks.
- You can potentially explore formats (digital shorts, etc.) and/or reach audiences deemed too niche by big publishing.

And the minuses:

- There's an investment up front (typically $500 to $5,000 to get the book "out there" in a professional fashion) and no guarantee of return on that investment.
- You have reduced access to ancillary rights (film, TV, foreign), mainstream book reviewers, and physical book retailers.
- Some genres are weak in this arena (literary, YA).
- Self-publishing is easy to do poorly.
- Authors often find that all their eggs are in the Amazon basket.

YOUR NEW MANTRA: "DO BOTH!"

You look over those lists of pluses and minuses and think, *Jeez, which one should I choose?* Forget that. Jump up, freeze-frame heel kick, and yell: "I want to do all the publishing!"

Because you can. That's what being a hybrid author is all about: It's about leveraging the advantages of each publishing form against the other. That diversity maximizes the benefits and mitigates the disadvantages.

Step 1: Write Something Great

The first step to being a hybrid author is to write something amazing. Put your heart on the page. Bleed into the story. Practice your craft. Exercise your awesomeness. Write the best book (or novella, or short story, or comic book, or *whatever*) you can.

A great story is your first step and is also the best first defense against any problems that pop up on *either side* of the publishing fence. Anything less and you're doing yourself—and your future readership—a grave disservice.

Step 2: Write Something Else That's Also Great

Being a hybrid author means making multiple works available across a variety of platforms … and that means you can't just write one thing and nest on it like a bird.

You're a writer. So you're going to have to write.

Write two things. Three things! *Write all the things.* Write one story, and then, as you work to edit it, write another. To be creative means to *create.*

Step 3: Share—One for Me, One for You

A lot of today's most celebrated hybrid authors began in one publishing arena, found success there, and moved into the other when it made sense. Hugh Howey began as an author-publisher before his bestseller status garnered offers from agents and big publishers. Lawrence Block had decades of experience (and success and acclaim) in the traditional space before deciding to see what he could do on his own. Both now utilize both options simultaneously.

Finding success in one arena is of course a viable pathway to success in another. Maybe you're too busy right now to run your own small business (and be assured, self-publishing is exactly that) and so you'd rather leave your work to the vagaries of the traditional system. Or maybe you don't feel like waiting two years for your book to be on shelves and so you want to grab the reins and ride the horse instead of sitting in the cart. You can pick the one style of publishing that seems to suit you up front, and go that way, diversifying once you're more established.

Or you can form a plan for attempting both. Reserve one of your works to be published yourself. Assign a second work to have a go at the traditional system.

How to choose the project best suited for each model? This requires a bit of educational guesswork mixed with polling your intestinal flora (a.k.a. "gut feelings"), and at the end it's important to note that neither path offers a guarantee at success. The trick is trying to suss out which of your works will gain the most success in each space. This isn't math, where you can plug in variables and calculate an answer with certainty, but you *can* look to strategies other authors have employed that make good sense.

A strong foot forward is to reserve your riskier work to publish yourself and to designate the more, well, *traditional* work for the traditional space. If this seems counterintuitive, remember that riskier works are much more difficult to get past the publishing gatekeepers. Publishers are more comfortable publishing known quantities. They like the kinds of books that they know will sell. (And frankly, if you have the means to reach a niche audience on your own—say, through your participation in specialized online communities—you might be better equipped to do so than a publisher would be, so why not retain more of the profits from your efforts?) Traditional publishers also like certain genres and formats, and manuscripts of certain lengths. A publisher might not be likely to accept these things from a first-time author, for instance:

- a novella (note also that new platforms available to self-publishers, such as digital shorts and e-singles, have no real counterparts in the traditional space)
- a short story collection
- a nonfiction work by an author without a big platform
- an epic fantasy of inordinate length (200,000+ words)
- a novel that is not easily labeled with a genre

So if you determine, "I think my chances of this particular story passing through the traditional gatekeepers—and then performing well—are low," then you'd likely be better served by self-publishing that work while sending another, less risky story out into the traditional channels.

For instance, you might note that YA fiction does not do particularly well in the digital self-publishing space because teens have been slow to embrace e-readers. Further, YA is really big right now in the traditional space, and the advances reflect that. So you might reserve an adult work to publish yourself while submitting the YA book to publishers.

KEYS TO YOUR SUCCESS

Sounds simple enough, right? But as with everything, to be truly successful, there are some caveats to be aware of.

Caveat 1: Hybrid Authors Benefit from Having Agent Representation

You want an agent. First, you'll need one to get your work in front of most major publishers in the traditional space. Second, an agent can also help you carry your self-published work into other spaces later on—you have a greater chance of selling alternate rights (including print!) for *all* of your works with an active agent.

Note also that some publishers have certain contract terms—particularly noncompete and right-of-first-refusal clauses—that can be unfriendly to hybrid authors. Thus, it's important for you, an agent, or a lawyer to negotiate those, along with any other restrictive language that grants them unnecessary rights to your work (particularly in digital).

The way to secure an agent is to pitch him a single project for which you are seeking traditional publication. But once you have an agent's interest, you need to discuss *up front* that you intend to be a hybrid author. That means seeking out agents who are not only comfortable with that, but savvy in that arena. An agent interested only in the traditional space and unaware of the options available to author-publishers will not be the best representative for you. And a bad agent can do more harm to your career than no agent at all.

Caveat 2: Hybrid Authors Need to Self-Publish Well

Self-publishing is easy to do, but difficult to do well. Still, you're going to need to do it well in order to give your book a chance to succeed. Fortunately, there are myriad resources at your disposal to help you. Use them. Here's a preview of what you'll learn: Self-publishing well means putting some money on the table. It means professional editing. It means a great cover artist. It means putting out a book (or e-book) that looks as good as—no, *better* than—what you'd find on the shelf at Barnes & Noble. A poorly done effort will harm your chances in the traditional space, which means: No hybrid author for you.

Self-publishing well also means developing an author platform that you can rely on to increase the visibility of your work. This often starts with a strong social media presence—not one devoted to marketing, but one devoted to you being the best version of yourself and engaging authentically with your potential audience.

For hybrid authors, it's *vital* that all of your social media outreach and other platform-related efforts lead to a central online space (a professional author website or blog) that showcases your other work. If your books are going to be coming from multiple sources, the one place interested readers can visit to learn about all of your offerings begins and ends with you.

DOWN THE ROAD

The hybridization of your writing career isn't just to get you going: This is a long game, not a short stint.

Should you be able to get a series of book releases in the traditional space, you could use the gaps between them to release other material yourself to strengthen the loyalty of that readership. Or, should you get a positive response to your self-published works, you could leverage that to gain more support from the publisher(s) for your traditional titles. The energy and marketing of your releases feed off of one another. Meanwhile, with hope you'll be banking small-but-steady (and ideally growing) income from a variety of sources.

Note that diversity as an author can also mean working with a variety of publishers, big and small. And experimentation (Kickstarter! Kindle Worlds! Serialized fiction!).

Of course, to do this, you need a healthy crop of stories. Which takes us back to step one: Write. Finish what you start. Make it great. Then do it all again.

Chuck Wendig is the *New York Times* best-selling author of *Star Wars: Aftermath*, as well as the Miriam Black thrillers, the Atlanta Burns books, and the Heartland YA series, alongside other works across comics, games, film, and more. A finalist for the John W. Campbell Award for Best New Writer and the co-writer of the Emmy-nominated digital narrative *Collapsus*, he is also known for his popular blog, terribleminds.com, and his books about writing. He lives in Pennsylvania with his family.

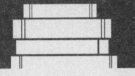

Part Five

INTERVIEWS WITH NOVELISTS

BEST-SELLING ADVICE
Readers

"The unread story is not a story; it is little black marks on wood pulp. The reader, reading it, makes it live: a live thing, a story."

—Ursula K. Le Guin

"All readers come to fiction as willing accomplices to your lies. Such is the basic goodwill contract made the moment we pick up a work of fiction."

—Steve Almond

"Write out of the reader's imagination as well as your own. Supply the significant details and let the reader's imagination do the rest. Make the reader a co-author of the story."

—Patrick F. McManus

"Always remember the reader. Always level with him and never talk down to him. You may think you're some kind of smart guy because you're the great writer. Well, if you're such a smart guy, how come the reader is paying you? Remember the reader's the boss. He's hired you to do a job. So do it."

—Jay Anson

"A cop told me, a long time ago, that there's no substitute for knowing what you're doing. Most of us scribblers do not. The ones that're any good are aware of this. The rest write silly stuff. The trouble is this: The readers know it.

—George V. Higgins

> ❝ You better make them care about what you think. It had better be quirky or perverse or thoughtful enough so that you hit some chord in them. Otherwise it doesn't work. I mean we've all read pieces where we thought, 'Oh, who gives a damn.'"
>
> —Nora Ephron

"I don't believe one reads to escape reality. A person reads to confirm a reality he knows is there, but which he has not experienced."

—Lawrence Durrell

"We all tell a story a different way. I've always felt that footsteps on the stairs when you're alone in the house, and then the handle of the door turning, can be scarier than the actual confrontation. So, as a result, I'm on the reading list from age thirteen to ninety."

—Mary Higgins Clark

"I don't care if a reader hates one of my stories, just as long as he finishes the book."

—Roald Dahl

"The critics can make fun of Barbara Cartland. I was quite amused by the critic who once called me 'an animated meringue.' But they can't get away from the fact that I know what women want—and that's to be flung across a man's saddle, or into the long grass by a loving husband."

—Barbara Cartland

"In truth, I never consider the audience for whom I'm writing. I just write what I want to write. ❞

—J.K. Rowling

66 If you can teach people something, you've won half the battle. They want to keep on reading."

—Dick Francis

"To gain your own voice, you have to forget about having it heard. Renounce that and you get your own voice automatically. Try to become a saint of your own province and your own consciousness, and you won't worry about being heard in *The New York Times*. **99**

—Allen Ginsberg

57

DAVID BALDACCI

....

Absolute Writer

_____

Jessica Strawser

While many authors struggle to find time to write, for David Baldacci it's more of a struggle to find time to do something *other* than write—and an unwelcome one at that, as there's clearly nothing he'd rather be doing.

Since splashing onto the scene with the 1996 Presidential thriller *Absolute Power* (swiftly snatched up by Hollywood for a feature film starring Clint Eastwood), he's written more than thirty novels for adults and five for young readers. Although he's known best for his books of action-packed suspense and his vibrant characters, such as secret agent Shaw, Army special agent John Puller, government assassin Will Robie, and Amos Decker, a man with total recall of his life who debuted in 2015's *Memory Man*, he's also penned a wide range of well-received stand-alones, among them the family drama *One Summer*, the Appalachian historical *Wish You Well* (the indie film adaptation, which Baldacci wrote and coproduced, was released in 2015) and the holiday tale *The Christmas Train*.

A former lawyer, Baldacci still attacks his writing career as if preparing for a high-stakes defense. His typical day currently involves several hours a day on one or more manuscripts, and *another* few hours on a screenplay. "During the course of the day I might work on three or four different projects, but only when I run out of gas on one do I move on to another," Baldacci says. "I write until my tank is empty each day. I don't count words or pages or whatever—that seems like an artificial goal for me."

Clearly it's a big tank, powering an energy-efficient engine with a lot of horsepower. And while he now has an office staff helping with the day-to-day admin that comes with such success (maintaining his website and responding to the hundreds of reader letters he gets every week), he still rolls up his shirtsleeves for causes he believes in, serving on the Mark Twain House & Museum board of trustees (where he is the benefactor of the $25,000 Mark Twain American Voice in Literature Award); cofounding, with his wife, Michelle, the Wish You Well Foundation to foster and promote family literacy; and advocating on behalf of authors during the much-publicized dispute in 2014 between Amazon and his publisher Hachette.

Baldacci broke away from his computer screen for an hour with *Writer's Digest*—unhurried, down to earth, insightful, and inspiring.

Memory Man is a huge hit—4.5 stars on Amazon with some six thousand reviews. Where did the idea for Decker come from? Is his videographic memory a real condition you researched, or is it of your own devising?

Hyperthymesia is a very real [but very rare] condition. Most people are born with it—the most famous example is the actress Marilu Henner, who starred in *Taxi*. It's very easy for her to memorize her lines! [Laughs.] I've been fascinated by the brain for a long time. The brain is our most critical part of what we are and also controls our personality. So to delve into that, I wanted to take it to the extreme and have this guy who had been a normal person and had suffered a debilitating injury and came out of it as someone else. I wanted to create a character who had some baggage that I could explore dramatically in the course of the novel, and also give him this unique attribute that would work very well for him as a police officer and a detective—but there are lots of things in his life that he'd prefer to forget, and for him time doesn't heal wounds. Putting him into a mystery that challenged his strengths and his baggage at the same time was an interesting challenge. Usually I write about characters who are in an agency, or a police office, or the federal government—hard charging, ambitious, fit. He was the exact opposite, and I just wanted to get out of my comfort zone and chase something that would make me stretch and do something different.

How do you keep an emotional distance when writing a character like Decker? A lot of stuff in this book—losing a child, a school shooting—falls into the "worst nightmare" category. Yet to write this I'd imagine you'd have to put yourself in Amos's shoes, and for a lot of the story, they're an awful place to be.

Absolutely. You want to try to keep a bit of a distance just because you're sane, but I had to sort of personally live that horror through Decker. You have the choice—you don't have to write about these types of subjects. But if you do, it's

David Baldacci

almost like being an actor playing a role—you just have to immerse yourself and go for it. I needed to feel what he was feeling and project my emotions through him onto the page, because it had to be a big thing to move Decker in the way that I needed him to move. It's uncomfortable, but if you take it on, you have to jump in with both feet.

Did you always intend for Decker to be a series character?

Yeah, I always intended him to come back. There's just a lot left to him. He was one of the few characters that I knew sitting down with the first book that he was going to be part of a series. Some of the others, like The Camel Club and even King and Maxwell, I wasn't really sure until I got to the end of the book that I was going to bring them back. But with Decker I was pretty certain.

When *The New York Times* asked you about the key to a great thriller, you said a "contortionist writer at the helm who manages to stay a step ahead of even the most astute/cynical story gobblers. You make it look easy and seamless, when actually it's the hardest thing you've ever done in your life and the whole thing seems held together by fraying duct tape and spit." What are your favorite contortionist techniques?

If you can take a little slice of the world and a little piece of dirt and really focus on details, you can drive large, seemingly spectacular movements. *Memory Man* was a great example. It was a very small stage that I created. It was this teeny town, and Decker lives in this Residence Inn, and most of the action takes place in a school. So the contortionist in *Memory Man* was, Okay, I've got this very intimate stage, and I've got a very few number of characters, and mostly you're going to see this big lumbering fat guy walking around, and a lot of it is this interior monologue of how he sees things in that school, walking those corridors. … It was like a Hitchcockian film set, and you're trying to figure out where the parts are. So for me it was very much in those little details that are really hard to assemble properly. You want to show everybody everything, but you don't want them to say, "Oh, I know where that's going," and then go on Amazon and say, "Predictable. One star!" [Laughs.]

While laying the groundwork and foreshadowing and trying to be fair, I try to do something else, almost like a magician—I'm showing you what you need to see, but with my other hand, I'm doing a trick and drawing your attention away. So while Amos Decker is lumbering through the school, piling up deductions and inductions and conclusions, other bits of action are flaring all over the place. People interrupt him; something else happens … not just to distract and deflect but to keep the action moving forward and keep the readers on their toes, going, *I thought I knew where this was going, but all of a sudden there's something else totally different, so I need to pay attention.*

You've said you do a lot of writing in your head without doing strict outlines in advance. How can writers with similar approaches fill their tool kits with the right "duct tape and spit" to pull these kinds of plots together?

You have to retain a sense of childlike wonder. You know, there's nothing wrong with outlines. I do many outlines as I'm working through the book, but I don't plot everything from *A* to *Z*. When I first started writing Decker, how could I outline the guy? I had no idea who he was. I had to get on the page and kind of feel around and talk to him and see what he could do.

There is sort of some type of structure even though you're flying by the seat of your pants with duct tape and spit. I always have an idea of where I'd like the story to go, where I think I might end up, though that could change. It depends on you exercising your full imagination. Daydreaming a lot. Sensing what possibilities are out there. Not being afraid to change your mind on something. And that's why I think sometimes these full-book outlines are counterintuitive and even destructive. Even if it doesn't feel right as you're writing it on the page, you feel like, *I spent four months writing this outline, I'm sticking to the damn thing.* But as a writer, it's like you're a fighter in the ring. You have to bob and weave and juke and move and change direction and tactics all the time based on what your instincts are telling you about what's happening on the page, and I can't emphasize greater how important that is. *That* is going to determine whether the story turns out well.

There's a perception that sometimes when writers get to a certain level they start kind of phoning it in. You're obviously not—the phrase "hardest working guy in showbiz" comes to mind. Why work quite so hard?

Certainly financially I don't have to do this anymore. I spent fifteen years of my life writing short stories, because I *love* short stories—and trust me, I'm sure you well know this, you're never going to make a living selling short stories. That's one reason I went to law school. I never thought writing was going to be my occupation—it was going to be my curious sort of hobby, and I wrote because I couldn't *not* write. To this day, people ask me, "Don't you ever take a break?" and

I'm like, "My whole life is a break!" [Laughs.] Because I get to do exactly what I want to do every day, and I actually get paid to do it. As a lawyer I spent enormous amounts of my life billing my time out in increments of thirty minutes—and I didn't dislike being a lawyer, I think it gave me a lot of good skills and discipline, but it wasn't how I wanted to spend my life—so I had a very big dose of, *Gee, I'm going to spend my life doing something I really don't love.* Now the fact that I am a storyteller and I've always been a storyteller and I did it for free for a long chunk of my life, and now I get to do it every day—it's amazing. I work hard because I just love what I'm doing. And once it's not a job, then it just doesn't seem like you're working anymore.

I know there are some writers who get to a certain level and then they start turning out a lot of books, and they have other people's names on them, too. People ask: "Would you ever write with someone else?" and my standard response, and it's true, is that I do not play well with others. [Laughs.] For me to have somebody come in and I give them an idea and they write the story—that takes all the fun out of it. *I* want to be the one seeing it through.

You've avoided being pigeonholed as a thriller author. Yet you wrote your first fantasy while hitting all your thriller deadlines and without even mentioning it to your agent until you were finished.

Here's how I approached *The Finisher*: My wife gave me this blank journal on Christmas Day in 2008—and I tell people, "Never give a writer blank paper on a major holiday, because you will never see them again for the rest of the day!" So off I went to my little cubby, and I started writing Vega Jane. That took five years: Four-and-a-half of sweat equity, trying to figure out what the story was, and then six months of just enormous spurts of writing.

But I didn't want people to publish it [just] because it was me. So I sent it out to lots of different publishers under a pseudonym, Janus Pope—Janus is the Roman two-faced god. And Scholastic was the publisher that seemed so excited about the book. I showed up at their headquarters to meet them—and I'd written years ago a book for them in the 39 Clues series—and they were like, "Oh, why are you here?" and I said, "Well, you just bought my book." And, "What book is that?" "*The Finisher.*" And they were like, "Holy shit! *What? Where's Janus Pope? We thought he was a Brit!" [Laughs.]

So that was really more of a challenge to yourself?

Absolutely. I had no interest in going to Hachette and saying, "I want to write a fantasy, and I'll have it to you soon, and you're going to publish it." I wanted

The Complete Handbook of Novel Writing

people who really knew fantasy to look at this book, think it was by an unknown person, and render their judgment. And if nobody had bought it, then it would have been five years of my life gone, but that's okay, because I've had lots of ups and downs in the writing business. You know, early on, where you get thousands of rejections and everybody's telling you [that] you should do something else because you're never going to be a writer—so I was kind of bulletproof on that stuff. But I wanted [to know], "Hey, is this good, or not good?"

How do you think you've grown as a writer?

I think I've gotten better at understanding the story. I always do a lot of research— I think in my earlier books I kept too much of it in. These days a month of research might end up being two sentences in the beginning, a paragraph in the middle, and a sentence at the end. I think I'm better at moving the narrative of the story forward at a good clip. I go back and reread some of my earlier stuff and go, *I could've said that entire page in a sentence and a half.* You get a lot more economical. My plots are sharper. Earlier on I had too much going on. My agent would lament [when] I'd turn in a book, "This is a fantastic book. You know, it could be *three* books ..." [Laughs.]

Do you ever have to scrap a project that's just not working, or have you moved beyond that now?

Earlier on, yes, I've had to scrap projects. These days, I really have crystallized it enough where it's gotten to the level of development in my head where I know it's a go. It's like when pilots are going down the runway, approaching takeoff speed, and then the co-pilot will tell the pilot, "V1!" V1 means you're going up, whether you want to or not. We're at the point of no return; you can't abort the takeoff anymore. So I've gotten better at waiting until I'm at V1 and I know I'm going up before I sit down and I start to spend enormous amounts of time on a particular project.

But even given that, it's that latitude where you might have written a lot of it, but if it's not working, you've just got to say, "You know what, it's not working. And I'm pissed! And I'm going to go have a drink. [Laughs.] But I'm going to come back, and I'm going to cut the hell out of this, because I have to." You can't take so much pride in ownership of something that you are unwilling to do what's right for the story. You just have to be brutal.

You spoke out during the Amazon/Hachette dispute and have expressed concern about trends in digital publishing damaging authors'

profits. What do you think newer authors should be most wary of in today's publishing climate? And what's your best advice?

The first thing is that no one on earth is going to care more about your career than you. Not your agent, not your publisher, not friends in the industry. At the end of the day, you need to take responsibility for your career. And I know it's hard when you've got your first book and you're so excited that you're like, "I'll let other people take care of the royalties and all that—I'm just so excited, there's my book on the shelf!" But at the end of the day, everything matters.

As a lawyer I never wanted to see people taken advantage of. You need to be your best advocate. You need to understand the financial side of the business, because if you don't, then you by default are going to be taken advantage of by people who do pay attention to those details.

I've always maintained that no publisher should make more money off of a book than the writer does. They publish thousands of books a year—but this is the only one (or two) I'm going to do. This also applies to the Amazons of the world. We the writers should be king of the hill because we provide the content. Kindles, Nooks, e-readers are great devices—*if* you have something to read on them.

So writers need to lead from a position of strength that we are a special commodity, and people need to be fair to us. But just because people *should* be fair to you does not mean that people will. We got a good dose of that, even veteran writers, with this thing with Hachette and Amazon. And the industry really can't survive too many more of those episodes, I don't think.

On the plus side, there are opportunities for self-publishing now in a way that gives you a platform that was never available before—but the caveat is, if it looks too good to be true, it often is. So put on your business hat and your writing hat. You have to have both these days.

You're on the board that helps protect Mark Twain's legacy. What do you hope your legacy will be?

I'll tell you this story. In the early nineties, before my first book sold, I had this hot script, kind of like *Die Hard* in the White House, and I had an agent in L.A., and it was going to make it around to the studios. Everybody was like, "This is going to be huge, Warner Bros. and Paramount are all over this, could be a bidding war, blah blah blah." I was up in New York—I was practicing law and our client was buying a bunch of banks, and I'd been sent up there to review leases. So I spent all day reading stuff that would make you want to slit your wrists after ten minutes. And I went back to my hotel that night, and because it was L.A. time versus East Coast time, around 11:00 I get a call from my agent. And he goes, "Well, Warner Bros. passed on it, and because they passed all the other studios thought there must be something wrong with it, so everybody passed. I'm sorry." I remember looking out the window and thinking, *Okay, I've been doing this for seventeen years—trying to get stuff sold and published—and I just spent three days of my life reviewing bank ground leases, and maybe this is going to be it. I'm going to have my little hobby, and I'll write for me only.*

But I went back to D.C., and I had an idea for a book. I remember thinking, *I'm going to be the only one who ever reads it, because obviously the breaks are just not going to happen for me.* But the drive, there it was. I spent the next three years writing *Absolute Power* because it was a story that I wanted to tell.

So I guess my legacy is, I'm a guy who's always had a story that he's wanted to tell. And that's all I ever think about. And trust me, never in my wildest dreams did I ever think that *Absolute Power* was going to take off. When I sent *Absolute Power* out to a bunch of agents, I had already started writing my second novel, because I figured, *I'm not going to hear back from these guys, I'll just write another novel and have some fun with it.* That's me—just a guy who's always chasing the next story.

Jessica Strawser is the editor of *Writer's Digest* magazine.

58

LEE CHILD

······································

The Rise of Reacher

─────────────

Zachary Petit

A man named Jim Grant had just been canned.

The Coventry, U.K., native had been working at the once-revered Granada Television channel in England for close to twenty years. But in 1995, he was let go. He was thirty-nine. "Corporate restructuring."

Fortunately, like a certain soon-to-debut protagonist, Jack Reacher, Grant is resourceful. Smart as hell. And he can roll with a punch.

He'd write a thriller.

"It was just a question of showbiz—entertainment was all I knew," he says. "It seemed like writing this kind of book was the way to go."

He gave it a shot.

And in the most unexpected ways, the foundation of his literary career began to take shape. At the supermarket, an old woman asked Grant to reach something on a high shelf for her. He obliged. His wife joked that if his novel-in-progress didn't pan out, he could take up a career as a *reacher*.

Jack Reacher was born.

Later, Grant was on a train with a Texan who was chatting with him about his French Renault 5, branded in the U.S. as Le Car—which the man pronounced "Lee Car." Grant and his wife playfully began appending a "lee" to everything—including their new daughter: *Lee Child*.

A best-selling penname was born.

And it didn't take long for Child's leap of faith to pay off. He signed with the first agent he queried *and* the first publisher they pitched it to, and *Killing Floor* debuted in 1997. The book introduced Child's master creation—ex-military police major Jack Reacher, a nomadic vigilante who travels the country with little more than a toothbrush, encountering trouble and doing what's right to squelch it (often with a head butt). *Killing Floor* won a bevy of awards and launched a best-selling series that to date has sold some 100 million copies in ninety-five countries. The second Hollywood adaptation of the series, *Jack Reacher: Never Go Back*, starring Tom Cruise, hit theaters in October 2016, and the twenty-first installment of the series, *Night School*, was released in November 2016.

Child's readers love him not only for his protagonist but for his signature style, in which he utilizes simple, almost Hemingway-esque sentences and deft pacing to craft taut narratives. Fellow writers agree—in 2009, he was appointed president of the Mystery Writers of America.

These days, Child maintains homes in New York, England, and France. In person, he exudes a quiet Zen. Despite residing partly in the United States, he remains quintessentially British—funny, wise, and dry, a slight smile often playing on his lips.

Here, he reveals why coming late to a writing career can be a great thing, why he's sticking with Reacher for the long haul, what film adaptations can (and can't) do, and much more.

You launched your fiction career after being fired from your long-time TV job. What do you think readers can learn from your story about the power of rebounding?

I think they can learn a lot. It's a terrible feeling. We're sort of trained or accustomed to thinking it's a disaster—and it is, you know, it's a major disruption. ... You've got to look on the positive side. I was about to turn forty, and that's halfway through your working life, basically: You've been to college, you're going to work till you're in your sixties, so you're exactly halfway through. That's not a bad time to start something else. It's not too late. You've built up twenty years of work habits, skills, all that kind of thing. You're not the jerk that you were when you were twenty-two. It's good in some ways, especially for writing. I honestly believe that writing is possibly the only thing that not only can you [do later], but you *should* do it later. I think writing fiction especially is something that is unnatural when you're young, because you haven't absorbed enough, you haven't seen enough, you haven't developed your own mental space or your thoughts and all that kind of thing.

Where did Reacher come from, and how did he translate from your mind to the page?

I'd learned in television that there's one intractable rule, really, which is that you cannot design a success. Success is always accidental, and the only way to really make a second-rate product is to sit down and think about what you're going to do. You think, *I've got to do this; you've got to do that; this is popular; that's popular; women like this; men like that.* If you start thinking about that and start putting it into a laundry list of things you've got to cover, then it will be a terrible product.

So I just thought, *All right, do it with your eyes closed, metaphorically, just close your eyes and [write] and see what happens.* And Reacher is what happened. And I didn't really care to think about it because I thought the more I investigated it, the more danger there was of overanalyzing it. Clearly he came from the previous reading I'd done. Reacher is a fairly standard mythic character that has been around in various iterations for many, many centuries.

Do you think that's what makes him resonate so much?
Absolutely. There's no question about that. Here's the mysterious stranger, the knight errant, the noble loner that has been invented or exploited or loved over and over and over again. I suppose if you really analyzed it academically, you'd probably figure [he pops up in] fifty-year intervals, stretching back to Homer, probably, and the ancient Greeks. ... So here's something that's being constantly desired by the audience.

Do you ever foresee stepping outside of the Reacher universe?
I doubt it very much. You know, whereas, yes, absolutely this is a creative business, and the art and the craft and so on are absolutely paramount, it's [still] a *business.* And you've got to be at least a little bit sane about your relationship with the marketplace. It's evident that people like Lee Child the author and Jack Reacher the character. But I think it would be very misguided and arrogant to say, "People like Lee Child the writer, so they'll like whatever I give them." That's an unproven assumption, and there's no reason to believe that. What they want is Reacher.

It's obvious that you still have a genuine interest in the character. The books don't seem stale.
Yeah, because he's a very timeless character, and he's a very capacious character inasmuch as I leave him undescribed a lot of the time, I leave him unexplained, and so he can do pretty much what he wants. Also, [every book is set] in a different place. That was one strategic decision I took at the beginning, which was

that it would not be employment based, and it would not be location based, because at the time everything else was. *Everything.* ...

We talk a lot about good writing advice. What's the worst writing advice you commonly hear?

The worst is probably *Write what you know.* Especially in this market. In the thriller genre, for instance, nobody knows anything that's worth putting in. There are three people in the world who have actually lived this stuff. And so it's not about what you know. [Write] what you *feel* is really excellent advice. Because if you substitute *Write what you feel,* then you can expand that into—if you're a parent, for instance, especially if you're a mother, I bet you've had an episode where for five seconds you lost your kid at the mall. You turn around, your kid is suddenly not there, and for five seconds your heart is in your mouth and you turn the other way, and there he is. So you've gotta remember the *feel* of those five seconds—that utter panic and disorientation. And then you blow that up: It's not five seconds, it's five days—your kid has been kidnapped, your kid is being held by a monster. You use what you feel and expand it, right up as far as you can, and that way you get a sort of authenticity.

You've said that a book is like a snapshot of who the writer was when they wrote it. I love that.

I think it is. And now that I know the process better and I know people—you know, a lot of writers are now my friends—I read their books partly to read a great new book, but it's also kind of like getting a letter from a friend. This is basically telling you about what was on their mind last year, and you can really decode that. It's good fun.

What vices do you need to write?

I think you've got to be very nosy. And that sort of gives you an excuse. I love eavesdropping, I love people watching. It's terrible—if someone invites you to their house, you say, "Excuse me, I'm just going to go to the bathroom," but actually you're not, you're poking around in the mail on the kitchen counter, you're checking the computer. I think you've got to be intensely interested in people and things.

Vices—I mean, writers are portrayed always as drunkards. I don't drink at all, hardly at all. I'm not a teetotaler or anything, but I'm not much more than a social drinker. I don't think you necessarily need vices.

I have to ask the question I'm sure you're sick of—the one about fans objecting to the casting of Tom Cruise as Reacher.

Point One is: I'm just unbelievably grateful that anybody has an opinion. If people are reacting one way or the other, I'm thrilled with it, because it means the thing has worked. The series is out there, and people own it, people love it, and they are sufficiently motivated one way or the other—in this case, mostly the other—to vocalize what they feel about it. And that's a total thrill. If you say to any new writer, "Imagine fifteen years from now there will be Facebook pages complaining about what somebody is doing to your character"—you know, God, yeah, you'd give your right arm for that. So I'm totally thrilled about that.

Then Point Two would be, I am—I think all of us, always, we're in a bubble here, the writer/reader bubble. It's a very intense bubble. And one of the things I notice when I venture outside of it—suppose I'm on a plane somewhere and you've got a chatty person next to you. They say, "What do you do?" And you say, "I'm a writer." Inevitably, without fail, if it's a normal member of the public, the next question will be, "Oh, have any of your books been made into a movie?" … For them, a book is a weigh station to becoming a movie. The book is a half-finished product, and the endgame is to have it made into a movie. That's the public perception.

Therefore, Point Three: I'm kind of surprised at the book people. Here's how I view it, as a metaphor: Here's me the writer, here's you the reader, and the book is the thing. The book is the entire subject for the conversation. I'm writing it, you're reading it, we're talking about the book. And then, as your career goes along, there begin to be sort of foothills, the valley gets filled up with other stuff, like fame and websites and this and that. I've met two babies who are called Jack Reacher. You know: first name Jack, middle name Reacher, surname. They come to signings—the father brings the birth certificate to prove it. So the book is still there, the absolute pinnacle, but the valleys are now getting filled up with these little bits of extraneous matter. And to me the movie is another of those extraneous things in the valley. I'm glad it's happened, just like I'm glad people have named their kids Jack Reacher. But it's not the book.

Is there anything we haven't yet touched on that you think is important in a discussion of writing overall?

Writing overall is in such a state of flux at the moment, with all this conversation going on about digital versus physical, legacy [publishing] versus self-[publishing] and all that kind of stuff, but ultimately those are such trivial details. All that matters is coming up with a great original story. And yeah, then you do have a sort of procedural problem with how to publicize it. It's only a different medium. It's no bigger deal than when paperbacks were introduced. The problem is that if this revolution removes traditional publishers—I mean, what are traditional publishers? People try and analyze what is their core function, and they say, "Well, they've got a lock on print distribution." That's not a publisher's core function. That's like saying a baseball team's core function is to charter an airplane. That's just a necessary evil. A publisher is basically a publicizer.

Now, if the ability to push great stories towards the marketplace is lost, then we really do have a level playing field. And people say *level playing field* as if it's a good thing. A level playing field is a terrible thing. Because nobody will get heard. It's most unfair that only a few people get heard now, but the alternative is nobody will get heard. ... To say that a future without major publishers is bad is not an arrogant thing, it's actually a humble thing, because we are very aware of how dependent we are on somebody else's expertise.

Where else would you like to take your writing before all is said and done?

My ambition is to stay on this path but get out just before the peak. I think if you say, "I wanna quit at the top," then what you're doing is you're predicting that you will be able to tell when you're at the top. And my experience is most people are late with that judgment. They think they're at the top now—well, sorry mate, you were actually at the top two years ago. So I think my ambition is to keep it going until I feel like I would be letting myself down. I'd like to go out with one final book that leaves everybody desperate for more rather than keep it going until the point where they're like, *Oh God, that guy ... that guy jumped the shark years ago.*

Zachary Petit is the content director of *HOW* and *Print* brands, editor-in-chief of the National Magazine Award–winning publication *Print*, a freelance journalist, and a lifelong literary and design nerd. Alongside the thousands of articles he has penned as a staff writer and editor, his words regularly appear in *National Geographic Kids* and have also popped up in the pages of *National Geographic*, *mental_floss*, Melissa Rossi's What Every American Should Know book series, *McSweeney's Internet Tendency*, and many other outlets. He is also the author of *The Essential Guide to Freelance Writing: How to Write, Work, and Thrive On Your Own Terms*, and co-author of *A Year of Writing Prompts*.

59

PATRICIA CORNWELL

A Life of Crime

Jessica Strawser

To say that Patricia Cornwell is a force to be reckoned with—whether at a crime scene, in a forensics lab, at her keyboard, or on your bookshelf—is a grotesque understatement. Not only is the novelist touted as the world's number one best-selling crime writer, she's become a forensics consultant in her own right through the course of researching what she calls her "nonfiction fiction" series featuring medical examiner Dr. Kay Scarpetta. A founding member of the National Forensic Academy and founder of the Virginia Institute of Forensic Science and Medicine, in addition to influential roles at other respected institutions, Cornwell is arguably as well known today for her books—a staple of bestseller lists (and airport kiosks) everywhere since her series began with 1990's *Postmortem*—as she is for her advocacy of psychiatric research, criminal justice, literacy, and animal rights. She's also been credited with whetting the American public's seemingly insatiable appetite for the forensic genre, the popularity of her series spurring shows like *CSI* and *Cold Case Files*.

Some attribute her success to a determination that took root during her childhood years in foster care. Others say her steadfast persona is a reflection of her start as a journalist, her hands-on approach to research, and her adult life lived in the public eye—she's drawn notice from the start, with her debut book, a biography of longtime family friend (and wife of the prominent preacher) Ruth Bell Graham; her self-financed investigation into the identity of Jack the Ripper, culminating in the controversial book *Portrait of a Killer: Jack the Ripper—Case Closed*; her relationship with FBI agent Margo Bennett, whose husband was convicted of his wife's attempted murder after allegedly discovering her affair with Cornwell; her marriage first to Charles Cornwell, a professor seventeen years her senior, and presently to Harvard psychiatry instructor Staci Ann Gruber; and her successful defamation suit against a writer who accused her of plagiarism and waged an Internet war against her character.

One thing is certain: Cornwell isn't going anywhere anytime soon. And neither is Scarpetta. A film is in development at Fox, with Angelina Jolie attached to the project, and Cornwell's twenty-fourth book in the series, *Chaos*, was released in November 2016.

It's not easy to picture the crimes you write about, or to imagine people capable of committing them. How much can you afford to immerse yourself in your stories? Is there a way to maintain a distance as you work?

Yes, and I think that is a judgment call that's different for every individual. You know the saying: *If you're going to dine with the devil, use a long spoon.* We all have to know what our boundaries are, and certainly my boundaries are much broader than a lot of people's, because this world I write about is something I've found extremely interesting, going back to the earliest days of my development as a writer, when I was a journalist [on] the police beat. I always wanted to know: *What happens to the body when it disappears from the crime scene? Where's it going? What are they doing with it?* This was in the late seventies, and nobody talked about that sort of thing back then. But I was fascinated by the body and what you could tell from it.

And I think the reason I'm comfortable with what people would call "gruesome" is I look at it as an excavation. When I was a kid, one of my dreams was to be an archaeologist, and if you think about it, working a crime scene is a reconstruction of a past life, and a death, and trying to figure out everything you possibly can from the artifacts that are left behind, whether they're injuries, or the way they're dressed, or a fleck of paint, or a fiber—all of these have a story to tell. *That* is what I find so intriguing, and that tends to overwhelm the gross factor. Because, yes, crime scenes and the morgue are offensive to all of your sensibilities. But for me, the idea of figuring out what happened is far more compelling than my repulsion by the unfortunate aspects of it.

So I know my boundaries. For example, if a pathologist said, "Have you ever done a Y incision on a dead body? Would you like to try?" I'd say, "Absolutely not." There are things I won't do, because to me it's over the line. Maybe the farthest I would go is to, if I were studying a bite mark done postmortem, for example, bite on a piece of raw chicken and then brush my teeth really well. I [once] went to a tattoo parlor, had a turkey roaster tattooed, and then did forensic tests on it for *Black Notice*. So I do things, but I have limits.

One thing I've always been careful of is I don't want to spend a lot of time with the people who commit these types of crimes. I've interviewed people on death row and been to prisons, but a little of that goes a long way. Direct exposure to what I call "monsters" disturbs me. It doesn't feel safe when I *write* about them. I wrote in the third-person point of view for a while, and when you do that, you have to take on the perspective of the killer—and I found it was really uncomfortable, so I don't do that anymore.

You've said you don't know what's going on with your characters' personal lives until you start to write. How much do you know about your central, crime-based plot before you begin? Do you have an outline?

No, I'm a very organic writer. I started out doing poetry when I was young, and I think I have a little bit of a poetic approach to writing a book, where I start with an image. For example, in *Red Mist*, I knew Scarpetta was going to have to go to Savannah, but I had no idea what was going to happen. And then I just continued to have this image of her driving this old white van through the swamps on this hot summer day. I thought, *You don't drive something like that. I must have mixed images in my head.* But she wouldn't get out of it. I kept seeing it, and I thought, *You know what, just go with it. But I sure as hell don't know what she's doing in this piece of crap—it's not even a rental car!* And that becomes a very important part of the story: what she was doing in that, and who it belongs to, and what's in store for her—she's been lured into sort of a trap. So I basically started spinning this whole story based on this image.

Sometimes it goes really smoothly, and sometimes I get stuck. But I can't imagine outlining a book and then just sitting down and writing it. I think it would lose its emotional being—the effervescence, the sparkle. It would get flat, I'm afraid, if I tried to do it that way. But I know that works for some people. Everybody has to do what works for them.

How much do your writing and researching processes overlap, then? Your plots hinge on those factual details.

They're inextricably connected: [Research] is where I get my ideas, and I continue to do research as I'm writing a book, and it all evolves together. I get an idea, and then when I look into it, that gives me other ideas. Sometimes one single thing somebody shows me on a research trip becomes the genesis of the entire story. ...

One of the things that inspired *The Bone Bed* is that I was invited to go on a dinosaur dig, and I went. So what I would say to writers is: *Go out and do something.* Don't just read other people's books. Go have adventures! When you read Hemingway, you know he's had that beer, he's eaten that food, he shot that elephant. Now, I'm not recommending people go around shooting elephants, but go out and do something. Get real-life experiences you can describe.

What's your daily writing routine?

I try to start first thing in the morning, when my mind is clear, and work as long as I can. In the early stages of a book, that might only be four or five hours. Then there might be times I'm working eight to ten hours a day. I get the most done by secluding myself. My partner is very understanding about my running away from home, because I sometimes just have to go. I set up an office in a hotel—on the water, that's my favorite—and I isolate. Then I'm just living with what I'm doing, and even when I'm not writing it, I'm thinking about it, and I can get an incredible amount of work done in two or three weeks. So I tend to write in spurts.

One thing I'd advise is: Treat your writing like a relationship and not a job. Because if it's a relationship, even if you only have one hour in a day, you might just sit down and open up your last chapter because it's like visiting your friend. What do you do when you miss somebody? You pick up the phone. You keep that connection established. If you do that with your writing, then you tend to stay in that moment, and you don't forget what you're doing. Usually the last thing I do before I go to bed is sit at my computer and just take a look at the last thing I was writing. It's almost like I tuck my characters in at night. I may not do much, but I'm reminding myself: *This is the world I'm living in right now, and I'll go to sleep and I'll see you in the morning.*

A lot of writers feel locked into a style after they've established a series, but you've changed things like tense and POV. How have you found that freedom?

You have to be willing to take risks, especially if you're going to be out here for a long time. If you get bored or frustrated, then your readers are going to be bored and frustrated. I'm not saying change is always good, but it may be necessary. When I finished *The Last Precinct*, in 1999, I said, "I'm banging on the walls of [Scarpetta's] skull. This is so confining, writing from her point of view. I don't think I can do this anymore." So I made a decision to try writing the next [book] from the third person. And I needed to do that, to become a better writer and to sort of broaden my stage. But after a while, I realized I like it better writing from her point of view, so I've gone back to it. And technology has changed so much in the last decade that now you can write from somebody's point of view and still take them lots of other places and have them see different things because of surveillance cameras, the Internet, and all that. ...

You're going to have one side love that you did something different, and then another side that doesn't like what you do. [But] you have to adapt to the world that you're in. If you want to stay viable, you have to.

You have experts review your manuscripts before they're published. Why is it so important to you that the facts in your stories be meticulously accurate? Are you ever tempted to take creative license?
I do take creative license sometimes—I invent things that aren't out there yet but I know will be—but there's no reason to make gratuitous mistakes. If you get a forensic instrument wrong because you're too lazy to check it out—*that* I won't do, and I think that goes back to my starting out as a journalist. I have rubbed shoulders so much with people in those professions, that out of respect for them I try to get it right.

I write a sort of nonfiction fiction. I weave stories out of factual material, and that is grounding to me—it's the tether that holds my balloon in place so I don't go drifting off into chaos. That doesn't mean everybody has to do that. But I do think that if you're trying to capture a certain world, such as law or medicine or forensics or a historical novel, there's no reason not to try to get the facts correct, to do that research. And I think if people go to the trouble to do it, it'll become more vivid to them, and they'll write better stories as a result.

You've been credited for starting the rash of forensic-based books, TV shows, movies, you name it. Do you see yourself as having spurred your own genre?
Yeah, Scarpetta really opened the door to what I call the forensic genre—and it's not that I was smart enough to think of that, it's just that I inadvertently threw myself into the research, because this world fascinates me. And obviously people in the entertainment business realized there was enormous potential there.

That became the tail chasing the dog in my case. I had to adapt what I do, because of what people see every day. I'm not going to spend ten pages describing what a scanning electron microscope is, because people see them on television now. I don't need to tell you twenty pages of what the morgue looks like when you're watching reality shows that take place in a morgue. So I've had to adapt *how* I tell my stories, but also I have to always keep one lap ahead of the competition. Whatever they come out with on some show, I'm going to make sure I do research and know something they don't know, and [put] it in my next book. And then *that* gets recycled in some TV show, and then I do the next book and show you something else new, and it all ends up on television anyway—which is the way it works. I mean, I don't own forensics. But it created a situation I never would've imagined. I'm like someone who's running faster all the time and trying not to look back. *Run, run, run, they're gaining on you!*

This is one of the reasons, too, that I switched back to Scarpetta's point of view: The *one thing* I do better than anybody, and nobody has ever repeated, is this one character. I don't care who else is out there; there's not another Scarpetta. She is my gold—all of my characters are. So I have become much more character driven, and much more about what's going on in their lives. Of course they're going to be extremely technically sophisticated, and I'll never cheat anybody on that, but the main characters aren't forensics and science and medicine anymore.

Some novelists are constantly reminding people their work is fiction, but you're often consulted as a forensics expert. When did you become okay with that distinction being blurred? And do you think it's an advantage for fiction writers to become experts on their subjects?

I do think it is. I'm a strange mix. I started out as a poet and an artist, but I also have this other side where I absorb this information. If I'm at a crime scene or an autopsy, I completely understand what these professionals are talking about, and I feel like I'm one of them, while at the same time I know who they really are as opposed to me. I always give them the respect they deserve—I don't ever mess with the real thing, and I never am presumptuous—but over the years, these are sort of my colleagues. When I go riding with the detectives, we're sort of working the case together. I never cross boundaries in a way that's inappropriate, but it's just become natural for me to live what I do—again, knowing the limits.

And the truth is, that's what's fun. It makes it fun for me. The biggest enemy when you have a series is that you get bored with it. …

One thing I'd remind writers is: Writing is hard work. It isn't just sitting around fantasizing, or having a drink with somebody and talking about how cool it would be if you wrote a story. It's work. And if you don't make it work, and you don't devote yourself to it, you're not going to write anything very good. I think writers who consistently produce, they're going to tell you they don't always feel like doing it. It's the hardest thing, to sit down at that blank screen.

And research isn't easy. But if you're going to have a character who's a musician, you should learn everything about that you possibly can. When I decided Lucy was going to be a pilot, I started taking lessons—how could I describe what that feels like unless I've sat in that seat? That's important: I want you to see it, smell it, taste it. I want you to go through the looking glass of the words on the page and be in the world I'm describing. And the audience can do it painlessly. But those of us who create that have to work very hard for it.

You once said, "I am just as insecure for my new book as I was for my first one." Is that still true today?

Absolutely. I always think, *I'm not sure I can do this—what if it's not any good? Oh my God, what a terrible paragraph—erase it before somebody sees it!* [Laughs.] I don't think I'll ever get over that. A part of me knows I can pull it out somehow, but it's daunting. It gets easier and harder at the same time. I know the characters better, but that's also a drawback, because you want to do something new with them.

I think a little insecurity is a good thing. I'll be honest: When somebody has written their first novel and they tell me how fantastic it is, I know it's probably not very good. It's usually the person who says, "I don't know, I'm not sure what I think, but I'm afraid to do much else to it because I don't want to ruin it," and then you look at the thing and go, "Now *that* is really special." So it's not bad to be a little insecure. It makes you work harder and pay attention.

It's like when people tell me, "It must be so relaxing to fly a helicopter," and I say, "If your pilot says that, do not get in!" That should *not* be relaxing—you should be hypervigilant and alert. Why? Because you're *a little bit insecure*. Because you're in this very powerful machine that's off the ground.

When you sit in that chair, that should be your cockpit. You should be hyper-, hypervigilant, and alert, and a little bit nervous about what you're doing, and you'll do a good job.

You've been referred to as "a woman who writes like a man." How can writers sidestep labels like those?

If you worry about labels, about what a publisher's going to think, you're worrying about the wrong things. You should be telling your truth and pulling it out of your soul. You should go see something and interpret it in a way nobody ever has. … You should be worried that you can't describe a full moon in a way that somebody hasn't one hundred times before you. The poetry of what you do, the imagination of it, and the startling enlightenment of what you might present to an audience, *that* should be what you're worried about.

You had three books rejected before *Postmortem*, which was also rejected before finding a publisher. What can you say to struggling writers today?

Quitting can't be an option. You don't become a writer—you are one. And if you really are a writer, it's like telling a songbird to shut up—you can't.

You have to be willing to be bad at something to be good at it. You will never be good at writing the first time you try, any more than Nadal hit a tennis ball the way he does now the first time he picked up a racket. You're going to trip over your own feet, you're going to have awkward sentences and terrible dialogue, and the only way you get better is to just do it all the time. And if this is the inevitability of how you express yourself, you're still going to get up after failures. Some people are lucky, and their first book gets published and is well received. For me it took a lot of warm-ups, and those books should have been rejected. They were a learning process; I would never try to publish them today. And *Postmortem* did *not* deserve to be rejected by practically every major publishing house before it was accepted, but it was because it was so different [that] people didn't know what to do with it. I think something that's unique is going to get passed over a lot of times—and then it gets published by some little off-beat press and takes the world by storm. ...

I worked in the morgue for six years, because I had so many failures. And Scarpetta knew I needed to do that to be qualified to write about her. She says, "I hate to do this to you, but you don't have a clue, girl. You need to be down here every day going to the labs, going to the morgue, going to crime scenes, riding with the detectives, going to court. And then, *maybe*, you can begin to have a concept of what it's like to be me, and *then* I'll let you tell my story." And she *still* does that to me.

60

KATHRYN CRAFT

....

How Structure Supports Meaning

─────────────────

Janice Gable Bashman

In *The Far End of Happy*, Kathryn Craft novelizes her first husband's suicide standoff with the police by confining the story to its true twelve-hour time frame. Adding a ticking clock is a well-known way to inject edge-of-the-seat tension into thrillers and suspense novels, but Kathryn co-opted the technique for her women's fiction. The novel's one-hour blocks add a sense of weight to each unfolding moment of that fateful day. While Kathryn expands the frame of the story with pertinent events that brought the characters to this moment in time, and while she suggests the ramifications for their futures should they not be able to face their issues, the reader senses the dividing line: Because of this day, where one man's life hangs in the balance, these characters' lives will never be the same. She further divides each hour between three points of view that show the impact of the standoff on the wife, the wife's mother, and the despondent man's mother, as each woman sifts through her memory for clues as to "how the heck she got there this day."

Kathryn's interest in weaving backstory threads into the ongoing narrative reveals her fascination with why people do the things they do, placing her firmly in the psychological subgenre of women's fiction. She had already experimented with such techniques in her first novel, *The Art of Falling*.

In addition to her two novels from Sourcebooks, Kathryn is a contributor to the book *Author in Progress,* a no-holds-barred look at what it takes to get published, authored by the blogging team at the online writing community Writer Unboxed (www.writerunboxed.com). Her decade of work as a freelance developmental editor at writing-partner.com follows a nineteen-year career as a dance critic. A longtime leader in the southeastern Pennsylvania writing scene, she has served on boards for the Greater Lehigh Valley Writers Group, their annual Write Stuff conference, the Philadelphia Writers' Conference, and in several volunteer capacities for the Women's Fiction Writers Association. She hosts lakeside writing retreats for women in northern New York State, leads writing workshops, and is a member of the Tall Poppy Writers.

Here, Craft shares her insights on structuring a novel, using backstory to fuel readers' engagement, and developing rich character arcs within a short time line.

The word *structure* can mean different things when referring to novel writing. How do you define it?

I see it two different ways. The most crucial decisions an author makes are in terms of storytelling structure, which really isn't about "telling" at all. It's about how you will raise questions in the reader's mind about whether your character can achieve her story goal. Storytelling structure fuels the novel with backstory motivation that creates a deep desire for the protagonist, suggests the stakes should the character not succeed, and creates a yardstick by which to assess the protagonist's progress ("Yes, this is just what he needed," or "Oh no, things aren't looking so good for him just now!"). With the right kind of overarching span and page-by-page tension, the desire to answer the story question will pull the reader all the way to the end of a book.

While wrestling down the myriad decisions of storytelling structure, though, we writers sometimes forget to tend to the way the larger structures of a book—what I call "macrostructures," ([or] how it's divided into chapters and sections and perspectives)—can contribute meaning. One of my favorite examples is the novel *The Secret Life of Bees,* in which Sue Monk Kidd begins each chapter with a nonfiction epigraph about bees. As the novel progresses, the astute reader can't help but seek parallels in human and insect behavior.

How did the craft of communicating through structure first occur to you?

As with many discoveries, it happened by mistake. In early drafts, *The Art of Falling* opened with Penelope Sparrow's moment-by-moment actions as she parted from a high-rise balcony and landed on a bakery truck fourteen stories below. The chapter's tension and drama earned the chapter an award in a statewide contest, but it couldn't fool my advance readers, who could not engage with Penelope. I finally figured out why: The question raised by this opening is "Oh my gosh, will she survive?" Well, guess what happens when the reader turns the page and sees Penelope waking in a hospital room? When the story question is answered, the story is over. I needed a structure that would raise book-length questions, not answer them.

So was that complicated to set up?

In a word, yes. I needed to create an inciting incident—that incident that changes everything in my protagonist's life and incites her to set a story goal—that would raise questions about both the ongoing and backstory threads. I found my solution in creating a slight disconnect in perception among my characters as to what that incident really was. My secondary cast—new friends outside the dance world, the local dance critic, and Penelope's doctors—helped me raise the first question, since they all perceive the inciting incident as being the fall. They ask Penelope outright: What happened out on that ledge? By this point the reader wants to know as well.

Penelope's ongoing inner conflict causes her to see things differently. While her body brings her life joy and meaning, she blames its imperfections for the loss of her dream career. Now the strength and resiliency of that same body has caused her to survive what should have been a deadly fall. The aforementioned disconnect is revealed: For Penelope, the inciting incident is not the fall. If she had died, her soul would have been released from the burden of her imperfect body and free to dance with the gods. No, for Penelope, the inciting incident was surviving the fall.

The two story questions are now opened: (1) What put Penelope on the penthouse balcony, at the height of what [appeared to be] her dream career, and (2) How can she remobilize her life in a more meaningful way now that she's hit ground zero? Those questions drive both the backstory and present storylines, which intertwine until we get the missing piece at the end. The piece Penelope's traumatized brain has been unwilling to face, and the piece I had mistakenly, at first, opened with—what happened between the balcony and the ground. By making a personal mystery of it, and waiting until Penelope had learned some important lessons before showing what happened, I was able to sustain reader interest all the way until the end.

You use similar backstory interweaving in your second novel as well. Did you employ the same process?

In a way, but in *The Far End of Happy* there is no misperception about the inciting incident, which is painfully clear. In the opening my protagonist is sitting on the guest room bed, writing in her journal. Here, she presses her pen "to a cool, fresh page" and writes:

Today Jeff is moving out.

She would not have predicted this day in her marriage. Its impact was impossible to fathom. How could she write beyond such words? Ronnie shut her journal. Only one sentence, but it was a good one. Full of hope but also one of the saddest she's ever written. She'd have to sort her feelings tomorrow. Today was a day for moving forward. She capped the pen and placed the notebook on the growing pile of journals beneath the bed.

When instead of moving out Jeff shows up drunk and armed, and holes up in a building on the property, the story question is set: Will Ronnie be able to move forward if her husband is determined to stand off?

Again, I used secondary characters to open the backstory thread. Since the police are coming to the situation cold and seeking context, they ask, What happened? How was your husband this morning? Has he exhibited signs of depression recently? Each of the questions leads the reader back in time, until she too wants to know how a life that once held such promise has come to this.

Other writers might have examined the protagonist's life both before and after the suicide standoff, or started the story earlier in the marriage and ended on the day of the standoff. Why did you choose to start and end the novel on the day of the standoff and keep it confined to its one-hour blocks?

Since the novel is based on true events, I originally drafted this story as a memoir that explored how such a happy marriage had devolved, over fifteen years, into my need to divorce and my husband's threats of suicide. Frankly, I needed that story. But the knowledge of what was to come colored everything. As I sorted through my journals in search of the most relevant scenes from my marriage, my thoughts kept snapping back to the suicide: Had my husband been in a bad mood that day, or was this a clue? Had this been manipulation, or love? I realized the daylong standoff was the perfect metaphor for exploring one partner's deep need to keep things the same even as the other must honor her deep need for change. What better way to highlight how these twelve hours changed this family's life forever than to devote the whole novel to it? This was easier done in fiction than in memoir, since I'd have to compress the time line of actual events to complete my protagonist's arc in just twelve hours. But the high stakes, tough choices, and nagging shameful secrets would now be palpable in every single minute.

You further divide the one-hour blocks into chapters, each limited to one of three points of view. What difficulties did you face when

structuring the novel like this, and how did you manage to make it all come together in one cohesive story that keeps the pages turning?

The multiple points of view were key to my decision to novelize. A memoir would throw the spotlight on what happened to *me* and what I learned. I wanted to suggest the widespread impact of suicide. I gained this meaning through the perspectives of the mother who has to watch her daughter pay such a high price for love and the mother who must face that she cannot save her son.

As to how it all came together, well, ahem, that took several rounds of trial and error. At one point I had chapters sitting all over my floor with character codes and key words scrawled at the top, arranged in twelve fanned stacks like a giant game of solitaire, so I could see how best to balance perspectives and backstory within each one-hour block.

How did you manipulate the novel's structure so that the backstory threads, which are told in three points of view, wouldn't pull the reader out of the story tension and make her want to set your novel down?

The secret here is to raise a question about the backstory for which the reader desires an answer. For me this often comes in the form of a little question bomb at the end of a chapter—a reveal about the past that makes the reader sit up and say, "Wait, *what*?" Then I'd break away for another bit of forward-moving story, ending only when a new question was raised. The reader doesn't want to stop reading then, either, but she still wants to know the answer to that backstory question, so she'll gladly delay moving on to circle back for more complete knowledge.

I used those same techniques in *The Art of Falling,* but in that book, it helped that there was a troubled romance in the backstory thread. Readers rarely mind cutting away for romance.

Giving three point-of-view characters a growth arc over a twelve-hour period sounds challenging. How did you create believable growth arcs for these women?

One way I met this challenge was to firmly root each character's desire in the backstory and then allow the inciting incident—the start of the standoff—to intensify that desire, allowing for a longer arc. An example is the backstory of my protagonist's mother. Beverly has unresolved issues involving suicide that she's hidden from her daughter, Ronnie. The tension she feels in watching her daughter go through this standoff is palpable—Beverly knows the stakes all too well. This long backstory tail [makes] Beverly's arc the most profound, because it gives us some sense of what will be needed for Ronnie to heal. It sets up the possibility for hope.

Not all arcs are equal, though. Jeff's mother has allowed denial to define her relationship with her son for his entire life, so one small step in the right direction by day's end will be huge for her. These backstories suggest the stakes: If these women can't support one another in facing this [crisis] head-on, this suicide will cripple Ronnie for the rest of her life. Completing the arc in twelve hours didn't leave me much time for a resolution, so I allowed symbolic actions to do much of the work.

What advice do you have for authors who might want to use a macro-structure to support meaning in their novels?

I suggest you pull way back and think about what you are trying to accomplish. An accurate synopsis will help you see the story all at once. In *The Art of Falling*, I wanted to show that Penelope's whole life, like modern dance itself, is about effort and surrender (gravity provides the metaphor). To support this meaning I divided the novel into four sections—Fall, Recovery, Contraction, and Release—based on the philosophies of early American model dance pioneers. [I used] as epigraphs quotes from both dancers (to represent body experience) and critics (to represent societal judgment). In this way I tied the healing journey she undertakes to the source of her conflict. Dance critic John Martin's quote for "recovery" is a metaphor for storytelling structure itself: "All movement can be considered to be a series of falls and recoveries; that is, a deliberate unbalance in order to progress, and a restoration of equilibrium for self-protection."

Ask yourself: What is this story's organizing principle (also known as theme, premise, or what choreographer Twyla Tharp, in her book *The Creative Habit*, calls a spine)? Is there a way you could reinforce it through the way you name your chapters or sections? No one who has read Mark Haddon's *The Curious Incident of the Dog in the Night-time* will forget that his novel begins with "Chapter 2" because his protagonist prefers prime numbers. Such structural considerations can help your project stand out in a crowded market.

Janice Gable Bashman is the Bram Stoker–nominated author of *Predator* and *Wanted Undead or Alive*. She is the publisher of *The Big Thrill*, the International Thriller Writers' magazine. Visit Janice at janicegablebashman.com.

61

ROBERT CRAIS

....
Fired Up

Jessica Strawser

Write what you love to read: The advice, oft touted, sounds simple enough. But few embody this approach as successfully as Robert Crais, whose slickly-plotted, tough-talking, wisecracking crime novels continue to prove worthy of comparison to the hard-boiled classics he cut his teeth on—while showcasing a style that still manages to be his own.

An Emmy Award–nominated writer for *Hill Street Blues*, *Cagney & Lacey* and *Miami Vice*, in the mid-eighties Crais traded in his lucrative TV credits for his dream of having a spot on bookshelves. He put his own team on the case, and Los Angeles private eye Elvis Cole and his partner, Joe Pike, have been collecting fans since their introduction in *The Monkey's Raincoat*, which won the 1988 Anthony and Macavity awards and was nominated for an Edgar. They've starred in sixteen of Crais's twenty novels to date, making their author a number one *New York Times* bestseller and Mystery Writers of America Grand Master. His latest, *The Promise*, pairs Pike and Cole with the stars of his 2013 bestseller *Suspect*, LAPD cop Scott James and his K-9 partner. A seventeenth in the series is slated for early 2017.

How his writing has evolved along the way—and what we can all learn from it—is, like many things in the writing life, best described by the author.

You've talked about your 1999 hit *L.A. Requiem* as a turning point in your career. What in your approach and perspective changed at that point?
I grew up as a crime fiction junkie. I write in this field because I grew up reading in this field. ...

You grew up in a family of law enforcement, too, correct?

In my family there are I think now five generations of police officers. That may not be in reality how it sounds—it's not like growing up in a TV show—but the true benefit for me, I think, was in seeing police officers as human beings, and understanding who they are in real life. That gave me an appreciation for the nuance of their characters in detail that hopefully I've brought to the characters of my novels.

So I grew up reading this stuff and loving it; my favorite writers in those days were the classic American detective fiction writers: Raymond Chandler, Dashiell Hammett, Robert B. Parker. So when I created Elvis Cole and set about writing my books, that was coming from a place of enthusiasm; I was a fan. And the first seven books were written in the style of the traditional American detective novel: first-person point of view of the detective, everything is seen through the detective's eyes, because I thought that's what you're supposed to do.

But as I wrote them, I began to feel constrained by that limitation. I wanted to tell stories that were broader than one could tell frozen in that traditional pattern. So by the time I got to number eight, which was *L.A. Requiem*, I just decided to take out the jams and combine all the different types of crime fiction and thriller fiction that I like to read.

It wasn't an easy decision. I'd had this traditional approach [that was] proving to be pretty popular. Part of me was saying, *You're about to shoot yourself in the foot.* But I felt strongly that I could tell the stories I wanted to tell if I expanded the canvas. I brought in points of view of other characters, cut from good guys to bad guys, did the flashback thing, and was still so unsure that when I sent it to my agent, I told him, "If the publisher hates it, I'll give the money back."

Luckily, it worked out. I've had this saying I've used forever as a self-motivator, a little sign in my office that says, *Trust the talent.* What that means to me is, when you're at your darkest moments and you think you're writing the worst thing that's ever been written, and it's going to be a failure, you just want to give up and go to Madrid, the best thing you can do is simply give yourself over to your instincts.

So you still have those dark moments sometimes?

Of course. After twenty books people must say, "He must knock this stuff out now." But most of the writers I know don't escape the effort that goes into writing. In fact, I think if you're doing the job correctly it gets more difficult, because each time you go back to the well, you have to dig deeper.

Robert Crais

When you begin, no writer knows where you're going to end up—and I'm not talking about the plot. I plot things out—I know where the story's going—but what I never know is: *Can I pull this one off? Can this all add up to be what I want it to be? Is it true, is it real, is it strong, does it have the right energy?* You face those questions every day. And especially when it's damn hard, and the words aren't coming, and you really have to bash your head into the wall, you do have those dark moments.

The only difference between me today and me then is that I've now been through it twenty-plus times, so I have a greater level of confidence that I'll be able find my way out of the darkness. At the beginning I didn't know, and that was *really* scary. Now I have more faith that even though I'm lost right now in this moment, history shows I can probably figure my way out of this. Just keep pushing, just keep typing, just keep writing.

So what is your process? You said you plot things out.

I have to figure it out before I write. Otherwise, I'm just lost. Maybe that comes from my TV days, where there's this fairly rigid professional process: You think up the story, you have to pitch the story to someone, a bunch of people sit in a room and talk out the story, you come up with an outline, all the themes are broken down, there it all is before you ever write the screenplay.

I actually wrote a couple of manuscripts, prior to my first published novel, with the high-minded idea that an artist would never, ever plot out a story in advance. If you were a true artist, you simply started typing. It was like magic: You know, your eyes rolled back in your head, and the story came to you and you were just glowing with inspiration, and days or weeks later you came out of your trance and had this beautiful novel. Well, I tried that twice, and they were just terrible. One had a five-hundred-page beginning and a fifty-page ending and there was no middle. I mean, these things were so bad I never even submitted them. Even I knew they were bad—why inflict them on anyone else?

So when it came time to write the next book, I said, *Listen, you've failed twice in a row, why don't you do it the way you're comfortable with?* And what makes sense to me is to figure stuff out in advance.

With a lot of writers, we're not talking about the same thing when we say we *outline.* Many people believe outlining is an intellectual process: *Chapter One: Elvis walks into a room, and a woman wants to hire him. Chapter Two ...* And you come up with forty or fifty of those, and there's your book.

The Complete Handbook of Novel Writing

But it isn't that at all. I'll spend three or four months figuring a story out before I ever begin to write it. And it's never sequential for me. In the beginning the ideas or thoughts come to me sort of globally. I always start with a character—character is what motivates me, what interests me. There's some human aspect to the nature of a particular character that has to get its hooks in me. Thereafter I just sort of free-flow scenes with that person or with that person's problem, with general situations that interest me, and I end up with sort of this mass of random scenes, but little by little some of them begin to connect, because I find them the most interesting or the most relevant.

After many weeks of this stuff, 80 percent of those random scenes and notions I've come up with are in the garbage, but I begin to see a story arc there, and the story arc comes together. All those scene notes, character notes, I put on little notecards and pin them up on blackboards in my office. I'm very visual; I like to see it laid out in front of me. After three or four months I have something that actually works as a story. I don't need 100 percent of everything figured out, but I typically need 75 or 80 percent. I have to see the beginning, the middle, and the ending I want to reach: This is what I'm trying to do with this particular story and these characters. When I'm confident in that, I'll begin to write. ...

[All told, it typically takes] around ten months, give or take a little bit. I usually don't write all the chapters or all the scenes sequentially. As I'm figuring everything out, getting closer and closer to the process, I'll write scenes that end up [coming much later in the story].

Voice is important with recurring characters especially. When developing a new character, what are some techniques you use to make him sound distinctive?

Always it begins with an emotion. Sometimes that emotion's not definable at the beginning. I'll see an image or imagine the character doing something that I don't understand but that fascinates me.

To give you an example, the first novel where Joe Pike is the main character was *The Watchman*, and the very first notion that eventually became that book was this image I had of a young woman in a convertible. Her hair is flying because she's driving really, really fast, hands on the wheel at ten and two, knuckles white, wind is screaming past her, she's pretty and her eyes are clenched closed. That's all I saw, but what grabbed me was that her eyes were closed, and I was hooked. I thought, *There's something about this woman—I want to know why her eyes are closed, I want to know how she came to this place. Who is she?* It's always like that, with all the characters.

From something like that, I'll begin to think about a character, and if need be I'll research a character. One of my (now continuing) characters is former Delta [Force] operator/now mercenary Jon Stone, and it was the same sort of genesis for him, though because of the nature of his work, I ended up doing an enormous amount of research on private military contractors. ... Contrary to the stereotypic image of muscle-bound, professional warriors, you find people who are Rhodes scholars. You find people who are voracious readers who read and write poetry. You find all these fascinating things. And brick by brick the character becomes real to you—you use your imagination to connect the stilts of reality that you found through research. You can hear the way he sounds, you can see the way he walks.

And pretty soon they come to life. I mean, I'm not saying when *I'm off my meds* they come to life, but they become the kinds of characters *you* want to read about. I'm going to give that book a year of my life, and [when you think about it] that way, you want to spend it with people you find interesting and care about and have grown to love.

You do a lot of hands-on research with the LAPD, FBI, bomb squads, and the like. How much do those experiences change the course of what you plan to write, versus informing the plots you have in mind?
Constantly. First of all: Research is the best. Research is more fun than writing. Research, you get to go outside!

Do you find it's best to do it while outlining or writing, or do you finish research before the story starts?
I begin researching a particular subject or character when I'm first conceiving it. If I need to know something about police K-9 dogs, or private military corporations, or how to make a bomb, whatever it is, I'll begin researching, and the more real-world research I can do, I pick up a ton of small stuff that adds enormously to the writing.

I do that research in the beginning, but you find that as things develop over the course of creating the book, you need to find out other things. Again and again, you trip over a pothole where you think, *I don't know that,* or *How do they do this?* When I'm in the heat of the writing, I'll make crap up, because I want to keep going. But that's never good enough, and I'm always bothered by that, so in the coming days or weeks, I'll retro-research it, and then if I have to revise or add things, I can do it.

Research is never finished—not until the project is over. It simply goes on throughout.

Some newer writers are intimidated by the idea of that kind of research, especially not knowing if the book will ever be published. They worry about not getting access, or not being taken seriously. What would you tell writers who are feeling that way?

I was once the person who didn't have twenty novels published, so what I learned firsthand is that if you present yourself professionally and respectfully, you'll be treated professionally and respectfully.

But the notion that, *I don't want to spend a lot of time researching this because someone might not buy it*, I think is a recipe for failure and is also disrespectful to your own work. Why write it if you're not going to try to make it the strongest, most powerful, most alive thing you can? You've got to throw yourself into it. If you're writing about a world in which you need to do research to learn about it, then feel passionate about it. If you're not passionate about what you're writing, you're writing the wrong thing.

I cannot stress how much I believe that. I don't know how other people feel, but writing, whatever I'm writing, is an emotional event for me. The intellectual part of it comes later, as almost the mechanical part of getting the emotional stuff right, getting it all typed up and ready to go. Successful writing is all about passion, to create a world that's full and complete and engrosses the reader. And remember: First and foremost the reader is you.

Why write about anything if you're not going to write about something you're passionate about, characters who you're fascinated by, a world in which you want to be in, even if it's only for a short period of time? That passion is the engine that has to fire the whole thing, drive the whole experience. Every one of the books I've written—hell, all the TV scripts I've written—at some place in the genesis of those things I found something that I was really hungry to write—because I wanted it there. I wanted to create it and see it and have it in front of me. And I think it's a mistake for anyone to somehow disassociate themselves from that passion, to think that the creation of a compelling piece of fiction can be had simply on intellectual terms. It becomes cold, and I don't think you want cold. You want heat, you want fire. That's what we gather around and warm our hands with.

Robert Crais

62

EMMA DONOGHUE

Room with a View

Jessica Strawser

When Emma Donoghue claims she's never written with the goal of being a best-seller, you can't help but believe her.

Since earning her Ph.D. in English in 1997, Donoghue has been enthusiastically amassing a body of work inspired solely by her personal passions, with little concern for the market. As diverse as she is prolific, she's written historical novels; literary criticism in the forms of articles, essays, and three complete books; countless short stories and fairy tales; both historical and contemporary fiction exploring lesbian themes; and plays for stage, radio, and screen; in addition to editing anthologies of fiction, nonfiction, and poetry.

That impressive range goes beyond form and genre. A Dublin native now living in Canada with her partner and two children, the forty-one-year-old has published in several international markets, with varying degrees of commercial success, over time garnering modest awards and even her first taste of best-seller status in the United States and abroad for 2000's *Slammerkin*—the story of a prostitute in eighteenth-century London, inspired by an actual murder case from 1763—which showcased her ability to enthrall readers with her reimaginings of real life.

And then, in September of 2010, she published *Room*.

Room wasn't just unlike any other book Donoghue had written—it's unlike any other book, period. Told from the perspective of a five-year-old boy who was born to a kidnapped woman and knows nothing of the world beyond the room in which they're held captive, *Room* is a haunting, powerful tale of the effects of isolation as well as the bonds between mother and child. The public may have first taken notice when Donoghue admitted she'd been inspired by the notorious

Elisabeth Fritzl kidnapping case, but readers and critics alike soon recognized the book for its remarkable achievements in voice, perspective, and story. The international bestseller landed Donoghue on the 2010 shortlists for a trio of giants—the Man Booker Prize, Canadian Governor General's Literary Award, and Galaxy International Author of the Year—and won both The Hughes & Hughes Irish Novel of the Year award and the Rogers Writers' Trust Fiction Prize for the year's best Canadian novel.

But if you think this means a new, mainstream direction for Donoghue, think again. Read on for her take on the intersections between inspiration, work, and unexpected success.

You've had a prolific career, but *Room* has garnered unprecedented attention. What's that been like?

It's like when you get a new haircut, and suddenly all your friends are going, "Oh, I'm so relieved you've got this haircut! This is ten times better than your hideous old hair!" You're obviously thrilled that people like the new haircut, but also mildly insulted that clearly everybody despised your previous haircut. I remember the [literary director] of the Man Booker Prize, Ion Trewin, said of me something like, "Here's this woman who's been writing for years and getting nowhere, and now suddenly she's on the Booker list."

And you know, I still maintain I was *not* getting nowhere. I think to support yourself as a writer is a great mixture of merit and good luck anyway, and I've always felt a great connection with my readers—they're just far more numerous this year. So I'm bemused by the sudden increase in my reputation, but from my point of view, I've been a success since the age of twenty because I've never needed to get a job.

Are you already feeling pressure for the next book?

Definitely. Some journalists even slightly scold me, like, "Now you've learned how to be commercial. Will you do this again next time?" And I say, "No, it doesn't work that way." There would be no surer way to write a complete failure of a book than to try and in any way recapture *Room*. Bestsellers are completely unpredictable, and you certainly don't manage to be original by looking over your shoulder at your possible readership and trying to guess what they will like. The only way to succeed as a writer—in literary fiction, anyway—is to follow your personal obsessions. And once in a while, your obsession will happen to overlap with the obsessive interests of a lot of readers.

Emma Donoghue

In a publishing climate where writers are often advised to develop one niche, you're quite diverse. Is that something you consciously strive for?

You know, maybe I'm lucky nobody ever told me that. I know what you mean, in terms of marketing and making a brand of yourself. It would be logical to develop one niche.

But I've always had a very good agent who's always emphasized the sure interest of each book or play. She's never approached my work with that hard-boiled, *Will this appeal to your previous readership?* attitude. I know my publishers are occasionally a bit bemused by, you know, what am I going to throw at them next, but nobody's ever said, "Oh, Emma, you have to give us more of the same thing."

How would you describe what drives you as a writer, or what lies at the heart of all the writing you do?

I think I'm what in the academic world—when they're talking about historians—they call a revisionist. Revisionist historians take a particular era and look at what the prevailing wisdom on that era is, and find a sort of countermovement and a different way of interpreting the same evidence.

Sometimes I literally do historical revisionism, like if I take eighteenth-century London and focus my narrative on a working-class prostitute [as in *Slammerkin*]. And sometimes I do a more symbolic revisionism where I try and find voices for people who have not been very much represented in contemporary literature. I am certainly interested in the marginal, in outsiders.

Another thing that's coming up quite a lot is emigration. … I'm interested in people who, like myself, have ended up far from home, and in the parallels between that geographical journey and the other ways people end up far from where they started. [And] I have an obvious interest in women's history and women's lives, but not an all-exclusive one.

You write books at a steady pace, and still regularly publish short pieces. I assume that means you're often working on more than one piece at a time?

Yeah, I often am. I think some writers are very intense in their process. I'm not like that at all. I'm much more in the tradition of Jane Austen, who wrote on her lap, and whenever visitors arrived she would just put a cushion over her work and chat. I'm intensely absorbed in each project, but not such that it disrupts my life, and it's not one at a time. I can be writing intensely on one thing in the morning, and then something else in the afternoon. I wouldn't usually have two novels on the go, but I would certainly have the writing of one novel and then research for the next one.

I think that's the main way I avoid writer's block is that if I'm feeling a bit sluggish or uninterested in whatever my main project is, I will either go do a bit of research, or write a short story. These things give me little breaks from the slightly claustrophobic monotony of working on one project.

Your novels, as varied as *Slammerkin* and *Room*, have been inspired by an element of truth from real life—
It's funny, *Room* has such a tiny little connection with fact. ...

It's been sort of blown out of proportion.
Oh, it has. I was naive—I didn't realize that if you get associated with a notorious case in any way, the next thing you know, it'll be, "Fritzl Novel Wins Prize," which makes me shudder. I hate being evasive, so I thought I was better off just saying up front, "Yeah, it happened to be the Fritzl case," but I don't know. It would make me wary of writing anything else which has any connection with the headlines.

But I've often written *closely* based on fact [in my historical fiction]. So it's sort of ironic that I ended up being punished for the hint of fact in *Room* when [it's] one of the least factual books I've written.

What is it about a story in life or in history that will compel you to tell it, or to imagine what might have been?
I get this burning curiosity—really just for my own benefit I want to find out what happened. And when I get to the cliff edge where the fact runs out, I switch from historian to novelist, and I start to think, *Ooh, I can imagine what happened.*

You might say I could have just made it up in the first place, but I find it more thrilling if my inventions are rooted in fact. I find that moment where the facts fall away a very stimulating one. Because often the historical facts are just so wonderfully unpredictable and gritty.

So how do you decide when research is warranted?
I research at least five things for every one thing I actually write. The key moment for me is ... that click when I suddenly see who my main character will be, and in a way that tells me what the story will be, too.

Emma Donoghue

How does your formal education in literature influence the writing you're doing today?

Well, it's not like it's necessary—I've met wonderful writers who've barely finished school. I don't know any good writers who don't read a lot. Whether you get it through reading or from an education, it comes to the same thing: You have to immerse yourself in many other people's words and ideas before you will be able to express your own very well.

But doing a degree in English taught me how to analyze texts, and it made me more clear-sighted about my mistakes, because I can write a bad review of my own work in my head very easily. Doing a Ph.D. made me uninhibited about research. [And] it gave me years of uninterrupted work time.

What about your father—being a literary critic and a professor, has he been an influence?

Definitely. He's very wide-ranging in his intellectual interests. He'll point me in the direction of interesting texts, and once or twice he's given me ideas for particular stories. But mostly the effect he's had on me is that I grew up confident of my power to write books, because my father's name was on the backs of books all over our house, so it just seemed a thing to do, you know? Grow up, write some books, go get published. I realize this is not the normal attitude!

Do you think about readers at all as you write fiction?

I think about them in the most helpful sense: I'm aware at every point of, okay, what does the reader know yet? That hint I dropped, will the reader have picked up on it? ...

The most important conversation I ever had on that subject was with my agent, when I first met up with her. She told me that my [debut] novel *Stir-Fry* was good, but that I'd written it clearly for an audience of Irish women. And she said, "Your readers could be anyone in the world, so rewrite the book assuming nothing on their part." Since then, I've tried to think of my readers as just about anyone.

So many writers find that the middle of a book is the hardest part. What helps you to push through?

I often get a bit bogged down. Or sometimes the first chapter can be a killer, because there's so much information to include. I sometimes wish I could say to readers on about page 5, "Please bear with me! All this will pay off!" ...

But then, yes, there's another possible slump, which is in the middle. Sometimes it means that you've planned it badly. I'm a big planner, and if there's a boggy bit in the middle, sometimes it's that that chapter doesn't need to be there.

Do you outline?

I do, in quite a lot of detail. I find if you plan, it allows you to leap more dramatically from one necessary moment to the next. I also write down what revelations the reader is getting at each point, so I can see whether I'm giving away a lot in chapter one and then no new information until chapter five. What you're trying to do is to keep up the reader's energy at every point. You're looking for spots where things would sag or get lost or come off the rails.

You have a great deal of experience publishing internationally. What's the most valuable thing you've learned?

My experience of the publishing process really does vary wildly from book to book. When your book is not doing well, it's just deeply, deeply quiet. Whereas when you're successful, suddenly publicists are constantly ringing you up. So right now I'm experiencing the industry a bit like children constantly wanting me to tie their shoes. But they're being really, really nice to me, as well—you feel like a star. The more usual experience is just very quiet.

Something I've learned is to take charge of representations of my work. I'm careful to write a blurb that will be the basis of the cover blurb. The terms you set in your initial synopsis, they're going to turn up in reviews for the rest of that book's life. ... So it would be unwise to write your book and then just say to publishers, "Oh, you do all that." You might think a book would be self-explanatory, but in fact, people are going to summarize it, sometimes in a single sentence. So if you're the one who gets to set those terms, then you can really stop the book from being misunderstood.

Your career has taken so many turns. What would you say to writers who are frustrated with where they are?

We all have bad times. Two of my novels weren't published in Britain, because my career there had fallen into oblivion—and that was just before *Room*.

I suppose getting focused on how to achieve success is really not the way to write great books. Keeping your mind on, you know, what is the story you would *really love* to tell, that actually is the best route to success.

63

JOE HILL

The Once and Future King

Zachary Petit

One day, a funny thing happened: An unknown, frustrated writer named Joe Hill got an envelope in the mail.

A small one.

He'd been sending his short stories to *The Atlantic* for a while now, and thought he was getting close to breaking in. The rejection letters usually came in big envelopes containing his manuscript, but this one was different: It was small. *Like, say, something you'd mail a check in.*

Hill was married at the time, and he ducked into a pay phone to call his wife.

"I said, 'I'm so excited, I'm so excited, I think I just sold a story to *The Atlantic*—I'm going to rip the letter open and I'm going to read it to you right now—"

She said she was so proud, so excited, it was wonderful—

"—And I ripped the letter open, and it was a form rejection," he says. "And scribbled on the bottom was, '*Sorry, we lost your manuscript.*'"

Hill erupts in a laugh.

"I was like, *What the hell am I doing this for? I'm so sick of it.*"

Hill had been keeping a secret for years: He'd been writing under a pen name. His surname is actually *King*. And his father, Stephen, is widely considered to be the most well-known writer alive.

Creative types sometimes wax and wane about whether writers are made or born. Sometimes, it would seem, they're both.

• • •

Joe Hill was born Joseph Hillstrom King in 1972, two years before his father released his first book, *Carrie*, and nine years before his mother, Tabitha King, released her debut novel, *Small World*. He'd come home from school to find his dad working in his office, and his mom banging away on her IBM typewriter.

"It just kind of seemed like the most natural thing in the world to go up to my room and play make-believe for an hour on the assumption that eventually you'd get paid for it," he says.

As a kid, alongside his older sister, Naomi King (now a Unitarian Universalist minister), and his younger brother, Owen King (now a literary writer whose debut novel, *Double Feature*, came out in March 2014), he *lived* storytelling.

"It sounds really Victorian, but when we sat around the dinner table, our conversation was all about books," Hill says. "After dinner we would go into the living room, and then instead of turning on the TV, we would pass a book around and read it."

After all, he adds, this was Bangor, Maine—there were only three TV channels.

It was natural, then, that Hill started writing on a steady basis when he was twelve. He estimates that by the time he was fourteen, he'd set a daily goal of seven pages, which he could sometimes pull off in forty-five minutes. At fourteen (!) he wrote his first novel, *Midnight Eats*—a story about a school with a satanic dean … and a cafeteria that (literally) serves up students who'd found him out. Even as a high school freshman, Hill says he had a feel for his future genre of choice.

But in his mind, that genre already belonged to his by-then famous father. So when Hill entered the writing program at Vassar College, he made two decisions: to avoid the horror and fantasy genres, and to drop his last name from his byline. His reasoning for the latter was this: He was "deeply afraid" that a publisher would see a way to make a quick buck off of him, and it would result in a bad book with his name on it. He wanted a career of doing what he loved, not a fling.

"[Readers] may buy your first book because you're the son of someone who's famous," he says, "but if the book's no good, they won't buy the second one."

So Joseph Hillstrom King became Joe Hill. And in time, the pen name gave Hill an essential dose of freedom. He realized he could play in whatever genre he wanted. Under his real name, he says he might have been judged harshly for writing horror and fantasy, stories sometimes not far off from the sort of stuff his dad wrote—but as it stood, no one knew who Joe Hill was. No one cared.

He produced *a lot* of stories. Around 1995, he queried literary agent Mickey Choate with a novel Choate describes as short and very dark, "but more literary than horror or dark fantasy." Choate took a chance on him without knowing his true identity, and the two never met in person—which was probably a good thing, given that Hill is a dead ringer for a young Stephen King (they even *sound* remarkably alike).

But ultimately, publishers far and wide rejected Hill's manuscripts. When his agent couldn't sell a certain fantasy novel Hill was fond of, Hill was heart-broken—"but in retrospect, [it] seems like it was a case of the pen name doing good work, because it wasn't good enough to sell on its own merits, and so better it didn't sell at all."

Hill's anonymous approach was not without exception in other arenas, though: After all, he says, he needed to make a living, and so he *did* collaborate on a pair of screenplays with his brother under his real name. They sold one, but ultimately it wasn't produced.

As Hill was beginning to think that maybe he just didn't have a novel in him, he had a breakthrough in another realm: comic books. Marvel bought a Spider-Man story he'd written. (Had his fiction career not worked out, he says he'd have been happy as a staff writer at a comic book publisher.) He'd also been having some success publishing short stories. Hill would keep half a dozen in the mail at once so that when a rejection came through, it seemed as if he'd been only one-sixth rejected.

"I got to a point where I kind of felt like I'd rather sink with the ship than drop the pen name," he says. "I wanted to be able to say to my kid that I had a passion for something, I had a dream for something, and I stuck with it on my terms and made it work."

Eventually, his persistence paid off: A small publisher in England bought his short story collection *20th Century Ghosts* and released it in 2005. After almost a decade, Hill finally revealed his identity to his agent and went on tour to support the book.

And as soon as he stepped foot onto the promotion circuit, people started to put it all together. The cat was beginning to creep out of the bag—but by then it didn't matter. The writing had come first. The pen name had done its job.

• • •

When you're writing about Joe Hill, a part of you longs to be able to relegate all mentions of Stephen King to a passing footnote. Here's why: Joe Hill can terrify. He can humor. He can sadden. He can shock. His characters are deep and vibrant, his plots mesmerizing, his prose genuine. Simply put, he's a damn good writer, and you feel like you're selling him short.

After *20th Century Ghosts*—which won several awards, including a Stoker for Best Fiction Collection—Hill released his first novel, *The New York Times* best-seller *Heart-Shaped Box*, in 2007. The tale earned Hill another Stoker, this time for Best First Novel. He followed it up with the popular Eisner Award–winning comic book series Locke & Key, and *Horns*, a 2010 horror novel with a romance component (which has been adapted into a film starring Daniel Radcliffe). His 2013 novel *NOS4A2* (sound it out), is a seven-hundred-page supernatural thriller about a mother, her son, and a man who abducts children and takes them to a terrifying place called "Christmasland." It was released to enthusiastic early reviews, and has been dubbed by Hill as his "Master's Thesis in Horror Writing."

For *NOS4A2*, Hill says he wanted to go big. He wanted to write something that spans many years, something with a lot of characters and subplots, and something truly scary. When he was younger, he says, he read a lot of great books in that vein—among them, his father's unforgettable clown classic, *It*.

"In some ways, *NOS4A2* is my rewrite of *It*," he says, laughing. "That kind of goes back to where we started this conversation, because I feel like most of the stories I write are partially a conversation with my dad, and my mom, and my brother and sister—that we're still having that same conversation we had around the dinner table."

As for being able to execute a novel of *NOS4A2*'s magnitude—or any great horror story, really—Hill says the genre is all about making readers care about someone, giving them a character they can root for, and then putting that person through the worst. He adds that when a piece of horror writing fails, it's often because the characters have transgressed into slasher-movie cutouts—characters you actually *want* Freddy Krueger to kill.

"If one of my characters is in danger, I want the reader to *feel* it and to *care* about what happens, not be hoping someone's head gets sliced off," he says. "I mean, I can match gore with the best of them … but I do want the characters to be all there."

Moreover, he says bad genre writing too often involves characters acting out the expected emotional response: Something bad happens, someone cries. Something scary happens, someone runs.

"I don't think real people are actually like that," he says. "Sometimes something awful and sad happens to you and you feel blanked. It doesn't hit you until three days later."

Another way Hill suggests keeping a piece of fiction fresh: Drop the bear. Hill did a comic book adaptation of his story "The Cape" with his friend Jason Ciaramella. In the second issue, some police officers think a character murdered his girlfriend (which he did). The character, who has a cape that allows him to fly, soars to a zoo and gets a bear cub. The cops are in a convertible. He drops it in on them. Mayhem ensues.

"Since then, I've sort of joked that in every story, there has to be a moment where you drop the bear," he says. "It's sort of like the opposite of jumping the shark. You're looking for that moment where the readers' eyes pop a little, and you hit them with the punch they didn't see coming."

While Hill may keep his stories free of formula and cliché, he doesn't hide from genre labels. He's one of those refreshingly candid writers who calls it like it is, identifying his horror novels as, well, horror novels. ("It would make me crazy when I'd be reading an interview with some director who'd say, 'I don't really think of myself as a horror director.' And the movie he just directed is *Sorority Slasher Babes 7*. And I'm like, dude, no offense, you ain't [f-ing] Fellini.")

Hill doesn't see genre writers as a totally different species than "literary" writers. After all, he says, everything an author such as Neil Gaiman does with imaginative prose is at its core literary. On the flip side, he adds that many contemporary writers commonly thought of as "literary"—Jonathan Lethem, Michael Chabon, Karen Russell—are incorporating genre techniques into their work in wonderful ways, too.

"They're opening up the genre toolbox and playing with everything in it," he says. "It sort of returns genre to the larger literary family. It has helped make genre respectable again."

• • •

Given that his parents are who they are, you may be wondering: What's the best piece of writing advice they've ever given him? Hill says it's this: *Finish the book. Finish the book, regardless of how bad it is. You can make it better in a rewrite.*

To that end, Hill describes himself as a big believer in habit. He usually begins his day by tapping in changes to the previous day's work, then writes five new pages, reads those pages over, and makes notes for the next day. Like his father, he works every day (weekends included) and writes organically—no outline. Which, seemingly, would be a good thing for father and son to have in common, given that they recently collaborated for the first time in print, co-authoring a couple of novellas. Readers of both father and son also will have undoubtedly noticed Hill's allusions to King's work in his own books—to the fictional town of Derry in *Horns*, to "the Pennywise Circus" in *NOS4A2*—tiny Easter eggs for the "Constant Reader" that Hill says he's more comfortable featuring now than he would have been earlier.

Given that his parents are who they are, you may also be wondering which of Hill's books is their favorite. Well, he says, always the most recent one, of course.

"They offer good advice, they have interesting things to say about [mine and Owen's] stories, but you have to remember that they're also parents. And so to a degree it's kind of like when your third-grader brings you a picture of an elephant, and [you] say, 'It's the best elephant ever!'"

When asked about what he wants to accomplish in his career before all is said and done, he pauses for a moment. Ultimately, the job of the day, he says, is to just write one solid scene. When you have one, you write another. When you have a stack, you have a short story or novel.

"I think for now I'm just paying attention to what I can see in my headlights. I'm not worrying about what's beyond them. One of these lines you hear a lot is, *Live like it's your last day on earth!* That's a really terrible piece of advice for a writer." He laughs. "You kind of have to live instead like you're immortal. You know, there's no rush to finish the book. It'll get done when it gets done. You sort of put off the idea that there's gonna be an end."

· · ·

So: Are writers made or born?

While an author profile that fails to mention Hill's background is inherently incomplete—a crime of omission for the simple fact that storytelling is in his blood—fiction that fails to do so isn't. A story speaks for itself.

So forget writers being made or born. Perhaps a more meaningful question is: *Do you like the book you just read?*

Good stories, like Joe Hill's name, stand perfectly alone.

BEST-SELLING ADVICE
Purpose

" The writing of a novel is taking life as it already exists, not to report it but to make an object, toward the end that the finished work might contain this life inside it and offer it to the reader. The essence will not be, of course, the same thing as the raw material; it is not even of the same family of things. The novel is something that never was before and will not be again."

—Eudora Welty

"When I sit down to write a book, I do not say to myself, 'I am going to produce a work of art.' I write it because there is some lie that I want to expose, some fact to which I want to draw attention, and my initial concern is to get a hearing."

—George Orwell

"[The writer] has to be the kind of man who turns the world upside down and says, lookit, it looks different, doesn't it?"

—Morris West

"Indeed, great fiction shows us not how to conduct our behavior but how to feel. Eventually, it may show us how to face our feelings and face our actions and to have new inklings about what they mean. A good novel of any year can initiate us into our own new experience.

—Eudora Welty

"I write in a very confessional way, because to me it's so exciting and fun. There's nothing funnier on earth than our humanness and our monkeyness. There's nothing more touching, and it's what I love to come upon when I'm reading; someone who's gotten really down and dirty, and they're taking the dross of life and doing alchemy, turning it into magic, tenderness, and compassion and hilarity. So I tell my students that if they really love something, pay attention to it. Try to write something that they would love to come upon."

—Anne Lamott

"The only obligation any artist can have is to himself. His work means nothing, otherwise. It has no meaning."

—Truman Capote

"I've always had complete confidence in myself. When I was nothing, I had complete confidence. There were ten guys in my writing class at Williams College who could write better than I. They didn't have what I have, which is guts. I was dedicated to writing, and nothing could stop me."

—John Toland

"You need that pride in yourself, as well as a sense, when you are sitting on page 297 of a book, that the book is going to be read, that somebody is going to care. You can't ever be sure about that, but you need the sense that it's important, that it's not typing; it's writing."

—Roger Kahn

"The real writer learns nothing from life. He is more like an oyster or a sponge.

—Gore Vidal

> **"** I think most writers—and I'm excluding now the adventure and mystery writers—will write about episodes meaningful to them in terms of their own imaginations. Now that would include a great deal of what they experience, but I'm not sure there's an autobiographical intention so much as the use of experience. That's been true in my case: I believe I'm telling the truth when I say that, when I wrote *Catch-22*, I was not particularly interested in war; I was mainly interested in writing a novel, and that was a subject for it. That's been true of all my books. Now what goes into these books does reflect a great deal of my more morbid nature—the fear of dying, a great deal of social awareness and social protest, which is part of my personality. None of that is the objective of writing. Take five writers who have experienced the same thing, and they will be completely different as people, and they'd be completely different in what they do write, what they're able to write."
>
> —*Joseph Heller*

> "They have to be given some meaning, the facts. What do they mean? The meaning's going to be influenced by a lot of things in you and your own culture. And some of these things you may be unaware of. But every historian has some kind of philosophy of life and society. ... All kinds of strands and currents and factors are involved. You have to separate and put together and from that we should deduce that there's no situation in the present that's simple, either. No simple answers. And the historian, when he looks over one of these situations, is going to try and consider all these things and try to be objective and fair and balanced, but what he picks out as the meaning will, of course, be what he himself believes. **"**
>
> —*T. Harry Williams*

64

KHALED HOSSEINI

Moving Mountains

Jessica Strawser

In peaceful Kabul, Afghanistan, many years ago, there was a young boy who, like most young boys, loved his family, loved his country, and loved great stories. He was taken by his culture's tradition of oral storytelling and soon discovered a deep love for reading fiction, and writing it, too. When his father's work took the family to France, it was meant to be temporary. But then, a war began back home. They lost their belongings, their land, their way of life.

When the boy was fifteen, his family came to the United States as political refugees. He saw his educated, affluent parents resort to paying for groceries with food stamps. He spoke only Farsi and French on his first day in a California high school. And as he watched his family struggle to rebuild, his dream of writing now seemed "outlandish." He learned English by immersion and, determined to "make something" of himself—and make his parents proud—went on to study medicine. He became Khaled Hosseini, M.D.

But the boy who became a doctor never let go of writing as a hobby. In fact, he began writing in English, his third language. Then one of his short stories, a tale of boyhood friends in Afghanistan that was inspired by a real-life Taliban ban on kite flying, seemed as if it held the potential to become something more. Now a husband and father, he began getting up at 5 A.M. to write every day before work. But as he neared the end of the manuscript, the attacks of September 11 occurred. He almost abandoned the novel, in doubt that there was now a market for such a story, and not wanting to seem "opportunistic." His wife insisted he keep writing.

In 2003, that novel, *The Kite Runner*, was published. At first, sales were slow. Then word of mouth began to spread. The unknown writer's book went on to spend a staggering 103 weeks on *The New York Times* bestseller list and eventually became a major motion picture.

Hosseini soon left his career in medicine. In 2007, he followed with *A Thousand Splendid Suns*, a tragic story of women in war-torn Kabul. The two novels combined have sold more than *38 million copies* in more than *seventy countries*.

The next time you're having one of those days when your writing dreams seem out of reach, you might try opening up a book by Khaled Hosseini.

And if you've ever wondered if good writing still has the power to make a difference, take heart. The literary career that has brought compassion to his native country's plight has opened other doors for Hosseini, now a goodwill envoy for the United Nations Refugee Agency and founder of his own humanitarian aid foundation for Afghanistan.

In May 2014, Hosseini ended worldwide readers' six-year wait for more from the novelist with the release of *And the Mountains Echoed*, the story of an Afghan family devastated by circumstance but bound forever by love. Here, he discusses his inspiration, the writing craft, and hope.

When you wrote *The Kite Runner*, you hadn't yet been back to Afghanistan since your childhood. But your subsequent novels clearly have been influenced by the humanitarian trips you've since taken. Why use fiction as a vehicle to tell these stories? I'd imagine you could have written nonfiction accounts drawing on similar themes.

Well, I think that presupposes that I wanted to write about Afghanistan and that I thought the best way to do it was to go through fiction, where it's really the reverse: I always wanted to write fiction, and the story I was interested in telling was set in Afghanistan. ... I've loved writing fiction my whole life, it's been a lifelong passion, and I've never really been all that interested in writing nonfiction.

Are there any specific experiences that inspired the story behind *And the Mountains Echoed*?

In the winter of 2008, I read in the newspaper stories about impoverished Afghans selling their children so they could give the kid that they were selling a chance at a better life—an education, a roof over their head—and also so they could take care of the remainder of their families. It struck me as unbelievably sad. And at the time I thought it was another consequence of living in a country where the economy is so battered—that it was a legacy of thirty years of conflict and displacement. But then I showed the story to my father, who grew up in Afghanistan, and he told me, "Oh, that used to happen, back in the forties and fifties." *Woah.*

So that kind of sat in the back of my head for a long time, and I began thinking of a family to whom this would happen, and what would be the consequences of that. As a writer, the draw of a story like this, of having a parent who has to give away a part of themselves to save another part of themselves, was irresistible.

The story spans multiple generations, with a large cast of characters. How did you go about crafting a novel of this magnitude?
The structure is very complex. I wanted something that would have the arc and the heft of a novel, but I had so many characters in mind, and so many different storylines, that I just couldn't see how I could get it done through a traditional linear structure. So I decided that each character would get his moment in the sun, and that I would find the links between them, and allow each character to step up and tell their part of the story, and then the next and the next—like listening to a choir, except one voice at a time, and then cumulatively they would erupt to a chorus of big songs.

I wanted each chapter to answer questions that came before, and raise additional questions. I wanted each chapter to reveal an epiphany, whether it be minor or major, and illuminate a part of a much bigger story. But I also wanted each chapter to be structurally more or less complete, freestanding, and yet still be part of the scaffolding for this much bigger story.

It's *so* intricately woven. Did you write it chronologically?
No, it was really hopping from character to character rather than proceeding chronologically. For instance, in the second story, we have what appears to be kind of a tough, unpleasant, embittered woman in the stepmother character. And I was interested in trying to find out where she came from and what gave her this disposition. What's her backstory?

So what would happen is I'd write a chapter and a particular character would pique my interest. Then I'd follow that character and see where it went and see how their story overlapped or coincided with some of the other characters' stories, and find connections. It wasn't until much later, when all the stories were done, that I decided to arrange them in a chronological way. [Now] the book progresses from the fifties to the present day, and it also expands from the small to the much bigger—it starts in a village, then to Kabul, then to Greece and France and the United States.

So it was really just following the scent of one character to the next—which made it difficult, because it was easy to lose track of time, lose track of space, lose track of *where was I with that character, where was I with this one?* It became an act of spinning a bunch of plates simultaneously.

Even your minor characters are very well developed. What are some techniques you use to make them seem so real? It sounds like you're a very organic writer.

I don't plan anything out. I *wish* that I was a more organized writer and I would plot everything out, and then it would be a matter of simply writing it. It just doesn't work for me. I lose patience with it, number one. And two, I always feel boxed in; I feel confined by the parameters of my outline.

One of the things I really love about writing is all the spontaneous moments, all the surprises, all the unforeseen developments that pop up and give you an insight into how different things might be connected or how differently things might be arranged than you originally thought, which would make for much more interesting storytelling.

So I don't plot out. And my characters ... I try to remove myself from them. My first book was probably the most autobiographical, the second less so, and then the third even less so—I try to let the characters just kind of get away from me and have their own voice, and have their own life. And at some point, it happens. It rarely happens in the first draft—my characters in the first drafts, particularly my central character, tend to be flat—but it really is through reviewing the story and writing a second, and then a third, and a fourth, and often a fifth or sixth draft, that slowly that working over finally stirs a character to life, and those unexpected things happen, and I begin to see how small changes here and there make a big difference.

I've found that for me, revising a character is sometimes even more about removing rather than adding—deleting things that you just don't need, that are weighing the character down. So I just work my way through it, and eventually I hope that at some point the character will start having their own voice, and I won't hear myself and there won't be a mouthpiece for my voice.

I saw an interview where you said you love to revise ...

Yeah.

A lot of writers *hate* to revise. Can you explain a bit about your process and what makes it so enjoyable?

It's kind of like moving into a house. For me the first draft is all about carrying all the furniture, and the bed, and the armoire, and the cabinets, and all the mattresses, and shoving it in the house, you know, everything that you have, all these belongings—and it's just hard, laborious work.

But for me the revising process is like, okay, now you've got all the stuff that you need in here, pretty much—you're going to throw some of it away—but now it's a matter of arranging things in such a way that makes it feel like a home, that makes sense and is pleasing. *This painting looks better on that wall, let's move the bed over here, and this couch looks really good here.* That's sort of the way I work through it.

I love having written something, to come back to it two, three, four months down the road, and so clearly see what works and what doesn't. And come back at it with a fresh idea of how it can be improved, what can be added, what can be taken away, so that it becomes much more alive. I really love doing that, because it's during the revising that suddenly I begin to see characters come to life. And for obvious reasons I find that very enjoyable, very rewarding.

Critics have said that your work just keeps getting better. What are some ways you think you've grown as a writer, and what are some lessons you could share?

I hope I've grown—that's really up to others—but I think one way in which I've grown is … [with my themes,] I've moved away from archetypal notions of good and bad. The epigraph at the beginning of [*And the Mountains Echoed*] is by Rumi, and it says, "Out beyond ideas of wrongdoing and rightdoing, there is a field. I'll meet you there." As I've written more and I've gotten older, I've become more interested not so much in *What's a good person and what's a bad person?*, which is quite obvious in *The Kite Runner*, but whether that kind of question can even be answered. So the new book is, I think, much more full of ambiguity—I think the characters, their motivations, stand for more nuanced, more complex, more surprising, more contradictory, and in the end hopefully more interesting places. It's less black-and-white.

And part of it is trusting. There's something that the novice writer does: worry that the reader won't get what she's trying to say. It's just [learning to] trust the reader and resist the urge to nail things down too much.

What do you still find most challenging about writing?

Oh, there are so many things. But, ultimately, the most difficult thing about writing is outlasting the beast [laughs]—lack of stamina, really. Because writing a novel is a very demanding task. And there are, in the course of writing it, multiple, multiple times when it threatens to take you over and basically just beat you down.

There are going to be many times where you're going to be frustrated, where you're pretty sure that you've just wasted the last four months of your life, where you think that this is something that somebody in junior high would write [laughs]. There are multiple crises of confidence and episodes of self-doubt. And what I've learned is that you just have to weather those. You really have to fight through them, no matter how unpleasant it is. Just be kind of blue-collar about it: Come in, do work, check in every day, check out at the end of the day, do what you have to do, trust in the process, and hope that something miraculous will happen down the line, and it will all be worth it.

I think one of the other difficult things is to accept that you actually *have* wasted the last four months of your life [laughs], at least in terms of what fits into the manuscript. What you've written may be fine, or it may not be, but it's just not going to work in this particular book you're writing. And so, do not be afraid to start over. Do not be afraid to just take that and put it in the trash pile, and move on.

That's extremely unpleasant—and I've done that multiple times with this book, and with all the previous books as well. But the bright side is there's no writing that you do from which you can't learn something. Even if it's a "mistake," even if it's not very good, there's always something you can draw even from your "failures." Sometimes I've had entire, you know, 150 pages of work that I've stashed away and [later] I've found some of it salvageable, just in a different context. So I always save them, because I never know.

Your stories have a lasting quality about them, where they stay with you long after you've finished reading. What do you think it is about them that gives them that longevity? Is that something you consciously strive for?

The only thing I consciously try to do is write as well as I can. … Everything that happens after that [is] a by-product of that. It's not something that I set out to do.

It happens that I'm interested in things that are universally human regardless of race, culture, ethnicity, religion, language, and so on. … The things that have always appealed to me about books are all the ways in which people seem to falter, and the ways in which they're weak, and the ways in which they're good, regardless of where they're from. That's one of the reasons why I'm so interested in the theme of family. There's an inherent push and pull between people within a family that I find fascinating. All the great themes of literature, in fact the great experiences of being human—you know, love and loyalty and duty and sacrifice and conflict and all those things—are very much alive within families. And so I write about families a lot—in fact, you could say all three of my books really are family stories. And that's something that's very universal and enduring and appeals to people regardless of where they're from.

It does seem the success of your work shows that a powerful piece of fiction can actually be one of the best ways to humanize stories from within a region or culture that is often misunderstood. But you say that's just a happy side effect?
It is, and I'll say that I don't think it would be particularly effective if I consciously set out to do that, because occasionally I've tried to do that—I've had an idea that I want to write about, that I feel is an important idea, and then I try to find a story around it—and those stories always turn out too political and agenda driven. I much prefer telling a simple story, or sometimes not so simple, but focused on character and inner thoughts and the interaction between different people, and how something emerged from that may be telling a bigger story than what's actually going on on the page.

[For example,] the interaction [in *And the Mountains Echoed*] between two boys, one the son of a warlord, the other the son of a refugee: It's a story that revolves around their encounter and the ways in which they're basically boys, both of them, but also how different their lives are and what different experiences they've had. You know, if through that there's a statement that comes through about where Afghanistan is today, how the rebuilding process has gone, what the legacy of the Soviet war has been, the class structures that seem to have formed almost overnight in Afghanistan, the incredible wealth some people are enjoying and the abject poverty other people are living in, partly as a result of what happened after September 11, then fine. But that wasn't my intention. My intention was about the awakening of this insulated and kind of innocent, to some extent, boy, who worships his father and is slowly awakened by this incident to who his father really is, and who *he* really is, and how you make peace with the unpleasant and sinister sides of not only the people you love but of yourself.

Do you think of your writing career as linked to your humanitarian efforts in any way?
I'd be very hesitant to say that my writing has any kind of humanitarian [link]—but my [humanitarian] travels and conversations and the things I've seen and

heard certainly have informed my writing. As you pointed out earlier, particularly in my last two books my encounters in Afghanistan have made their way onto the pages and have helped provide backstory, or sometimes much more than that, to my characters. So my travels have certainly informed my writing. But the writing also gave life to an opportunity for me to work with the U.N., and the opportunity for me to start my own foundation, and the success of my books and the wide readership that I've been lucky to enjoy has opened this door for me and allowed me to do something that I strongly believe in, something that makes me very happy, and something I hope makes a difference.

What do you think is the most valuable thing you've learned that you could pass along to writers who are hoping to enjoy the kind of success you have?

The temptation to give up, to surrender, is very, very strong. And you have to have faith in the work that you're doing. You have to have faith that as dark and unlikely and as dreary as things may seem, that it's worth pursuing, and that there's a good chance you'll be glad you did. Writing a novel—this is a cliché—is like a marriage. There are ups and downs, there are times when you just want to leave and close the door, you just want to be alone, you don't want to hear that voice, and so on and so forth, but it's well worth it, and I've learned that—to stick with it.

You know, I came close to abandoning all three of my books—very, very close, multiple times—where life seemed so much more pleasant if I just didn't have to try to work my way through the impasse. But I kept working, and I'm thankful every day that I did.

65

HUGH HOWEY

....
Brave New World

―――――――
Rachel Randall

At first, Hugh Howey's decision to walk away from a small press contract and self-publish didn't seem all that remarkable. After assuming complete control of his work, he kept his day job and began writing and releasing e-books (as well as some print books) in his off hours, happy to be simply sharing his stories with any readers who might find them. But when one of those books, *Wool*, unexpectedly took off, everything changed. Howey found himself at the top of e-book bestseller lists—and at the forefront of a new age of publishing.

The opening chapters of *Wool* first appeared as a $.99 e-book novella via Kindle Direct Publishing in July 2011; Howey had written the post-apocalyptic story, about a community of people living underground in giant silos, without intending to immediately follow it up with more installments. "I self-published it and went right back to my next work," he says. But by October, Howey noticed *Wool* was eclipsing all of his previous works and was positioned to sell one thousand copies by the end of the month. "I figured this was going to be the pinnacle of my career," he says. So he promptly tabled the unrelated project he'd been planning for National Novel Writing Month and instead focused on writing more of the *Wool* saga.

What happened next is a story that rivals the success of self-made sensations Amanda Hocking, John Locke, and E.L. James. The subsequent, rapid releases of the next four e-book installments of *Wool* rocketed Hugh Howey's name to the top of Amazon bestseller lists in several categories. In January 2012, he released the *Wool* omnibus (the combined five parts), which spent two weeks on *The New York Times* e-book fiction bestseller list and received the Kindle Book Review's 2012 Best Indie Book Award in the science fiction/fantasy category. By that summer, Howey was selling twenty thousand to thirty thousand digital copies of *Wool* a month ... and making a monthly salary of $150,000 from e-book sales alone. He quit his day job.

Publishers began to take notice. But instead of accepting the first offer that came along, Howey partnered with a literary agent, Kristin Nelson, and embarked on a mission. The pair began having conversations with publishers about the type of contract they were seeking—one that would allow Howey to broaden his reach to bookstores worldwide while still thriving as a digitally self-published author.

Not surprisingly, a lot of publishers weren't even willing to discuss a print contract that didn't encompass digital rights—and really, even Howey didn't expect to land that kind of deal. He saw himself as advocating for an eventual shift that might help other authors in the future. "We figured that ... it would take twenty or thirty published authors like myself having these conversations before some author down the road got the kind of deal we envisioned," he explains.

But then something else amazing and unexpected happened: Holding his ground worked. After walking away from several six-figure advance offers *and two seven-figure advances*, Howey became the first self-published author ever to be offered a print-only contract—and a significant six-figure advance—by a major publisher. Simon & Schuster released *Wool* in both hardcover and paperback in March 2013.

The nature of Howey's author-centric conversations with publishers speaks to his inherent altruism—a quality that seems to be at the core of his success. Howey has since self-published the second and third omnibuses in the Wool universe, *Shift* and *Dust*, which were also traditionally published as well. From his Florida home, where he resides with his wife and dog, Howey continues to advocate for more power in the hands of both traditional and self-published writers. Here, he discusses his unconventional road to success, his love for the science fiction genre, and his best advice to other hybrid authors in the making.

What influenced your initial decision to self-publish rather than pursue the traditional route?

Largely, my impatience. I went the traditional route with my first manuscript. I [had] shared that manuscript with some friends and people I knew on forums— I was going to put it on my website for free—and they said, "This is as good as anything I've read in the bookstore. Don't put this out there for free; you need to submit this to publishers and try to get an agent." So I begrudgingly went that route, and I was surprised: Within weeks I had some small publishers offering me advances. I was thrilled.

[But then,] watching that first book get published, I realized that all the tools were available to me. There were these new digital tools, and I could do it all myself. So when I got a contract for my second book, it was a difficult decision to make, but I told the publisher that I was going to try to do it on my own.

When did your literary agent come into the picture?

When [Kristin Nelson] got in touch with me, [*Wool* had become this breakout success and] I was turning away offers of representation. I just didn't think I needed an agent because I was enjoying what I was doing in the U.S. and I was making enough to not need a day job. But she explained that I could … give the Hollywood market a much bigger attempt and that I could attack the foreign markets. … Kristin has taken something that was doing really well domestically and expanded it in ways I never would have been able to.

You were having fantastic success through e-book sales alone. Why take *Wool* to a traditional publisher?

When I hooked up with Kristin, we discussed the fact that there was very little chance we would actually sign a deal with a traditional publisher. They would want the digital rights, which was how I was making a living, and they would want to take the [e-book] down. It could take a year before I saw any sort of payment, and I was getting paid monthly [at the time]. So we had these conversations [in order to] get publishers used to [ideas] they were uncomfortable considering, and we figured it would help some author years from now. …

Finally, Simon & Schuster came up with a contract that was everything we were looking for. It was a print-only deal, [and there was] nothing to hamstring my self-publishing career. They embraced what I was doing on my own, and they just wanted to offer this book to a wider market. … And it's gotten a lot of attention in the publishing industry. Another author, [Colleen Hoover], has [since] gotten a similar deal, so that's exciting to me.

So you believe traditional publishers are becoming more open to negotiating hybrid models?

I think of all the industries that have been revolutionized by digital media, publishers have done a great job [of adapting]. They've gone from [stigmatizing] self-publishing to looking at the bestseller list to find people who aren't signed, snatching them up and giving them much fairer contracts, and embracing the fact that they can publish several books in a year and have this huge fan base they can bring with them. It just makes complete sense, you know? There's so much risk involved in publishing a book. If you can print a bestseller that's already self-published, a lot of the risk is removed.

Do you feel that luck has played a role in your success?
Absolutely. I'm uncomfortable ascribing my success to my writing prowess. So much of it is timing. If I had been doing this five or ten years ago, I never would've gotten my stories out there. And if I would do it ten years from now, maybe my stories wouldn't be good enough to compete with all the other works being self-published.

Now that you've had experiences with both traditional publishing and self-publishing, would you say being a hybrid author is the best of both worlds?
Absolutely. I not only have the great royalties that come from the dual rights, but I've been picked up by major publishers overseas [such as Random House in the U.K.]. I get to work with wonderful editors at Random House and Simon & Schuster and go on a book tour, things that I would never be able to do on my own. But being self-published means that I get to produce three works a year. I get to price my works where they'll sell instead of pricing them so high. So there are advantages to both, and trying to pick the best from both worlds, to me, is ideal. It just requires a bit of good fortune to get to a position with your self-publishing career that you can get into the traditional world. And it also requires some bravery from traditionally published authors who want to become hybrid to break out and do some self-publishing. Some *New York Times* bestselling authors are now self-publishing in order to augment their earnings, and I think that's brilliant.

What advice can you offer to authors who are trying to build a hybrid career?
Well, if you're already traditionally published, examine your contract and see if [self-publishing] is something you can do. It's a wonderful way to build your readership. My recommendation to anyone who's got a backlist or a career in a traditionally published model is to break out and test the waters in self-publishing. It's not going to do anything but good for your career.

For those who want to self-publish [from the start], embrace that. There's no stigma from publishers, so if you want to become a hybrid author, the goal is to get as many works published [as possible]—high-quality stuff—build an author platform, and trust that ten years from now you have twenty works available and one takes off and a publisher will approach you. You have as good a chance of winning a publisher over by getting sales going through your self-published works as you do submitting to the slush pile.

Both routes are fine … but if you're really weighing the pros and cons [of] self-publishing, maybe you're earning twenty dollars or fifty dollars a month with the six or seven titles you have out there, and you're busy writing your next work. You're not thinking about landing an agent. You're not writing query letters, you're writing stories. And meanwhile, [your e-book sales might be] paying your cable bill. … Instead of [having your manuscripts] in a drawer or in self-addressed, stamped envelopes, you have them out there where readers can find them, and maybe one of them will take off. That's something I advocated before *Wool* had any sort of popularity, so it's not just anecdotal. The fact that it worked I think lends credence to the idea of it working for others.

You've said that you wrote *Wool* for yourself rather than for a specific audience. Do you think this approach has had something to do with its success?

Oh, for sure. I think readers are looking for something new, something they haven't experienced before, and that's been my passion behind everything I've written. … I'm writing the stories that I wish were already out there. With *Wool*, I wrote a story that was short and dark, and it seemed completely uncommercial to me, but it was the kind of story I wished I could encounter as a reader. … I never thought it would have this sort of success. You're not sitting there thinking any of this is possible when you're writing. You're thinking, *I'm going to enjoy this, my wife is going to enjoy it, I'm going to self-publish it, I'm going to get on to the next thing.*

What is it about the science fiction genre that appeals to you?

To me, the beauty of the genre is its ability to [satirize] the human condition and really speak to what it means to be alive and to exist as a person. Of all the genres, science fiction gives you the best ability to exaggerate some feature of the human condition or some feature of our environment and see how your characters will respond to that.

I was struck by the complexity of the world you built in *Wool*. Did you do extensive planning before you began writing, or was your approach more organic?

I have an idea of where a story is going to end before I [start writing]. I'll even write a very rough outline of the last scene or the last chapter, so I know where everyone's going to end up and where the story is going to finish. I read some books and they're just meandering and trying to find their ending, and I like for my characters to have a destination. [I leave] some room for wiggling, and for characters to interact organically with their environment or each other. I don't plot heavily, but I definitely know where the story is going to end up, and that's necessary for me. I want to avoid what [the TV show] *Lost* did, which was to make it up as they went along. [Laughs.]

What's the best piece of advice you can give to other writers?

Support one another. Wherever you are in your career, there's something you can do to help someone else out. The unusual nature of our industry is that we are not direct competitors to one another. … What I've learned from being a bookseller is that we will never have so many books that someone is not going to read your book because they're reading everyone else's. We can all do well, and the way we do that is by making reading as pleasurable as possible and by turning more and more people on to it.

Rachel Randall is the editorial director for Writer's Digest Books.

66

STEPHEN KING AND JERRY B. JENKINS

....
Writing Rapture

———————————

Jessica Strawser

One is arguably the best-known writer of our time. The other made his name writing the end of the world as we know it in the Left Behind series. If this unique pairing seems unlikely, look closer. A conversation with the two yields both parallels and polarity—and candid insights as well as mutual respect.

How did the two of you meet?

JENKINS: We happened to have the same audio reader, a brilliant voice actor named Frank Muller. In November 2001 Frank was in a horrible motorcycle accident that left him brain damaged, incapacitated, and barely able to speak. One of Frank's brothers started a foundation to assist with the obscene expenses, and Stephen became aware that I was helping out.

Stephen was carrying the lion's share, undoubtedly contributing more than half of the total the foundation raised, but he called me one day to thank me for my part and to suggest other ways we might be able to help Frank. Needless to say, when my assistant told me Stephen King was on the phone, I quickly ran through my list of practical-joking friends to decide how to greet whoever was claiming to be him. But, just in case, I said my usual, "This is Jerry."

I had to squelch a laugh when he said, "Steve King."

Who calls Stephen King "Steve"? Well, Stephen King does. We learned that we read each other's stuff and laughed about being strange bedfellows. Then we agreed to [meet to] visit Frank at a rehabilitation facility.

Your works are in some ways polar opposites, but in other ways parallels can be drawn. What do you think of each other's books? Do you imagine you share an audience?

KING: I got to know [Jerry] through the Left Behind series, which has a lot in common with *The Stand*—both are stories about the end of the world, with Christian overtones (mine has more four-letter words). While I'm not a big believer in the Biblical apocalypse and end-times, I was raised in a Christian home, went to church a lot, attended MYF (Methodist Youth Fellowship—lots of Bible drills, which every writer could use, Christian or not), and so I knew the story. The Left Behinds were like meeting an old friend in modern dress. I very much enjoyed *The Youngest Hero*, which is a crackerjack baseball story written by a man who must be a serious stat freak. Jerry writes sturdy prose and plots well. He's also warm and compassionate. Understands families inside and out. There's a lot there to like.

JENKINS: Much of my audience tells me they read Stephen's works. Others, of course, find horror horrifying, and some of his stuff pushes the envelope of comfort for them. Even for me, I lean more toward *The Green Mile* than, say, *Carrie*, but regardless of what one thinks of the genre, Stephen's talent is no longer up for debate.

What compels you to write?

JENKINS: I write because I can't do anything else. I like to say I don't sing or dance or preach; this is all I do. But I [also] have a passion for my subject matter. I was a sportswriter as a teenager (after being injured playing sports) but felt called to full-time Christian work. I thought that would mean I'd have to give up writing and become a pastor or a missionary. I was thrilled to find out I could use my budding writing gift and accomplish the same thing.

KING: Jerry's direct and correct: I can't do anything else. And every day I marvel that I can get money for doing something I enjoy so much.

What do you need to consider in writing about belief systems and other themes that are intensely personal to your audience?

JENKINS: It's one thing to preach to the choir, as we often say. It's quite another to try to make a particular faith understandable, palatable, and hopefully even attractive to the uninitiated or the patently hostile. I'd had some experience writing to a crossover audience (the general market) because I had done many sports personality books (Hank Aaron, Walter Payton, Orel Hershiser, Nolan

Ryan, et al.), but when Left Behind crossed over in a big way, I quickly realized the spot I was in.

Here I was, writing fiction with an overtly Christian theme (the Rapture of the church at the end of time) to an audience that suddenly seemed to include everybody. I tried to remember always where my readers were coming from and to be sure to stay away from insider language.

Of course, the singular challenge I had was to allow the message to come through without letting it overwhelm the fiction. The story has to be paramount. Readers must fall in love with the characters and want to keep turning the pages. The minute your novel starts to read like a sermon, end of story.

KING: The old Robert (*Psycho*) Bloch witticism applies here: "Thou shalt not sell thy book for a plot of message." Jerry said it, and I'll double down: Story comes first. *But*—and I think Jerry will agree with this, too—what you write ought to be about *something* you care about. Why else would you spend all that time and expend all that effort?

What are your secrets for making readers suspend their disbelief and immerse themselves in your imagined worlds?

KING: Making people believe the unbelievable is no trick; it's *work*. And I think Jerry would agree that belief and reader absorption come in the details: An over-turned tricycle in the gutter of an abandoned neighborhood can stand for everything. Or a broken billboard. Or weeds growing in the cracks of a library's steps. Of course, none of this means a lot without characters the reader cares about (and sometimes characters—"bad guys"—the reader is rooting against), but the details are always the starting place in speculative or fantasy fiction. They must be clear and textured. The writer must have a good imagination to begin with, but the imagination has to be muscular, which means it must be exercised in a disciplined way, day in and day out, by writing, failing, succeeding, and revising.

JENKINS: Ironically, the definitions of nonfiction and fiction have flip-flopped these days. Nonfiction has to be unbelievable, and fiction has to be believable. So, to my mind, the task (and I agree with Stephen that it's no trick) of getting readers to buy your premise and temporarily suspend disbelief is to *yourself* believe your premise with all your heart.

For me that meant that for the Left Behind series, I believed the biblical prophecies are true and will happen some day. Then I went about trying to show what it might look like, all the while owning it. When Stephen writes about what

Edgar Allan Poe referred to as the phantasmagorical, I imagine him pecking away in the dark, all the while telling himself, "This could happen."

As to why people like to escape into other worlds, that has to do with this world. People are longing for something beyond themselves and their current circumstances. They want either hope or escape—or both.

What do you think it is about your books—and each other's books—that keeps people up at night? While writing, do you ever frighten yourself?

JENKINS: From my perspective, Stephen's gift is this incredible ability to recognize and exploit details of life and squeeze from them every ounce of meaning. I'm reading his *N.* right now and find myself constantly saying, "That's how I would feel! That's how I would say it!" (I'm speaking of identifying with the characters, not with the author. If I could say it the way Stephen says it, the Left Behind series would be just one of a string of megahits rather than an anomaly in my career.)

As for frightening myself, it happens that by, in at least this sense, being part of the Stephen King school of fiction (trying to put interesting characters in difficult situations and writing to find out what happens) allows me to have the same emotions the reader will have. Since I write as a process of discovery—even though I know this is all coming from my subconscious—I am often surprised, delighted, scared, disappointed, saddened, etc., by what happens. If it's serendipitous to me, it certainly should be to the reader, too.

At least it gives me an out when readers demand to know why I killed off their favorite character. I can say, "I didn't kill him off; I found him dead."

KING: I usually feel in charge. But not always. You know how Jerry says, "I didn't kill him, I found him dead"? That *does* happen. It happened to me in *Cujo* when the little boy died. I never expected that. I wasn't frightened, but I was sad when that happened. Because it seemed outside my control.

Why do you think the battle between good and evil never ceases to fascinate readers? In what ways does it continue to fascinate you?

KING: The battle between good and evil is endlessly fascinating because we are participants every day. Sometimes we see it on TV, as in the Mumbai terrorist attacks, and sometimes we see it on the street, as when a big kid pushes a smaller one or some maladjusted individual indulges in a little drive-by harassment. We feel it when we're tempted to skim a little money or do a little running around outside the relationship or participate in some deal we know damn well is skeevy. When evil is vanquished in a book, most of us feel cathartic triumph.

I think we're also looking for strategies to use in our daily battle. And, let's face it, we enjoy the conflict. That's what makes pro football such a ratings wow, not to mention [pro] wrestling. And—rule of thumb—those of us who root for the "good guys" are probably well adjusted. But writers must be fair and remember that even bad guys (most of them, anyway) see themselves as good—they are the heroes of their own lives. Giving them a fair chance as characters can create some interesting shades of gray—and shades of gray are also a part of life.

What are the challenges of writing for "constant readers," as Stephen calls them? What's fun about having a devoted fan base?

JENKINS: Readers come to respect you, believe in you, and set certain expectations for you. I always want each book to be better than the last, and sometimes readers want to stay where they're comfortable. People still ask for more Left Behind books. Sixteen was plenty. I'd be surprised if people didn't occasionally ask Stephen for sequels to some of his classics. But writers need to grow, too, and try new things.

Stephen, am I right? Do your fans obsess over the old stuff and want more of the same?

KING: They just want a good story, and I think they come to crave your *voice* even more than the story itself. It's like having a visit with an old friend. As for revisiting old stories … I remember a very young fan in Houston (it was my first book tour) telling me that he loved *Salem's Lot* and thought I should write "a squeal in that jenner." After a moment of frantic cranial cogitation, I realized he was saying "a sequel in that genre." I *have* thought of writing a "squeal" to one of my early books, mostly because I've never done it before.

Jerry, do you write from a place of uncommon spiritual insight?

JENKINS: I wouldn't say it's uncommon spiritual insight, but it does come from a lifetime of belief. In many ways writing Left Behind, a story I had been telling since I was a teenager, felt right because I grew up in a tradition that believed it. I am neither theologian nor scholar, but I understand the story and am fascinated by it. When I assisted Billy Graham with his memoir *Just as I Am*, again, it felt right, as if I had been prepared for it by a lifetime of passion for the same tradition.

When writers "outside" the faith attempt to write about these same things, the base audience senses their disconnect and their discomfort.

Stephen, a lot of your constant readers seem to think that, on some level, you must be channeling some sort of other world entirely. Is there any truth to that?

KING: I have no particular spiritual insights, but I think every writer who does this on a daily basis has a "back channel" to the subconscious that can be accessed pretty easily. Mine is wide and deep. I never write with an ax to grind, but I sense strongly that this world is a thin place indeed, simply a veil over a brighter and more amazing truth. To me, every ant, cloud, and star seems to proclaim that there is more to existence than we know. I suppose that sounds like naturism and pantheism, and to some degree it is, but I also believe in a power greater than myself. If I die and that turns out to be wrong, there's this advantage: I'll never know.

How has your writing evolved over time? In what ways do you feel your audience has evolved with you?

KING: For sure my audience has grown older with me, and to a greater or lesser degree, wiser. Certainly more sophisticated. I think I have a greater grasp on my narrative powers than I used to have (*that'll* start to degrade in another ten years or so, as the gray cells begin dying at a faster and faster rate), but I still refuse to recognize any limits to my gift. I think it's important to keep on pushing the envelope. I also like to think that I'm being "discovered" by younger readers, but who really knows? Certainly I haven't evolved as a writer by consciously trying to evolve; I just keep writing and hoping to find good new stories. In truth, I hardly ever consider the audience at all. And I don't think it's wise to. I have a built-in desire to please; that should be enough. Beyond that, I'm just trying to amuse myself. Usually that amuses others, too. Which makes me a lucky man. True for Jerry as well, I'd guess.

JENKINS: I hope my writing has become more spare and direct over the years. The longer I write, the less patient I am with needless words. That's fortunate, because my audience has kept pace with the culture, in which technology has reduced us all to short attention spans and sound bites.

That said, a good book can't be long enough for my taste. And a bad book can't be short enough.

You've both seen your work interpreted into film. What is most satisfying about such collaborations? What's the worst part?

JENKINS: For films, as I'm sure is true with Stephen, some I'm thrilled with, some I don't even acknowledge. I was particularly happy with what Hallmark did with *Though None Go with Me* and what my own son Dallas (Jenkins Entertainment) did with *Midnight Clear*. Stephen, you're on record for hating a lot of the film treatments of your work. Were there some you were happy with?

KING: Who gave you the idea I hate most of the film adaptations? There are at least eight really good ones, and the only one I can remember hating was [Stanley] Kubrick's cold adaptation of *The Shining*; spending three hours watching an ant farm would be more emotionally uplifting. But the ones that are bad … I just laugh and then forget them. I'm always interested in what happens, but my expectations are low, which makes life a lot simpler. My favorite adaptation is still Rob Reiner's *Stand by Me*.

JENKINS: Speaking just for me, I think the best film ever made of one of Stephen's works was *The Green Mile*. Usually watching a movie of a favorite book is disappointing, but in that case I kept remarking that it reminded me of what my mind's eye saw as I read.

Stephen, do you consider The Dark Tower series your magnum opus? How do you view it in relation to your complete body of work?

KING: I hope my magnum opus isn't written yet, but by length and ambition, I'm sure most readers would say The Dark Tower is the big one (when they're not naming *The Stand*, that is). Another sign: I don't feel done with it yet. Those seven books feel like the rough draft of one unified novel. I've already rewritten the first one, and I wonder if Jerry sometimes has the urge to revisit Rayford Steele and his buddies and spruce them up. Not saying they're bad as is; just saying sometimes you look back at a completed work and say, "Oh yeah! Now I know what I meant!"

JENKINS: I have made the mistake of saying that my latest novel, *Riven*, was indeed my magnum opus. Trouble is, I don't know how to do anything else, so more novels will be coming. And readers will say, "Didn't you retire? How does one follow his own magnum opus?"

So—any thoughts of retirement?

JENKINS: Retire from what? Why would I want to quit doing what I love? Slow down a bit, sure. See the kids and grandkids more, you bet. Retire? Nah. [My wife] Dianna says she's going to put on my tombstone, "Never an unpublished thought."

Stephen, it seems every few years someone breaks the big story that you've announced you're finished. Thankfully it's never proved true. Are you toying with them, or are there times when you feel the tank is empty? (As I've told you, after *Riven* I seriously wondered if I had anything left to say, and your counsel was to not make any rash decisions while recuperating. That proved great advice, and I'm back at the keyboard.)

KING: There was a time when I thought I would, because I'd had an accident, I was hooked on pain medication, and everything hurt all the time. Things are better now. When I wonder if I really have any more to say, I pick up a novel by John Updike or Elmore Leonard … which gives me hope of another twenty productive years.

How do you think having written a book for writers helps define your career? Might you pen another?

KING: I think I've said what I have to say about writing, and I'll be interested to see how Jerry answers this question. For me, *On Writing* felt like both a summing-up and an articulation of things I'd been doing almost entirely by instinct. I thought it would be an easy book to write, and it wasn't. I also thought it would be longer than it turned out to be. But you know what we used to say when we were kids, playing Hearts? "If it's laid, it's played"—meaning you can't take back a card once it's on the table. Nor can you invent new cards. I said everything I knew then, and if I added what I know now, it would probably amount to, "Don't write long books, because the critics rip them," and, "Don't end sentences with a preposition." Which I might have said in *On Writing*!

JENKINS: I didn't write *Writing for the Soul* to define my career, but it did give me my only chance to be overtly autobiographical, so in some ways it accomplishes that. Because of my ownership of the Christian Writers Guild, I may have another writing book in my future. This would be more nuts-and-bolts and less personal, probably.

KING: Last but not least—we're all amateurs at this job, really. It's always new. For me (to quote Foreigner), it always feels like the first time.

67

DENNIS LEHANE

....
Pride of Ownership

———————

Steve Boisson

Like many writers, Dennis Lehane started with short stories. He wanted to create the kind of beveled truth nuggets crafted by Raymond Carver, but he didn't feel his efforts met that mark, so he didn't submit a one. In 1990, two years out of college, twenty-five-year-old Lehane decided to try his hand at a crime novel instead. The first draft came pouring out in three weeks. Many rewrites and a Master of Fine Arts later, *A Drink Before the War* was published in 1994, earning a Shamus Award for Best First PI Novel.

Lehane's star investigators are Patrick Kenzie and Angie Gennaro from Dorchester, the tough, working-class Boston neighborhood where Lehane grew up. In that first book, they're childhood friends turned professional associates, but they soon develop a relationship that turns on-again-off-again through *Sacred*, *Darkness Take My Hand*, *Gone Baby Gone*, *Prayers for Rain*, and *Moonlight Mile*. Lehane isn't your average crime novelist, and Kenzie and Gennaro aren't your average PIs. Unlike many of their fictional counterparts, Lehane's protagonists carry the psychic cost of the violence they've suffered, witnessed, or perpetrated from book to book.

Five books into the series, Lehane stepped away to write 2001's *Mystic River*, a complex story about three men whose lives take disparate paths after a disturbing childhood incident. In it, Lehane pushed the boundaries of crime fiction—the present-day murder is secondary to the emotional consequences of a past crime. It hit the bestseller lists shortly after its publication in 2001, and was adapted into an Academy Award–winning film directed by Clint Eastwood.

Most of Lehane's subsequent work has similarly been informed by crime, though not strictly crime fiction. *Shutter Island* explores the psyche of a troubled U.S. marshal in deep denial over his demons. *The Given Day* is a sprawling historical novel, the first in a trilogy introducing a new family of characters, the Coughlins, encompassing the influenza pandemic of 1918, the Boston Police Strike of 1919, European anarchists, and Babe Ruth. Its saga continues in the Edgar Award–winning *Live by Night*, featuring patriarch Thomas Coughlin's youngest son, Joe, a romantic though nonetheless criminal underling of a mob boss, and *World Gone By*, Lehane's twelfth novel, in which Joe's new life as a respectable businessman is threatened by events from the past.

From pushing genre novel boundaries with *Mystic River* to writing scripts for a Scorsese–helmed *Shutter Island* spin-off, Dennis Lehane's success has carried him coast to coast, but Boston will always be home—in his heart and on the page.

How did your first novel come about?

The bottom line is I was unbelievably broke that summer and I couldn't afford to go out. So I decided to try my hand at crime fiction because I've always liked it. It kind of blew out of me, whereas short stories—I thought I was a short story writer—could be painfully slow. So that was kind of an "aha moment" in my maturation as a writer.

I sent it to a friend of mine, Sterling Watson, a Tampa writer, and he said it was really terrible but structurally very strong. He suggested I rewrite it, and I did, several times, and each time it got deeper and better written. He sent it [to an agent he knew] on my behalf, and about six months later she called and asked to be my agent. For two years it kept going out and getting rejected. And just as I was finishing grad school, the same week, it was accepted by [Harcourt].

There were several conditional rejections of the book: Several publishers would accept it as a paperback; I said no. A couple said, "If you change the fact that the lead female character is a battered wife, then we'll take the book." I said no. My ability to stick to my guns stemmed from two things: One, I had a great agent who believed in me. Two, I was living so far below the poverty line nobody could make me any poorer.

You've spoken about a renaissance in crime fiction, beginning with the 1978 publication of James Crumley's *The Last Good Kiss*.

It's straight-up *literature*. It's got astonishing depth of prose. It's one of the greatest novels about the 1970s ever written. Just because you're published in literary fiction does not make it literature—and just because you've published in genre does not make it *not* literature. I felt that way when I read Crumley; I felt that way when I read James Ellroy's *L.A. Quartet*; I felt that way when I read James Lee Burke. The finale for me was when I read Richard Price's *Clockers* and it got no serious literary recognition that year. And if the most important book published that year didn't get respect because it was an urban novel with a cop at its center, then the whole system's screwed. That's when I said, "Maybe I ought to try my hand at genre."

Do you follow a writing schedule?

I do now because I have two kids, but I never [used to]. I think it's really important to write every day. You have to do an hour a day minimum or the muscles get atrophied.

Before you start a novel, do you know the ending?

Usually I know three things about a book, and the end is usually one. I know one thing in the beginning, one thing in the middle, and one thing at the end, and I don't know anything else. And I just dive in. *One step forward, two steps back* is usually how I write. That's why books take me a long time.

In *Mystic River*, you show the various characters' points of view while remaining in the third person. Yet Dave Boyle, suspected of murder, doesn't reveal his innocence until three-hundred-plus pages into the book.

Once we know that, I don't think there's much suspense. There's not much mystery in *Mystic River*. There's *Who killed Katie?* which I don't think is terribly mysterious. I throw the suspect right out in front of your face, as quickly as possible. This is the least important thing to me, so if somebody figures it out, great. And then, *What happened to Dave that night? Why did Dave have the blood on him?* That was the mystery of the book. So how do I show readers the damage to this guy's psyche so they believe in the end that he would admit to a crime he didn't commit? And the only way I could do that was to withhold information as fairly as I could, staying in Dave's psyche because [having been molested as a child] Dave's in denial about a lot of what's inside himself. I was a little concerned about that, but in the end I think it worked.

The rule is you've got to play fair. That's always been my thing. I meet people all the time who say, "I figured out who killed the girl in *Mystic River* in the first forty pages." This is a book about how one stone hits the pond and ripples, and we have no idea how far those ripples are going to go or who they're going to affect.

You've worked with physically and sexually abused kids ...

I worked both in Boston and Florida as a therapeutic counselor, usually in group homes. At the place I worked the longest, we would pick kids from juvie who we thought were just on the right side of the line between victim and victimizer. And we'd try to save them before they became victimizers, because that's usually the standard: If you get beaten long enough you end up being a beater. ... That directly inspired *Mystic River*, working with those kids.

Gone Baby Gone also depicts child abuse.

Gone Baby Gone started with the question, "What is the worst type of child abuse?" I think we can all agree it's sexual child abuse. But then you start getting into grays. Is physical abuse as bad as neglect? So *Gone Baby Gone* was looking at every single aspect. ... That's what Amanda represents. Joy has been robbed from her.

After Amanda has been kidnapped, her aunt turns to Kenzie and Gennaro, Dorchester people like herself. It seems unique to Boston, the neighborhood loyalties of the working class.

Oh, yeah. It's sort of blind loyalty. It can be pretty destructive. At the same time, I come from a place where your word was your bond. That and work ethic were the two most important qualities of a person: the value of their word and the value of their work. I get asked if the neighborhood people get pissed at me [for writing about them], and I say, "No, they don't mind as long as you write about warts and all—as long as you're not some carpetbagger coming from the outside judging them." I'm from the inside, so I can say, yes, there's a lot of racism, there's a lot of tribalism, there's a lot of violence, intergenerational violence, intergenerational crime. But there's also an amazing amount of goodwill and neighborliness, for lack of a better word, and again, a strong sense of loyalty and integrity. I wouldn't change a thing about having grown up there. It's been the luckiest break I've ever had, really. I don't know what kind of writer I'd be if I'd grown up in Aurora, Illinois.

You traveled back in Boston history for The Given Day. Did you know it would expand into a trilogy?

I knew it was going to sprawl out on me. I could see I was putting a lot of people in the dugout, so I could use them at various times should I choose. For now that saga is over. But that doesn't mean that someday I won't go back and look into [another one of those characters] for a book.

What inspired you to bring Babe Ruth into the story?
He just walked into the book. He walked in early, and he was so great and so much fun. That was really the beginning of the modern celebrity, and I wanted to run with that. I wanted to run through this incredible year that I think was one of the most exciting years in American history, September 1918 to September 1919, and Babe Ruth was in the middle of it all. As I used to say when I was teaching, sometimes the reason to write something is because it's cool. Because you enjoy it. Because you're having fun. Because you just think, *Hey, why not?* Those are reasons that sometimes get lost in the more schematic ways we approach writing. Sometimes if you get excited, guess what? The reader's going to get excited, too.

Is it possible to do too much research?
Very much. I lost a year on *The Given Day*. A complete waste of time. Ever since *The Given Day*, I write, and as I'm writing and I get to a moment where I need a fact—"What did a pack of cigarettes cost in 1921?"—*then* I look it up. I research as needed. I don't pre-research—never again. I know a bunch of facts about 1918, and unless I get on *Jeopardy* and it happens to be a category, they're completely useless to me.

Your writing is very evocative of place: bug-infested swamps in Florida, dank bars in Boston.
I'm one of those people who get depressed if I'm in a place I don't like, the way other people are affected by weather. I couldn't care less about weather, but if you put me in a place I don't like, I become very depressed very fast, even if I'm only there for a few days. I have a very strong reaction to the physical world I am in. I don't like writing about places unless there's something exciting to write about them. I love trains, so you see Luther's train ride in *The Given Day*. Yeah, I usually write about evocative places.

You've written teleplays for *The Wire* and *Boardwalk Empire*. Are the limitations of TV writing—characters created by someone else, a fixed length and pace—liberating when compared to the challenge of a blank slate?

Yeah, it's great. But at the end of the day you don't take pride of ownership. I'm really proud to have been associated with *The Wire*, but pride of ownership goes to David Simon and Ed Burns. I'm just a guy who came in to paint a room. It's a wonderful feeling and it's a very relaxing thing to be working on a TV show that's not yours. *Boardwalk* was a complete joy. But it's not the same pride of ownership.

I've written screenplays, but you don't know what's going to show up on the screen. When you write a book, you go over proofs with your editor, and that's it. It doesn't happen that the book comes out a year later and you don't recognize half of it. That's exactly what happens when you write a script. Not that it's happened to me in film, because on *The Drop* I was treated beautifully. But I've written scripts, I've been paid for them, and I've seen what they become, and they're not even close to what I wrote. Richard Price said to me once, "I don't care what scripts you wrote, you don't put it on a shelf." And that's it. *Clockers* is on a shelf. *The Wanderers* is on a shelf. You look at them and say, "I did that."

Steve Boisson is a Los Angeles–based freelance writer whose articles have appeared in *The Boston Globe, Acoustic Guitar, American History,* and many other publications.

68

GEORGE R.R. MARTIN

At the Top of His Game

Rich Shivener

"Sometimes you have to wait."

It's a Tuesday afternoon, and George R.R. Martin is talking about A Song of Ice and Fire, his epic fantasy series that began in 1996 with *A Game of Thrones*, now a hit HBO series of the same name. He knows that fans are clamoring for the series' final two books, *The Winds of Winter* and *A Dream of Spring*, and he knows that a very vocal batch of them want them *now*—rendered impatient by the five-year gap between the third and fourth books and the six-year wait for the 2011 release of the fifth. But they'll have to be patient. After all, the books are heavy volumes, averaging 850 pages.

"I've never been a fast writer, and I've never been good with deadlines … and the vast majority of my fans seem fine with that," Martin says. "I get tons of great letters saying, *All we care about is how good the books are. Take as long as you want.*"

For Martin, the path to best-selling success was not a rush to the finish, either. Early in his career, he wrote short stories and novellas, graduating in 1977 to his first novel, *Dying of the Light*, which garnered Hugo and Locus nominations. He wrote two more to similar praise, but the big commercial failure of his fourth, 1983's *The Armageddon Rag*, soured his outlook on the form, and he shifted his focus to teleplay writing for CBS. There, he penned episodes of *The Twilight Zone* and *Beauty and the Beast*, and between TV gigs edited short story collections and anthologies. All of that work and more, plus a love for medieval history, would ready Martin to return to novel writing and create his magnum opus: A Song of Ice and Fire.

His flagship series about rival kingdoms unravels in a universe riddled with lust, treachery, and family affairs—and has racked up a mountain of accolades and awards along the way. His new home at the top of bestseller lists led *Time* to brand him "The American Tolkien" in 2005; by 2011, he had even earned a spot on *Time's* 100 Most Influential People in the World list.

Martin writes with a certain magic that transcends fantasy and science fiction, roping in audiences far beyond the usual genre boundaries. As a result, the series has transformed the writer into a living pop-culture phenomenon. These days, it can be nearly impossible to catch up with him. Here he's at home, writing the next Ice and Fire books and editing anthologies. Here he's at Comic-Con, posing for a curious Random House photo-op with Fifty Shades author E.L. James. Here he's at BuboniCon. ChiCon. ConQuest. LoneStarCon. ConCarolinas. MystiCon. The Clarion Writers Workshop.

Still, he generously found time to talk with *Writer's Digest* and share some words for writers wondering how they might tap into Martin's kind of magic.

A Song of Ice and Fire has such complex storylines. How do you juggle them so deftly?

With a certain amount of difficulty. Sometimes I think I threw one too many balls in the air, and I rather wish that instead of juggling twelve storylines, I were juggling six. Once you have thrown a ball in the air, you are obliged to keep on juggling it as best as you can. Sometimes this is where rewriting comes in—especially if I neglect something or a contradiction sneaks in. Not to beat the juggling metaphor to death, but it's like I drop the ball and have to pick up the material.

On a good day, how much do you write?

Probably no more than four or five pages. I think on the best day I've ever had in my life I wrote twenty pages, and that was twenty years ago. I'm happy if I can finish a few pages in a day.

The process with the Ice and Fire books involves a great deal of rewriting. The first thing I do when I get up in the morning is pull up what I did yesterday and start revising it, polishing it, and making it a little better. Hopefully, by the time I've dealt with whatever I did yesterday, I've built up some momentum, then I can go in and add some new pages.

Do you spend more time revising and editing than writing?

It's all kind of continuous. I don't write a first draft and then go back and write a second draft. I'm writing new pages as I write old pages; I'm restructuring, etc., etc.

It's interesting for a guy my age to reflect on how different my working methods have become since the seventies, when I was writing everything on a typewriter. There was a great deal less revision then because it was so cumbersome. I think the ease of restructuring and repolishing on a computer leaves one to do more of it.

Are stories ever really finished?

You could always use more time, but sooner or later you have to pry it out of your hands and get it out there. ... The question is, *When* is it finished? I think every writer faces the situation where you're suddenly two weeks away from the book being due, and what do you do? Some writers slap on an ending and work very hard to wrap it up. I decided long ago not to do that. I wish I could make the deadlines, but I'm a slow writer, and I think I'm overoptimistic when I sign contracts. The question is, *When is the book ready? When is the book in the condition that I want it to be in?* That's when I send it in.

A segment of your fans is known for being vocal that you're not releasing books as fast as they'd like. How do you respond to that?

There is really no answer that will satisfy anyone, which is something I learned more than ten years ago. Ultimately, the only thing that is going to matter is how good these books are. If people are still reading me fifty years from now, as they're still reading Tolkien, the people who pick this up in 2070 are not going to be saying, "How long did he take to write these books?" They're just going to be judging if the books are good or not. That's my criteria.

In addition to the hit TV show, *A Game of Thrones* has also been adapted into popular games and even a graphic novel series. Have those adaptations influenced your writing?

They haven't, really. All of these secondary projects—be it the TV series, the critical essays, the games—have their value, and fans seem to enjoy them, but the only canon is the books. The stories have their own demands, and the characters and the worlds are very real to me.

Your prose is often praised for being so vivid, and for its flow. Can you describe how you craft a sentence?

In my first drafts, I tend to be wordy, and then in my final drafts, I tend to be cutting things. I probably overdescribe. I'll write, *John got up from the chair and walked across the room and pulled up the Venetian blinds, then lowered the win-*

dow, latched it, and returned to his chair. Then I change it to, *John got up and closed the window.* [Laughs.]

Your characters are also strikingly multifaceted. What's your best advice for crafting characters?

One of the big things that distinguishes the strongest fiction from writing that's perhaps without depth is a real understanding of what real human beings are like. From my point of view, I don't see heroes and villains; I see very flawed human beings. All of us have good in us; all of us have evil in us. All of us are capable of acts of heroism, acts of selfishness, cowardice, or what we might call villainy. We all have reasons for what we do. You don't just have people who wake up in the morning and say, "What evil things can I do today, because I'm Mr. Evil?" People do things for what they think are justified reasons. Everybody is the hero of their own story, and you have to keep that in mind. If you read a lot of history, as I do, even the worst and most monstrous people thought they were the good guys. We're all very tangled knots.

You've been a faculty member of the Clarion West Writers Workshop. What do you find aspiring fiction writers most often need to focus on improving? Plot? Character?

It really depends on the writer. I do think with a lot of them it's the structure of the stories. You see a lot of young writers who have interesting ideas and a certain skill with words, but their story is not a *story* … it's more a vignette.

Writing is something very hard to teach in the abstract. That's a great virtue of Clarion [which facilitates intense critique sessions with students and instructors]—you're dealing with actual stories. You're not giving general lectures. You're dealing with a specific work of art, and saying what works about this story and what doesn't. It's a great process for pulling people apart and putting them back together so they work better.

Over the course of your career, what have you learned about the business of writing?

The field is constantly changing—that's the one thing about a career in writing. Just when you reach the stage that you understand how publishing works, and how to build your career, then all the rules change. I had it all figured out by 1977, but then the rules changed completely, and they have several times since. And now with e-books and self-publishing, we're seeing another watershed change. It's not a career for someone who likes security. You have to constantly adapt—

whether it's to new modes of publishing or a new subgenre, fashion, or entertainment. A writer needs to be flexible, and I think I am.

You also edit collections and anthologies. What do you look for in a story? What makes a story great?

I think the characters. I think it's the setting, too. I want a story to take me to a place that I've never been to before and make it come vividly alive for me.

I hate stories that are predictable. I want to get engrossed in a story and not know what's going to happen next. I always try to make my own fiction a little unpredictable, and as a reader, I love stories that surprise me and delight me.

Where do you think science fiction and fantasy are heading?

Right now, science fiction is in a down cycle—it has been for a decade, but I think it's coming back. There are some very popular and accomplished young science fiction writers who are bringing back classic space opera, and tales of spaceships and aliens. I think epic fantasy is a major genre, and I think it will continue for quite a while.

How has your experience writing for TV shaped your other work?

As William Goldman said in his book *Adventures in the Screen Trade*, structure is everything. And I think my sense of structure has improved, and so has my ear for dialogue. Writing dialogue that actors are going to have to speak aloud is very different than writing dialogue that just appears on the page. I think my dialogue got sharper, funnier, and better, all told.

Also, the act-break technique that I learned from *Twilight Zone* and *Beauty and the Beast* is a technique I carried over to Ice and Fire. Even though we don't have commercials between the chapters, I do alternate between points of view. I end each chapter with a cliff-hanger, resolution, a turn, a reveal, a new wrinkle … something that will make you want to read the next chapter of that character. But of course you can't, because now you have to read about the other six characters, so you're always anxious to read more. At least, that's the theory.

Where else would you like to take your writing?

I have a lot of other books that I want to write. Science fiction books, fantasy books, horror novels. … I have ideas for hybrids that don't fit anything, and I would like to try something different.

What's the hardest part about writing a series, and this series in particular?

It's all hard. The juggling of all the plotlines and characters is hard, and maintaining the chronology also has some difficulty. Meeting my deadlines is extremely hard, so hard that I haven't done it for years. Fortunately, I have very forgiving editors and publishers who are willing to cut me some slack. ... In the early part of my career, I did everything possible to avoid having deadlines. I wrote my books before I sold them. Nobody even knew I was working on a novel until it was finished, and that worked very well for me.

It doesn't work with a long series like Ice and Fire, unless I wanted to vanish from public sight for twenty years while I finished all seven volumes.

What else is hard? The words are hard. You get these visions in your head of what the scene is going to be. You have a big battle scene, let's say, or a feast, or a lovemaking scene. It doesn't matter what the scene is. You can see it and you can hear it, but you're still staring at a blank screen. That's the nuts and bolts of writing. It's great to see the cathedral, but you still have to build it one stone at a time. A tremendous amount of effort goes into finding the right words.

Rich Shivener is a teacher and journalist based in Cincinnati.

The Complete Handbook of Novel Writing

69

BRAD MELTZER

Walking the Line

Jessica Strawser

If you're a history buff, you might know Brad Meltzer from the two History channel shows he's hosted: *Decoded* (an investigation of unsolved mysteries and conspiracy theories) and *Lost History* (a search for missing artifacts). If you read suspense, perhaps you know him for his legal thrillers (Meltzer has a law degree and was once an intern on Capitol Hill), or for his Culper Ring Series of secrets and symbols in Washington, D.C. (the latest, *The President's Shadow*, was released in June 2015). If you're a parent, it may be the Ordinary People Change the World picture book series that comes to mind (he released four in 2014, including number one bestseller *I Am Amelia Earhart*), or his inspirational collections *Heroes for My Son* and *Heroes for My Daughter*. Or perhaps you're a fan of his comics, inspiring TED Talks, the old WB teen drama *Jack & Bobby* he co-created, or even just his popular Twitter feed.

But no matter what you know Brad Meltzer *from*, if you've seen any of his work, you know Brad Meltzer. It's his passion that's the calling card of everything he writes, and he pours himself into his work with geek-level enthusiasm, an unassuming likability, and good humor. Here, he talks with *Writer's Digest* about jumping fences to greener pastures, keeping yourself hungry, and never letting anyone tell you no.

How do your novels and your History channel shows feed off of one another?

No question, they are just both part of me, and so they can't help but feed each other. Anything that you work on, if you're being honest, shows your personality in it. ...

There are things like the Knights of the Golden Circle that as I started researching them we started seeing them on *Decoded*, and they became characters in *The Fifth Assassin*. You can't help but look at history and find good stories.

In the bigger picture, whether it's my novels, the nonfiction, the kids' books, the comic books, *Decoded*, or *Lost History*, all of them have one thing in common: It's my core belief. I believe *ordinary people change the world.* And I don't care where you went to school or how much money you make—that is utter nonsense to me. I believe in regular people and their ability to affect change on this planet. And so each of those things always reflects that. In that way, they feed each other in the most basic, primal way.

I think that core belief is important for other writers, too, because so many of us work on manuscripts wondering if anyone will ever even see them.

Listen, my first novel still sits on my shelf, published by Kinko's. It got twenty-four rejection letters. There were only twenty publishers at the time—that means some people wrote me twice to make sure I got the point. But I don't look back on that and say, "I was right and they were wrong, ha-ha." Whatever it is you do, my advice is simple: Don't let anyone tell you no.

Was there anyone back then who gave you bad advice?

The only bad advice I got was advice that really I gave myself. And that was [for] my second novel. I had this high-concept idea about Cain and Abel in the modern day, and my editor said, "Are you crazy?" I had just gotten on the bestseller list for a legal thriller, and it was the time of legal thrillers, and they said, "Why would you want to jump into *historical*?"

Between college and law school, I was accruing debt by the moment, and I was terrified that any success was going to go away. So rather than sticking to my guns, I said, "I'll write the kind of book you want me to write." And although I'm proud of the way it came out, I still think it's the one book I'm the most critical of, because I didn't follow my gut. After that, I said, *I'm never doing that again.* And the book after that, when I went back to doing what I wanted to do, wound up being, at that point in time, the best-selling book we ever did.

Writers these days are often advised to create a brand. But you do so many different things. ... Do you feel that's a better course for other writers to pursue?

I wish I knew. None of this is a calculated endeavor. I think if I was smart, I should just write thrillers. Even my publisher will say they just want more thrillers. That's what feeds my family. But I feel like if I did that, I wouldn't be being true to myself. ...

A very famous writer said to me at one point—about his recurring character that was so terrific—he said he wanted to put a gun in his mouth if he had to write him again. I *never* want to be that writer. We all know the grass is always greener, right? Whatever you're doing, anything someone else is doing automatically seems more interesting. So I use the different mediums and I treat it as my own fence, and I get to jump over to the other grass.

Jumping into different genres is what charges me up to do each one. Plus, just the challenge that everyone says you can't. When I did comic books for the first time, people told me, "You're going to wreck your career. You're a novelist, why are you lowering yourself?" And I thought, *What are you talking about?* There's no pyramid with literary fiction at the top and everything else at the bottom. It's a flat line. It's just a matter of how you want to tell your story. And I just like being able to walk across that line.

So how did you end up on the History channel?

I ask myself that question *all the time*. Here's what happened. One of the heads of the History channel read my novel *The Book of Fate* and said, "We want to do a show like that." They liked the name *Decoded*, and they wanted it to be something about the Freemasons. And I said, "That's fine, but that's not a show. That's a setting, I guess. You need stories." And they were like, "Well, do you have stories?" And I'm like, "Yeah, that's all I have!"...

The truth was they wanted me just for my name. I was supposed to just be the guy who introduces the story at the beginning and then at the end said goodbye. And they were doing some kind of promo for the show, and the network kept saying, "We don't like this or this or this, but we want more Brad." My wife kept laughing—she said, "That's the silliest thing I've ever heard." Over time they were like, "You're going to host this thing," and I couldn't help but laugh, either.

Off camera, how much do you drive the content?

I came up with the idea for *Lost History*. I was researching in the National Archives for my novel *The Inner Circle*, and they told me they have a department that tracks down lost and stolen artifacts. And I was like, "What do you mean?

What's gone?" The idea wasn't even really about doing the show, it was about, *How do we get the items back?*

We have a team now that, once the show got greenlit, is helping with the research. (I do all my own research for the novels, but for the TV show I just physically don't have the time.) I'm very particular about the writing, so they send me every episode, and then I put it into my voice.

You're known for doing extensive on-scene research for your novels. How do you soak in those experiences?

I think I'm very good at the full-on experience of how it feels there. I just have a really good memory for what I see. Most of the time I don't even know what I'm looking for. If I knew what I was looking for, I'd know before I got there. You go for a world that interests you, and then you find something else that makes you go, *Oh, that's interesting.* I think the better use of research is talking to people where they develop a trust and tell you their greatest story. If you go in there and you know what you want to write and you just want to write it, then why bother them? But you're there and taking their time because they have something amazing to share, and as a writer, all you're doing is trying to look through someone else's eyes.

You answer a lot of FAQs on your website. Do you tend to get bombarded by questions from readers?

We used to, and then we started putting an author's note [in] each book. People just wanted to know what was real.

I think of how after *The Da Vinci Code*, it seemed as if Dan Brown spent years reminding people it was fiction.

Yeah, and in a strange way he opened that door for all of us. When Dan Brown came out, if I had asked to do Cain and Abel then, they would have said, "Oh, go ahead, everyone loves history!" I think his sales were a huge help for me in terms of convincing editors that you can do real historical research and make it fun. I owe him for that.

Your novel *The President's Shadow* is the third The Culper Ring book. Will the series continue?

This one concludes where we are. The next book will not be a Culper Ring book. I definitely want to do it again, so this certainly is not the last, but after doing three books in a row on the same subject, I feel like trying something new.

The Complete Handbook of Novel Writing

What were the biggest challenges and rewards in continuing with Beecher White's character?

I remember saying I never wanted to do a series. I always thought series were for someone who ran out of ideas and just wanted to milk one forever. And then I had done seven or eight books and just wanted to know, *Can I pull it off?* What I've learned is that the hardest part is, you can't start a book unless that character is going to change in some way. Character is the best plot. What I couldn't figure out for so long is, *How do you keep giving a character an arc and always make it something different, and always make them evolve?*

We meet James Bond and Jason Bourne as superheroes. But what if you meet them when they're novices and the journey is that you get to watch them become that great person? I have no interest in the great person. I have interest in the regular person who finds it within them to have that great moment. So that's what Beecher was for me. But six years in, I think of that character in such a different way, a more complex way. And that's been the best reward.

Are there any other genres you have your eye on?

I definitely want to do young adult. And we did do nonfiction historical writing in *History Decoded*, but I'd love to try a longer form, really tackle one subject.

It seems as if you've built a career on your passions.

Someone years ago sent me a question that said, "I have two ideas for a book. One I think I can sell for a lot of money, and it's fine, but it's pretty by-the-numbers, and the other book is my obsession, which is the druids, but nobody cares about the druids. Which one should I write?" And I said, "You've got to write about the druids." The X factor on every page is, does the writer love what they're writing about? Anything you love that you've read in your life, from page 1, you feel the writer's passion. That's the thing that you can't put your finger on. And when you read Book Ten of a series, and you go, "Man, it's just not as good," it's because the writer just doesn't care anymore. If you want to find your answer as a writer, follow whatever you're passionate about.

You've written about real-life heroes. What sorts of heroes do you think writers in particular should look to?

I think these days, what I admire most in a writer is honesty. When I first became a writer, every interview [with me] was like reading an interview with a rookie sports player: *one game at a time, just happy to be here....* I was the first in my family to attend a four-year college, so the idea that someone was going to buy a book that I wrote was a miracle to me. My dad read seven books in his life—my seven. My mom, the same. I was so thrilled to be able to be a writer that I was terrified to say that life wasn't perfect because it would make me look thankless. And I think if I'm anything over the years, I'm just more honest, and it's okay to say, "This was a hard year—my parents died, and I struggled with this book." I can't say I'm a better writer over time, but I'm certainly a more honest one. I think that's what I admire more these days.

But those aren't real "heroes" to me. If you made the bestseller list, who cares? That doesn't make you a better person. It means nothing. It means people buy your books. The question is, what do you do beyond your God-given gift? Any first-time writer that will e-mail me and say, "Will you help me plug my book?" I'll plug it every time, all the time. Use your power for good. Help other people. To me, that's a hero.

That's so great. If we print that, you'll probably get bombarded, though …

[Laughs.] That's okay. You know what, I don't care. I'd be happy to. When I was starting out, you know how many blurbs I had on my first book? Zero. So if I can help someone and make them feel good to put their book out there, great, that to me is the best use of my Twitter account.

Do you still have doubts about your own work?

Oh, every time. Every day when I sit down to write, the one thing I do is I remember when my true first novel was out there trying to be sold. I went to New York to have these meetings with two editors who were like, "We really like it, we think we're going to buy it," and my agent said, "I'm going to call you tomorrow and tell you how much they're going to pay for it." And I was like, "Oh my gosh, the offers are coming in!" And I picked up the phone and she said to me, "Sorry, kiddo." They both bailed, and the book never sold.

Every day that I sit down to write, in my head I paint that scene again, and I picture that crappy Formica desk, I picture that lint that was floating through the air, I picture the corded phone that was in my hand, I picture every detail of that moment, and then I picture my agent saying to me, "Sorry, kiddo." Because the moment you think you're done, and the moment you think you've made it, you're finished. The best motivator is to remember what it's like to have nothing at all—to keep yourself hungry.

70

JOJO MOYES

....

Going Global

Jessica Strawser

It's always come down to two things for Jojo Moyes: writing and motherhood.

The London native worked as a journalist for ten years, including time at *South China Morning Post* in Hong Kong and *The Independent* in the U.K. But once she and her husband started a family, she aimed for a more manageable work-life balance and decided to try her hand at a different kind of writing. In 2002 her first novel hit U.K. bookshelves, and for almost a decade she made a rather quiet, sustainable living writing books marketed largely to romance readers.

She started drawing more notice—and more mainstream fiction audiences on both sides of the pond—with 2011's *The Last Letter from Your Lover*, an intricately plotted tale of parallel romances spanning decades.

And then, she struck a nerve.

Me Before You was the surprise smash of 2013. It tells the story of plucky, working-class Louisa "Lou" Clark, hired in spite of her total lack of experience to care for Will Traynor, a handsome, adventure-seeking executive paralyzed in a freak accident. As an unlikely bond develops, Lou discovers that what Will wants most in the world is something that will shatter hers. He wants to die. And he wants her help.

Transcending the hot-button right-to-die debate, the book has sold more than *5 million copies worldwide*. In June 2016, it also became a feature film, for which Moyes wrote the screenplay and worked grueling days on set to adapt the script scene by scene. Her subsequent novels, *The Girl You Left Behind* (featuring parallel love stories, set during WWI and in the present, that have a piece of stolen artwork in common) and *One Plus One* (following an ensemble cast on a road trip) have been immediate international bestsellers, and much of her backlist has now been released in the United States.

But it's still *Me Before You* that draws overwhelming volumes of reader mail. And Moyes—now living on a farm in Essex with her husband, a writer for *The Guardian*, and their three children—still personally answers every letter. "Sometimes people are sending you a page of very emotional stuff about their lives, and you can't just say, 'Oh, thanks for reading the book!' You have to answer them properly," she tells *Writer's Digest*. "And I suppose because I was a fairly unsuccessful author for so long, I also feel an obligation because, you know, there's *always* a part of me thinking, *Thank you for buying my book!*"

Now, Moyes has gifted those fans with something more: a sequel. *After You* meets Lou a couple of years after *Me Before You* leaves off. Here, Moyes talks about navigating career turns with grace, relearning to write a novel with every story, and nurturing her books and children above all else.

In a letter to your readers you explain why you wrote this sequel. Why did you feel that an author's note was necessary in this case?

I don't know if it was necessary—it's just that over the last few years I feel like I've developed such a dialogue with the people who read my books that it seemed to make sense to speak to them directly.

I wrote eight books before I wrote [*Me Before You*], and the thing that has really marked this book out for me is the fact that people felt compelled to talk to me about it—and that's been extraordinary. I get e-mails every week, I get tweets, I get Facebook messages, [all] from people who want to talk about their own lives, or about Lou, or how she reflected something in their life, and that's never happened to me before. People had such a fundamentally personal reaction to it that [a letter to readers] felt like a nice way to do it, I guess.

There were readers who voiced some really strong opinions online at just the news of you writing a sequel—ranging from jumping-up-and-down excitement to "You'd better not mess this up!"

That's been terrifying. I have to say, once I committed to the idea of writing a sequel, I thought it was going to be easy. I thought it was just going to be me revisiting these characters that I knew and loved. And what turned out to happen was the absolute opposite of that. Because you're constantly asking yourself, *Is this interesting enough? Does this match up to* Me Before You *enough?* But also you're conscious that readers have really strong opinions about these characters.

The flip side of people feeling very invested in your characters is that they're going to have very strong opinions about what you do with them.

I had to reach a point where I just reconciled myself to the fact that, hopefully a lot of people will love what I did with the book, but there's quite possibly going to be a lot of people who disagree. That doesn't trouble me. What *does* bug me is people who get upset with the *idea* of writing it and try to persuade other people not to read it. Because you just think, *I don't care if you read it and hate it, that's absolutely your prerogative, but don't give me one star because you don't like the* idea *of it! That's not on!* [Laughs.]

At any point in writing *After You* did you start thinking, *I don't know if this story is going to come together*?
Oh, sure. I wrote the first three chapters again and again over a period of several months. Originally Lou was a paramedic. But the tone of the book went missing—it felt like I was writing a medical drama rather than Lou's story. And I had to reach a point where I gave up on the idea of her having that job, and once I did, and once I hit on the idea of [her working at] the airport, her life suddenly made sense to me again.

Frequently I will write chapters that I end up having to ditch. And they might be beautifully crafted, they might contain things I'm really proud of, but you have to be ruthless. There comes a point when you know in your gut something just isn't working or isn't as good as it should be. What I've found over the years is that I've never regretted anything I've ditched—I've only regretted stuff I've left in.

I think some people assume that once you're multipublished the manuscripts just flow out of you.
No—I think it gets harder. You know, when I wrote *Me Before You*, I was between contracts. I had a small, loyal readership, but I'd never troubled the best-seller charts. I don't think anyone would have really jumped over themselves to see what I wrote—and that actually was quite liberating. Because I could write the exact story that I wanted to write. I didn't think about how anybody would receive it. My husband and I used to joke that *Me Before You* was going to be the book that finished my career entirely because of the [controversial] subject matter. And I just wrote the book that I wanted to write.

What happened with *After You* was I kept feeling the weight of expectation. And that was new for me.

How much of the plot do you know before you begin?

I do outline. I'm always amazed by these people who say that they just start and see where the story takes them. That makes me actually kind of [shake] with fear—I couldn't do it. So yeah, when I say I ripped up three chapters, I ripped up three chapters of written work, but then I had to replot the entire book, because I had to work out who she was if she wasn't a paramedic. I ripped up an entire book.

For anybody who thinks that you can just suddenly work out HOW TO WRITE, in capital letters, and get on with it: Every time I start a book, I think, *I have no idea how I did this the last time. No idea.* All you can do is rely on your tricks. I always say to myself, "I'll write the first chapter, and I'll probably get rid of it at some point, but at least it will get me writing." Because sometimes you don't know your characters until you're a third of the way into the book, or two-thirds in, and then you have to rejig the existing book. But I have confidence tricks that I play on myself just to get me going. And sometimes you have to do that. This time my editor and my agent got quite firm with me at one point because I was so worried about it. I think my editor's phrase was, "Stop thinking and get writing."

So what is your process? If you diverge from your outline, do you stop and re-outline, or keep going?

It varies, but in general I have a vague outline, a rough plot, and then I have themes that I want to look at within that plot, so my subplots and possibly even the main plot will be informed by what I think the book is actually about. Often I'll tape the phrase "What is this really about?" over the top of the monitor so that I don't lose sight of that. So I try to keep those two things in my head all the time, and the reason I think for quite a long time before I start work is because they often won't marry.

After You, for example—yes, it's about Lou moving on with her life, and whether she'll find love with someone else, and how much responsibility she shows to somebody linked to Will's past, but it also is about the cost of individual decisions. In a world where we're told to follow our dream and do what we want to fulfill ourselves, what is the impact on the people left to cope with that decision, whether it's the children of divorcing parents, or a mother who had done nothing but look after her family for forty years and suddenly decides that she'd like to try something else? Although they may seem like disparate plot points, I try to make sure there is a current running through them.

It seems fortunate if a writer can hit on concepts from which to grow a story rather than one single plot idea, or even a character, because there are so many ways you can approach them.

It's interesting to me that my books only really took off once I started to view them in that way. And maybe I'm somebody that just had to teach herself as she went along. But [*The Last Letter from Your Lover* was] the first book where I really started to look at that. And since I've really been thinking it through in that way—and quite a calculated way—before I start, either my books have really improved or people have just responded better to them, I'm not sure.

How does your background as a journalist influence your fiction writing?

I think the first thing is the ability to see stories. You learn to use your antennae. I can see stories pretty much everywhere. I just think it gives you that way of looking at the world. The other thing is it teaches you to work everywhere—you're not precious about waiting for a muse. I work on train station platforms, departure lounges, you name it. I'm happy to just get my laptop out and hunch over and get to work. But also I'm quite good at meeting deadlines. I have a very high work ethic, because I love what I'm doing, so it makes it easy.

How do you think you've grown as a writer?

I *hope* I've gotten better. I think I've gotten better at analyzing what is working and what is not working. I have a litmus test where, for example, if I'm writing a very emotional scene, I know that if I'm not laughing or crying at my own work, the reader isn't going to. I've tested this by asking people—*Where did you laugh? Where did you cry?*—and it's always the pages where I did. And I'm pretty ruthless about stripping stuff out. I've only started using humor in my books since *Me Before You*, but I think I've discovered that I like using humor and that it's a useful foil to the more depressing aspects of a book. So I don't know really. But it's nice to get bigger sales finally! [Laughs.] It took a long time.

Are there any secrets you've discovered to writing humor in a way that adds warmth to a tough scene?

I feel like I'm still learning that one. It can be really hard. I think part of it's your mood. My biggest tip for writing is: If you get stuck, move forward to a scene that you're looking forward to working, and that just tends to give you your joy back. And then often you'll find that the space between them is actually a lot smaller than you thought it was, and maybe a kind of easier way to work it.

The thing I've *really* learned is the importance of leaving time between finishing your book and then going back to it before sending it off. Because you see the holes in a way that you just can't see when you're up close to it. In fact, it's one of the reasons why I find it very hard to read the books that I've written, because all I can see is the faults—they become so clear to me that I just want to howl and say, "Why did anybody let that through? It's just awful!"

So what is your revision process, exactly?

Well, I don't have an exact one—I just revise *all the time*. I might write 1,000 words one day and delete 999 the next. I'm not somebody who can craft a perfect sentence. I try to hit on the emotional truth of a scene, and then after that I'll just keep polishing until the language feels right.

Earlier in your career you talked a lot about the challenges of juggling raising kids with your writing time. Has that balance changed at all in recent years?

It's a *constant* struggle, and it's one that I never feel I quite get right. I've grown to accept maternal guilt as something that comes with success, and what I try to do is make sure that I carve out enough time and special little events with the kids so they feel there are some advantages to me doing what I do and not just disadvantages.

I have a really supportive husband. I have help at home. I heard a saying awhile ago—I can't remember who said it, but it was somebody I admired, and she said, "If you have children, you can only do one other thing well." That stuck with me. So I try to write well. And I am unapologetic about contracting stuff out. I hate this pretense that women can do it all, because you can't. Or you can, but you end up tearing your hair out, and that's no good for anybody.

Work out what you want to do most, other than work. For me it was literally sitting on the sofa giving my kids a cuddle. I felt like there were two years where all I said to them was, "In a minute," "I just have to do this," "I just have to do something else," and I hated the sound of my own voice. And I thought, *What are they going to remember from this? That Mom was always working?* No. So I don't do the other stuff anymore. And that's one of the benefits of success.

71

ANNE RICE AND CHRISTOPHER RICE

....

Blood Bond

Zachary Petit

If you try to envision the family tree of mother-and-son bestsellers Anne and Christopher Rice, it might seem fitting to picture, say, a live oak—one of those great, gorgeous Southern behemoths they both grew up under in New Orleans, the same moss-draped giants that occasionally populate their novels.

But if you were to envision their lives as writers, they might seem to have come from different seeds entirely. Consider:

Anne's initial subject matter: Vampires. Erotica. Christopher's: Crime. Gritty mystery.

Her writing style: Elaborate, ornate, philosophical. His: Stark, unembellished, masculine.

Her first book: the iconic *Interview with the Vampire*, published when she was an unknown thirty-four-year-old. His: the best-selling *A Density of Souls*, published when he was a *known* twenty-two-year-old. Neither had an easy start, and their writing lives began—and evolved—quite differently.

Anne was born in New Orleans. (Her father, Howard O'Brien, also wrote some fiction.) Anne moved West, and along the way married the poet Stan Rice. Her defining moment as an author came when she was in the Ph.D. track at the University of California, Berkeley, and found herself alienated within the program and bored with an essay she was reading on Stendhal. "I thought, *I really want to be a writer—not study other writers*," she recalls.

She switched to a master's in creative writing. And then her life changed: The year she graduated, 1972, her five-year-old daughter died of leukemia. In an often-told story, Anne retreated to her writing. The eventual result: *Interview with the Vampire*. She met her agent at the Squaw Valley Writer's Conference, and the book sold and was later released in 1976.

Christopher was born two years later. He attended Brown University and the Tisch School of the Arts but left to take a crack at screenwriting. He "joined the family business," as Anne says, when he wrote *A Density of Souls*. He showed it to his father, who said the book would change his life. Stan was right—Anne sent it to her agent, and it launched Christopher's writing career.

Christopher is often branded "the son of Anne Rice," but that hasn't stopped him from writing critically-lauded books. He's also often pegged simply as a "gay writer" (despite the fact that some of his protagonists have been both straight and female), but that hasn't stopped him from achieving mainstream success. All of his subsequent thrillers—*The Snow Garden*, *Light Before Day* (which Lee Child deemed a "book of the year"), *Blind Fall*, and *The Moonlit Earth*—went on to become hits. He had four bestsellers by the age of thirty.

As for Anne, she moved home in the 1980s and became a legend of New Orleans, and over the years she followed *Interview* with eleven more vampire novels, the Lives of the Mayfair Witches trilogy, pseudonymously-penned erotica (the Sleeping Beauty Trilogy), and other books. To date, she has sold more than 100 million copies of her work. (Along the way she even helped her sister, the late Alice Borchardt, launch her own historical fiction/paranormal writing career.)

In the late 1990s, Anne made a much-publicized return to the Roman Catholic Church and said she'd dedicate all of her future writing output to God. She released two novels in her Christ the Lord series in 2005 and 2008, but had an equally much-publicized withdraw from the church in 2010.

Regardless of her beliefs, Anne's impact on modern fiction—especially when it comes to the supernatural genre—is deep and undeniable. Following the death of her husband, she left New Orleans in 2005, partly to be closer to Christopher. The two now each reside in California. *Writer's Digest* met up with them in New York at ThrillerFest 2013, where Anne was accepting the award of ThrillerMaster—the International Thriller Writer's lifetime achievement honor.

In person, as on the page, Anne and Christopher might seem as different as they come.

But on that family tree, on that live oak, all the branches trace back to the same massive, unshakable base, that deep-seated root system that includes Howard, Stan, Alice, all of them. They're *writers*. They're family.

The Complete Handbook of Novel Writing

And Anne's and Christopher's branches have, after all, finally intertwined: For the first time, mother and son are sharing a release date. In October 2013, Anne returned with a new supernatural novel—*The Wolves of Midwinter*, the sequel to her 2012 werewolf bestseller *The Wolf Gift*—and Christopher released his first, *The Heavens Rise*.

On the following pages, they discuss what led them to this intersection—and the importance of following your own path in the writing world.

Christopher, you've previously said you would never touch the supernatural, and Anne, you've said you would never go back to it. [Laughter.] What changed?

ANNE: Well, that's really kind of a long story. I did at one point say I would never go back to the despairing, dark supernatural novels that I [wrote], and I don't know that I ever will. I think any supernatural novels that I write now will not be dark and despairing. And I don't think *The Wolf Gift* and *The Wolves of Midwinter* are dark and despairing. They're much more upbeat; it's a different tone, so I like to believe I'm being faithful to what I said, and I'm doing something new. And you can see from the responses that some people don't care for *The Wolf Gift* and my new hero, Reuben, because they want the more dark, troubled, despairing heroes that I wrote about in the past. But *I'm* loving [the series].

Also, another thing happened. Werewolves were always off limits to me because my sister had written about them—Alice Borchardt—she'd written three different novels with werewolves, and we lost Alice in 2007, and about two years ago a friend, Jeff Eastin, the TV producer who does *White Collar* and *Graceland*, he actually suggested to me that I do a werewolf book. And for the first time I thought, *Well, maybe I can do it; we've lost Alice, we have her books, and we'll always have them, but she's not working in that field anymore.* She had never asked me, by the way, not to write about them—it was all in my brain that I wouldn't. So I started thinking about it, and I started seeing a completely new approach to the material, and that's why I went back. And frankly, I just wanted to go back. I mean, I love writing about the supernatural. Even when I was writing my books about Jesus Christ, they were really about the supernatural.

CHRISTOPHER: I said for the first few years that I didn't want to do anything supernatural, and then I began to come up with ideas for supernatural books and was actively discouraged from pursuing them by people in publishing. There was really a belief that I needed to assert myself as something more distinct from [my mother], and [as] a mystery and thriller writer. And I got sick of being told "No," really, is what happened. The inception of *The Heavens Rise* had to do with this character Niquette Delongpre, who I knew was missing, who I knew cast this shadow over everyone who had loved her and cared about her, and I couldn't figure out in a real-world setting: What was it about her that had led her to go? I mean, was she a drug addict? I'd written so many stories about drug addicts at that point, I was just tired of it. And then it clicked: She's got a gift. She's got a supernatural ability that she doesn't want to reveal to the world around her, and so she's living in shadows and isolation. And the story began to catch fire. It was related to character for me, more than anything else. But I think all of the supernatural ideas that I'm interested in pursuing are pretty down here on earth. They're pretty muddy, if you get the term. The focus is definitely on the human characters contending with the intrusion of a supernatural force into their ordinary world.

If you had to pinpoint one key that differentiates good supernatural writing from bad supernatural writing, what would it be?

ANNE: One has to write about the details pertaining to the supernatural as precisely and realistically as one writes about the details about ordinary life. The ordinary and the extraordinary have to be written with the same attention to detail. That's what makes good supernatural writing. You can't suddenly change your writing to something airy and lofty-sounding when you confront the vampire or the witch or so forth; you have to describe that person just as meticulously and scrupulously so that the whole thing has the feeling of reality. Because that's the way I see it and feel it—as reality. But when I approach other people's writing and I see a sudden shift, you know, it's like a gauzy filter has gone over the camera lens because the supernatural character's on the stage. It's not convincing.

CHRISTOPHER: They say a similar thing about action scenes in thrillers that aren't supernatural—that you have to be as literal and as descriptive as you would be of anything else in the book, and that the temptation is to make the language florid and over the top in those moments. Your commitment is to display, you know, to bring the reader in. I think that's an important element, too. It's absolute commitment, is what I think she just described. Absolute commitment.

ANNE: That's it, yeah—absolute commitment. The supernatural is as real to me as anything else in the novel.

Looking at your bodies of work, you've both moved around to different genres. Do you think it's good for a writer to play in different genre sandboxes?

CHRISTOPHER: Well, your publisher never wants you to play in different sandboxes. That's the thing: They have a track for you that they think they've figured out in advance. And there are great stories of writers—like Ken Follett, being told *Pillars of the Earth* was a terrible idea, and he should never do it, and then he goes and he does it and it's a great idea. I think you could tell the same story about [Anne's] first Christ the Lord book—

ANNE: Oh yeah, yeah. But one thing about [my publisher Alfred A.] Knopf, is they've always prided themselves on publishing distinguished voices, and they would never say, "Don't do what you want to do." It might enter into business negotiations with an agent—she might say, "There will be more money on the table if you agree to do another vampire novel," or something like that—but I mean, that's the agent's job, to talk like that. … You know, it was wonderful when I reached the point where they didn't ask me for any pages. Because they'd never *see* it. I mean, you can give them the best idea in the world, [and they say], "Well, I don't know, where are you gonna go with that?" When *Interview with the Vampire* was just a manuscript, I took it to a couple of writers' groups where friends invited me just to sit in, and they read a chunk of it. And I remember them saying, "Well, I don't know where you can go with this idea for three hundred pages—how are you going to ever sustain this?"

CHRISTOPHER: At some point you have to say, "I'm the writer, it's my job to figure out where I'm going to go with it," you know? [Laughter.]

ANNE: I don't think we should discuss ideas. I think we should just write, and then go in with the book and say, "Here's the book." Now, sometimes you have to say something. But I wouldn't listen to what they say back—because they're not prophets. … Agents particularly are really not in the business of being prophetic. They know what *has worked*, and that's it.

CHRISTOPHER: Right. With *The Heavens Rise*, I went off and wrote it on my own, in large part because I had heard this. And it was the best course of action because I know along the way they would have said critical things that would have thrown me off my game.

ANNE: You've got to protect your voice and your vision from everybody, really. Even the best-intentioned editors. And I mean, I love my editor; I've been with Vicky Wilson for over thirty-five years. She's wonderful, and her remarks on the finished manuscript are always terrific. But I don't go to her to discuss a germinating idea.

CHRISTOPHER: You learn, as I think she's describing, the ways in which different types of people in the business respond to writing. There's a way that agents respond. ... Then there's a way that other writers respond, which is they'll just tell you how they would have written it themselves. And if they're a romance writer, their opinion of your horror novel isn't going to be that helpful. But it's not that you don't necessarily engage those people, it's just [that] you learn the filter by which you're going to assess their feedback.

Anne, critics and readers have focused heavily on your religious shift and your shifts in subject matter. Do you think that's something they should care about?

ANNE: I think it's caused a lot of confusion for my audience. I wish that I had never discussed my personal beliefs. I didn't actually plan to; I went out with Christ the Lord in the marketplace and I found that the questions were inevitable—they were unavoidable. "Do you believe in him yourself?" And I ended up answering them, and with pleasure. But it was a mistake. Because really it's nobody's business what you believe. The book should stand on its own. ...

In terms of craft advice, it's constantly said that writers should write every day. Anne, I've read that you don't.

ANNE: I don't think there's any rule. I don't write sometimes for months. Of course, I write e-mails every day. I write in my diary every day. I may not touch the manuscript at all, or anything pertaining to it. And I was discouraged very early in my college years by people who told me I wasn't a real writer because I didn't write every day. Things like that should not be said. And anybody who says anything to you like that, you have to ignore them. You know, there are no rules. Whether [or not] I hit the keyboard, I'm writing in my head. I'm working on my books all the time. I write best in short, intense periods. A period, say, of three or four months—very intense work. And then I draw back and I read, and I do other things. Again, I don't think there's any rule to any of this. It's the greatest profession because you do it all in your own way.

CHRISTOPHER: I think [writing every day is] a very limited piece of advice. I'm working on different things. I have an Internet radio show ["The Dinner Party Show"] that has forty-five minutes of scripted content, so when I go into the studio to record it, am I not writing? If you have a mono-focus on getting a specific novel out, or getting novel after novel after novel out, that's fine, but what we consider writing—and I think if you really interrogate writers about this, what they consider writing, or part of their workday—is pretty inclusive. And it should be. You know, making yourself a slave to a daily word count is a bad thing, in my opinion. And I think you should be flexible with yourself because if you set the bar too high, you'll have an experience like she described, feeling like, *Well, I [didn't] make it, I shouldn't even try if I'm not going to hit these benchmarks.*

ANNE: People have been telling me ever since I can remember that I'm not a real writer. Sophomore in college, the teacher said the fact that I wrote on a typewriter meant that I wasn't a real writer. [Laughter.] She said, "Real writers actually write with pen in hand." [Laughter.] I've been told all my life that I was not a writer! I just marvel at it.

CHRISTOPHER: So was James Lee Burke. James Lee Burke was told that his grammar was simply too bad.

At this stage in each of your careers, what do you find to be the hardest aspect of the craft?

CHRISTOPHER: The isolation and the loneliness.

ANNE: The voice. It's really hard for me. I can see the whole novel and don't know if I have to go in in first person or third person. That's the biggest problem for me, is the beginning—getting into the story. I can see the whole thing. The whole shape, all the characters, what they're doing, and I can't seem to find a way to break in. And I rewrite the opening pages over and over and over again. It's like OCD—it's like hand washing. And finally I get so frustrated that I go and pick up something like *The Godfather* by Mario Puzo, which is great storytelling, but just any way he wants to do it. I mean, he may introduce Luca Brasi here, and never get to physically describing him until fifty pages later, to never get to telling who he really is until one hundred pages after that. And that clears up my OCD. *Okay, just plunge—just start. Just go.*

And so how do you know when you have it right? Is it just a feeling?

ANNE: I force myself, finally. I just despair and say, "Okay"—

CHRISTOPHER: But do you ever know? I never know. I just know when I haven't stopped.

ANNE: I know when it starts rolling, when I've got two or three hundred pages in, and it's really rolling, and I know then that I'm not going to quit. But the first hundred pages are the hardest to complete without quitting.

What's the biggest lesson of the craft that you've learned from each other?

ANNE: I've been inspired from the beginning by Christopher's ability to use the third person—to write in the third person and to write from the point of view of many different characters. I'm always trying to learn that because I always fall back on one point of view. It's almost compulsive. And even in a book like *The Witching Hour* I only had a few points of view that I was working with, and then it would have to be for the whole chapter. But Christopher, that freedom to just range, and the characters' reactions on both sides of a conversation, I really find that inspiring. …

And also, Christopher has a really great ability to write about what's happening to him immediately. With me there was always quite a delay; several years had to pass before I could write about something, and there was always a symbolic remove—I might set the story in the eighteenth century. But he had this ability to just write about New Orleans, write about the high school he went to, write about college, write about the town, and I'm trying to learn from that.

CHRISTOPHER: It's her commitment and her fearlessness. It really is. It's her absolute commitment that's constantly, constantly inspiring, and her lack of cynicism in everything that she writes. And her ability to love her characters, which a lot of writers don't have—it's very easy to hate our own characters, and to punish them and to set them up to fail and all of that. And [her] incorporation of scholarship into an intricately constructed supernatural world.

All of the things that everyone else loves her for are the things that have inspired me as a writer. Obviously I know her as a mother as well, but the things that are extraordinary about her work are encouraging to me. And they're encouraging to me even as I don't seek to emulate her. They're like counterbalances on what my instincts are. Like, don't go for the cheap laugh line in this scene, go for the emotional core of what's happening with these two people, even if they aren't human. I think that's incredibly inspiring. There's the content side of it and then there's the work ethic side of it. Even though she says things like she "hasn't written for months," her work ethic is incredible. She's constantly engaged in a kind of study that feeds everything that she's ever written. And there was always a sense that—well, I'll put it this way: The number one piece of advice she gave me was, *Write the book you want to read.* And if you're not writing the book you want to read—

ANNE: Something's wrong.

CHRISTOPHER: Something's wrong. Like, what's your agenda, pal? Are you trying to win an award because you think it'll make you look cool? And the reason her story overall is so inspiring is because it's similar to so many other success stories, where everybody said, "What were you thinking?" I mean, when she went into writers' workshops in the Bay Area in the 1970s and wanted to write about vampires, they thought she was crackers. And yet here she is, having reinvented this entire genre, with a whole issue of *Entertainment Weekly* full of contemporary vampire writers saying it's all because of her—

ANNE: They aren't all saying that.

CHRISTOPHER: They did. They totally did. It was like the Anne Rice issue. And yet, everybody along the way told her that it was a foolish endeavor. And I think that's what's inspiring. It gets back to that William Goldman line about the film industry: *Nobody knows anything about what's going to work.* Nobody does. And so the only choices you have are to commit fully to what you love and what you are passionate about, and to that book that you want to read.

Christopher, what would you like to accomplish in your career before all is said and done?

CHRISTOPHER: Well, I love the movie industry and I would still like to work in the movie industry, and I have some things that are developing on that front. … So there's always that. But I'm not going to throw all my chips [in any] hat and wait fifteen years for something to get made. I feel very situated in the supernatural genre now. I have a lot of different stories I want to tell. I feel like a new doorway has opened. I feel like I did a lot of different things over the course of three really true detective mysteries, and I'm not saying I'll never write a mystery again, but I think this is the beginning of something for me that excites me.

Anne, what do you want your legacy to be?

ANNE: Oh, boy. All of the books I've written, I guess. You know, all of it. I go book by book, and I hope my best books are ahead of me. I want to keep going; I want to do a lot of different things. I think I've done as much erotica as I want to do, and I do want at some point to do a Christ the Lord book, the third one, to sort of finish the trilogy. But I think it's going to be very difficult to do that, and it may be a very long time before I try it, and it may not happen. But, I'm just as excited about the next book as I ever was. I want to keep trying things and doing things. I want to write a lot more about ghosts.

Would you ever do more installments of your classic vampire series?

ANNE: I wouldn't say no to anything. …

Is there anything either of you would like to add about the craft or the writing life overall?

ANNE: Protect your voice and your vision. Protect it—and if going on the Internet and reading Internet reviews is bad for you, don't do it. [Laughter.] It's awfully rough right now. It's a jungle out there.

Do what gets you to write, and not what blocks you. And no matter where you are in your career, whether you're published, unpublished, or just starting out, walk through the world as a writer. That's who you are, and that's what you want to be, and don't take any guff off anybody.

72

JANE SMILEY

....

Smart Luck

Adrienne Crezo

Since Jane Smiley's 1980 debut novel, *Barn Blind* (an American pastoral centered on a family fraught with clashing ambitions), and through and beyond her 1992 Pulitzer Prize–winning *A Thousand Acres* (a modern American reinterpretation of *King Lear*), she's been a self-proclaimed fiddler—a writer who toys with form, plucks at connective threads, and pulls notes from history both near and ancient. This fiddling, says Smiley, comes from a deep sense of curiosity. And that curiosity shines through as she talks: *Interesting, think, know, learn,* and *understand* are words she uses frequently in conversation, and it's apparent in her body of work that she has a broad range of interests.

The Iowa Writers' Workshop alumna and former Iowa Writers' Workshop professor has written twenty-one books of fiction of seemingly every variety, including a series of young adult novels (Horses of Oak Valley Ranch), a murder mystery (*Duplicate Keys*), historical fiction (*The All-True Travels and Adventures of Lidie Newton; Private Life*), humor (*Moo; Horse Heaven*), a Norse epic (*The Greenlanders*), contemporary fiction (*Good Faith; Ten Days in the Hills*), short stories (*The Age of Grief*), and novellas (*Ordinary Love and Good Will*).

Smiley has also written nonfiction works about everything from mountain-town artisans (*Catskill Crafts*) to horses (*A Year at the Races*) to famous figures (*The Man Who Invented the Computer: The Biography of John Atanasoff, Digital Pioneer*) to the challenge and evolution of writing (*13 Ways of Looking at the Novel*).

And now, for the first time, Smiley has written a literary trilogy. The three books of The Last Hundred Years, each equal in length and span of time, follow the Langdon family and their five children (Frank, the character Smiley describes as "probably the protagonist—he would say that he is, anyway," Joe, Lillian, Henry, and Claire) from 1920 through 2019—from their farm in Iowa to a handful of major American cities and far-flung countries, and through the births and marriages and deaths of some forty characters—as the world experiences war, economic flux, social upheaval, and climate change. The saga begins with 2014's *Some Luck* (fans of *A Thousand Acres* will recognize the Denby, Iowa, location), continues in April 2015's *Early Warning* and concludes with *Golden Age*, released in October 2015. All three books were immediate bestsellers.

What will the Langdon family's future hold—or the author's own? Here, Smiley speaks with us about the trilogy, the craft, how publishing has changed since she started, and why she's the luckiest woman she knows.

In The Last Hundred Years, each chapter covers one year, and the three books encompass a full century. That's an ambitious project. What inspired the idea?

The idea started with the title of the trilogy, and so out of that the structure came. … I wanted the characters all to come and go and to be equal in some sense.

I wanted to have each year be equal over the course of one hundred years. I didn't want to give any extra importance or weight to any particular year. And then I wanted to weave the stories into the years. It may be that somebody else has done that, but I haven't read any books that have done that. I thought it would be an interesting concept, and I wanted to see where it led.

I hope it's a new idea. It didn't start out as a new or daring idea. It just started out as *Let's try it*, you know? *Let's see what happens.* And then I got drawn in by the characters and their relationships with one another and I stuck with the form because I found the form interesting, but the ways that the characters talked and interacted with one another really drove me forward. I really did want to see what they did and I really did want to see how they related to one another and what sort of families they had and what sort of lives they built, and it was incredibly fun. You know, some books are more fun than others, and this one was incredible amounts of fun.

What was your process for choosing which parts of history to touch on?

I read a lot of the history, and some of it was very detailed. My main goal was to give each character certain characteristics, and then to set them up. And then I sort of sent them out into the world. I did my best to understand the world that they were going out into, and then I had them react to it according to their individual temperament and other experiences. So of course Frank, who's quite well coordinated and brave and quite daring, and you might say a little self-involved—he's going to go out into the world differently from his brother Joe. I didn't quite know how it was going to turn out. I mean, I knew what the history was in general, so I knew what they were going to have to deal with, but a lot of stuff just cropped up.

How did you handle the years 2015 through 2019 in *Golden Age*?

Well, I fiddled. I kept fiddling all along. My main concern in these books, I would have to say, because it starts on the farm, is climate, weather—those kinds of issues. I think it's pretty clear what our future is in terms of climate and weather issues. So I fiddled a little bit with the details, and I did make a president in the 2016 election. We'll see if I'm right or not. We'll see. … I thought it was time to try it out. Basically, you know, make it work—predict a little bit of the future and see if I was right. I went back and forth and back and forth and back and forth on what I should do with the future.

You've had a long, varied, successful publishing career. Do you feel as if the industry has changed too much for new writers to achieve similar success?

You know, I don't really have any idea. You'd have to ask my friends from the Iowa Writers' Workshop if they felt that. Some of us have been very successful, some of us have been not so successful, some of us gave it up long ago, some of us are still working at it. I think we had one advantage, which was that publishing wasn't such a big deal. It was very diverse in terms of how many companies were publishing books. There was a big small-press presence, and so there were a lot of entry doors. And most of the entry doors were very small.

My best friend, who was in the Iowa Writers' Workshop with me, moved to New York and became an editor. She was a very promising writer, but she decided she didn't want to write books, so she gave up writing and became an assistant editor. Her boss liked her a lot and he gave her a certain amount of freedom, and so he let her publish a couple of my books. And that gave me the entry that I needed. And those were [what I think of as] "practice books" and I was no big deal, and every so often I would get a pat on the head and it was a wonderful thing to do. So that was a good way [to get started] in *those* days.

These days, the entry doors are a little bit different, but there are still ways in, not only through publishing but also through self-publishing. So the real question is not *Can I get published?* but *Can I make any money?* And nobody knows the answer to that. That's a thing that you can only discover retrospectively. And if you're lucky you can say, *Well, I guess I did*, and if you're not so lucky, you can say, *Well, I guess I didn't*.

But I don't have any advice, really, because it's not just that the publishing world has changed since I started, it's that the publishing world is always changing. There was an article by the writer Chris Offutt about his dad, who wrote hack porn for years. I think it was on the order of hundreds of novels, and [at that time] there were people who wrote hack mysteries, and there were people who wrote other kinds of popular novels, and those [all] went by the wayside. When Dickens started, he serialized his books in magazines, and then *that* went by the wayside.

To me, what is really important is that there seems to be a persistent audience for reading books, for reading novels. Hooray, you know? As long as there's a persistent audience for reading novels, then there's going to be some way for them to be published.

Do you think it's easier now to find a writing community than it was pre-Internet?

My daughter works at Book Country [Penguin Random's online writing community, bookcountry.com]. I feel compelled to ask her advice. Book Country is a really interesting website because it's like an online writers workshop. You can just go on and connect with people and read things and learn from it and get advice. I think it's fascinating, and I'm glad she works there, and I think she's learning a lot. I try to get advice from *her*; she doesn't get advice from *me*. [Laughs.]

It seems to me that the history of writing is closely connected to the history of people being able to find a community that helps them write work, learn from each other's work, and understand their own work. It's very rare that a person just shows up and they've got a book and they wrote it all on their own and they don't know anybody. Usually the first thing they do is get into a social system or social group that is interested in writing. Those people encourage you and give you the criticism that you need. That's the way it happened with Shakespeare, that's the way it happened with Virginia Woolf, that's the way it happened with Charles Dickens. It's good for you to do that, especially when you're young; that way, you are eased into the literary world, and you always feel connected to people around you, and you always feel that you're learning from people around you.

It is inevitable in our world that people are going to do this on the Internet. Is that better? Is that worse? I have no idea. It's just another form of something that's been going on since Athens. Literature is a form of communication. When we first start—whether it's in a workshop or hanging out by the Parthenon—it's because we want to communicate. We just modify our ways of communicating as the world changes. The tool changes, but the desire to communicate, the desire to tell stories, that seems to be continuous.

You called your early novels "practice books."

Yes! I was so lucky. I'm a big fan of Anthony Trollope, and one of my favorite novels of his is one called *The Kellys and the O'Kellys*, which he wrote when he was in Ireland, and it sold very poorly in England. Both of his Irish novels, *The Kellys and the O'Kellys* and *The Macdermots of Ballycloran*, sold very poorly. And yet he got the chance to write those novels in obscurity. … I realized that he had had a mildly similar experience to mine. He got to write a couple of novels, he got them published, he got a few readers, he got that sense of how to do it. And then when he went on to write *The Warden*, he already kind of knew what he was doing because he had gotten those practice novels.

I think it's harder—I don't know from my own experience, but it looks like from the outside—that it's harder if you strike a big success with your first book, because what do you know? You don't know nothin'. And then the pressure is on you. The great thing about your practice novels is that there's no pressure. Nobody cares. And so you get to do the best you can and learn from it, rather than having a big, hit novel.

You're hoping to improve, but eventually, or at least in my case, you're doing what you want to do because you're curious about that idea. My motivation for writing has always been curiosity. I prefer to write about things that I know a little about, but not a whole lot about. Then when I write the novel, it becomes completely interesting to me because I'm finding out about things I didn't know before.

When I was first starting out, pretty early on, I came up with several ideas. And then I worked out those ideas as I grew into them. I had the idea for *The Greenlanders* years before I started it, but I knew that I wasn't going to be able to do it because I didn't have the skills. One of my practice novels is a murder mystery—*Duplicate Keys*. … I'd read a lot of murder mysteries when I was a kid, especially Agatha Christie, and so I knew that if I worked on a murder mystery that I would be able to learn how to do a plot. Once I had done that, I felt as if I had at least a little more knowledge. And so then I felt I could contemplate *The Greenlanders* more.

A *Thousand Acres* gets a lot of attention, even twenty-four years after it won the Pulitzer and so many books later. Do you feel it's your best work?

I don't ever say "best." I think it's all personal. So for me, it's not *What's your best?* but *What's your favorite?* Because you can't be objective. It all depends on what suits you. I don't believe in "best" lists. I just think it's all a personal choice. I would say that I'm quite fond of *The Greenlanders*, I'm quite fond of *Horse Heaven*. I love *Moo*. Comic novels never get to be "the best" because their audience is always quite particular—much more particular. And I also love *Early Warning*.

I don't think too much about *A Thousand Acres*. I understand that I've been lucky. If you're lucky, it gets better and better.

Do you feel lucky?

Absolutely! How could you not? I mean, the biggest piece of luck is that you get to do what you want, and once you get to do what you want, then you are defined as lucky. And in some ways, that is the definition of success, as far as I'm concerned. You're lucky if you don't have to subordinate the things you want to do in order to survive.

Of course I understand that it's luck. But I'm not going to walk away from it for that reason. ... I understand that I've been lucky and that my job is to continue on and keep going.

73

GARTH STEIN

....
Illuminated

Jessica Strawser

Garth Stein has never been a stranger to small audiences. He's stage-managed "theater at sea" on cruise ships. He's written stage plays produced by community theaters. He's made documentary films. He's written well-reviewed novels published by independent presses. Put it all together, and he's done the very thing so many people aspire to do but so few accomplish: simply make a living by making art.

And then, he did what some might imagine to be the equivalent of literary suicide: He wrote a book from the point of view of a dog.

It was called *The Art of Racing in the Rain*. And the unique perspective of its canine narrator, Enzo, who longs to be a human race car driver, had so much heart that its 2008 release did find a *slightly* bigger audience—to the tune of more than *4 million copies* sold and over *three years* on *The New York Times* bestsellers list.

Where do you go from there?

Well, if you're Garth Stein, you buckle in for the ride of your life. You go on tour. You sell movie rights. You create a special edition for teen readers (*Racing in the Rain: My Life as a Dog*) and a picture book adaptation (*Enzo Races in the Rain!*). You pay it forward, joining forces with other published writers to create a successful and growing nonprofit, Seattle7Writers. ("We should be marshaling our energy for the greater good," Stein told me, describing the organization as a "win-win-win" for author-members, local bookstores and libraries, and the reading and writing public.)

And eventually, of course, you write something new.

A Sudden Light, centered on the descendants of lumber barons and the fate of their crumbling mansion, is part coming-of-age story, part ghost story, part reminder of the price nature has paid for man-made fortunes. In October 2014, a few weeks after its hardcover release, it made a brief appearance on *The New York Times* bestsellers list. And then ...

Well, the next chapter has yet to be written. Can lightning strike twice for the same author? Stein spoke with us about what it takes to write a book you truly believe in.

If *The Art of Racing in the Rain* had been narrated by any other character, it would have been a very different book. And while *A Sudden Light* evolved from your play "Brother Jones," that title character is not the narrator of the novel. So how do you choose a narrator?
Well, with *The Art of Racing in the Rain*, I knew from the very beginning the only way that story could be told was from the dog's point of view. Otherwise it would just be a family drama that's been done before. [But] with *A Sudden Light*, it took me a long time to find the narrative voice because it was a much larger novel in terms of spanning multiple generations, and I like having a first-person [POV].

I spent quite a long time—years—writing five generations of the Riddell family history. I thought that was my novel. I wrote 100,000 words of the family from 1890 through 1990, and I thought it was good, but then I stepped back and looked at it and said, "Oh, this isn't my novel. This is research I've been doing in *preparation* to write my novel."

So then it became: I wanted to write the present-day story of the family, and the idea of redemption and how this family resolves its issues over generations, but do it from the contemporary vantage point. Who can narrate *this novel*?

Like you said, Brother Jones was the protagonist—and I have to say, that's one of the flaws of the play. He's too—well, his son calls him a "waffle." He's a little too waffle-y. To be a good protagonist you have to have a clear and substantial goal. Whether or not you achieve that or that's *really* what you want, it gives momentum to propel the story forward.

So that's where Trevor [Jones's son, and the narrator of the novel] came from. Jones did not have a son in the play. And so I brought the son in because he is untainted by the dark history of the Riddell family. He knows nothing about it, in fact—his father has never spoken about it. So [when his parents separate and his father takes him to the Riddell house], he comes in completely clean and has a simple, clean, objective goal, which is, *I want my parents to stay together. How am I going to achieve that?* Now, the path of that goes many directions, and as

The Rolling Stones say, you can't always get what you want, but if you try, you'll get what you need—and I think that's a good protagonist, right?

Then there came this problem with having Trevor as the protagonist: He would have to learn everything [about the family's history] through discovery, and that becomes very awkward. That's when I put the lens in of the story being told by thirty-eight-year-old Trevor to his children and his wife, who he's returned to the estate with, to tell them what happened to him when he was fourteen years old.

That lens gives perspective from a more mature voice as someone who has been able to process everything that's gone on and so can add some clarity to what happened. It [also] allowed me to set it in 1990, a really innocent time, pre-digital. I wanted young Trevor to be isolated in a strange world. He leaves The North Estate [only] twice in the book—I wanted him to have that sense of isolation. His mother, who he loves and is depending on, is some distant voice [on the phone from her own family's house in] England; his father is reticent at best; his grandfather may or may not have dementia; and his aunt is always playing a game—he can't get a straight answer out of her. The only person he can come to depend on is the ghost of Benjamin Riddell. So that's how the whole scheme came together.

As you alluded to, you're not afraid to end a story in a way where readers don't get everything they've been hoping for. Do you know the end before you start? I suppose not, if you threw out 100,000 words. ...

That was just my self-deception. You know, when you work on something like that, you're not going to sit down and say, "You know what I'm going to do? I'm going to sit down and spend two-and-a-half years writing character sketches!" That would be demoralizing. You just wouldn't do it. So you say, "Oh no, my book isn't *this* now; there's going to be a Part One and a Part Two"—that's how I convinced myself. The Part One is the history, and the Part Two is the contemporary story. You know, that's just self-delusion. We *have* to do that as writers, though. We're building mountains, not molehills, and it takes a long time to do it, and I find that most writers—when I teach a writing workshop—think their book is done, and it's just not. You've got to get it [written], and then have smart people give you feedback, and then spend another year or so working on it, and then you've gotta do that again. And again. And it's just not done yet. But we want it to be done so badly, we convince ourselves it must be.

I do know *an* ending, always. I feel you have to write *to* something—you have to aim for something or you're not going to get anywhere. You're just going to be wandering around the countryside. The ending, though, has to be true to the drama, and so therefore the ending may change. You may have *an* ending, but it's not the right ending.

I went to film school, so I have a pretty strong background in dramatic structure. I do a whole outline, and as I work it gets progressively more detailed. But if something happens in those spontaneous moments of writing that's different than my outline, I go with the spontaneity and change the outline to suit it.

Because the spontaneity, that's the *art*. My intentions are the *craft*, right? That's what I'm *trying* to do. But what is *being done* is where the magic is. I like to say that the first draft of anything I write is about me: It's about, *I have an idea and I'm trying to write a story*. Every subsequent draft is all about the characters and the story, and it's my job to shepherd the story. It's fiction, but it has to have a dramatic truth that people will believe. So then it's not about the writer anymore, then it's about the work.

The writer has to step aside and acknowledge that, because otherwise that's where the contrivance happens. Everyone's read those books. You're like, "I was really into it until this happened, and I just don't buy it." Because the writer has tried to do something that is contrary to the true nature of his story or his characters. And you *cannot* do that. If you want something to happen, you've got to set it up. If you want something to happen on page 180, you better fix it back on page 17 so that the character takes the reader where you want the reader to go.

How else does your background as a filmmaker influence the way you approach a novel?

I wanted to be a writer, but when I was going through college it was pretty irresponsible to say, "I'm going to be a novelist!" So I got my MFA in film. But I hated screenwriting, just hated it—I had kind of an allergic reaction. I was really lucky that I got the attention of a documentary filmmaker who was teaching at Columbia: Geof Bartz. He saw that I was struggling and was like, "Let's go into the editing room," and he showed me how to tell a story using found objects, which is what documentary filmmaking is. It's nonfiction, but it's still got to have a story. It's still got to have a protagonist or an issue people care about; there has to be some obstacle involved; there has to be a crisis, a climax, a resolution; it has to follow dramatic structure. And I *loved* editing films. I went into making documentaries and worked for nearly ten years doing different aspects of filmmaking, making my own films as well, and that gave me a lot of time to develop as a person and as a storyteller. ...

I'm a big fan of telling young writers to take all the detours they possibly can, both in life and in writing. Those detours are going to lead you to where you need to be. If someone says, "How would you like to spend two years working in the Czech Republic for the state department?" you should do that. You can always get back to your novel. You need to have as many experiences as possible.

It's the same in writing a book. If a new character walks in or your character does something unexpected, you have to go with that. If it's a dead end, you can always get back to your map. But chances are it's happening for a reason.

The craft is something we can teach. The art is the inspiration that we can't teach. We want the art, that's what we're aiming for. We're aiming to suppress our cautious editor who always tells us what to do. I think one of the big writers said, "Write drunk, edit sober." I say: *Write fat, edit lean.* In that first draft, put all the extra stuff in, anything that comes into your head. What happens is we self-edit as we're writing—*Oh, that's not going to make it in the final.* Don't worry about that. Put it in. It's going to add flavor, and it's going to inform the text. Once you're done with that, *then* go through and put it on a diet. You know, we *want* a fat baby. They've got the chubby cheeks, the chubby arms, the chubby fingers—we love that! That's good. When the baby grows up, *then* we want the lean muscle.

I've interviewed other authors who were releasing new books years after a mega-hit, and they all acknowledged the pressure that can come with that. How do you think that has affected you?

Uh, gray hair? My son says I have "vintage" hair. [Laughs.] It's very difficult, because there *are* expectations, and there's, *What did I do, and how do I do it again?*

I've never worked under contract before, and I don't like it—I feel guilty, because it took me longer to write the book than I expected—but I told them right on, turning out books in a similar vein, I can't do that. All the books I've written [are] similar thematically. But I invented a rule, by the Writers Guild of the Universe: One dog book per writer per lifetime, and that's it. So I kind of had to hold firm to that.

Did you any get pushback?

I didn't. ... But in terms of the pressure, the thing is, I'm not going to put out a book until it's the best book I possibly could've written. It's just not fair to do anything other than that. So if it takes twenty years, it's going to take twenty years.

Garth Stein

Writers and readers have a trust. You give me your time, and I'm going to give you a really good story that's provocative, and it's going to make you think and it's going to make you close the book and have that feeling of catharsis: *I wish I could spend more time with these characters.* And if you're not there yet, *don't* put your book out there; it's a betrayal of the trust. So in that sense, if you adhere to that, like I've tried to, the pressure is in just getting the book to that level.

Sometimes, though, you do have to say, "Okay, this book isn't going to get to that level," and then you have to set it aside. But we can't be depressed about that. We just have to say, "Well, I was learning about my craft and learning about myself as a writer and I was practicing—that's good time."

What's it like now, being on such an extensive book tour?

I'm doing *such* a long tour. It's really important that I get this book out there and stand behind the book. To *me* it's important. Because everyone expects me to fail. In general, [for other recent authors who've had a runaway hit] the follow-up hasn't done as well. Will I succeed? I don't know. I'll try it. If I have to go put the book in every person's hand and start reading with them, like I do with my seven-year-old, then I'll do that, because I do believe in this book.

There's a *Racing in the Rain* movie in development. Are you involved with that at all?

Not at all. ... You know what was great? It was done as a play by Book-It Repertory Theatre in Seattle, and there was an actor playing Enzo. I remember sitting next to this guy, and he was having none of it, and clearly his wife had cajoled him into coming. And I leaned over finally and said, "It sounds ridiculous, I know. But stick with it. Because by the end of the play, you're going to believe that actor is the dog." And at the end I looked over at him, and he had tears coming down his cheeks. If the film could get some of that magic, it would be amazing. So I have my fingers crossed.

The Complete Handbook of Novel Writing

PERMISSIONS

"Training Your Ideas" by N.M. Kelby: Reprinted from *Writer's Digest*, January 2010. Used with permission of the author.

"Bend It, Amp It, Drive It, Strip It" by Elizabeth Sims: Reprinted from *Writer's Digest*, November/December 2012. Used with permission of the author.

"The Taming of the Muse" by Paula Munier: Excerpted from *Writing with Quiet Hands* © 2015, with permission from Writer's Digest Books.

"Testing the Strength of Your Story Ideas" by Fred White: Reprinted from *Novel & Short Story Writer's Market 2017*. Used with permission of the author.

"Fire up Your Fiction" by Donald Maass: Excerpted from *The Fire in Fiction* © 2009, with permission from Writer's Digest Books.

"The Hero's Journey" by Paula Munier: Excerpted from *Plot Perfect* © 2014, with permission from Writer's Digest Books.

"The Two Pillars of Novel Structure" by James Scott Bell: Reprinted from *Writer's Digest*, January 2013. Used with permission of the author.

"Weaving in a Seamless Backstory" by Karen Dionne: Reprinted from *Writer's Digest*, January 2013. Used with permission of the author.

"The Essential Endgame Structure" by Larry Brooks: Excerpted from *Story Engineering* © 2011, with permission from Writer's Digest Books.

"Supporting Stories" by Jessica Page Morrell: Excerpted from *Between the Lines* © 2006, with permission from the author.

"Behind the Scene" by James Scott Bell: Excerpted from *The Art of War for Writers* © 2009, with permission from Writer's Digest Books.

"Character Study" by Alice Hoffman: Reprinted from *Writer's Digest*, February 2007. Used with permission of the author.

"Mining for Diamonds" by David Corbett: Excerpted from *Author in Progress* © 2016 by Therese Walsh, editor, and the Writer Unboxed community, with permission from Writer's Digest Books.

"Map Your Novel with a Reverse Outline" by N.M. Kelby: Excerpted from *The Constant Art of Being a Writer* © 2009, with permission from Writer's Digest Books.

"Creating a Flexible Outline for Any Story" by K.M. Weiland: Reprinted from *Writer's Digest*, February 2014. Used with permission of the author.

"Plantsing" by Jeff Somers: Reprinted from *Writer's Digest*, May/June 2016. Used with permission of the author.

"Rough It Up" by Elizabeth Sims: Reprinted from *Writer's Digest*, February 2009. Used with permission of the author.

"Titling Your Story" by Steve Almond: Reprinted from *Writer's Digest*, June 2008. Used with permission of the author.

"The Geyser Approach to Revision" by James Scott Bell: Excerpted from *Revision and Self-Editing for Publication, 2nd Edition* © 2013, with permission from Writer's Digest Books.

"Your Revision Checklist" by Josip Novakovich: Excerpted from *Fiction Writer's Workshop, 2nd Edition* © 2008, with permission from Writer's Digest Books.

"The Great Revision Pyramid" by Gabriela Pereira: Reprinted from *Writer's Digest*, September 2015. Used with permission of the author.

"Literary Lust Versus Commercial Cash" by Jodi Picoult: Reprinted from *Writer's Digest*, December 2006. Used with permission of the author.

"Understanding the Elements of Literary Fiction" by Jack Smith: Reprinted from *Writer's Digest*, November/December 2013. Used with permission of the author.

"World Creation in Science Fiction" by Orson Scott Card: Excerpted from *The Writer's Digest Guide to Science Fiction and Fantasy* © 2010 by Orson Scott Card and the Editors of Writer's Digest, with permission from Writer's Digest Books.

"What 'High Concept' Means in Any Genre" by Jeff Lyons: Reprinted from *Writer's Digest*, July/August 2013. Used with permission of the author.

"Write This, Not That" by Elizabeth Sims: Reprinted from *Writer's Digest*, May/June 2010. Used with permission of the author.

"The Stuff Series Are Made Of" by Karen Wiesner: Reprinted from *Writer's Digest*, September 2013. Used with permission of the author.

"Writing Investigation" by Hallie Ephron: Excerpted from *Writing and Selling Your Mystery Novel Revised and Expanded Edition* © 2017, with permission from Writer's Digest Books.

"Blurred Lines" by Michelle Richmond: Reprinted from *Writer's Digest*, July/August 2013. Used with permission of the author.

"Love Gone Wrong" by Leigh Michaels: Excerpted from *On Writing Romance* © 2007, with permission from Writer's Digest Books.

"Between the Sheets" by Deborah Halverson: Excerpted from *Writing New Adult Fiction* © 2014, with permission from Writer's Digest Books.

"Know Your Young Audience" by Mary Kole: Excerpted from *Writing Irresistible Kidlit* © 2012, with permission from Writer's Digest Books.

"Making Magic" by Kristin Bair O'Keeffe: Reprinted from *Writer's Digest*, July/August 2014. Used with permission of the author.

"Basics of a Solid Three-Paragraph Query" by Ann Rittenberg: Excerpted from *Your First Novel* © 2006 by Ann Rittenberg and Laura Whitcomb, with permission from Writer's Digest Books.

"Your Guide to an Effective Novel Synopsis" by Chuck Sambuchino and the Editors of Writer's Digest: Excerpted from *Formatting and Submitting Your Manuscript 3rd Edition* © 2009, with permission from Writer's Digest Books.

"Straw into Gold" by Wendy Burt-Thomas: Excerpted from *The Writer's Digest Guide to Query Letters* © 2009, with permission from Writer's Digest Books.

"Author Platform 2.0" by Jane Friedman: Excerpted from *2013 Writer's Market* © 2012, with permission from the author.

"Going Public" by Elizabeth Sims: Reprinted from *Writer's Digest*, September 2013. Used with permission of the author.

"Revise Your Path to Publication" by Jane Friedman: Reprinted from *Writer's Digest*, July/August 2011. Used with permission of the author.

INDEX

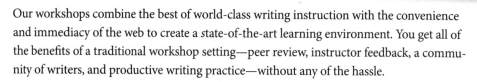